HTML Plus!

JAMES E. POWELL

Virginia Polytechnic Institute and State University

INTEGRATED
MEDIA
GROUP

An Imprint of Wadsworth Publishing Company
I$\textcircled{T}$P® An International Thomson Publishing Company

Belmont • Albany • Bonn • Boston • Cincinnati • Detroit • London • Madrid • Melbourne
Mexico City • New York • Paris • San Francisco • Singapore • Tokyo • Toronto • Washington

For Chris Waters, Melanie Waters, and Michael Powell Jr.

New Media Publisher: Kathy Shields
Assistant Editor: Tamara Huggins
Production: Vicki Moran
Composition: Publishing Support Services
Copy Editor: John T. Selawsky
Print Buyer: Karen Hunt
Cover Design: Bay Graphics Design
Printer: Quebecor Printing Fairfield, Inc.

Printed in the United States of America
1 2 3 4 5 6 7 8 9 10

For more information, contact Wadsworth Publishing Company:

Wadsworth Publishing Company
10 Davis Drive
Belmont, California 94002, USA

International Thomson Editores
Campos Eliseos 385, Piso 7
Col. Polanco
11560 México D.F. México

International Thomson Publishing Europe
Berkshire House 168-173
High Holborn
London, WC1V 7AA, England

International Thomson Publishing GmbH
Königswinterer Strasse 418
53227 Bonn, Germany

Thomas Nelson Australia
102 Dodds Street
South Melbourne 3205
Victoria, Australia

International Thomson Publishing Asia
221 Henderson Road
#05-10 Henderson Building
Singapore 0315

Nelson Canada
1120 Birchmount Road
Scarborough, Ontario
Canada M1K 5G4

International Thomson Publishing Japan
Hirakawacho Kyowa Building, 3F
2-2-1 Hirakawacho
Chiyoda-ku, Tokyo 102, Japan

Library of Congress Cataloging-in-Publication Data
Powell, James E.
      HTML plus! / James E. Powell.
          p.   cm.
      Includes index.
      ISBN 0-534-51626-2 (pbk.)
          1. HTML (Document markup language)   I. Title.
QA76.76.H94P68   1996   96-17875
005.75–dc20

 This book is printed on acid-free recycled paper.

TABLE OF CONTENTS

PREFACE

HTML Plus! is more than just a tutorial of the current and upcoming versions of the Hypertext Markup Language; it also provides hands-on tutorials for hypertext authoring, CGI programming, text search engines, Perl, Java, VRML, Acrobat, and SGML. Each of these technologies coexists with and compliments HTML on the World Wide Web, so *HTML Plus!* doesn't just gloss over them. You will build a search engine, a Web server, a half dozen Perl CGI scripts both for processing HTML forms and presenting dynamic content, two Java applets, and a VRML world. Whether you are an absolute beginner or a veteran HTML author, you will find *HTML Plus!* a valuable learning tool and reference. In addition to detailed tutorials, there are HTML tag and attribute summary tables at the end of each chapter, which will guarantee that your copy of *HTML Plus!* will become dog-eared in no time.

HTML Plus! covers each type of markup, each programming language, and each topic as if this were your first exposure to it. And it doesn't cut corners by presenting shallow examples. Most chapters include detailed projects with source code solutions. The HTML projects range from building a simple home page, to a self-scoring HTML forms-based exam, to building a complex HTML 3 Web page for a fictitious travel company. Other projects include building a Perl/CGI-based VRML editor, an HTML search engine, a language translator in Java, and a model of the solar system implemented with VRML. Upon completing these projects you will have more than an idea of what these technologies are, you will know how they work and have working examples that you can modify and expand to suit your own needs.

HTML Plus! is divided into five sections:

Part I is an introduction to today's HTML: HTML version 2.0. These six chapters will teach you everything you need to know to create a basic Web page. You start out by learning what text markup is, what HTML tags, attributes, and character entities look like, followed by an overview of the structure of an HTML document. Complete chapters teach you how to build a document header and body, fill it with headings and text blocks, tag phrases and text, make hypertext links, and finally, how to add images to your page. All of these topics are presented with an emphasis on building structured documents, not just producing glossy platform-dependent pages. In addition to these tutorials you will find information about image compression and the new Portable Network Graphics image format (PNG) designed specifically for delivering images on the Web. Plus, there are handy sidebars that cover anchor and icon design do's and don'ts, projects that demonstrate each topic (including HTML source code), and complete tag and attribute summary tables.

Part II covers advanced HTML 2.0 markup including forms, image maps, and browser-specific HTML extensions such as those developed by Netscape Communications and Microsoft. The remaining chapters in this section cover HTML 3.0. Entire chapters are devoted to HTML 3 document structure, the new Cascading Style Sheet (CSS) standard, HTML 3.0 tables and math, Netscape frames, and creating multilingual documents for the Web. Again, projects are provided for each chapter and tag and attribute summaries provide valuable reference material that will help you use HTML 3 to its fullest potential.

Part III discusses issues related to contributing documents to the Web. It begins with a chapter that examines current practices related to building Web home pages. The next two chapters examine hypertext issues and hypertext styles that you can use to build large coherent collections of documents to teach, inform, or entertain. Other chapters in this section examine the problems and potential solutions for providing maximum access for users with physical disabilities, publishing HTML on CD-ROM, and various classes of HTML editing tools you can use to manage large collections of documents.

Part IV delves into advanced Web concepts and introduces several programming languages that have become as essential to the Web as HTML. You start out by building Common Interface Gateway (CGI) scripts to accept HTML form data and return responses, but this is only the beginning. The next chapter is a tutorial on the Practical Extraction and Report Language (Perl), followed by chapters devoted to search engines, building HTML documents "on the fly" from relational databases, and presenting hypermedia content on the Web. Two chapters devoted to the Java programming language round out Part IV. These chapters do more than simply introduce Java. They cover the Java Development Kit, the Java API, introduce object-oriented programming concepts, and demonstrate step by step how to build Java applets and embed them in HTML documents. You will create a Java-powered language translator that could easily be expanded to translate hundreds of words or even handle multiple languages, just like a hand-held translator, only embedded in a Web page!

Part V introduces other ways of publishing documents and information on the Web. Two chapters are devoted to the Virtual Reality Modeling Language (VRML). Among the topics covered are VRML browsers, editors, and the VRML language itself. Once again you are exposed to the inner workings of the technology as you build a complete model of our solar system in VRML without using a graphical design tool. The next chapter introduces Adobe Acrobat and the Portable Document Format (PDF) for distributing highly formatted documents in a platform-independent manner. Finally, *HTML Plus!* ends where it began. The last chapter introduces yet another markup standard: the Text Encoding Initiative (TEI) SGML application. This chapter not only introduces TEI, but also shows you how to browse and publish SGML content other than HTML to the Web using the Panorama SGML document browser.

HTML Plus! closes with more material designed to make the book a valuable reference as well as a teaching tool. Appendix A includes a table of HTML character entities. Appendix B is a color code table for building Netscape and CSS style sheet color values. Appendix C presents Java keywords and a brief overview of the Java API. Appendix D contains a list of links that point you to essential documentation, software, and resources on the Web, organized by chapter.

Whether you are a magazine editor in New York using a Macintosh, an architect in Tokyo using a Windows-based PC, or a biochemist in Geneva using a UNIX workstation, *HTML Plus!* will teach you all you need to know in order to evaluate Web technologies, and use those technologies to publish what you have to say. Many of the examples and projects in *HTML Plus!* are devoted to human languages. It cannot be emphasized enough that the World Wide Web is a global phenomenon. By presenting projects that teach languages or attempt to overcome communications barriers, *HTML Plus!* is continually reminding you that when you publish on the Web, your audience is the world.

ACKNOWLEDGMENTS

Like climbing a mountain, writing a book is an adventure. You cannot do it alone. A special thanks to my very own in-house editor, Tim Buck for taking the time to read and reread chapters as I progressed, for encouraging me and for providing countless suggestions that have made this book better.

Thanks to the members of the Southern Ohio chapter of the American Society for Information Science for asking me to speak to their group, and a special thanks to Karen Ruud at the University of Cincinnati. You all set things into motion! Thanks to my supervisors Susan Olivier and Gail McMillan for allowing me to invest time and energy to this project. I also want to thank my coworkers, some of whom helped out directly while the rest put up with me during this stressful time (no small task!): Melissa Obenhaus, Stephanie Sanders, Curtis Carr, Scott Bowman, Russ Fenn, Vicki Burnett, John Lewis, Beth Lancaster, Peter Haggerty, Charla Jenrette, Bill Vandervoort, Debbie Cash, and Jerry Moore. Thanks to Mark Samsel for helping identify and fix a Java applet bug when the clock started winding down! Thanks to the University Libraries Web Team members for thought-provoking Fridays: Richard Sapon-White, Pat Murphy, Brenda Hendricks, Ginger Young, Tamara Kennelly, John Lewis, and Alan Armstrong. Thanks to Lon Savage, former head of Scholarly Communications Project of Virginia Tech, for giving me the opportunity to get into this field and for encouraging me to write a book on something. Thanks to Howard Frederick, Emerson College; Michael P. Harris, Del Mar College; Christopher Marler, San Francisco State University; and Lee Montgomery, Southern Utah University for their helpful comments on the manuscript. Thanks to my late grandmother, Hazel Powell, for believing I'd do this one day—I hope you know. A big thank you to my family who let me disappear for months: Mom (Virginia), Dad (James Sr.), Mike and Valerie, Carolyn and Keith, Steven and Melissa.

1

Windows
on the Web:
Web Browsers

CHAPTER AT A GLANCE

- What Web browsers are and how they differ
- Netscape menus
- How to use Netscape navigation aids effectively
- Modifying preference settings for Netscape
- *Where Can I Get Netscape for My Computer?*

The World Wide Web is a veritable jigsaw puzzle of software applications and standards. Pieces include the Web server and client software, HTML language and editors, uniform resource locators, and gateway programs. While years of effort have gone into making the Web a success, the component that captured the imagination and fueled sudden enthusiasm for hypertext and the Web was the first graphical Web client to run on more than one type of computer. Mosaic initiated the exodus from primitive, text-based information tools to the rich multimedia World Wide Web we know today. It was developed at the National Center for Supercomputing Applications (affiliated with the University of Illinois) by Marc Andreessen and Eric Bina. It quickly became popular because it supported graphics and because it ran on different types of computers. NCSA's team provided the client for several different UNIX systems plus the far more common Macintosh and Microsoft Windows environments. Until then, the Web had been a text-only system supported by tools for relatively uncommon systems such as NeXT computers, on which it was originally developed. Even with its bugs and its half-completed and now almost forgotten support for group annotations, Mosaic version 1.0 was a great success.

A Web client has to do a lot of work. Not only do Web clients communicate directly with Web servers using the hypertext transfer protocol (HTTP), they also understand and use uniform resource locators to find the correct server and then ask for the appropriate document. They can communicate directly with ftp servers, logging in as an anonymous user, changing directories, issuing directory and get commands as needed just as you would if you were ftping to a site manually. They pretend to be gopher clients when retrieving files from a gopher and present the gopher menu as a hypertext document built locally on your computer. They even know how to decode and display several types of graphic image formats such as XBM (X Windows bitmap), GIF, and JPEG compressed full-color images. No wonder underused functions such as group annotations and combined editor/browsers were discarded!

Like the Web, the Internet is in transition. Escaping from military-funded labs where it was developed as the ultimate uninterruptable communications link, the Internet turned out to be an insecure, uncensorable communication medium unsuitable for military use. But it launched a revolution that will ultimately be more significant than the introduction of the personal computer. We are approaching the day when the individual computer is less important than the network connectivity available to it. The supercomputer has gone from being an almost mystical nitrogen-cooled behemoth to a mundane collection of moderately speedy workstations scattered about the planet and connected by a fast, reliable network.

Revolution in communication means revolution in commerce, and the Web is the first tool attractive to corporations that want to conduct business on the Internet. So it is no surprise that big business lured Mosaic's developers away to rebuild Mosaic from the ground up and improve it. From these pioneers has come the first of the third-generation Web clients called Netscape Navigator, which is often referred to simply as Netscape.

Netscape's browser is quite popular, and is most definitely being used by more people than ever used Mosaic. But Mosaic and other clients paved the way for Netscape, and there were Web clients even before the bright inventors at NCSA had ever seen the Web. As many as 30% of the people using the Web today are not using Netscape. So what are they using?

Some people still use terminals. Terminals are text-based display stations that are usually not computers themselves but are connected to one nearby. For text-only displays the University of Kansas created Lynx. CERN (the European Laboratory for Particle Physics, where the World Wide Web began) also built a text-only client but it relied on a crude and clumsy scheme of numbered anchors, that required the reader to enter a link's number in order to jump to another document. Lynx uses a more intuitive link-highlighting mechanism allowing the user to cycle between the current set of links on the screen with the up and down arrow keys. The highlighted link can be accessed by simply selecting it and pressing the Return key:

```
telnet - nebula.lib.vt.edu default<1>                           _ □ ✕
File   Edit   Setup   Help

                                 www.ukans.edu default index (3/15/95) (p1 of 2) ▲

                        WELCOME TO THE UNIVERSITY OF KANSAS

      This server is operated by Academic Computing Services at the
      University of Kansas, which is the home of

          * KUfacts, the KU campus wide information system,
          * KANREN Info, the KANREN information system,
          * HNSource, the central information server for historians, and

          * the Lynx and DosLynx World-Wide Web (WWW) browsers. The current
            version of Lynx is 2.4. If you are running an earlier version
            PLEASE UPGRADE!

      OTHER UNIVERSITY OF KANSAS SERVERS
          * The University of Kansas Medical Center--Pulse
          * Atmospheric Science
          * Electrical Engineering and Computer Science
          * Mathematics
          * Physics
      -- press space for next page --
       Arrow keys: Up and Down to move. Right to follow a link; Left to go back.
      H)elp O)ptions P)rint G)o M)ain screen Q)uit /=search [delete]=history list
```

The Web found many early converts in the legal field and so a browser called Cello was developed especially for those users. This Windows-based program attempted to achieve a paper-on-screen effect, defaulting to black text on a white background. It had one of the friendliest interfaces of its time, associating icons familiar to most computer users with Web navigation functions. Some users found the way it displayed links to be less obvious and more distracting than other browsers. Each hypertext link was surrounded by a series of dashed lines, instead of the more common underline/color convention established by hypertext systems such as Microsoft Windows Help and Mosaic.

WinWeb and MacWeb were developed by a commercial indexing project for the Web. Each featured a very simple interface, with a minimal complement of navigational controls such as the standard Previous and Next document buttons (left and right arrows) and the Home document icon (an iconified house). These browsers were not the speediest, failed to support a few tags correctly in their earliest versions (such as <TEXTAREA> for forms), and didn't differentiate themselves enough to achieve any loyal following.

Other less common platforms ended up with their own Web browsers because they were not considered mainstream enough to have a version of Mosaic ported to them. OS/2 now bundles a Web browser called Web Explorer. It is an attractive application well-integrated with the OS/2 environment. Users can easily grab graphics and blocks of text from a Web page displayed with Web Explorer. It provides the same types of controls as Mosaic and other browsers.

A direct descendent of Mosaic is Microsoft's Internet Explorer. This browser satisfactorily handles HTML 2, some Netscape Navigator extensions, and even a few extensions of its own. But it contributes little to the field and pales in comparison to the performance and cross-platform support available with Netscape.

There are several Web browsers for NEXTSTEP, the birthplace of the Web. NEXTSTEP is an innovative object-oriented operating system that simplifies programming tasks to more easily manageable, self-contained pieces called objects. Its role in the birth of the Web was probably due to the ability of programmers and even nonprogrammers to rapidly create a mock-up of an application with NEXTSTEP. The original NEXTSTEP Web browser developed by CERN featured editing capabilities but did not support inline graphics or the complete HTML 2 tag set. OmniWeb, the most successful browser for this environment, is a commercial application. Early versions of OmniWeb were quite slow, due in part to its strategy of calling an external graphics application to render inline images and then send them back to the Web browser. Newer versions are dramatically faster but do not match the Netscape browser's performance under Windows on an identically configured PC. It has also lagged behind other clients in supporting new tags, an unhappy fate for one of the parents of the Web.

Several other Web browsers have become commercial applications. A version of Mosaic called Spry Mosaic is now sold or bundled with books on the Web and operating systems. It is a less buggy and speedier version of the original Mosaic. And of course there's Netscape. Developed by many of the same people who created Mosaic, Netscape Navigator is a fast and reliable Web browser that was made available free to all academic users shortly after its completion. Netscape supports the complete HTML 2 tag set, a set of nonstandard extensions referred to as the Netscape extensions, and some HTML 3 elements and attributes. By most estimates, Netscape is used by as many as 70% of the people using the Web today. Netscape is used extensively in this book since the vast majority of its readers will already have it or will certainly be able to get a copy.

Before we delve into HTML, let's take a tour of the Netscape browser. For purposes of this tour, we'll use Netscape version 1.22 running under Microsoft Windows 95. Version 1.22 of Netscape is almost identical across all other supported platforms. To launch Netscape, locate the icon that looks like this and double click it:

Early versions of Netscape featured a purplish "N" that pulsed like a beating heart. The new logo was designed to coincide with the first official version of Netscape. A contest was announced to find a suitable replacement animation for the pulsing "N" that used the new logo. The shooting stars animation that displays whenever Netscape is locating or loading a document was the winner. Others included a giant "N" marching over the globe and an animated Mozilla character, the cartoonish dinosaur mascot of Netscape.

Tour of the Netscape Menu

Like all Windows and Macintosh applications, Netscape has a set of pull-down menus:

| File   Edit   View   Go   Bookmarks   Options   Directory |

File provides access to window, document, and printing controls:

- *New Window* to display different Web documents in different windows simultaneously
- *Open Location* for accessing a remote document on the Web
- *Open File* to open a local HTML document
- *Save As...* to save the current document to your hard drive
- *Mail Document* to mail the current document to yourself or a friend
- *Document Info* to display the document title, URL, last update date, and character set for the current document
- *Page Setup* to configure printing options
- *Print* to print the current document
- *Print Preview* to see how the document will look when printed
- *Close* to close the current window
- *Exit* to quit Netscape

Edit includes the standard suite of text manipulation tools:

- *Undo, Cut, Copy, Paste, Find*

View provides control over the content of the document being viewed:

- *Reload* to re-retrieve the current document
- *Load Images* to retrieve all the images in the current document if they haven't already been retrieved by the *Auto Load Images* option
- *Refresh* to redisplay the current document
- *Source* to display the HTML tagged document behind the current Web page

Go is a pull-down menu of items that also appears on the navigation bar:

- *Back, Forward, Home, Stop Loading, View History,* and an automatically updated list of recently visited sites

Bookmarks lets you save or edit a collection of pointers to Web pages:

- *Add Bookmark, View Bookmarks,* menu items followed by your bookmarks list

Options allows you to configure the Netscape toolbar and preferences (described below):

- *Preferences, Show Toolbar, Show Location, Show Directory Buttons, Auto Load Images, Show FTP File Information, Save Options*

Directory contains a collection of pointers to Netscape and Internet Web pages:

- *Netscape's Home, What's New!, What's Cool!, Go to Newsgroups, Netscape Galleria, Internet Directory, Internet Search, Internet White Pages, About the Internet*

Help is a mixture of additional Netscape Web documents and locally stored help files:

- *About Netscape, Registration Information, Upgrade Information, Handbook, Release Notes, Frequently Asked Questions, On Security, How to Give Feedback, How to Get Support, How to Create Web Services*

The underlined character in each option name can be used together with the Alt key on a PC or the Command key on a Macintosh to select that option without using the mouse.

Netscape also features a navigational toolbar:

Back and *Forward,* when highlighted, allow you to move backward and forward through a list of previously viewed documents. *Home* takes you to a document you have configured to be your default home page. *Reload* will cause the current document to be retrieved as if you had never viewed it, so any changes that might have been made to it while you were reading it will appear. *Images* loads the images in the current document if you have the *Auto Load Images* option turned off (the *Images* button is always disabled if you have this option turned on). *Open* brings up a panel in which you can enter the uniform resource locator of any document on the Web and immediately retrieve it. *Print* lets you print the current document. *Find* displays a text entry panel in which you can enter a word to search for in the current document. *Stop* cancels a document retrieval already in progress.

Some of these navigational controls were conceived of and implemented in other hypertext systems before the Web was developed. HyperCard has the concept of a home stack (a stack is a set of hypertext-linked cards similar to Web pages but more compact) and uses a similar icon. Keeping the user of a hypertext system oriented is a primary concern in a system where links can lead users around the world in a matter of minutes. Other ways Netscape provides navigational control are by displaying the address of the document you currently have open:

Location: | http://scholar.lib.vt.edu/ |

or by allowing you to view a history of recently visited documents:

History   [x]
IUMA, Welcome to IUMA   :   http://www.iuma.com/
Yahoo   :   http://www.yahoo.com/
Scholarly Communications Project of   :   http://scholar.lib.vt.e
University Libraries Information Sy   :   http://www.lib.vt.edu/

[Go to]   [Create Bookmark]   [Close]

or to save and use pointers to documents you found interesting on the Internet:

Netscape Bookmarks   [x]
File   Edit   Item
📂 Personal Bookmarks
— 📄 Carnivorous Plant Database
— 📄 Scholarly Communications Project of VPI_SU
— 📄 TheContinental Homepage
— 📄 ** HIT ME!! **
— 📄 Yahoo
— 📄 PERL -- Practical Extraction and Report Language
— 📄 University Libraries Electronic Reserve
http://reserve.lib.vt.edu/

These pointers are called "bookmarks." Countless Web pages have started out as the author's bookmark collection. Not only do bookmarks help you keep track of interesting sites but they are also a great way to start building your own personal home page since they are stored in an HTML file called bookmark.htm.

Netscape has a set of unique buttons for quick access to several Netscape Communications home pages including *What's New!*, *What's Cool!*, and a page about upgrading to new versions of the browser software:

The navigation toolbar, location field, and Netscape home page buttons can all be turned off under the *Options* menu. Usually, you will want to keep at least the navigation bar around, but sometimes turning off the other features gives you valuable vertical space in which to view longer documents. You can turn these off by pulling down the *Options* menu and then deselecting the feature you want to disable so that it does not have a check mark next to it. Be sure to select *Save Options* under the *Options* menu if you want this feature disabled by default whenever you run Netscape:

Under *Preferences* you will find a huge collection of options that give you some idea how much information a Web browser must be able to process or pass along to other applications:

WHERE CAN I GET NETSCAPE FOR MY COMPUTER?

The Netscape Navigator Web browser is licensed free of charge to individuals who are *"students, faculty members or staff members of an educational institution (K–12, junior college or college) or employees of a charitable non-profit organization."* So if you fall into one of these categories, you can simply retrieve the software from the Internet without being required to pay for it. There are versions of Netscape for the Apple Macintosh and PowerMac; Microsoft Windows, Windows NT, and Windows 95; and several UNIX systems including DEC Alpha, IBM RS/6000, Linux systems, and SGI and Sun workstations.

Continued on next page

Continued from previous page

There are a couple of ways to retrieve the software. You can use an FTP client application such as Fetch for the Macintosh or Winsock FTP for Windows and connect to one of the sites listed below. Or you can use any other Web browser to access one of these sites by placing *ftp://* in front of the ftp site address and appending the path information (e.g., *ftp://ftp.netscape.com/pub/navigator/*). Easier still is to point your Web browser at *http://home.netscape.com/* and follow the instructions provided.

Once you retrieve the program, you will have to install it. For Macs, Netscape Navigator is provided as a compressed, BinHexed program that must be decoded and decompressed before it can be installed. Netscape Navigator for Windows is provided as a self-extracting archive. Once you retrieve the .exe file, run it from the Program Manager or *Start* menu to extract the installation files, then run the setup.exe program that is included. Netscape Navigator for UNIX systems is provided as a tarred and compressed file (using the GNU zip utility). Use gunzip filename.tar.gz to decompress the file and tar xfv filename.tar to extract Netscape and related files from the tar file.

Here are some FTP sites that distribute Netscape Navigator in North America:

ftp.netscape.com in /pub/navigator/
ftp2.netscape.com in /pub/navigator/
ftp3.netscape.com in /pub/navigator/
ftp.cps.cmich.edu in /pub/netscape/
sunsite.unc.edu in /pub/packages/infosystems/WWW/clients/Netscape/

Styles determines the look of the navigational toolbar, the default home page, how links should appear, and how often you've visited links before they should expire. Until they expire, they are displayed in a different color than links you have not visited to remind you that you have already viewed the documents the links point to.

Fonts lets you select a default font for document body text and preformatted text blocks, as well as multilanguage font sets for non-English Web documents.

Colors controls the colors of followed and not yet visited links, as well as text and background colors for documents as you view them.

Mail and News provides access to the configurations necessary to send mail with your Web browser (*mailto:* URLs need this information) and to read Usenet newsgroups. The values to fill in here are available from your Internet service provider.

Cache and Network controls how much memory and disk space is used by Netscape as you surf the net. You can also turn on, restrict, or turn off automatic document verification. If verification is turned on, Netscape asks the Web server that houses the current document if it has changed. If so, it performs an automatic reload; otherwise, it loads the locally cached version of the document.

Applications and Directories sets the default telnet application for use in following *telnet:* URLs. It also determines where your bookmarks file is located and where non-HTML files are temporarily stored when retrieved by Netscape. The *View Source* configuration item lets you select a text or HTML editor in which to load the HTML document when you choose the *View Source* menu item to see how a particular document was constructed.

Images and Security controls how images are displayed and when warnings should pop up when interacting with Web servers that support security features such as data encryption for Internet business transactions.

Proxies sets information for computers that serve as intermediaries between you and the Internet. You can access the Internet without being directly connected to it by configuring a proxy server for each information service listed here. The proxy server is directly attached to the Internet and issues requests on your behalf.

Helper Apps associates programs on your computer with types of information that Netscape cannot display alone. Netscape will run the specified program whenever one of these types of files (such as a sound or motion video segment) is encountered. This is how Netscape and other Web browsers function as hypermedia (multimedia hypertext) applications. With helper applications, you can configure Netscape to support new document formats that don't even exist today!

When you are viewing a document with Netscape, you can select text and copy it to other documents with *Edit* menu options. Graphics can also easily be captured by right-clicking (or just clicking on a Macintosh) on the desired image. While Netscape does not provide any HTML editing capabilities, these edit options and the *View Source* function allow you to quickly learn about HTML and grab examples for your own documents.

Now you are ready to begin using Netscape to design and test your own Web pages. Chapter 2 introduces the basics of text and HTML markup.

Introduction to HTML

2

HTML— the HyperText Markup Language

CHAPTER AT A GLANCE

- Text markup
- HTML tags
- Generalized and specific markup
- Character entities
- Table 2-1: *HTML Special Characters*
- *What Is an HTML "Editor"?*
- The basic structure of an HTML document

Markup

HTML is a text markup language. If you've ever peeked at the codes behind a WordPerfect document or used some old-style text formatting system, then you are probably familiar with markup. Markup is the hidden codes or tags used to mark the insertion point for a graphic, or to indicate that a certain piece of text should be bold, italics, a paragraph, indented, a different font size. Some types of markup are like road signs. They are equivalent to the signs on a highway where the speed limit changes with the terrain. Sometimes the sign warns the user to proceed more slowly due to numerous intersections or hairpin curves, while later signs encourage drivers to return to a higher speed (and some drivers add five or ten miles/kilometers to this amount!). These sign-style tags set a mode that stays in effect until a new tag is encountered. Once a bold tag is located, all text following it is bolded until some other font style tag is encountered.

Script/GML is a type of markup used on IBM mainframes to generate formatted documents. It is a sign-style language where one type style is set and stays set until another tag is encountered. Here is an example of specific markup using the Script/GML language:

```
.bChapter 1
.iIntroduction to markup
```

Here each tag is preceded with a period and immediately precedes document text. The ".b" tag causes all text that follows to be displayed in bold. The ".i" tag later changes the font style to italics. Script/GML has fallen out of favor over the years as word processors with WYSIWYG ("What You See Is What You Get") capabilities have proliferated. But ironically it is a direct ancestor of HTML.

HTML markup is a container-style markup. Just as most food products in a grocery store are wrapped, boxed, or bagged, pieces of text in a document are enclosed, or tagged, by HTML markup. Without proper containers, text in an HTML document might look fine or, like milk without a container, pour all over the place making the page unreadable. Unlike food containers however, HTML tags are hidden from the user when the finished document is displayed by a Web browser. They are only visible during the editing process.

SPECIFIC VERSUS GENERALIZED TAGS

HTML contains markup for encoding both specific and generalized information about a document. Specific markup is used to control exactly how a piece of text should look when displayed. Script/GML is an example of a specific markup language, where tags correspond to formatting styles such as bold, italics, or underlining.

Here is an example of specific markup in HTML:

```
<B>Chapter 1</B>
<I>Introduction to markup</I>
```

Notice that each segment of text is contained by matched tags, rather than simply preceded by a tag that specifies a mode switch.

In both examples, tags are added to the document to encode additional information about the document text. The process of adding these tags is referred to as marking up or tagging a document. The markup is interpreted by the computer or other output device and converted to formatting information which is then applied to the marked text. In this case, **Chapter 1** is **bold** and *Introduction to markup* is *italicized*. In each example the computer or laser printer has little choice about how to display the marked text, since there are definite rules that determine how bold or italicized text should look. This is the essence of specific markup. It is inflexible and has no relationship with the structure of the document in which it occurs, only the appearance. If HTML were just a specific markup language, you would never need to see or learn about its tags.

HTML is also a generalized markup language. Generalized markup is not always obvious to the user. It encloses document structures such as paragraphs, lists, and headings. Because of these markup elements, an HTML author needs to be familiar with and insert these tags with an editor. Since generalized markup encapsulates structures within a document, it is left up to the display device (in most cases a computer with a World Wide Web browser) to determine how to display the tagged structures. Here is an example of generalized markup in HTML:

```
<HTML>
<HEAD><TITLE>Chapter 1</TITLE></HEAD>
<BODY>
<H1>Chapter 1: Introduction to markup</H1>
</BODY>
</HTML>
```

In this example, the entire document is enclosed by the <HTML> tag. The first <HTML> tag is called the start tag. Since HTML tags are containers, it is paired with an end tag, beginning with a forward slash, that occurs after the text that it marks: </HTML>. This is how all HTML tags look. In a few cases, an end tag can be omitted, but it is good practice to always include an end tag even when minimization is allowed. Other tags in this example include the <HEAD> tag, which encloses the document header. An HTML document has only one header, which is located at the top of the document. The actual textual content of the document starts after the <BODY> tag. Here tags such as <H1> can be used to mark headings. Headings mark section titles such as chapters or parts.

It is up to the display software (the Web browser) to decide how to display the text marked with these tags. The contents of the <TITLE> tag in the <HEAD> section are typically displayed in the Web browser's title bar when it retrieves the document. The document contents start with the <BODY> tag; anything other than a comment between the <HEAD> and <BODY> tags is not valid HTML, and will be ignored. Headings (such as <H1>) can be displayed in a variety of ways and, in fact, are usually under the control of the reader. Browsers allow the reader to specify the size and even the font style for each HTML heading level.

It is difficult to avoid mixing specific and generalized markup when using HTML, but it is helpful to be aware of the differences. Authors who are not aware of the differences typically make mistakes such as relying on headers to emphasize text rather than to tag structures. The reader might have selected a very small font for that level header on their browser. The impact of their document is greatly reduced since they did not use specific markup, such as the bold tag, to control the appearance of this portion of text.

ATTRIBUTES

So far, we've seen two types of HTML markup: start and end tags. All HTML tags look like those in the examples above. Each starts with a less than sign (<), followed by the tag text, followed by a greater than sign (>). Many HTML tags contain additional information between the "<>" that further defines the tag. These pieces of information are called attributes. Attributes define additional characteristics of a tag. Some have predefined values, or only one possible value, whereas you can define the values of others. An attribute is assigned a value by including the attribute name followed by an equal sign (=) and the value. If the attribute allows you (the author) to define a value, then the value should be enclosed in double quotes (" "):

    <IMG SRC="worldmap.jpg" ISMAP>

In this example, the <IMG> tag's SRC attribute is assigned the value "worldmap.jpg" by the author. The ISMAP attribute has only one possible value, ISMAP=ISMAP, so you can abbreviate it by simply listing the attribute name. Adding the ISMAP attribute to this image tag makes it an image map instead of a regular inline graphic.

END TAGS

As we saw in our first example, HTML start tags have corresponding end tags. An end tag looks like the start tag but a forward slash follows the less than sign like this: </HTML>. End tags close a section of markup. If a bold <B> tag is not closed with a </B> tag, then all remaining text in the document will be bolded (like milk without a container!). Some end tags are not often used because it is clear by the next tag that the previous tag has ended. The paragraph tag <P> is typical of this. One almost never sees a </P> tag because the next <P> tag makes it clear to the software that the previous paragraph has ended. In practice, it is best to insert the begin and end tags in all cases, unless you are using an HTML markup tool to enter tags, in which case it is often not practical and too time consuming. Also, if you are hand tagging a document or part of a document, it is helpful to capitalize the text of the HTML tag: <P> rather than <p> since this makes the markup easier to distinguish from the text. However, both uppercase and lowercase make valid HTML tags. A few tags do not have end tags, such as the <IMG> tag, since it is not used to markup text but rather to specify that an image should be included at this point in the document.

CHARACTER ENTITIES

Another type of HTML markup is the character entity. You can use any ASCII character (A–Z, a–z, 0–9 plus a few standard punctuation and mathematical symbols) in an HTML document by simply typing it. To use characters not found in ASCII, such as characters from the ISO Latin-1 character set (characters used in many western European languages), you insert character entities. Character entities are markup which indicates that a special character should be inserted where the entity occurs in the document. Character entities start with an ampersand (&) and end with a semicolon (;). For example,

please look in /ãftp/pub/incoming for your homework assignment

is displayed as

please look in /~ftp/pub/incoming for your homework assignment

Character entity text should be lowercase, unless you are specifying an entity for an uppercase letter, in which case only the first letter should be capitalized. &ATILDE; would be incorrect in the above example. A character entity is treated exactly as a single ASCII character, so it can be used anywhere an ASCII character can appear in a document and can be bold, italicized, etc.

Since the less than, greater than, and ampersand are part of HTML markup, they also have character entities that must be used when you want to include one of these characters in a document:

The HTML tags for bold and italics are <B> & <I>

is displayed as

The HTML tags for bold and italics are <B> & <I>

If these characters were inserted into the body of the text unencoded, they might be misinterpreted as part of a tag. Then when no matching end tag is found, the entire document might be improperly displayed. Occasionally you might slip up and include one of these characters, only to find when you view the document that you have a hypertext anchor spanning many lines, or text has disappeared. Double quotes can often be inserted with no ill effect but if they appear within a tag, weird things can happen. It is good practice to always insert entities for characters used to construct HTML markup whenever you are hand-editing a file. Table 2-1 lists some of these characters, their meaning in HTML, and the character entity you should use whenever you want to include one of these characters in your document text.

TABLE 2-1   HTML SPECIAL CHARACTERS

Character	Meaning	Entity Equivalent
<	Opens an HTML tag	&lt;
>	Closes an HTML tag	&gt;
&	Starts a character entity	&amp;
"	Encloses attribute values	&quot;

You may also insert non-ASCII types of characters by using numeric entities. Numeric entities are similar to character entities but the ASCII character code is used instead of the abbreviated name. For example, { is the entity for a left curly bracket ({). A complete list of character and numeric entities is available in Appendix B.

HTML editing tools can even do some of the work for you. One extremely useful tool, rtf2html, converts documents saved in Microsoft's Rich Text Format to HTML. It constructs a valid document structure, and converts as many formatting attributes as it can to HTML tags. Newer tools incorporate conversion engines like these directly into word processors and page-layout tools. Software packages such as PageMaker and WordPerfect can already save files in HTML. They can recognize a paragraph or bolded text and perform the markup for you. But no such tool is likely to work 100% of the time when attempting to perform markup on citations, lists, blockquotes, etc., because there are several accepted standards for formatting this type of information. That's why it is important to learn HTML.

WHAT IS AN HTML "EDITOR"?

HTML was developed in 1991, long after word processors had become fairly common. So naturally, the first World Wide Web browser was also an HTML authoring tool—an HTML editor. Most HTML editors list tags that are available and allow you to select portions of text around which the tags should be inserted. Once you select some text, you usually click a button for the appropriate tag or select it from a pull-down list. The first HTML editor, written for computers running the NEXTSTEP operating system, had a feature that allowed you to build hypertext links between documents. Once you'd selected the text for a link, you browsed through your files and selected a file to which you wanted to link this text. Of course, the file to which you were linking had to be on the same machine as the HTML document you were creating, which was not always convenient. Other editors have a "validation" feature, which attempts to make sure you use tags correctly by looking for improperly nested tags, invalid attributes, missing end tags, etc.

Continued on next page

Continued from previous page

Word processors such as Microsoft Word can be used as HTML Editors

NESTING

If two or more tags are to be applied to the same text, they should always be nested within one another. It is incorrect to have one tag start within another and end outside it. For example,

<B><I>Important Announcement</B></I>

should instead be:

<B><I>Important Announcement</I></B>

If you find this difficult to remember, think of Russian "babushka" dolls. These small wooden ornaments are actually containers for smaller dolls. Each tag is a doll, and your text is on a slip of paper inside the smallest doll.

Of course, not all tags can be nested. For example, the <HEAD> tag cannot occur within <BODY>. Conversely, many tags can only occur between certain other tags. Tags are said to be elements of other tags when they can only occur between them. All HTML tags are elements of the <HTML> tag as this tag encapsulates the entire document. The <TITLE> tag is an element of the <HEAD> tag as it cannot occur outside the document header.

HTML and SGML

HTML is defined using the SGML (Standard Generalized Markup Language) metalanguage. SGML not only defines the tags, attributes and their allowed values, and the character entities, but also where these items can occur in a document; thus SGML defines the structure of the document. All of this information is defined in a document called a document type declaration (DTD). Meant to be human readable, DTDs are often too dense and obtuse to be digested in one or two readings (far better to find a book like this that tells you what tags to use where!). Since HTML is defined using SGML, it is often referred to as SGML. In fact, it is more precisely an application of SGML. But you will be forgiven if you persist in generically referring to it as SGML.

SGML utilizes some standard terminology for describing tags and document structure. The places where a tag may be used in a document is, in SGML parlance, its permitted context (Figure 2-1). For example, the permitted context of a title tag is the header of a document. Paragraph and list tags are examples of HTML tags that have multiple permitted contexts for they may be used anywhere in the body of a document whether inside an HTML form or on their own:

```
<BODY>
<P>HTML markup is easy
<DIV CLASS=abstract>
<P>It only takes a few hours to begin creating documents in HTML. HTML is the
best tool currently available for communicating information on the Internet. This
guide aims to show you the language and how to use it effectively.
</DIV>
<H1>HTML Tags</H1>
```

In this example, the permitted context of the HTML 3 <DIV> tag is anywhere within the body of a document, that is between the <BODY> start and end tag. Using a <DIV> tag in the header section is not allowed according to this rule. Elements and permitted context are synonymous.

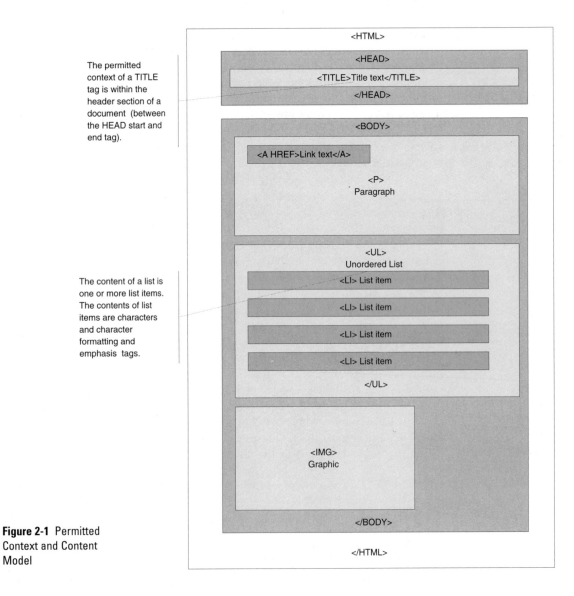

The permitted context of a TITLE tag is within the header section of a document (between the HEAD start and end tag).

The content of a list is one or more list items. The contents of list items are characters and character formatting and emphasis tags.

Figure 2-1 Permitted Context and Content Model

Tags also have a content model (Figure 2-1), that specifies what types of tags and data may appear within them. A paragraph's content model is text, which means document text (ASCII characters and character entities) and textual and character markup (such as bold and italics tags) may occur between a paragraph start and end tag:

```
<P>
The <B>header</B> of a document is a separate structure from the <I>body</I>.
The header &amp; body are the content model for the &lt;HTML&gt; tag.
</P>
```

Let's review what we've learned so far. Tags are text containers that come in two flavors: generalized tags that record what kind of text is tagged (heading, title, body) and specific tags that tell the Web browser how a piece of text should look when it is displayed. Attributes refine tags. Character entities let you safely include non-ASCII characters and characters that normally make up tags in a document. Putting the pieces together, HTML markup consists of tags, attributes, and character entities that you (the author) use to encode the structure and some basic formatting information for presenting a document on the World Wide Web. Now on to the tags!

3

An Introduction to Basic HTML

CHAPTER AT A GLANCE

- When and where to use **<HTML>**, **<HEAD>**, and **<BODY>** tags
- HTML document header elements
- *The "Tree of Knowledge"*
- HTML 2 Project: *Structuring Documents*
- General Document Tag Usage and Attribute Summaries

HTML 2

The most basic version of HTML in use today is HTML version 2. The next eight chapters will cover various types of HTML 2 tags. Each chapter will describe a set of tags and demonstrate their use with a project. You should follow along with each project by using a text editor to create and markup the example document. The projects in this book were developed with BBEdit for the Macintosh and Programmer's File Editor for Microsoft Windows–based PCs. Both are available as shareware or freeware from the Internet. Any word processor that can save as "text only" (e.g., WordPerfect, Word) is also suitable for use with these projects. Do not use a specialized HTML editor to insert tags for you because the goal of these projects is to demonstrate tags and their correct usage. Once you become adept at HTML markup, you may wish to use an HTML editor to assist you with large projects. There are many fine programs available for both Macs and PCs.

For each project you will also need a Web browser such as Netscape. The projects in this book were extensively tested with Netscape 1.22 for Windows, Mac and UNIX, Microsoft Internet Explorer for Windows 95, and Mosaic 2.0 for Windows. Any of these browsers is suitable for HTML 2 projects. HTML 3 projects (HTML 3 is covered in later chapters) were tested with the Arena browser for UNIX. When necessary (e.g., for Java and VRML), other browsers were also employed; these will be mentioned when used. Most examples for HTML 2 in this book are displayed using Netscape, unless otherwise noted. As stated in Chapter 1, Netscape 1.22 is free for all academic users.

HTML 2 documents should start with the <HTML> tag and end with the </HTML> tag. Currently, the <HTML> tag is not required. However, future versions of HTML will likely require this tag along with a VERSION attribute that tells the Web browser what version of HTML the document was tagged with. Each document has one header section tagged with the <HEAD> tag, and one body tagged with the <BODY> tags. So the simplest valid HTML 2 document looks like this:

```
<HTML>
<HEAD></HEAD>
<BODY>
</BODY>
</HTML>
```

This document has no header or body content, but it is valid HTML. It takes a few more tags, and of course some text, to make a useful document. Since many programming language texts often feature a "Hello, World" application, it seems appropriate that we start off with a "Hello, World Wide Web" document example:

```
<HTML>
<HEAD><TITLE>Hello WWW</TITLE>
</HEAD>
<BODY>
<P>Hello, World Wide Web.
</BODY>
</HTML>
```

Launch your text editor and type this document in exactly as shown. Save it as hello.htm, and then launch Netscape to view it. Select *Open File* from the Netscape menu:

Now, browse through your files until you find hello.htm. When you do, select the filename and click OK to open it:

You should see a very short document with the title bar "Hello WWW" and one line of text displayed by Netscape (Figure 3-1). In this example we have expanded the shortest valid HTML document to include text between the <TITLE> start and end tag, and one sentence in the body. All header elements can occur only within the <HEAD> start and end tags. The permitted contents of the <HEAD> tag include <TITLE>, <BASE>, <ISINDEX>, <LINK>, and <NEXTID>. Comments are also allowed (we will look at them shortly). Untagged text is invalid in a document header. As you continue reading, you will find that no header elements have end tags except for the <TITLE> tag. This is because only the <TITLE> tag marks text that is usually displayed to the reader while the other header tags store information about the document and its relationship to other documents on the Web.

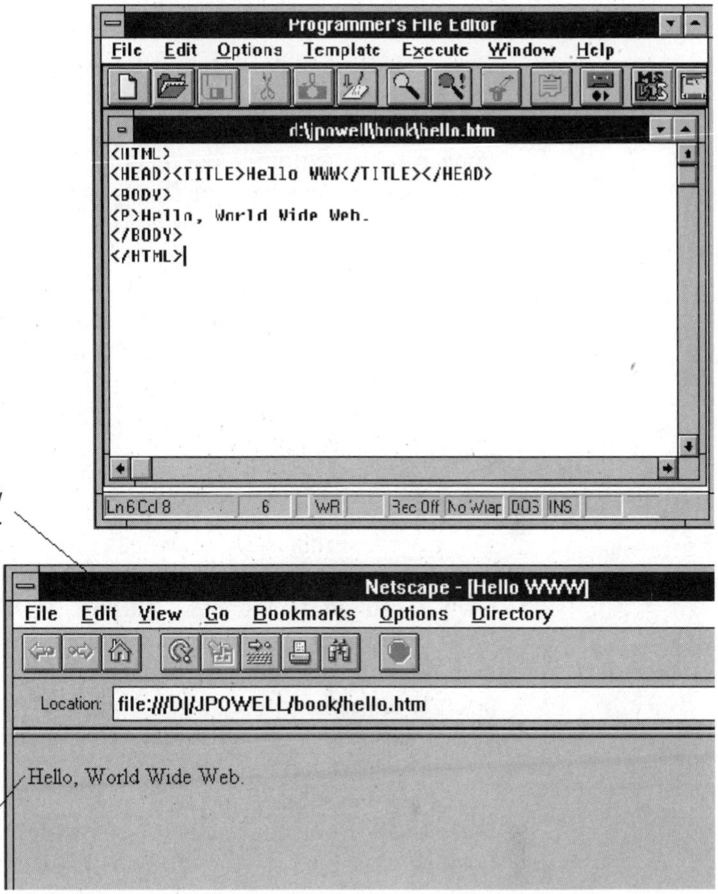

Figure 3-1 Text editor and Netscape displaying "Hello, WWW" document

```
Programmer's File Editor

File   Edit   Options   Template   Execute   Window   Help

d:\jpowell\book\hello.htm

<HTML>
<HEAD><TITLE>Hello WWW</TITLE></HEAD>
<BODY>
<P>Hello, World Wide Web.
</BODY>
</HTML>

Ln 6 Col 8        6      WR      Rec Off No Wrap DOS INS
```

<TITLE>Hello WWW
</TITLE>

```
Netscape - [Hello WWW]

File   Edit   View   Go   Bookmarks   Options   Directory

Location: file:///D|/JPOWELL/book/hello.htm

Hello, World Wide Web.
```

<BODY>
<P>Hello, World
Wide Web</BODY>

THE "TREE OF KNOWLEDGE"

The Web can be thought of as a stand of giant, many-branched trees. As you "surf the Web," think of yourself as a squirrel leaping from tree to tree looking for that kernel of knowledge that fits your immediate information need. HTML authors build these trees by building documents, which are themselves miniature trees. The author constructs a document from individual characters that form words, adds markup and punctuation, then groups these words into sentences and phrases. More markup creates paragraphs and text blocks until suddenly the main branches appear; the header and body, and finally the trunk—the document itself—rises from the electron dust. Structures *within* documents help lead a reader just as surely as links *between* them. A poorly structured document is as frustrating to read as a poorly planned collection of connected documents is to navigate.

<TITLE>

Every HTML document should have a title. The text marked with the <TITLE> tag should be unique and descriptive for the document in which it occurs. The contents of the title tag, as with any elements of the document header, do not appear in the text of the document. Title text is usually displayed in the title bar of the document when a user opens it with a Web browser. It is also saved as the name of an entry in their hotlist or bookmarks if they choose to mark your document for return visits. So it is very important to make this title meaningful. An introduction to a larger set of documents would be poorly served with the title "Introduction" but would be much more memorable and useful if it were instead called "Introduction to HTML." Longer titles are allowed, but many browsers display only the first 50–70 characters in the title bar. Multiple titles will be ignored and are not valid HTML.

<BASE>

There are several other tags whose permitted context is the header of an HTML document. The <BASE> tag sets a base-line uniform resource locator (URL) for a set of related documents. URLs are an addressing convention for the World Wide Web that uniquely identifies a document by server type (gopher, http, etc.), computer on which it is located, and directory path and filename. They can also point to a particular section within a document, known as a fragment. Other URL types point to e-mail addresses and even telnet sessions. URLs will be covered in more detail in Chapter 6.

<BASE> is useful for building links between a large collection of documents that reside on one computer. A book with many chapters, diagrams, and related documents might start with a table of contents that includes *<BASE HREF= "http://server.lib.vt.edu/texts/HTML_book/">*. This base URL is prepended to all HREF attributes in the remainder of the document, eliminating the need for server type (*http* stands for hypertext transfer protocol and means the server is a Web server), computer name (*server.lib.vt.edu*), or path (*/texts/HTML_book*) in the hypertext links to chapters and related documents in the table of contents. Any file in this directory on this server can now be referred to simply by filename:

   📁 /texts

      📁 /HTML_book

         📄 contents.html

         📄 chapter1.html

         📄 chapter2.html

```
<HTML>
<HEAD><TITLE>HTML Plus! Table of Contents</TITLE>
<BASE HREF="http://server.lib.vt.edu/texts/HTML_book/">
<BODY>
<H1>HTML Plus!</H1>
<H2>Table of Contents</H2>
<UL>
<LI><A HREF="chapter1.html">Chapter 1</A>
```

Hypertext links between documents normally require that all of this information be repeated for each link in the document, so <BASE> saves rekeying full URLs in the same document every time they are used. It also makes documents easier to maintain because if they are moved only one URL needs to be changed within the document, rather than each occurrence.

<ISINDEX>

The <ISINDEX> tag specifies that the browser should treat this document as a searchable index. Usually, the Web client will display a text entry field near the top of the document so the reader can enter search keys. This tag is usually associated with a program on the server that performs the search for the user. These programs, called scripts, will be covered in greater detail in Chapter 28. Without a script to process the search request, the user will not receive a reply to their search.

<NEXTID>

Another tag you might encounter in the header of some documents on the Web is the <NEXTID> tag. This tag is used by some automatic markup software to keep track of available anchors within a document. You would never place this tag into a document header yourself. A few automatic HTML markup programs can use hints from the original non-HTML document to build hypertext links using <NEXTID> as a mechanism to keep track of these links.

<LINK>

The <LINK> tag is used to indicate a relationship between this document and other documents. Essentially, it is a user- and developer-defined tag. You must have some documentation for the browser that supports link options in order to construct them since HTML does not define any link NAME attribute values. Some browsers use <LINK> to point to a URL or a local document such as a glossary or index. It is up to the browser to decide how to display the <LINK> tag. Such links would most likely appear as a toolbar (on each of a set of related documents), which a user could rely on to navigate quickly between a table of contents, a set of chapters, and perhaps an index or bibliography:

```
<LINK NAME="ToC" HREF="contents.html">
<LINK NAME="Glossary" HREF="glossary.html">
```

As many links as needed could be placed in the document header to define relationships.

<META>

Information intended for the client software but not part of the document is included in the header with the <META> tag. Here you can include information such as the last revision date or information describing how to access this document. Each <META> item in the header must have a name/value pair that is expressed with either the HTTP-EQUIV or NAME attribute combined with a CONTENT attribute. HTTP-EQUIV means this name corresponds to a documented server header field such as Expires, Keywords, or Reply-To:

```
<META HTTP-EQUIV="Last-Modified" CONTENT="Aug 03, 1995">
```

<META> should only be used when no other header element is suitable for conveying the information you wish to include in your document, such as a <LINK>, <TITLE>, or a comment. If the client does not understand the content of a particular <META> item, it will ignore it. Figure 3-2 shows a Netscape document information panel displaying various header information including Last Modified data from a <META> header element. Another common use of <META> is for encoding Netscape push-pull animation sequences, which are covered in a later chapter.

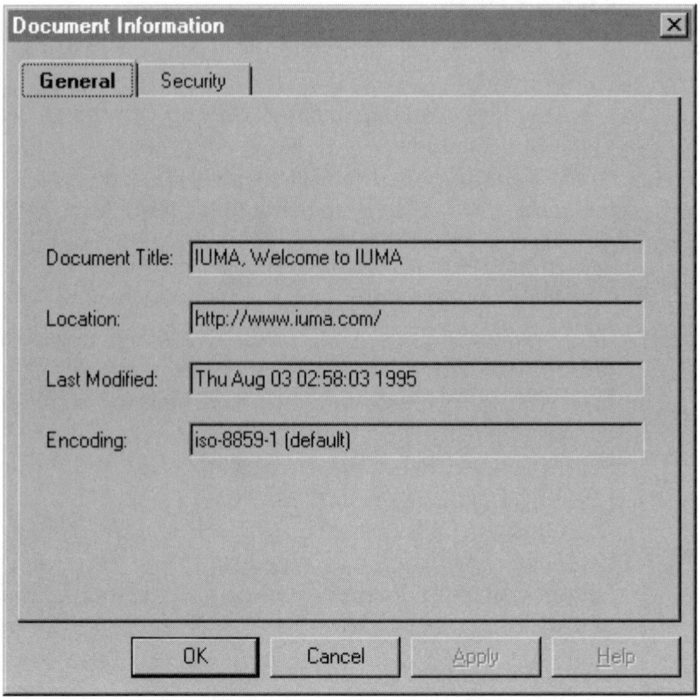

Figure 3-2
Netscape
Document
Information Panel

Document Information   ☒

| **General** | Security |

Document Title: IUMA, Welcome to IUMA

Location: http://www.iuma.com/

Last Modified: Thu Aug 03 02:58:03 1995

Encoding: iso-8859-1 (default)

| OK | Cancel | Apply | Help |

COMMENTS

The comment tag can appear in any part of an HTML document including the header section. A comment is a nondisplaying message to anyone reading the HTML source, such as the original author or additional author. A comment is preceded with <!-- and ends with -->. Comments can also appear in the document body and are often used to include document information such as version, creation date, last update, etc.:

```
<!-- Version 3.0, last updated July 20, 1995, JEP -->
```

Let's expand our "Hello, World Wide Web" example to include each valid header element:

```
<HTML>
<HEAD>
<TITLE>Hello WWW</TITLE>
<BASE HREF="http://server.lib.vt.edu/htmlplus/">
<META HTTP-EQUIV="Last-Modified" CONTENT="Sep 04, 1995">
<LINK HREF="glossary.html">
<ISINDEX>
<!-- HTML 2 header elements example -->
</HEAD>
<BODY>
<P>Hello, World Wide Web.
</BODY>
</HTML>
```

Header elements are a useful and often overlooked part of the HTML language. They can add flexibility and store useful information for both the author and the reader. Well thought out titles are particularly valuable to readers who might view dozens of documents a day and maintain large collections of bookmarks. HTML documents without valid headers could cause problems with some browsers making it even more important to include this structure in each HTML document you create for the Web. And don't forget that headers can also convey valuable information to maintainers with comments, links, and meta data elements.

HTML 2 PROJECT STEP 1: STRUCTURING DOCUMENTS

In our first project, we will create a simple language tutorial. Here are the first few paragraphs tagged with HTML markup we've covered so far:

```
<HTML>
<HEAD><TITLE>Introduction to Malay</TITLE>
<BASE HREF="http://server.lib.vt.edu/languages/malay/">
</HEAD>
<BODY>
```

Continued on next page

Continued from previous page

<P>Malay, or Bahasa Malaysi as it is known by those who speak it, is a language spoken in the southeast Asian nation of Malaysia. Malaysia is located on the same peninsula as Singapore, to the west of Thailand. Part of the country is also located on the island of Borneo, the fourth largest island in the world. Slight variations of Malay are also spoken in Singapore, Indonesia, Thailand and Brunei. Over 200 million people speak Malay, nearly as many people as the population of the United States. Malay, like French or Japanese, is a distinct language but also includes words from other languages:
Arabic
Chinese
Dutch
English
Indian
<P>Malaysia has become a major economic force in the region producing everything from timber to automobiles to computers. They launched their first compact car model, the Proton, in 1994. Because of its economic boom, Malaysia is poised to supply products to much of Southeast Asia including China and the Philippines. With markets like these, no wonder multinational corporations are beginning to take notice. By learning Malay, you will have a definite edge when applying for jobs with corporations that deal with southeast Asia.
</BODY>
</HTML>

Here's how the document should look when you load it into Netscape:

Netscape - [Introduction to Malay]   _ □ ✕

File Edit View Go Bookmarks Options Directory   Help

| ⇦ Back | ⇨ Forward | 🏠 Home | ⊘ Reload | Images | Open | 🖨 Print | Find | ● Stop |

Location: file:///D|/JPOWELL/BOOK/PROJ1CH3.HTM   ▾   **N**

Malay, or Bahasa Malaysi as it is known by those who speak it, is a language spoken in the southeast Asian nation of Malaysia. Malaysia is located on the same peninsula as Singapore, to the west of Thailand. Part of the country is also located on the island of Borneo, the fourth largest island in the world. Slight variations of Malay are also spoken in Singapore, Indonesia, Thailand and Brunei. Over 200 million people speak Malay, nearly as many people as the population of the United States. Malay, like French or Japanese, is a distinct language but also includes words from other languages: Arabic Chinese Dutch English Indian

Malaysia has become a major economic force in the region producing everything from timber to automobiles to computers. They launched their first compact car model, the Proton, in 1994. Because of its economic boom, Malaysia is poised to supply products to much of Southeast Asia including China and the Philippines. With markets like these, no wonder multinational corporations are beginning to take notice. By learning Malay, you will have a definite edge when applying for jobs with corporations that deal with southeast Asia.

The title "Introduction to Malay" appears in the title bar. Paragraphs are separated by a blank line. We've also established a base address for this and related documents with the <BASE> tag. But there are no section titles or headings in the document body. It would also be nice to perhaps tag the list of languages at the end of the first paragraph so that it actually looked like a list. In the next chapter, we will add some more text and additional markup to address these issues.

GENERAL DOCUMENT TAG USAGE SUMMARY

Tag	Permitted Context	Content Model
<HTML>	around document	<HEAD>, <BODY>, <!-- -->
<HEAD>	before document body	<TITLE>, <BASE>, <ISINDEX>, <LINK>, <NEXTID>, <!-- -->
<TITLE>	within document header	ASCII characters, character entities
<BASE>	within document header	no contents
<ISINDEX>	within document header	no contents
<LINK>	within document header	no contents
<NEXTID>	within document header	no contents
<META>	within document header	no contents
<BODY>	after document header	text blocks
<!-- -->	anywhere in document	ASCII characters, character entities

ATTRIBUTE SUMMARY

Tag	Attribute	Value
<HTML>	none	none
<HEAD>	none	none
<TITLE>	none	none
<BASE>	HREF	a URL
<ISINDEX>	none	none
<LINK>	NAME	any quoted string up to 1024 characters
	HREF	a URL
<NEXTID>	NAME	any quoted string up to 1024 characters
<META>	NAME	any quoted string up to 1024 characters
	HTTP-EQUIV	HTTP header name
	CONTENT	any quoted string up to 1024 characters
<BODY>	none	none

4

Headings and Text Block Elements

CHAPTER AT A GLANCE

- Correct use of headings
- *What makes a good heading?*
- Understanding paragraphs and lists
- Determining when to use the preformatted text tag
- HTML 2 Project: *Adding Text Blocks*
- Text Block Tag Usage and Attribute Summaries

In the previous chapter, we looked at the document header and its elements. We also constructed a very simple "Hello, World Wide Web" document. In this chapter, we will continue our first HTML project using some generalized markup elements of the <BODY> tag. Our project will incorporate headings and several text block elements.

HTML documents tend to be short. Rather than overwhelm the reader with details, you can present information in short, easy-to-read segments. The typical HTML document has four to six paragraphs. Hypertext allows you to build links and relationships between these short documents explaining topics in more detail, defining new words, presenting examples, etc. When you write for the World Wide Web, you should assume your audience will be extremely diverse. Some users will be beginners who need extra examples, while others will be experts who may only consult your documents as reference material. Structure within and among a collection of documents helps keep your user on track.

In a well-structured document, all text belongs to one of the document's text blocks. Text blocks such as paragraphs or lists are containers for structures within the body of the document. Their contents are sentences and phrases which are themselves made up of characters, character entities, and character markup.

Headings <Hn>

HTML lacks the exhaustive set of structural elements found in other SGML applications. Still, there is a structure to the body of an HTML document. HTML provides six levels of headings that are usually presented in a font descending in size at each level. For example, a level 2 heading would by default be displayed with a smaller font than a level 1 heading. Since headings are generalized markup corresponding to the structure of the document, the browser and reader have the ultimate control over their appearance. Heading tags are <Hn> where n can be the numerals 1–6:

```
<H1>Chapter 1</H1>
<H2>The Document Header</H2>
```

Headings must always have an end tag. Each heading is always displayed on a separate line, and they are sometimes centered, depending on the Web browser. Headings should be brief, as their main purpose is to contain the title of a document section. Thinking of headings as titles of outline or book sections can help you understand how to use them correctly:

```
<H1>Part 1</H1>
    <H2>Section 1: HTML 2</H2>
        <H3>Chapter 1: Introduction to HTML</H3>
    <H2>Section 2: HTML 3</H2>
        <H3>Chapter 8</H3>
```

In this example, each section is a subsection of the previous. Each subsection gets a higher-level heading (up to <H6>), until a new, less-specific-level section is encountered (as in Section 2, which is tagged with <H2>). You can skip levels but it is incorrect to use sections out of order, such as having a level 2 heading occur before a level 1 heading in an attempt to achieve a certain look for your page. Headings should not be used to format text.

WHAT MAKES A GOOD HEADING?

Headings should be brief (2–5 words), descriptive titles for sections of your document. Like titles, they are intended to lure in and retain the readers long enough to get them to read your document. When you are authoring text for the Web, use headings like an outline. When you have outlined your entire document, use this outline as a table of contents. Then select the contents of different-level headings in your outline to indicate which topics should be in their own separate document, such as all level 2 headings. Then you can reuse heading levels in each new document (e.g., a level 2 heading in outline could become a level 1 heading in the document covering that topic). Use the headings from the table of contents as the new document title (with the <TITLE> tag), to help orient the readers and keep them on track.

Headings are not good for picture captions, as hypertext links, or as formatting devices. That's because Web browsers have always allowed the end user to select the font style and size for each level heading. So what looks good to you might not be displayed the way you intended by someone else's browser.

PARAGRAPHS <P>

Most of the text in a document will probably be in paragraphs. HTML has a paragraph tag for these types of text blocks: <P>. Paragraph end tags are not required since the next paragraph or text block start tag implies that the previous paragraph has ended. Most Web browsers insert a blank line before the start of a new paragraph. Paragraph tags are often abused to achieve vertical line spacing because of this. But they are structure, not formatting tags. Everything within a paragraph is treated as a sentence belonging to it and is formatted accordingly. So if multiple spaces or carriage returns are encountered, they are ignored:

```
<P>Paragraph tags  are used to tag paragraphs.
Every paragraph should start with a paragraph tag but end tags are not required.
<P>HTML supports other types of text blocks such as preformatted text and
address blocks.
```

is displayed as:

Paragraph tags are used to tag paragraphs. Every paragraph should start with a paragraph tag but end tags are not required.

HTML supports other types of text blocks such as preformatted text and address blocks.

PREFORMATTED TEXT <PRE>

Sometimes you will want to include text that is precisely aligned, such as a table, or other multirow and/or multicolumn text using a fixed font. The HTML preformatted tag will preserve multiple spaces (which are replaced with one space in normal body text), alignment, and carriage returns. The preformatted text tag is <PRE>. An end tag is always required with this tag:

```
<PRE>
                  January     February    March
Orders shipped    1000        1115        1300
Returns           17          23          29
</PRE>
```

As you can see, the text should already be aligned and formatted the way you want it to look in the final document. <PRE> simply preserves this formatting information.

From time to time you might find a document on the Internet that uses one of several <PRE> predecessors. In earlier versions of HTML, including plain text in a document was considered very important, but people disagreed as to how it should be done, so several tags were created to do it. Tags such as <PLAIN-TEXT>, <XMP>, and <LISTING> are still present in documents published on the Web today. Like <PRE> they were used both to preserve formatting and to hint at the content (<XMP> was generalized markup for an example) but their meanings were not well defined. Each of these tags has been superseded by the preformatted tag because that's essentially all these tags did. Preformatted text segments are more difficult to read since they use a fixed-width font and allow no other font variations. If you can find other tags to do the work, use them instead.

Text Flow Tags

Most text block tags automatically control the flow of their contents. Paragraph tags remove extraneous spaces and carriage returns to form a cohesive collection of sentences. Preformatted sections retain virtually all formatting and alignment. Other text blocks function like paragraphs by default, but you can use text flow tags to alter their formatting.

The break (<BR>) tag forces a line break wherever it is inserted. It is useful for presenting addresses and informal lists of information:

Thomas Jefferson
 Monticello
Virginia

would be displayed as:

Thomas Jefferson
Monticello
Virginia

Break tags are simply inserted where desired. They have no end tags because they do not contain any text.

Another tag that breaks up the flow of characters is the horizontal rule (<HR>) tag. Horizontal rules are horizontal lines that extend across the Web browser screen dividing two blocks of text from one another. They improve readability of complex texts such as those with forms or preformatted blocks.

<ADDRESS>

The address tag marks a text block that contains information about the author. This information can be his or her name, postal address, e-mail address, etc. The contents of the address tag are usually displayed in italics by the browser and formatted as a paragraph unless you use text flow tags to alter formatting (Figure 4-1):

```
<ADDRESS>
Letters to the Editor<BR>
care of the Blacksburg Bugle<BR>
Blacksburg, VA<BR>
bbugled@bugle.bev.net
</ADDRESS>
```

Address blocks should be placed at the top or bottom of the text body.

<BLOCKQUOTE>

Blockquotes are portions of text included from other documents. Long <BLOCK-QUOTE> passages should also be marked with paragraph tags just as they appear in the original document (Figure 4-1):

```
<BLOCKQUOTE>
L'&eacute;tat c'est moi.
</BLOCKQUOTE>
```

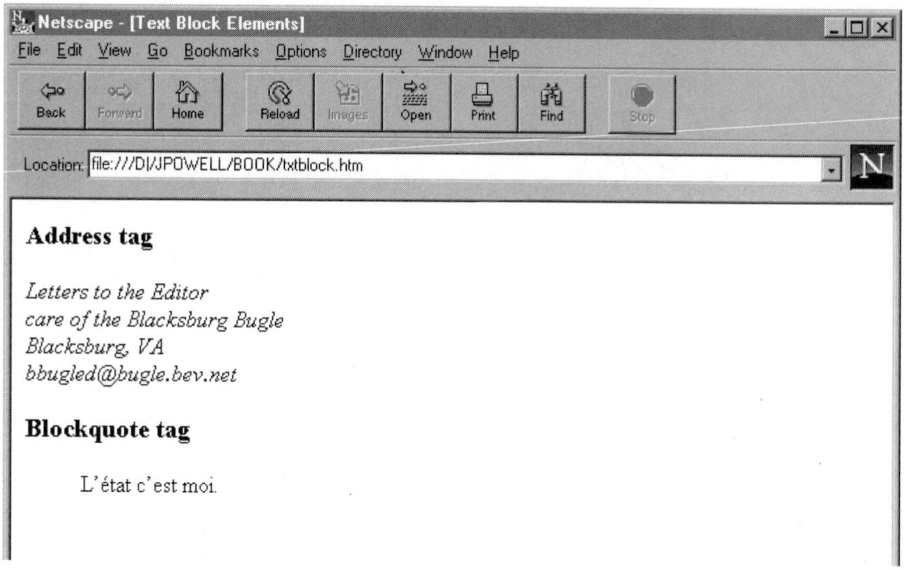

Figure 4-1
<ADDRESS> and
<BLOCKQUOTE>
tags

LISTS <UL>, <OL>, <DL>, <DIR>, AND <MENU>

HTML includes markup for five types of lists: unordered, ordered, definition lists, directories, and menus. The contents of lists are separated from the normal body text and each item is usually displayed on a separate line. All list types require start and end tags.

Unordered lists are lists of items that do not need to occur in a specific order. They are usually displayed as a bulleted list of items, one per line. Unordered lists are marked with the <UL> tag and each item is tagged with a list item <LI> tag. Every item in a list must have a list item start tag, so you do not need to use an end tag since it is implied by the next item tag (Figure 4-2):

```
<UL>
<LI>Canada
<LI>United States
<LI>Mexico
</UL>
```

Ordered lists are lists of items that should occur in a specific order. Each item is preceded by a number or letter that is incremented with each item. Ordered lists are marked with the <OL> tag and their items are tagged with <LI>, just like unordered lists. The Web client software decides whether to use numbers, roman numerals, or letters to number list items (Figure 4-2).

```
<OL>
<LI>janvier
<LI>f&eacute;vrier
<LI>mars
<LI>avril
<LI>mai
</OL>
```

Menus and directories display computer output. Neither can contain nested lists. Directories (<DIR>) are displayed much like unordered lists but each item should be brief (less than 24 characters) as they are sometimes displayed in multiple columns. The directory tag is useful for tagging a list of files. Menus (<MENU>) are displayed like unordered lists, but are more compact. Each item is displayed on a separate line. Both directory and menu lists use the list item tag <LI> to indicate individual list items.

Definition lists are used to present a list of terms and their definitions. Definition lists start with the <DL> tag. Definition lists are the only type of HTML lists that do not use the <LI> tag. Instead they use the definition term <DT> tag for each term, optionally followed by one definition <DD> per term. Each definition is displayed as a paragraph, which is typically indented to the right of the term it describes (Figure 4-2):

```
<DL>
<DT>malchance
<DD>bad luck
<DT>manger
<DD>eat
</DL>
```

Unordered, ordered, and definition lists have a COMPACT attribute, which tells the Web browser to display the list items with less vertical and horizontal space between them where possible. A definition list with the COMPACT attribute might be displayed with less vertical space between term/definition pairs and less horizontal space between the list items and the left margin.

Unordered and ordered lists can be nested. For example, you can have multiple levels of unordered lists or an ordered list as one item in an unordered list. The embedded list is treated as one element of the list in which it is embedded, meaning that all its elements are indented further to the right (Figure 4-3):

```
<UL>
<LI><B>Fruit</B>
<UL>
<LI>banane
<LI>pomme
<LI>p&ecirc;che
</UL>
</UL>
```

Figure 4-2 Lists

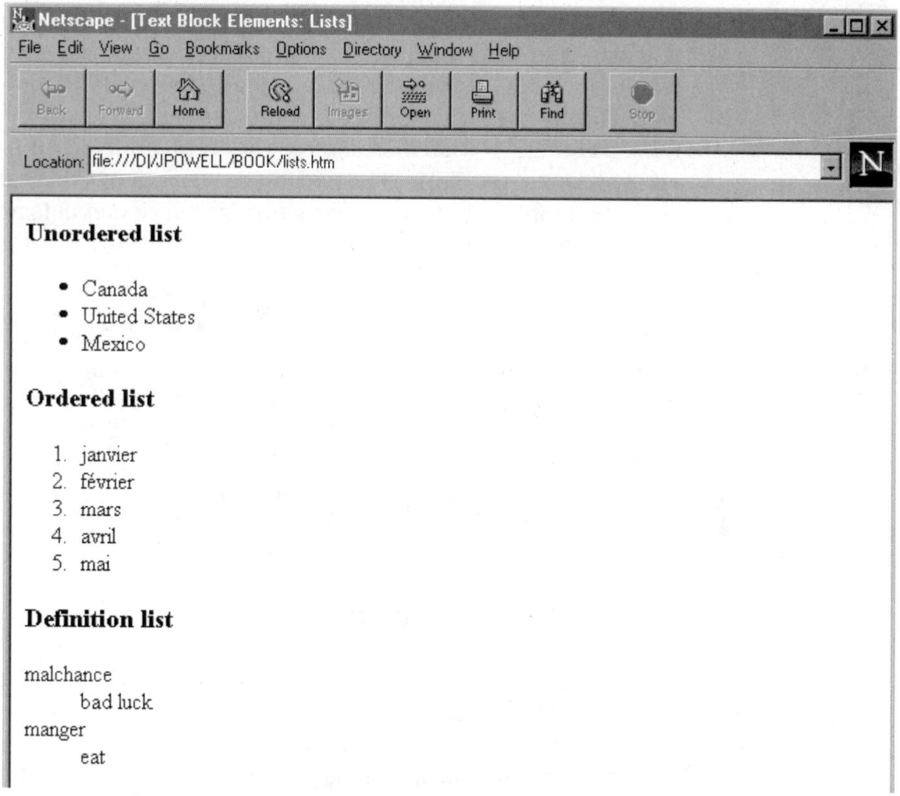

Netscape - [Text Block Elements: Lists]

File   Edit   View   Go   Bookmarks   Options   Directory   Window   Help

Back   Forward   Home   Reload   Images   Open   Print   Find   Stop

Location: file:///D|/JPOWELL/BOOK/lists.htm

Unordered list

- Canada
- United States
- Mexico

Ordered list

1. janvier
2. février
3. mars
4. avril
5. mai

Definition list

malchance
　　　bad luck
manger
　　　eat

Figure 4-3 Nested lists

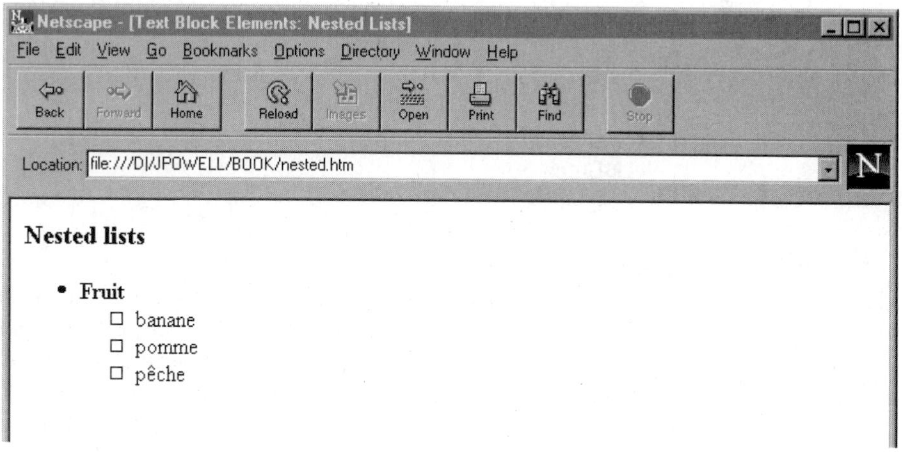

Netscape - [Text Block Elements: Nested Lists]

File   Edit   View   Go   Bookmarks   Options   Directory   Window   Help

Back   Forward   Home   Reload   Images   Open   Print   Find   Stop

Location: file:///D|/JPOWELL/BOOK/nested.htm

Nested lists

- **Fruit**
  - ☐ banane
  - ☐ pomme
  - ☐ pêche

Like document header and body sections, text blocks logically structure document content. All text within the body of an HTML document should be a member of some text block. Major sections of an HTML document should start with a heading that describes the content. Properly formatted HTML documents are collections of nested structures rather than blocks of free-floating text. As you will see later, HTML 3 is even more strict about this than HTML 2, so you should get into the practice of structuring your documents now to save time and effort when you revise them later to be HTML 3 compliant.

HTML 2 PROJECT STEP 2: ADDING TEXT BLOCKS

With step 2 of our project, we add text blocks to clarify and improve readability. Open malay.htm and add the **bold** text listed below:

```
<HTML>
<HEAD><TITLE>Introduction to Malay</TITLE>
<BASE HREF="http://server.lib.vt.edu/languages/malay/">
</HEAD>
<BODY>
<H1>Introduction to Malay</H1>
<H2>Malaysia</H2>
<P>Malay, or Bahasa Malaysi as it is known by those who speak it, is a language
spoken in the southeast Asian nation of Malaysia. Malaysia is located on the same
peninsula as Singapore, to the west of Thailand. Part of the country is also located
on the island of Borneo, the fourth largest island in the world. Slight variations of
Malay are also spoken in Singapore, Indonesia, Thailand and Brunei. Over 200
million people speak Malay, nearly as many people as the population of the United
States. Malay, like French or Japanese, is a distinct language but also includes
words from other languages:
<UL>
<LI>Arabic
<LI>Chinese
<LI>Dutch
<LI>English
<LI>various languages of India
</UL>
<P>Malaysia has become a major economic force in the region producing
everything from timber to automobiles to computers. They launched their first
compact car model, the Proton, in 1994. Because of its economic boom, Malaysia
is poised to supply products to much of Southeast Asia including China and the
Philippines. With markets like these, no wonder multinational corporations are
beginning to take notice. By learning Malay, you will have a definite edge when
applying for jobs with corporations that deal with southeast Asia.
<H3>Other Topics</H3>
<UL>
```

```
<LI>Vocabulary
<LI>Grammar
</UL>
</BODY>
</HTML>
```

Here's how the document looks when you load it into Netscape:

"Other Topics" includes links to two new documents for this project. We'll create one of those documents now. Create a new document with your text editor, enter the following text, and save it as vocab.htm:

```
<HTML>
<HEAD><TITLE>Malay Vocabulary</TITLE>
<BASE HREF="http://server.lib.vt.edu/languages/malay/">
</HEAD>
<BODY>
<H1>Malay Vocabulary</H1>
<P>For the tourist or businessman, it is often sufficient to learn a small number of
words and phrases of the local language. Phrases, or idioms, are important to
learn because they are difficult to guess since they do not literally translate well.
For example, if you had visitors who were departing you would say goodbye by
saying 'selamat jalan', which literally translates to safe road. Building a vocabulary
is also extremely beneficial. So let's start with a few words for common foods:
<DL>
<DT>bread <DD>roti
<DT>chicken <DD>ayam
<DT>egg <DD>telur
<DT>lemon <DD>li mau or jeruk sitrun
<DT>potato <DD>ubi or kentang
<DT>rice <DD>raw is beras, cooked is nasi
</DL>
Numbers are essential for any traveler:
<OL>
<LI>satu
<LI>dua
<LI>empat
<LI>lima
<LI>
</OL>
<HR>
Return to Introduction or go on to Grammar
</BODY>
</HTML>
```

TEXT BLOCK TAG USAGE SUMMARY

Tag	Permitted Context	Content Model
<H1>–<H6>	document body outside text blocks	ASCII characters, character entities
<P>	document body	ASCII characters, character entities, phrase and typographic elements
<PRE>	document body	ASCII characters, character entities, form elements
 	paragraphs, forms	none
<ADDRESS>	document body	ASCII characters, character entities, typographic elements
<BLOCKQUOTE>	document body	ASCII characters, character entities, typographic elements
<DIR>	document body	List items (<LI>)
<MENU>	document body	List items (<LI>)
<UL>	document body	List items (<LI>)
<OL>	document body	List items (<LI>)
<DL>	document body	Terms (<DT>) and Definitions (<DD>)
<LI>	lists	ASCII characters, character entities, typographic elements
<DT>	definition lists	ASCII characters, character entities, typographic elements
<DD>	definition lists	ASCII characters, character entities, typographic elements

ATTRIBUTE SUMMARY

Tag	Attribute	Value
<UL>	COMPACT	none
<OL>	COMPACT	none
<DL>	COMPACT	none

5

Phrase and Typographic Elements

CHAPTER AT A GLANCE

- Understanding how to apply phrase elements
- Using typographic elements sparingly yet effectively
- *Another Reason to Tag for Content*
- HTML 2 Project: *Adding Phrase and Typographic Elements*
- Phrase and Typographic Element Tag Usage Summary

No two sets of tags better represent the dual nature of HTML than phrase and typographic elements. Phrase tags, also referred to as logical style elements, are generalized markup used to emphasize important words or phrases. These tags indicate that the tagged text is more important than the surrounding text. They emphasize content but leave formatting to the browser. Typographic elements are specific markup that control how the text should look. The text may or may not be more important than the surrounding text. Typographic elements such as <B> for bold are specific markup that simply tell the browser how a character, word, or phrase should be displayed.

When you use HTML to markup a text, you should strive to select generalized markup elements when there are both specific and generalized tags that achieve similar effects. Generalized markup is difficult for an automated system to perform as it has little or no concept of content. Humans add significant value to texts when they can markup content. Computer programs can later be used to build lists of important points or keywords from a document with generalized markup, but less reliably so from a document by simply selecting passages an author might have decided to bold or italicize. As is often the case on the Web, bold or italics might be included in a document to make it look better rather than to indicate important pieces of the document.

Phrase Elements

Phrase elements are sometimes referred to as logical style elements. These tags indicate that a particular passage is more important than the surrounding text. Some are also used to tag specific types of data such as program source code. The <EM> tag indicates a section of text that should be emphasized. The <STRONG> tag is an enhanced <EM> tag meaning that the text should stand out more than the surrounding text, that is, it should be strongly emphasized. Some browsers display <EM> text in italics, and <STRONG> text in bold type. Figure 5-1 shows examples of phrase and Typographic Markup.

General text elements are used around textual structures such as definitions and citations. The <CITE> tag is used to indicate that the tagged portion of text is a citation from another source. You could, for example, follow a <BLOCK-QUOTE> element with a <CITE> element listing the original author and title of the work from which the quote was taken.

<DFN> marks a single definition. The text marked by this tag can be displayed or offset from the surrounding text in a variety of ways such as italics or indented. Unlike definition lists, you can include the term with the definition and need not supply additional elements.

Programmers and technical authors might want to use the HTML text elements available for program code and related text in online manuals and tutorials. The <CODE> tag is used to tag a section of program source code such as C or Perl language source. The <SAMPLE> tag is used to markup text output from a computer program. A software user's response can be tagged with the <KBD> tag if they are expected to hit a single key. Variables in the text are tagged with the <VAR> tag. Here is an example:

```
<CODE>
!#/usr/local/bin/perl
# catch any key and respond with a message
# output a line of text
print "Press any key\n";
read $_;
```

Continued on next page

Continued from previous page

print "this is a test";
</CODE>
will display the message
<SAMPLE>Press any key</SAMPLE> to
which the user can respond with a key such as <KBD>A</KBD> and the
program will respond with <SAMPLE>this is a test</SAMPLE>.
The user input is placed in the variable <VAR>$_</VAR>.

Figure 5-1 Phrase and Typographic Markup as viewed with Microsoft Internet Explorer

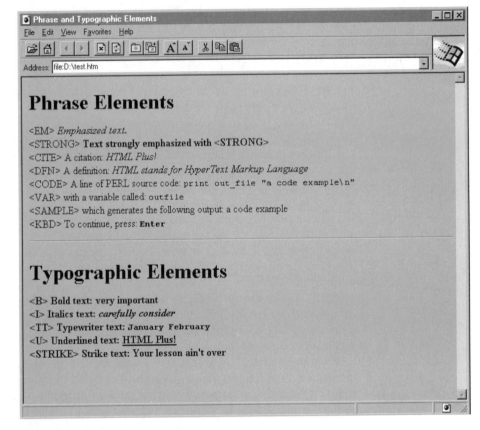

Typographic Elements

Everyone wants to publish the most attractive and easy-to-read document they can. Word processors have allowed us all to create far more attractive documents than we could have ever hoped to create without them. HTML markup is more concerned with content and structure than appearance but it does include a few tags whose sole purpose is to beautify documents. You should use

ANOTHER REASON TO TAG FOR CONTENT

HTML and the World Wide Web were originally designed to support a widely scattered group of people located around the world. These people were primarily involved in scientific research (specifically, high-energy-article physics at CERN). While they all had access to the Internet, they used different types of computer systems. The inventors of the Web wanted to eventually support anybody using any kind of computer, so they developed a system that would be platform independent—that is, documents could be displayed by any type of computer the user might have. That's why an SGML-based markup language was selected for the Web rather than a word processing format like Microsoft Word or WordPerfect.

SGML emphasizes document structure and leaves the display of these structures up to the individual computer. Some computers have more capabilities than others, such as high-resolution screens suitable for displaying graphics and multiple typefaces, while others might only be able to display text. If content is emphasized over appearance, then the computer can make formatting decisions by weighing the importance of the tagged content. Items tagged with <EM> are not as important as items tagged with <STRONG> so a browser might choose to reserve limited formatting styles for the most important items. This type of information is not available to the computer when text is tagged with specific elements such as bold or italics. So it might choose to ignore both or emphasize only one and could choose the item that the author considered less important. You might think everyone would use bold and italics consistently, with bold indicating greater importance, but in fact authors are often more concerned with a particular look and use these tags to make their documents more attractive rather than structurally sound.

Think about platform independence as you author for the Web. Remember that no matter how much you beautify a document, your efforts could all be lost at the other end. Spend more of your time tagging content with generalized markup tags and you will communicate more effectively on the Web.

them sparingly, and only where there is not a generalized markup tag for the type of content you are tagging. Inserting typographic elements should be thought of as a final, document-polishing step.

The bold tag <B> marks a section of text that should be displayed in bold typeface. Usually the bold start and end tags are placed around a word or phrase that should be emphasized for some reason. But they could also be used in other ways, such as to emphasize the first character of a new paragraph.

The italics tag <I> marks text that should appear in an italicized typeface.

Both bold and italics can be used together (if properly nested) to achieve a combined effect:

It is <B><I>extremely important</I></B> to save files frequently.

The typewriter text tag <TT> displays marked text in a fixed font. The text will often look like the output from a typewriter, hence its name. Typewriter text should be used on brief passages, shorter than one line, or on sentences that should not be spaced apart from the surrounding text. For multiple lines of fixed-font text, use the preformatted text block tag <PRE>.

Some Web browsers support two additional typographic elements. The underline tag <U> marks a section of text that should be underlined. Typically, underlining is used for titles of books or to provide extra emphasis for a word or phrase. But remember, underlining is not supported by all Web browsers, and the emphasis will be completely lost when displayed using software that does not render it.

<STRIKE> is used to indicate the tagged text should be removed from the document or ignored; the browser will display the text with a horizontal line drawn through it. Early on, the inventors of the World Wide Web envisioned that users would want to collectively author documents using Web browsers. The <STRIKE> tag was included to give editors or multiple authors a way to indicate changes using HTML. But until combination editor-browsers become commonplace, it is not likely that elements such as <STRIKE> will achieve widespread support.

Typographic HTML elements can improve the appearance of and, in some cases, the readability of Web documents. But authors run the risk of losing crucial information by using typographic elements instead of generalized markup such as phrase elements. Authors can add valuable information to a document by tagging content with content-specific markup instead of using tags simply to achieve a certain visual effect. As you will see later, HTML 3 provides a richer set of generalized markup elements, so developing a habit of marking content first, and tagging for appearance last will pay off as new HTML standards arise.

HTML 2 PROJECT STEP 3: ADDING PHRASE AND TYPOGRAPHIC ELEMENTS

Now let's add some phrase and typographic elements to our HTML 2 project documents. Open malay.htm and make the following changes (indicated in **bold**):

```
<HTML>
<HEAD><TITLE>Introduction to Malay</TITLE>
<BASE HREF="http://server.lib.vt.edu/languages/malay/">
</HEAD>
<BODY>
<H1>Introduction to Malay</H1>
<H2>Malaysia</H2>
<P><EM>Malay</EM>, or <STRONG>Bahasa Malaysi</STRONG> as it is known by
```

those who speak it, is a language spoken in the southeast Asian nation of Malaysia. Malaysia is located on the same peninsula as Singapore, to the west of Thailand. Part of the country is also located on the island of Borneo, the fourth largest island in the world. Slight variations of Malay are also spoken in Singapore, Indonesia, Thailand and Brunei. Over 200 million people speak Malay, nearly as many people as the population of the United States. Malay, like French or Japanese, is a distinct language but also includes words from other languages:

```
<UL>
<LI>Arabic
<LI>Chinese
<LI>Dutch
<LI>English
<LI>various languages of India
</UL>
<P>Malaysia has become a major economic force in the region producing
everything from timber to automobiles to computers. They launched their first
compact car model, the <I>Proton</I>, in 1994. Because of its economic boom,
Malaysia is poised to supply products to much of Southeast Asia including China
and the Philippines. With markets like these, no wonder multinational corporations
are beginning to take notice. By learning Malay, you will have a definite edge
when applying for jobs with corporations that deal with southeast Asia.
<H3>Other Topics</H3>
<UL>
<LI><B>Vocabulary</B>
<LI><B>Grammar</B>
</UL>
</BODY>
</HTML>
```

Save malay.htm. We don't need to make any changes to vocab.htm. Instead, create a new document, insert the following text, and name it grammar.htm:

```
<HTML>
<HEAD><TITLE>Malay Vocabulary</TITLE>
<BASE HREF="http://server.lib.vt.edu/languages/malay/">
</HEAD>
<BODY>
<H1>Malay Grammar</H1>
<P>One fascinating and often used grammatical construct in Malay is
reduplication. Reduplication is the practice of repeating a noun or adverb to
indicate an indefinite plural or to emphasize the word. Here is an extreme example:
<BLOCKQUOTE>
"Malam-malam dia bawa anak jalan-jalan satu-satu, dan kadang-kadang dua-dua
sekali." <BR>
Nightly she takes the children for a walk one by one, and occasionally both at
once.
</BLOCKQUOTE>
```

Continued on next page

Continued from previous page

```
<CITE>From Malay made Easy by A.W. Hamilton</CITE>
</BODY>
</HTML>
```

When you open this document in Netscape, it should look like this:

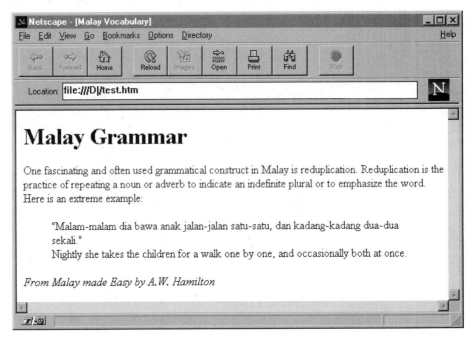

PHRASE AND TYPOGRAPHIC ELEMENT TAG USAGE SUMMARY

Tag	Permitted Context	Content Model
<CITE>	text blocks	ASCII characters, character entities
<CODE>	text blocks, sentences, and phrases	ASCII characters, character entities
<VAR>	text blocks, sentences, and phrases	ASCII characters, character entities
<SAMPLE>	text blocks, sentences, and phrases	ASCII characters, character entities
<DFN>	text blocks, sentences, and phrases	ASCII characters, character entities
<KBD>	text blocks, sentences, and phrases	ASCII characters, character entities
<EM>	text blocks, sentences, and phrases	ASCII characters, character entities
<STRONG>	text blocks, sentences, and phrases	ASCII characters, character entities
<B>	text blocks, sentences, and phrases	ASCII characters, character entities
<I>	text blocks, sentences, and phrases	ASCII characters, character entities
<U>	text blocks, sentences, and phrases	ASCII characters, character entities
<TT>	text blocks, sentences, and phrases	ASCII characters, character entities
<STRIKE>	text blocks, sentences, and phrases	ASCII characters, character entities

6

Making Connections

CHAPTER AT A GLANCE

- Understanding hypertext
- How to construct URLs (uniform resource locators)
- Table 6-1: *Uniform Resource Locators*
- Creating hypertext links between and within documents
- *HTML Anchor Do's and Don'ts*
- HTML 2 Project: *Adding Anchors*
- Anchor Tag Usage and Attribute Summaries

Content is as important on the Web as it is in any other publishing medium. But the ability to connect documents to one another across a global network is what makes the World Wide Web the most powerful publishing system ever invented. If HTML did not support links between documents, other languages such as PostScript might have usurped it as the document format for the Web. The ability to make connections between documents is what makes HTML a hypertext language. Hypertexts are documents that are connected to one another through links. Hypertext links provide the reader with multiple paths, hierarchical views, additional information, and routes to related documents. Each link is a word, phrase, or graphic that, when selected, causes another document to be loaded. The document pointed to is called a *target*. In HTML, links are also referred to as *anchors*. The target of an HTML anchor can be a different document, another portion of the current document, an image, or a variety of other multimedia data.

Many components of the World Wide Web work together so users can follow hypertext links around the Internet. Each document published on the Web is located on a computer running Web server software. When a document is published on a server, it has an address. The address includes the server name and filename, as well as other information describing where the document is stored on the computer and how it is to be accessed. The HTML anchor tag <A> marks text that is to serve as a link to another document or document fragment. Anchors are assigned the address of a published document or fragment within a published document. Web browsers make hypertext links selectable by the reader, and make them stand out by underlining, outlining, inverse text, or other variations in appearance. Finally, Web browsers communicate with servers using the HyperText Transfer Protocol (HTTP) to request and receive a document linked to by an anchor (Figure 6-1). You don't need to understand the HTTP protocol or Web server to create anchors but you do need to learn how to construct URLs and how to tag text to function as links and/or targets in HTML.

Constructing URLs

The uniform resource locator (URL) is the addressing scheme for the Web. A URL makes it possible to access a document on a remote computer as well as a file on the local computer. A URL can point to any type of data from an HTML file to a QuickTime movie to a software program that provides up-to-date stock market information. URLs can even point at resources that are not considered documents such as library online catalogs or e-mail addresses. Despite this flexibility, URLs are simple and have components as easy to recognize as the parts of a mailing address.

The first part of a URL identifies the type of program sending the data. Think of it as a label that says "FedEx" or "UPS." Program types are usually identified by an acronym, which expands to the name of a transfer protocol used to send the data. A protocol is simply a set of rules that determine what data is sent when and to where. In the case of the Web, a URL for a Web-published document would start with "http:". A Web browser strips "http" from the URL and then treats the next portion of the URL as an Internet address for a computer or document name. You can think of the computer name as the city, state, and country portion of a mailing address. If the Internet address of a computer is found, the browser connects to a Web server on the named computer and issues a GET /path/document.html command, where GET is an HTTP command, /path/ is a

Figure 6-1
Hypertext docu-
ments can span
the Internet. Here
three servers
each publish
pieces of a
document.

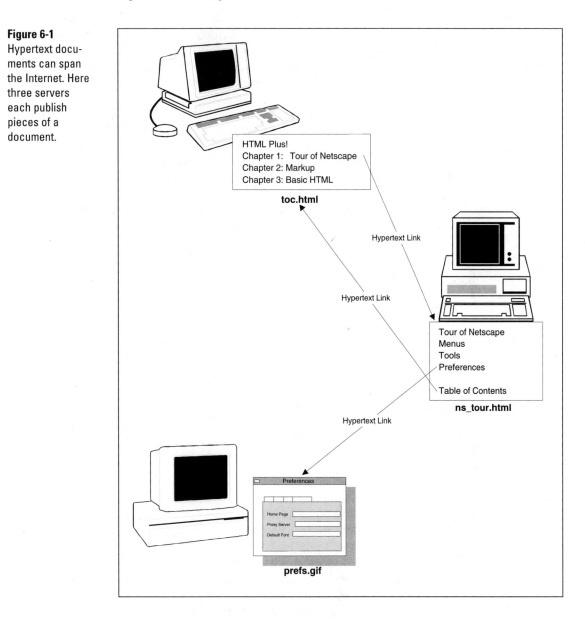

directory on the Web server and document.html is a Web document. The document path and address are like the street address and addressee of a postal
mailing address. You can pretend to be a Web client by telnetting to a Web
server (add a space and "80" to the address) and then typing "GET /":

```
telnet www.somewhere.edu 80
GET /
```

The HTML document text for the *root* or default document on that server will fill your screen until it is transferred, and then the connection will close. This trick is useful for systems administrators testing a new Web server since it is quicker than launching a Web browser, selecting "Open Location," and typing a URL.

URLs exist for most Internet information systems with simple request/reply protocols. An ftp URL such as ftp://wuarchive.wustl.edu/pub/ will ftp to the site wuarchive.wustl.edu, login as "anonymous" and issue a DIR command which causes the contents of the /pub directory to be displayed. The Web browser then builds a set of hypertext links, which are presented to the user, issuing additional DIR or GET commands depending on whether the link you select is a directory or a file. Gopher URLs cause the Web browser to act like a gopher client. The browser requests a gopher menu and then presents it as a list of hypertext links. You can even select "View Source" while browsing ftp or gopher to view the HTML source created during these transactions and use it to help you create your own links to these types of resources. Here's a complete list of URL protocol types, each followed by required punctuation for that URL type:

TABLE 6-1   UNIFORM RESOURCE LOCATORS

Protocol	URL Identifier	Example
E-mail (SMTP)	mailto:	mailto:jpowell@vt.edu
FTP	ftp://	ftp://scholar.lib.vt.edu/
Gopher	gopher://	gopher://gopher.vt.edu
Telnet	telnet://	telnet://vtls.vt.edu
Usenet News (NNTP)	news:	news:comp.infosystems.www
WWW (HTTP)	http://	http://www.microsoft.com/

The second component of a URL, as mentioned above, is a computer's Internet address. If no name is present, then the document is assumed to be on the local system. Internet addresses can be simply the name of the computer if it is on a local network, or a full Internet address such as "www.college.edu." Computers supporting Web browsers are often named "www" or often have an alias registered so that they can be identified by that name. If you are trying to find a particular site, a good guess is "www" plus the accepted abbreviation for that organization plus the extension "edu" if it is a university or "com" if it is a business. The named system must have a server of the type needed to respond to your URL; for example, if your URL is gopher://www.college.edu, then there must be a gopher server running on www.college.edu, or the connection will fail. If you create a link that generates a "Connection failed" error, you will probably find that you have specified an incorrect protocol or computer name.

The third portion of a URL is the document name and path. Documents are stored on the server in directories or folders just like they are on your own computer. Web documents in the Web server's root directory can be accessed with no path information. Directories can be accessed with no document name, unless you are simply requesting the "/" directory, in which case you will probably receive the home page of the server you are accessing. To access an HTML document called dogs.html in the pets directory on the dogvet server you would use the URL http://dogvet.vet.school.edu/pets/dogs.html. Directories and filenames mean nothing when accessing wais:, mailto:, or telnet: URLs. In these cases, the URL will simply be the protocol followed by a database and computer name or the e-mail address or computer Internet name only. Table 6-1 sorts out the various URL idiosyncrasies and provides examples of each.

URLs can also be used to access a specific section of an HTML document. Documents can have multiple named anchors, which are accessed by appending a pound sign followed by the anchor name. The section of the dogs.html document that covers "barking" could be directly accessed using the URL http://dogvet.vet.school.edu/pets/dogs.html#barking, provided the author has created a named anchor for that section. The Web browser will load the dogs.html document and display the line containing this section, rather than displaying the document starting from the top. URLs like these allow full hypertext links between and within documents.

Plans are underway for a naming system to replace URLs. The Universal Resource Name system will allow each unique document to be assigned a name independent of location or server type. URNs will be registered by authors with regional computerized database registries much like computer Internet addresses are today. When a document with a URN moves, the author simply requests that the URN registry update the location information stored with the name, so no links to it will break. The planned system would also allow authors to register multiple locations so that users in Europe might access a copy of the document from a British server while users in the United States would receive a copy from an American server. URNs will probably resemble ISBNs used to uniquely identify published books.

THE ANCHOR TAG <A>

HTML anchor tags have two uses: as end points for hypertext links and as pointers to other resources. Anchor tags consist of the <A> tag paired with an HREF and/or NAME attribute depending on whether the anchor is a pointer or marks a document fragment that serves as a target of a link (or both), followed by the anchor text, and then the anchor end tag </A>. Anchor tags without anchor text are inaccessible. Anchor tags with no end tag result in the remainder of the document functioning as an anchor, rarely the author's intent. The HREF attribute is assigned a URL, which can be as simple as a document name or as complex as a gopher menu item or hypertext link to a remote HTML document. The NAME attribute is assigned a label that is unique within the document. It is best to keep these names short and descriptive. Names can contain numbers and the letters

A–Z as well as underscore characters. Descriptive names are particularly useful if the link will be pointed to by other documents (such as our "barking" example above). All values assigned to HREF or NAME attributes must be preceded and followed by double quotes (" "). Double quotes cannot occur within these values. If they do, the result may be run-on anchors or disappearing text as the browser tries to figure out what to do with the incorrect link.

Anchor text can be tagged with various formatting tags such as bold or italics. The markup can be nested between the anchor start/end tags or placed outside these tags. Anchors and formatting tags cannot be intermixed as in the following example:

<B><A HREF="dogs.html#barking">Barking dogs and how to quiet them</B></A>

Markup such as this is incorrect and can cause unpredictable results.

Anchors are a powerful and flexible feature of HTML, useful not only in creating hypertext links within paragraph content but also links within lists, links within tables of contents, links to send e-mail to authors, directional buttons, and other navigational tools. Links can occur anywhere inside the body of a document and in conjunction with virtually all other HTML tags. One common use of links is to make a graphic function as a link, such as providing Previous and Next document buttons on each of a series of documents. Image tags nested inside anchor tags cause the image to function as a link:

<A HREF="chapter2.html"><IMG SRC="right_arrow.gif"></A>

When combined with image tags, anchors can be used to create documents that appear to the user as interactive tours, or control centers. But it is very important to be consistent when using images as navigational aids. You should select images that most people will quickly recognize the meaning of and continue to associate with their function while they are using your documents. And remember that images slow down document loading.

RELATIVE URLS

You will probably find that you gradually build up a collection of directories, each with several subdirectories, as you author for the Web. Long URLs can pose problems both for document maintainers and for browsers. Attribute values can be no longer than 1024 characters, and since HREF is an attribute, this means URLs cannot exceed this limit. 1024 characters sounds like a lot, but when you consider that URLs include protocol, system name, path and filename, and possibly even anchor name, it is not impossible to surpass this limit. Luckily there are shortcuts. Documents that reference other documents on the same system only need to specify the document path and name in an anchor. The safest route is to specify an absolute path to the file. If the file is in the directory /books/html/chapter1/ then make the anchor <A HREF= "/books/html/chapter1/page1.html">. The user will have entered your site through a full URL, so the browser has a copy of the computer name handy when it needs a new document. Somewhat trickier is the relative path. If all files pointed to by a set of documents reside in the same directory, you can safely drop the protocol, computer name, and path. The browser will look for the document in the same place as the file you are currently reading.

Some relative URLs are prone to failures and should be used only under certain circumstances. A URL that presents a path relative to the current path is easy to break if you need to move files around in the future. A URL such as "../chapter5/page1.html" attempts to step up a directory from the current location (perhaps "chapter1") and then enter the "chapter5" directory. If chapters 1 and 5 are both at the same level in the directory structure, and the user is viewing a file in one of those two directories, this will work. But if the author decides to move the "chapter1" directory to another directory called "section1" and "chapter5" to "section2", the URL will no longer work. A better solution would be to use the <BASE> tag in the document header to specify a partial URL such as <BASE="http://docserver.tech.com/book/"> and then build URLs relative to them: <A HREF="chapter1/page1.html">. Then you can change the <BASE> value if you change the directory structure, to quickly revise and preserve your links.

NAMED ANCHORS

Named anchors are easy to construct and provide additional paths through your document. They also publish document fragments to the Web, so that other authors can link to important passages in your document instead of simply pointing at the entire document. To make a piece of text capable of being the target of a link, tag the text with an anchor tag and a NAME attribute:

<A NAME="telnet_URL">A telnet URL</A> looks like this...

The same named anchor can also link to additional examples or other information if you add an HREF attribute:

<A NAME="telnet_URL" HREF="more_examples.html">A telnet URL</A> looks like this...

The attribute order does not matter. But remember not to use the same name in the document again. Here is an example of several items linked together in one document:

When changing a flat tire, first make sure you have a <A NAME="find_spare" HREF="#find_jack">spare</A> otherwise you better call a tow truck.
<A NAME="find_jack" HREF="#find_wrench">Now locate the jack</A>
If you have trouble finding the <A NAME="find_wrench" HREF="#find_space">wrench, look under the spare tire</A><P>
A <A NAME="spare">spare tire</A> is usually stored in the trunk under the carpet.

The anchor tag has several other seldom-used attributes. The HTML 2 standard has long provided a URN attribute even though the URN standard has not been finalized. URN would replace the HREF attribute. METHOD names the HTTP command that should be used to retrieve the document targeted by the link. The default is GET, but other methods include HEAD (retrieve document header only) and TEXTSEARCH (pass query string to the URL and request a search). Finally, HTML 2 supports REL and REV attributes. These attributes specify what relationship the current document has with the document pointed to and what relationship the target has with this document. Here's an example:

```
<A HREF="contents.html" REL="chapter1" REV="table_of_contents">
Chapter1</A>
```

In this example, the target of the link is "chapter1", and the current document is a table of contents. REV and REL are not currently implemented by any Web browsers, but they may be supported as document collections grow and authors demand more control over anchors.

HTML ANCHOR DO'S AND DON'TS

- Avoid the urge to make "Click here..." links. Instead, use titles or descriptive words for anchors.
- Add icons to indicate multimedia data.
- Be sure to use the ALT attribute with images that function as links.
- Try to avoid making every occurrence of a word an anchor. The first occurrence is usually sufficient.
- Avoid making anchors of headings. These are often easily overlooked.
- Don't dismiss menu-style anchor lists. They still work for gopher and can for WWW.
- Include file size with anchors if the link will retrieve a large document, file, or image.
- Make anchors a word or phrase, not a whole sentence.
- Use directional arrows with slide shows or tours. Use left/right or up/down pairs—as long as you are consistent.
- Include a "way back"—a link back to the home page or starting point document.

Anchors should be used whenever needed, but not overused. It is sufficient to make the first occurrence of a word that appears in a separate glossary an anchor, if you are certain readers will always be entering the document at the same point. Otherwise, if the word does not occur frequently, it is acceptable to make each occurrence a link to the external definition. Text that contains too many links is difficult to read, so evaluate each link to ensure it really will be useful to a large percentage of your readers. Sometimes it is also helpful to include a description of a link next to an anchor, but not as part of it. But you will find that most anchors are self-descriptive, and if they are not, then they probably should not be anchors.

The next two chapters will demonstrate how images can function as anchors and how links can also pass data to a target. Graphics can be used to create user-selectable icons for other documents or additional info. They can also be configured so that portions of the image point to different URLs. Forms are links that not only point to a target but also send user-provided data to it.

HTML 2 PROJECT STEP 4: ADDING ANCHORS

Now let's add some anchors to our project to make our three documents a hypertext tutorial. Open the malay.htm file and make the changes listed below in **bold**:

```
<HTML>
<HEAD><TITLE>Introduction to Malay</TITLE>
<BASE HREF="http://server.lib.vt.edu/languages/malay/">
</HEAD>
<BODY>
<H1><A NAME="introduction">Introduction to Malay</A></H1>
<H2>Malaysia</H2>
<P>Malay, or Bahasa Malaysi as it is known by those who speak it, is a language
spoken in the southeast Asian nation of Malaysia. Malaysia is located on the same
peninsula as Singapore, to the west of Thailand. Part of the country is also located
on the island of Borneo, the fourth largest island in the world. Slight variations of
Malay are also spoken in Singapore, Indonesia, Thailand and Brunei. Over 200
million people speak Malay, nearly as many people as the population of the United
States. Malay, like French or Japanese, is a distinct language but also includes
words from other languages:
<UL>
<LI>Arabic
<LI>Chinese
<LI>Dutch
<LI>English
<LI>various languages of India
</UL>
<P>Malaysia has become a major economic force in the region producing
everything from timber (<A HREF="http://server.envir.org/rainforest.html">see
rainforests</A>) to automobiles to computers. They launched their first compact
car model, the Proton, in 1994. Because of its economic boom, Malaysia is poised
to supply products to much of Southeast Asia including China and the Philippines.
With markets like these, no wonder multinational corporations are beginning to
take notice. By learning Malay, you will have a definite edge when applying for
jobs with corporations that deal with southeast Asia.
<H3>Other Topics</H3>
<UL>
<LI><A NAME="vocabulary" HREF="vocab.htm">Vocabulary</A>
<LI><A NAME="grammar" HREF="grammar.htm">Grammar</A>
</UL>
</BODY>
</HTML>
```

Notice that the document heading, "Introduction," can now serve as a target of a hypertext link. We've also added a link to a fictitious document about rainforests in the document body. Each of the two anchors in the "Other Topics" section is both a link and a target since each has both an HREF and a NAME attribute. Each HREF is only assigned the document name, since the remainder of the URL will be added using the <BASE HREF> value. For example, the "Vocabulary" link actually points to:

http://server.lib.vt.edu/languages/malay/vocab.htm

In order for these links to work properly on your computer, you will need to discard or modify the <BASE HREF> portion of the document header. So now remove or modify the following line in each of the three project files (malay.htm, vocab.htm and grammar.htm):

<BASE HREF="http://server.lib.vt.edu/languages/malay/">

Our vocab.htm and grammar.htm documents are now integrated with the introductory document. Whenever you create an anchor, you must be sure to test it, so load the malay.htm document now with Netscape and see if your link works. When you click on "Vocabulary," the vocab.htm document should be loaded, and when you select "Grammar," you should see the grammar.htm document.

ANCHOR TAG USAGE SUMMARY

Tag	Permitted Context	Content Model
<A>	document body outside text blocks	ASCII characters, character entities

ATTRIBUTE SUMMARY

Tag	Attribute	Value
<A>	HREF	URL
	NAME	ASCII characters
	TITLE	ASCII characters, character entities
	METHOD	HTTP server communication types
	URN	ASCII characters
	REL, REV	comma separated string listing relationships

7

Adding Images

CHAPTER AT A GLANCE

- Common graphics formats used on the Web
- *Images and Bandwidth: A "Catch-22"*
- Understanding the image tag and how to customize it
- How to create and use icons
- *Icon Do's and Don'ts*
- Selecting a graphics package for creating images for the Web
- HTML 2 Project: *Adding Images*
- Image Tag Usage and Attribute Summaries

One of the driving forces behind the World Wide Web was its pioneering ability to deliver images with text over the Internet. Gopher clients paled in comparison to Web browsers such as Mosaic, which captured the imagination of many who were not excited by the Internet publishing options that preceded them. Early Web browsers supported the limited XBM (X-Windows bitmap) format that displayed only black-and-white images, but the potential was recognized.

Users demanded color images, and today most Web browsers support full-color high-resolution image formats.

Documents combining images and text are certainly desirable in most situations. Images can illustrate certain details that might otherwise require pages of text. But as you might have imagined, using images in Web documents is not simply a matter of dropping a picture onto a page. It requires knowledge of how images are stored, image types, and options for image archiving. Creating images also requires some experience with computer graphics packages and/or scanning and imaging software such as Adobe's Photoshop. Photoshop can be an indispensable tool for Web publishing and we'll take a look at it later in this chapter.

GIF Images

Before we look at the HTML markup for an image, let's look at some image formats supported by Web browsers. The first color-image format supported by the Web was GIF. The Graphics Interchange Format is a bitmapped image format developed by CompuServe for transferring images between computers using a modem. Like all bitmap formats, a GIF file is a collection of data describing pixels on the computer screen. A pixel is the smallest addressable block on a computer display, like a tiny light bulb. If a computer has a 640 x 480 resolution display, this means the display consists of 480 rows of 640 pixels. GIFs can be one to eight bits deep, that is one to eight pieces of data describe a single pixel. And of course, a bit is the smallest piece of data a computer can store, a one or zero. A one-bit image is a black-and-white image, where the single bit per pixel is set to one (on) meaning white, or zero (off) for black. Here is a string of ones and zeros that might be used by a bitmap format to describe two rows of a checkerboard made up of 16 pixels:

10101010
01010101

All GIF images, regardless of their depth, store a string of eight ones and zeros for each pixel. In the example above, the two rows of ones and zeros would describe only 2 GIF pixels, instead of 16 pixels. But eight bits of color information is not a lot. So how do GIF images simulate true color despite the limited number of colors available?

All of the colors used in a GIF image are stored along with the image in a section called the palette. The palette is a color dictionary relating the pixel bits to a specific color. So each one to eight bits of data representing a GIF pixel is actually stored as a palette value, that is, a pointer to a color in the palette. Since the palette can be made up of any 256 colors, such as 256 shades of green, not just a sampling of the spectrum, the image can reserve the 256 palette values for just the colors it needs.

When more than 256 colors are needed, there are other tricks you can use to improve the quality of a GIF. Some graphics software can simulate intermediate colors through a process called dithering. Dithered images imitate lost colors with a blended region of pixels chosen from the available colors. For example, a pink might be simulated with a checkerboard pattern of red and white pixels. Dithering yields more consistent results on a variety of computer systems. Of course, on systems with few colors such as a gray-scale laptop display, the display software has to substitute shades of gray for the unavailable palette colors. No image format can overcome every limitation.

The built-in compression employed by GIF images is LZW (Lempel-Ziv-Welch) compression algorithm, which is patented by Unisys. LZW is also used with programs such as the UNIX compress and DOS pkzip utilities. LZW searches a file to be compressed for patterns of ones and zeros. It builds a dictionary of these patterns and stores the pattern with a much smaller string equivalent. Then the file is compressed by saving the smaller string equivalents and including this dictionary. Since GIFs have only 256 colors, there are only up to 256 possible bit patterns for a pixel. This means the dictionary can be discarded, making the file even smaller.

LZW is a lossless compression, meaning no information is removed or eliminated during compression. What you saw when you saved the document is what you will see the next time you open it. However, due to the color reduction required to save an image as a GIF file, GIF can sometimes be quite lossy, resulting in poor reproductions of photographs. This limitation and other developments set developers searching for other alternatives.

JPEG Images

In 1994, CompuServe announced and then shortly thereafter reversed their infamous licensing requirement for the GIF format. Some saw this as an opportunistic move by the communications giant to cash in on the popularity of their image format on the Web. Others saw it as just the push Web client developers needed to build in support for better image formats. The big winner was the JPEG (Joint Photographic Experts Group) format. JPEG is classified as a lossy compression type. JPEG discards information about subtle color changes such as those that cannot be perceived by the human eye. A JPEG graphic records millions of colors, compared to GIF's paltry 256, and is not even recommended for images with fewer than 256 colors. JPEG can compress images to various degrees (there are actually 100 different quality settings for a JPEG image), with higher compression values resulting in poorer quality. But medium- to high-quality JPEG compressed images are almost without exception sharper and more visually appealing than GIF because they include more colors. Whether an image has 256, 16,000, or 2 million colors, JPEG retains most of these colors. This makes JPEG ideal for photographic images. JPEG images do take slightly longer to decompress since there are up to five passes for decoding a JPEG compared to one for a GIF. But the difference is negligible on today's high-speed equipment.

GIF still has many uses and will probably always be a part of the Web. It is ideally suited for storing line art or gray-scale images such as graphs and charts or mathematical formulae too complex to represent in HTML. GIF is also popular for its ability to store transparency information. GIF images can be saved so that one selected color is invisible when the image is redisplayed by a Web browser. Instead of a logo on a white background, a GIF that has white replaced with transparency will seem to float or blend into the page. Even with only one transparent color, this capability, which is part of a newer GIF format known as GIF89, can be used to achieve dramatic results.

GIF images can also be saved as interlaced GIFs. Normally, GIF images are stored top to bottom, just like the HTML source in a text file. Interlaced images are saved so that all even rows of pixels are stored before odd rows. The Web browser reconstructs the image in four passes, displaying every eighth row starting with row zero, then every eighth starting with the fourth row, then every fourth row starting with the second row, and finally every second row starting with row one. By reconstructing the image this way, a Web browser can start displaying the entire picture with the effect of gradually "focusing in" on the final image as alternate rows are retrieved. It appears to the user that the image is transferring faster than it actually is. This provides them with an opportunity to stop transfer of an image if they determine they do not need to see it. Here are two frames of an interlaced logo as it is being transferred and displayed by Netscape:

PNG Images

A new graphics format designed especially for the Web is on the horizon. Portable Network Graphics (PNG) is a public domain image format developed specifically for Web use. PNG images can contain millions of colors (up to 48 million, also referred to as 24-bit color). They also have eight bits of transparency. This means there are up to 256 gradations of transparency available from nearly clear to almost completely opaque. PNG images can also be interlaced in two dimensions compared to one with GIF89. PNGs rely on a public domain data compression scheme, which means there's no need for concern that you will be hunted down and charged a fee a couple of years from now after converting all of your graphics to another format. PNG uses the GNU gzip compression scheme which is similar to the LZW algorithm employed by GIFs, and is lossless unlike JPEG. Many Web browsers already support this new format and it could replace both GIF and JPEG as the image format of choice for line art, logos, and photographic images on the Web.

IMAGES AND BANDWIDTH: A CATCH-22

Like the old cliché says, a picture is worth a thousand words. This is magnified on the Web where information is packaged in small hypertext chunks. But images slow down the retrieval of a document even more than you might think. That's because every image included in a document is retrieved as a separate file. The Web browser has to establish a second connection to a Web server and then receive and process image data while it is retrieving the document HTML text. And of course it is interpreting the HTML tags and decompressing the image at the same time. This is true for each and every image. Ten images mean ten more connections. Sometimes, the Web client may even have to wait for someone else to complete a request before they get a turn. Then there is the issue of bandwidth to further complicate matters.

Bandwidth is the speed at which data can travel from place to place on a network. On the Internet, some users have high speed connections called T1 lines. These connections carry gigabits of information a second, and support thousands of simultaneous users. At the other end of the scale are dialup connections. Home computer users and small businesses rely on modems and ordinary phone lines to connect to the Internet. Typically, these connections carry 14,400 bits of information a second, which slows the retrieval of even small GIF images to barely acceptable levels. JPEGs too, require more time than people are usually willing to wait for a computer transaction to be completed. So what is an HTML author to do?

Well, if you are building a graphical tour of an art museum, there's not much you can do. You can warn people at the starting point of the tour and include file sizes and descriptions with images, but for a presentation

Continued on next page

Continued from previous page

like this, the pictures have to be there. For less-graphics-intensive sites, there are some things that will help. The quickest way to reduce the size of an image is to reduce the resolution. Most computer screens are 72 dpi (dots per inch), so higher resolution images are usually displayed too large for the screen anyway. Reducing image resolution to 72 dpi will reduce file size, which reduces transfer time. You can replace gray-scale sketches with black-and-white line drawings, add transparency to logos, make all decorative graphics interlaced, and even consider providing a non-graphical collection of pages for impatient and bandwidth-impaired users.

Finally, consider your audience as well as the value of the information imparted by the images. If they are essential, use them and let the network bandwidth catch up with you!

THE IMAGE TAG <IMG>

The <IMG> tag is used to include an image in a document. Technically, <IMG> is an anchor tag. That's why you can click on an icon indicating that an image failed to load to attempt to reload it. But it is one of a small class of anchor tags that are normally processed without user intervention (others include <LINK>, <ISINDEX>, and some HTML form tags). <IMG> always has an SRC attribute to which you assign a URL for your image. Images can be stored anywhere on the Internet, not just on the server from which the HTML document originated. Each is retrieved separately while the document text is loading. Every image requires a separate connection to a server and must be decompressed separately, so it is very important to be sure the bulk of your users have the computing power and connection speed necessary to handle your page. Otherwise, many might turn away impatiently without ever viewing your page, or they might simply shutoff all image display while at your site.

Text does not flow around images placed in a document with the <IMG> tag because image data is treated as though it were a character. Small images can be mixed with text and can be made to look like characters, if they are small enough and appear on a transparent background:

<IMG SRC="equation.gif" ALIGN=BOTTOM>

$$\sum_{i=1}^{n} x_i = \int_{0}^{1} J$$

This is what many authors do when trying to represent a character not supported in the ISO-Latin character set, such as mathematical symbols. But larger images can appear awkward when displayed with text. HTML includes an ALIGN attribute that can improve the alignment with and appearance of mixed graphics and text. ALIGN can be set to TOP, MIDDLE, or BOTTOM to force the next line of text to align itself with the top, middle, or bottom of the image. This is particularly useful in lists and with headings, but still does not allow text to flow around an image.

The image tag also has an ALT attribute for assigning alternate text to be displayed either when a user selects not to retrieve images or the browser cannot display images. ALT attributes should always be provided with images used in or as anchors. Otherwise, the reader might see one or more anchors as simply the word *Image* underlined or otherwise highlighted. It is especially unlikely that a reader using a browser incapable of displaying images would ever select such a link, unless they had encountered this mistake before. ALT values can also be used to store descriptive information with an image tag that would be searchable if the HTML document were indexed. Image tags also have an ISMAP attribute for making sections of an image selectable. ISMAP is covered in more detail in Chapter 9.

ICONS

You can make your documents look more attractive by using images as anchors. Icons, rather than larger photographic-quality images, are usually used as anchors since they are small and transfer quickly. Icons are small images designed to illustrate the function that the link controls. They are often square but can also be rectangular or even round. Icons are usually between 16 and 64 pixels in length on a side. One use for an icon is to point a reader to the next page of a guided tour. The next page icon might be a small arrow pointing to the right side of the current Web page. Well-designed icons can make complex pages more intuitive and readable. But you should select such images with care and use them sparingly. You may increase image content with minimal penalty for the user if you add only a few new images per page as the user steps through your documents. If an image occurs frequently in different documents, most Web browsers will cache it—that is, store a temporary copy of the file on the computer locally, rather than retransfer every image each time it is needed. Select images that are small, consist of few colors, and are readily recognizable for their intended purpose. One common practice on the Web is to use images like the controls on digital audio equipment for forward, reverse, and the like. These icons represent back, forward, up, and table of contents, respectively.

Using familiar symbols such as these will reduce the amount of time a user requires to become familiar with your site. Use a custom-coloring or other accent to distinguish and add a sense of place to your pages. Replace large images, such as scanned page images, with miniature versions (called *thumbnails*), which load the full-size image when selected. Users will appreciate these considerations.

ICON DO'S AND DON'TS

- Use icons to reduce the amount of reading a user has to do. Even icons that the user has to think about a bit are better than two paragraphs of text serving as, or explaining, a link.
- Make your icons clear and bold. Use basic colors and try to achieve high contrast between the icon and its background.
- Make icons that function as links look like buttons. Sometimes borders can obscure the highlighting associated with hypertext links. If a button looks like something that can be pressed, the user will probably press it.
- Place directional controls near one another. Context helps make icon functions more apparent.
- Try to illustrate the action that will be performed if the user selects this icon. If the icon causes a larger version of a graphic to be displayed, make it look like a magnifying glass. If the link points to a movie, use an icon that looks like a bit of movie film complete with sprockets holes!
- Use color to enhance meaning. Reds and yellows draw attention and have familiar real-world analogies such as stop lights and school buses.
- Don't try to shrink a photograph down to icon dimensions. It almost never works.
- Don't use unnecessary or excessive color. Remember, some users have laptops with black-and-white screens that might mangle a colorful icon beyond recognition.

GRAPHICS TOOLS

Any graphics manipulation program that supports image formats such as GIF and JPEG is suitable for creating graphics for the Web. There are hundreds of file archives that include directories devoted exclusively to graphic editing and creation tools. Many programs, such as LView for Windows or Graphics Workshop for the Macintosh, are free or inexpensive shareware applications that can be found at many ftp sites on the Internet.

Photoshop from Adobe Systems is a high-end graphics-editing tool that is excellent for creating and modifying various types of images for the Web. When combined with a scanner and a scanner plug-in (a plug-in is software that adds functionality to Photoshop, such as the ability to scan or enhance images in new ways), it can be an indispensable Web authoring tool. Photoshop can open and save a variety of image formats at each format's maximum resolution and color depth. You can use its many built-in effects to sharpen or change image brightness, create buttons, and shrink or rotate images. You can scan an image of an

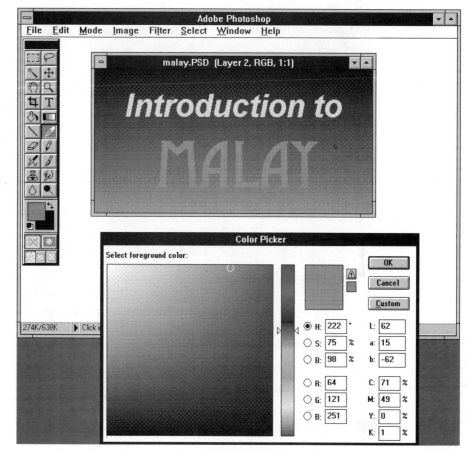

Adobe Photoshop

item intended as a logo, crop and rotate it, improve color contrast, and then reduce the number of colors so it can be saved as a GIF.

The impatient Web author's tour of Photoshop begins with the *File* menu. Here you can open and save images, as well as access plug-ins. *Edit* includes *Crop*, which is useful for trimming extraneous data from a scanned image, and of course the essentials: *Cut* and *Paste*. Under *Image*, the *Adjust* submenu contains controls for brightening and enhancing colors in an image (*Color Saturation, Brightness/Contrast*). *Image* also includes the handy *Image Size* option for reducing size and resolution of an image. *Image Size* can be used to scale down the size of an image, enlarge an image, and most important for Web publishing: reduce resolution. Most computer screens don't support more than 72 dpi, so reducing a scanned image from 300 dpi to 72 dpi can yield terrific file size savings. One tip when reducing color images: select RGB color mode before scaling, as the scaled-down image will be more attractive if reduced from a full-color image. Then reduce colors used in the smaller image after scaling. *Effects* (available under the *Filter* menu) such as *Emboss* are great for sprucing up logos and scanned images. Just keep your hands on the *Undo* key sequence to retract any undesired effect and return to your original image.

Two features missing from Photoshop are support for interlaced images and transparency. Various plug-ins, shareware, and freeware utilities are available from the net to add these final touches to graphics. Other commercial software providers offer graphics tools tailored specifically for use on Web pages. These typically include support for GIF and JPEG, interlaced and transparent graphics, as well as tracing tools for constructing image maps. These tools are usually less expensive and less memory- and CPU-hungry than Photoshop and are worth investigating if you're in the market for a graphics package specifically for developing graphics for the World Wide Web.

HTML 2 PROJECT STEP 5: ADDING IMAGES

Now let's add some buttons to our tutorial project. Open each HTML file, starting with malay.htm, and insert the following lines of text:

```
<A HREF="vocab.htm"><IMG SRC="vocab.gif" alt="Vocabulary"></A>
<A HREF="grammar.htm"><IMG SRC="grammar.gif" alt="Grammar"></A>
<A HREF="malay.htm"><IMG SRC="toc.gif" alt="Table of Contents"></A>
<A HREF="test1.htm"><IMG SRC="test.gif" alt="Test"></A>
<A HREF="help.htm"><IMG SRC="help.gif" alt="Help"></A>
```

When viewed, each document should have a set of buttons like the screen printed on the following page.

IMAGE TAG USAGE SUMMARY

Tag	Permitted Context	Content Model
<IMG>	within document body	none

ATTRIBUTE SUMMARY

Tag	Attribute	Value
<IMG>	SRC	URL of a graphic file
	ALT	ASCII text
	ALINE	TOP, MIDDLE, BOTTOM
	ISMAP	none

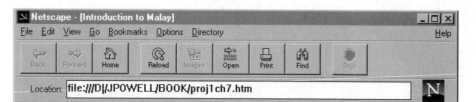

Malay, or Bahasa Malaysi as it is known by those who speak it, is a language spoken in the southeast Asian nation of Malaysia. Malaysia is located on the same peninsula as Singapore, to the west of Thailand. Part of the country is also located on the island of Borneo, the fourth largest island in the world. Slight variations of Malay are also spoken in Singapore, Indonesia, Thailand and Brunei. Over 200 million people speak Malay, nearly as many people as the population of the United States. Malay, like French or Japanese, is a distinct language but also includes words from other languages:

- Arabic
- Chinese
- Dutch
- English
- various languages of India

Malaysia has become a major economic force in the region producing everything from timber (see rainforests) to automobiles to computers. They launched their first compact car model, the Proton, in 1994. Because of its economic boom, Malaysia is poised to supply products to much of Southeast Asia including China and the Philippines. With markets like these, no wonder multinational corporations are beginning to take notice. By learning Malay, you will have a definite edge when applying for jobs with corporations that deal with southeast Asia.

Other Topics

- Vocabulary
- Grammar

Advanced HTML

8

Introduction to
HTML Forms

CHAPTER AT A GLANCE

- Recognizing forms as user-configurable hypertext links
- Designing a user interface using HTML form tags
- *Designing an Application Interface with HTML Forms*
- How to build script-ready forms
- HTML 2 Project: *Adding a Form*
- Form Tag Usage and Attribute Summaries

HTML form tags are a set of basic user interface design tools for creating fill-out forms and simple client applications. Forms pass their contents back to a server which then runs a program referred to as a CGI (common gateway interface) script. Web forms may not look like hypertext links, but that's exactly what they are. You can even simulate a form with a URL. Here's an example:

```
<A HREF="http://server/cgi-bin/script?first=John&last=
Doe&status=faculty&post_code=24060">John Doe</A>
```

Everything after the question mark is passed to the script as form contents. This is how the script expects to see the data. In this example data is hard coded into an HTML document anchor and cannot be modified. That's why forms were created—to allow users to specify values that can be passed to a script. This script either processes the form contents and generates a reply or modifies the input and passes it along to another application, thus acting as a gateway to an information server. The server can be an HTML search service, online library catalog, database system, or other resource. In this way, Web browsers can function as multipurpose client applications. In fact, many software vendors who sell client/server software are increasingly asked "Is there a Web interface?" when showing off their wares.

Forms are text blocks within the body of an HTML document. All tags valid within the body of a document such as paragraph, preformatted text, phrase and typographic elements like italics and bold, and image tags may be used inside a form. Forms also contain form-specific tags such as text input fields, selection lists, checkboxes, and the like. A document can contain multiple forms. Each form would be enclosed by a <FORM> start and end tag. It is more common for there to be one form per HTML file. A user presented with a multi-form document will be confused by multiple submit options interspersed with input fields and other form elements and may have difficulty distinguishing one form from another. Also remember that forms, like anchors, cannot be nested.

The <FORM> Tag

The <FORM> tag that indicates the start of an HTML form block has several attributes. Each form must specify a target for its contents using the ACTION attribute. The value assigned to ACTION should be a full or relative URL pointing to a script on a Web server. The ACTION attribute establishes a connection between the form and a script. But unless the script exists, the form will do nothing.

Every form should specify a METHOD type. Forms can send their data using two different methods. Each method is processed in a different manner. The rule to remember at this stage is that forms using the GET method are easier to process with a script than the POST, but GET forms run the risk of truncating data. This is because GET imposes a limit on the number of characters that can be sent. POST imposes no such limitation and will always send the complete contents of your form to the script, regardless of its length. So if your form is short, use GET, but if you are creating a long form or anticipate that some users may provide long answers to questions or long search strings, use the POST method.

```
<FORM METHOD=GET ACTION="http://server.com/cgi-bin/process">
```

The ENCTYPE attribute determines how the form contents should be encoded by the Web browser. When METHOD is set to GET, the contents of the form are encoded as URL that looks like this:

http://server/cgi-bin/script?name1=value&name2=value

The ACTION attribute value is the first part of the URL, to which a question mark (?) is appended. Then the name/value pairs from the form are added to the URL in the form name=value. The data is escaped, that is, reserved characters and spaces are replaced with alternate characters. Spaces are replaced with plus signs (+), nonalphanumeric characters are replaced with a percent sign (%) followed by a two-digit hexadecimal number (00-FF) representing the ASCII code for the character. The processing script unescapes the data, converting it back into name/value pairs for processing. POST data is encoded similarly, but is preceded by a header that includes information such as the sending application and the length of the data being sent. The POST header can include an alternate encoding method. The only value currently allowed for this attribute is "application/x-www-form-urlencode," which is the default. Only forms with METHOD=POST can specify alternate encoding options with ENCTYPE.

All form user entry fields are constructed from four tags: <INPUT>, <SELECT>, <OPTION>, and <TEXTAREA>. Each of these tags must have a NAME attribute. The NAME attribute specifies the variable name to be associated with a user input value or selection. Whether the field is a pull-down list, a set of checkboxes, or a text input field, they must all pass their setting or contents with a name. User input fields without names are inaccessible when delivered to a script. Some form attributes such as NAME require double quotes around their assigned values. This is because the value is not predefined by HTML. Other attributes such as the TYPE attribute can only be assigned certain values predefined by HTML. No quotes are required around these values:

<INPUT NAME="some value" TYPE=TEXT>

The <INPUT> Tag

The <INPUT> field is a multifunction HTML form tag. Depending on its assigned TYPE attribute an <INPUT> field can be a text entry field, a radio button or check box, a submission button, or a clickable image similar to an image map (see Chapter 9).

One of the most basic interface tools available in graphical user interface programs is the text input field. Input fields are ideal for accepting one line or a few characters of data from a user such as name, e-mail address, phone number, or other data unique to the user. To create a short text input field in HTML, use the <INPUT> tag with a TYPE=TEXT attribute:

Enter name: <INPUT NAME="user_name" TYPE=TEXT>

Enter name: [   ]

You can use additional <INPUT> attributes with text input fields, such as SIZE, to specify the length of the input field, MAXSIZE to limit the number of characters a user can enter in the field, and VALUE to specify the default value that should be displayed in the field. Here is a second example where a user is asked to submit a postal code up to nine digits:

Postal code: <INPUT NAME="post_code" TYPE=TEXT SIZE=12 MAXSIZE=11
VALUE="24060-9001">

Postal code: | 24060-9001 |

In this example, a default value "24060-9001" is displayed in the input field. If the user does not change the contents of this field then the default value is sent to the script upon submission. It is a good idea to specify a slightly larger SIZE attribute value than the maximum expected or allowed value so the data won't scroll as the user enters it. For example, a field for entering a phone number might be set as SIZE=15, even though you are expecting a value between 8 and 12 characters in length. This makes it easier for the user to check their input before submitting it.

TYPE attributes for the <INPUT> field support other form input types. TYPE=PASSWORD looks like a TEXT input field, but when the user types text in the field, it is displayed as asterisks, to obscure their password:

Enter password: <INPUT NAME="pass" TYPE=PASSWORD SIZE=10>

Enter password: | ****** |

If you want to create a set of radio buttons, use the INPUT tag with TYPE=RADIO. Radio buttons are ideal for presenting a set of options from which a user will be selecting one value such as a multiple-choice questionnaire. To create a set of radio buttons, you can create a series of input fields, each with the same value assigned to NAME and with TYPE=RADIO:

Status: Faculty <INPUT NAME="status" TYPE=RADIO VALUE="faculty">
or Student <INPUT NAME="status" TYPE=RADIO VALUE="student">

Status: Faculty ○ or Student ◉

Checkboxes are ideal for presenting a list of items that a user can select or deselect individually. Checkboxes input fields each have a unique NAME value and TYPE=CHECKBOX. Each input field should have a VALUE attribute assigned a unique value to be passed to the script if the user selects this radio button or checkbox:

<INPUT NAME="payment" TYPE=CHECKBOX VALUE="credit">Bill Credit Card

☐ Bill Credit Card

You can make a radio button or a check box selected by default by using the CHECKED attribute with an input field:

```
<INPUT NAME="payment" TYPE=CHECKBOX VALUE="credit" CHECKED>Bill Credit
Card
```

⊠ Bill Credit Card

Input fields can be used to send hidden values to a processing script. When TYPE is assigned the value HIDDEN, the field is invisible to the user. But a hidden <INPUT> field with NAME and VALUE attributes is accessible to the processing script. One example is creating forms that search different databases using the same script. The database name could be concealed from the user, simplifying the form:

```
<INPUT NAME="database" TYPE=HIDDEN VALUE="class_schedule">
```

Once a user has completed the form, they need to send its contents to the script. Form contents are submitted using an <INPUT> field of TYPE=SUBMIT. An <INPUT> field with TYPE=RESET clears the contents of the form when selected. <INPUT> fields with these types are displayed as buttons. The text of the button comes from the value assigned VALUE, or the TYPE name if no value is specified:

```
<INPUT TYPE=RESET VALUE="Clear"> <INPUT TYPE=SUBMIT VALUE="Send
contents">
```

You can even provide a NAME attribute for an INPUT field of type RESET or SUBMIT to pass along this field's value to the processing script. This might be useful if you want to have multiple submit buttons. The script would be able to tell which button was pressed by the VALUE it received:

```
<INPUT TYPE=SUBMIT NAME="submit" VALUE="Rush Delivery">
<INPUT TYPE=SUBMIT NAME="submit" VALUE="Regular Delivery">
```

Images can also function as input fields. An <INPUT> field with TYPE=IMAGE lets the user click on a portion of an image to select an option and submit the form contents simultaneously. The image input field passes a pair of coordinates to the script that describe where the user clicked. This is useful for building graphical controls and adding clickable image maps to textual input forms, such as allowing a user to select their geographic region from an image of a map. But since an image input field also functions as a submit button, a user can only select one image input field per form, even if there are multiple image input fields. An <INPUT> field of TYPE=IMAGE should have an SRC attribute that specifies what image should be used as a control:

```
<INPUT NAME="submit_campus" TYPE=IMAGE SRC="campus_map.gif">
```

All types of <INPUT> fields can be used in lists, paragraphs, and other text block elements. One common way of presenting a set of radio buttons is to make each button a list item in an ordered or unordered list:

```
<UL>
<LI> Faculty <INPUT NAME="status" TYPE=RADIO VALUE="faculty">
<LI> Student <INPUT NAME="status" TYPE=RADIO VALUE="student">
</UL>
```

The <SELECT> Tag

You can create pull-down lists and scrollable selection lists with the <SELECT> tag. The <SELECT> tag works much like a list tag, with each list item marked by an <OPTION> tag, the select equivalent of the <LI> tag for lists. A <SELECT> list allows only one item to be selected by default, but you can add the MULTIPLE attribute to let users select multiple list items.

```
<SELECT NAME="status">
<OPTION>faculty
<OPTION>student
</SELECT>
```

Use the SIZE attribute to display the selections as a scrollable list. The value assigned to SIZE should be the number of lines you wish displayed in the scrollable window:

```
<SELECT NAME="status" SIZE=2>
<OPTION>faculty
<OPTION>student
<OPTION>staff
<OPTION>other
</SELECT>
```

<OPTION> tags have two optional attributes. The SELECTED attribute causes an <OPTION> to be the preselected default for a selection list:

<OPTION SELECTED>faculty

Multiple items can be tagged as SELECTED if the MULTIPLE attribute is specified with the <SELECT> tag. You can also give each <OPTION> tag a VALUE attribute, which is formatted just like the <INPUT VALUE> attribute. If you do not provide a VALUE attribute, the text following the <OPTION> tag will be used.

The <TEXTAREA> Tag

The last (and least often used) type of <FORM> tag is <TEXTAREA>. <INPUT> fields are not always large enough to accept user responses to questions. Since input fields constructed with the <INPUT> tag are displayed as a box one character row high, they are not suitable for essay type responses. The <TEXTAREA> tag is used to build large input fields where users might enter detailed information up to many paragraphs in length. Unlike the <INPUT> tag, the <TEXTAREA> tag always requires an end tag. The end tag is required so that a default value of any length can be provided for a text area:

<TEXTAREA NAME="essay">This text could go on for paragraphs</TEXTAREA>

<INPUT> fields restrict the value of the VALUE attribute to 1024 characters. The dimensions of a <TEXTAREA> can be specified with the ROWS and COLS attributes. These indicate how wide and tall a <TEXTAREA> should be in characters, when displayed by a browser. This example creates a text area 60 characters wide and 10 characters high:

<TEXTAREA NAME="essay" ROWS=10 COLS=60></TEXTAREA>

DESIGNING AN APPLICATION INTERFACE WITH HTML FORMS

There are enough HTML form elements to create interfaces to databases, bulletin boards, and even networked games. But there are some limitations. You cannot check the contents of a form to ensure the user has specified an acceptable value. For example, you might provide a field for a user to enter their phone number. A web browser will allow a user to enter any characters into this field. It has no idea that these characters are not a valid telephone number. What's more, there's no HTML attribute to indicate that a field is required at all. So the script has to detect these problems, and generate an appropriate message such as "Phone number is a required field, please return to the form and provide a phone number." You should then tell the user to return to the form using the back arrow. They should find the form just as they left it, contents intact. If they follow a hypertext link or bookmark back to the form, the form will probably be reloaded and all fields reset.

The web is a *stateless* system. This means that once a request is made by a web browser, it stays connected to the information server only long enough to receive the requested document. Then the connection is broken. So some information services don't lend themselves easily to Web-based interfaces. Determine if this is the case for the resource you plan to build an interface to, and if the resource requires a stateful connection, like many online library catalogs, decide if it is worth the effort. See Chapter 26 for more information about forms and scripts.

FORM STYLE ISSUES

Forms should be simple and present various user input fields consistently. If your form is long and complex it is helpful to the user if you separate the document into sections with hard rules and heading levels. Aligning fields and using preformatted tags further simplify and improve readability of detailed forms. The preformatted text block is the best way to align fields and control the overall appearance of forms in HTML 2. As you will see later, HTML 3 table tags can also be used to organize document content including forms.

```
<FORM METHOD=GET ACTION="http://server.com/cgi-bin/get-address.exe">
<PRE>
Name:  <INPUT NAME="name" TYPE=TEXT SIZE=45>
Address: <INPUT NAME=address" TYPE=TEXT SIZE=50>
City:  <INPUT NAME="city" TYPE=TEXT SIZE=20> State: <INPUT NAME="state"
TYPE=TEXT SIZE=3>
<INPUT TYPE=SUBMIT VALUE="Submit">
</PRE>
</FORM>
```

If you do not want to place your form inside a preformatted text block, you should strive to make your form no wider than 60 to 70 characters by using line break (<BR>) or paragraph (<P>) tags. Use text block elements to clarify input options such as embedding checkboxes alongside their descriptions in a list block and breaking up long forms with hard rules and paragraph tags. If you allow form input blocks to flow as a user resizes a window, valuable information such as checkbox labels and input field descriptions can be displayed separately from the field.

```
<FORM METHOD=GET ACTION="http://server.com/cgi-bin/get-address.exe">
<P>
Name: <INPUT NAME="name" TYPE=TEXT SIZE=45><BR>
Address: <INPUT NAME=address" TYPE=TEXT SIZE=50><BR>
City: <INPUT NAME="city" TYPE=TEXT SIZE=20> State: <INPUT NAME="state"
TYPE=TEXT SIZE=3><BR>
</FORM>
```

Be sure to utilize hypertext links as needed to provide additional information about the form. Icons and other navigational aids are appropriate in forms as well. Navigation controls can also be returned by the script when it accepts the form input. If you are sure a user is arriving at your form through only one path, presenting a hypertext link back to the starting page is a good way to quickly get the user back on track. But avoid this practice if the user will be using this form to enter large amounts of data into a database or perform numerous searches, because following a hypertext link will add an entry to their history, while using the browser Back button usually does not. In addition, the user may not have to rekey some data if they simply backup to the form page locally, which can be a real time saver.

Hypertexts are by definition interactive. They allow users to specify a path of their own choosing through a collection of documents or data. HTML forms make hypertext links user configurable. Forms add an extra layer of interactivity to hypertext links. With forms, users might contribute comments to a set of hypertext documents or use a Web document in combination with a backend script to interact with remote software applications and databases. Forms are the ultimate anchors.

HTML 2 PROJECT STEP 6: ADDING A FORM

Now let's add a form to our HTML 2 project. Create a new document with your text editor and save it as test1.htm. This is a short, self-scoring quiz in HTML that sends its contents and is scored by the script score-test:

```
<HTML>
<HEAD><TITLE>Malay: Test 1</TITLE>
</HEAD>
<BODY>
<H1>Malay Test 1</H1>
<FORM METHOD=POST ACTION="/cgi-bin/score-test">
<P>
1. Malay is spoken in:
<SELECT NAME="q1">
<OPTION>China
<OPTION>Norway
<OPTION>Malaysia
</SELECT>
<P>
2. Malay includes words from (select all that apply):<BR>
a. <INPUT NAME="q2a" TYPE=CHECKBOX VALUE="English">English<BR>
b. <INPUT NAME="q2b" TYPE=CHECKBOX VALUE="Swedish">Swedish<BR>
c. <INPUT NAME="q2c" TYPE=CHECKBOX VALUE="Dutch">Dutch<BR>
d. <INPUT NAME="q2d" TYPE=CHECKBOX VALUE="Swahili">Swahili
<P>
3. What is the Malay word for rice? <INPUT NAME="q3" TYPE=TEXT>
<P>
4. Ayam means chicken. What is the plural?
<UL>
```

```
<LI><INPUT NAME="q4" TYPE=RADIO VALUE="ayams">ayams
<LI><INPUT NAME="q4" TYPE=RADIO VALUE="ayames">ayames
<LI><INPUT NAME="q4" TYPE=RADIO VALUE="ayam-ayam">ayam-ayam
</UL>
<INPUT TYPE=RESET VALUE="Try again"> <INPUT TYPE=SUBMIT VALUE="How
did I do?">
</FORM>
</BODY>
</HTML>
```

Here's how the test looks when you load it with Netscape:

FORM TAG USAGE SUMMARY

Tag	Permitted Context	Content Model
<FORM>	around HTML form contents	Body tags, <SELECT>, <OPTION>, <INPUT>, <TEXTAREA>
<SELECT>	around list of selectable options with an HTML form	<OPTION>
<OPTION>	within a <SELECT> list	ASCII text
<INPUT>	within an HTML form	none
<TEXTAREA>	within an HTML form	ASCII text

ATTRIBUTE SUMMARY

Tag	Attribute	Value
<FORM>	METHOD	URL (ASCII text)
	ACTION	GET, POST
	ENCTYPE	application/x-www-form-urlencode
<SELECT>	NAME	ASCII text
	MULTIPLE	none
<OPTION>	SELECTED	none
<INPUT>	NAME	ASCII text
	MAXLENGTH	numeric value
	SIZE	numeric value
	VALUE	ASCII text
	TYPE	TEXT, CHECKBOX, PASSWORD, RADIO, IMAGE, HIDDEN, SUBMIT, RESET
<TEXTAREA>	NAME	ASCII text

9

Image Maps

CHAPTER AT A GLANCE

- When a set of links might benefit from an image map
- *What About Lynx Users?*
- Constructing a functional image map on most common systems
- Table 9-1: *Image Map Shapes*
- HTML 2 Project: *Adding a Toolbar*
- Image Map Tag Usage Summary

Image maps make Web documents come alive. Any image can be an image map. You just need to create a mapping file that lists the coordinates for each region and the URL for a document that the Web browser should load when a user selects that region. Image maps can be used to mimic a variety of functions found in desktop software from zooming in on an image section to get a better view, to accessing large collections of information, to virtually touring a university campus. While tedious to create, image maps can be more intuitive for users than text and anchors, especially on introductory pages. They are also an excellent way to provide a consistent navigational toolbar in a large collection of documents. Aside from forms, they provide the greatest degree of interactivity possible between a user and a document.

In terms of HTML markup, image maps are a combination of image and anchor tags that allow a user to click on a point or region of a graphic to follow a certain link. The Web browser then sends the x,y coordinates of the user's selection to the server. Here's an example and the corresponding URL constructed by the Web client when a user clicks in the upper- left-hand corner of the image:

```
<A HREF="/cgi-bin/world_map><IMG SRC="world_map.gif" ISMAP></A>
/cgi-bin/world_map?0,0
```

The server consults a configuration file for the image. This file maps closed regions such as polygons to the URLs for other documents. The image map configuration file in this example is called world_map. ISMAP is actually the name of the script that accepts the coordinates and maps them to an anchor specified in the configuration file. This URL is sent back to the Web browser, which immediately loads the target document.

Uses for Image Maps

Image maps can be used to interact with large, complex sets of data at a higher level. For example, it is much easier for a user to locate and click on their state on a map of the United States than to provide latitude and longitude coordinates to retrieve a weather forecast. With an image map, hundreds of links can be concealed behind one easy-to-understand graphic. Image maps are also useful for providing consistent navigation tools between sets of documents. A bar with buttons listing various categories of documents can be added to a number of documents in the set without adding a lot of extra text or links to each document. Once the user learns how to use this bar, they can quickly navigate through the local collection of documents without having to track down a way back by reading. The author can add new features to the bar simply by updating the centrally stored graphic and mapping file.

WHAT ABOUT LYNX USERS?

Image maps don't work for everyone. All graphical browsers support the ISMAP attribute. However, even a Netscape user might occasionally forego image loading in order to follow links and retrieve documents more quickly. So what is an HTML author to do? At the minimum, put a warning on your documents that an image map is used. Often, the ALT image attribute is sufficient for these purposes. This allows users who can to move to a graphics-capable browser. If possible, provide an alternate collection of Web pages that contain only text. You can construct a satisfactory replica of a navigational toolbar with a row of hypertext links utilizing short titles for each function as link text. For example, if your toolbar included previous, next, table of contents, and search icons, you could construct the following ASCII equivalent using vertical bars and spaces as separators:

<A HREF="previous.html">Previous</A> | <A HREF="next.html">Next</A> | <A HREF="contents.html">Contents</A> | <A HREF="search.html">Search

Finally, accept the fact that there are sometimes no options for text-based users. Tell the user that they are accessing a page that contains a frog dissection that requires a graphical Web browser. Lynx users can't expect ASCII renderings of the anatomical structures of amphibians even if it were possible to construct them!

THE MARKUP

The HTML markup for an image map is quite simple. First and most important, the image must be a GIF image. This image should be made a link using the anchor tag. You should make the anchor's target (the HREF attribute value) be the URL of the imagemap program. Next, add an ISMAP attribute to the <IMG>. This ensures that when a user clicks on the image, the coordinates of the click point are sent to the server and the Web browser waits for a URL from the server. Clients supporting image maps will receive the URL and immediately load the document to which it points. Nongraphical clients and clients with image loading turned off cannot provide any access to the links behind an image map, so keep this in mind if you think some of your users will have nongraphical clients. You should provide some type of text-based access for them if possible, such as listing major cities in states for the weather map example discussed above.

Experienced Web users are aware of the difference between image maps and images simply used as anchors, but it is still a good idea to either label an image map as such or use familiar graphics, such as raised buttons, as part of the image. An ALT attribute or text label below the image will let users without graphics know what was there and might serve as the text for an anchor to a textual alternative. If the image map is to serve primarily as a navigation tool, select an image no larger than about 475 pixels across and 300 pixels high so that it fits within the typical browser window. Photoshop (see Chapter 7) is an excellent package for designing image maps. You can also use it to resize large images, reduce colors, and locate coordinate ranges for the mapping file.

IMPLEMENTATION ISSUES

Before implementing an image map, you must first determine if it is the best mechanism for the task. If the links would be just as understandable in the form of a list of anchors, use a list tag instead. However, if the list would be exceptionally long or you want multiple conditions to lead a user to the same anchor, an image map is a good solution. Try sketching an interface to your collection of anchors. The image you create can be as simple as a collection of buttons or as complex as a topographic map or the molecular structure of a complex chemical compound.

Next, make sure you can map enclosed areas to a hypertext link. Other enclosed areas can share the same link, but areas cannot overlap. Link regions can be shaped like rectangles, circles, or irregular polygons.

Now convert your sketch into an electronic image. You can scan the image and use graphics software to enhance and add color to your sketch. If regions of the image are not obvious, you may want to color each link area so users have some idea of the functions available. As you design your image, keep in mind the same rules that apply to using any images on the Web such as bold, clear designs and small file sizes. When you complete your image, insert it as a simple inline graphic with the <IMG> tag as a test. If the image is especially large, you may want to limit the amount of additional text surrounding it. Image maps are much less effective if the user has to scroll to see the entire image. This is especially true if the image is wider than the typical Web browser window, about 450 pixels, since Web browser windows tend to be taller than wide. Occasionally, wider images are unavoidable, but in these cases it might be better to create a set of image maps that a user might reach after selecting regions from a less detailed map.

MAPPING FILE FORMATS

Finally, you need to create a map file for your image. Mapping files have slightly different formats depending on the http server you are using. Most use the NCSA[1] style:

```
# NCSA style image map file
circle http://server/doc.html 20, 15, 10
rect http://server/doc2.html 10, 10, 40, 20
default doc3.html
```

The other style, CERN[1], switches the URL and the coordinate pairs, and expects parentheses around each coordinate pair, like this:

```
# CERN style image map file
circle (20, 15) 10 http://server/doc.html
rect (10, 10) (40, 20) http://server/doc2.html
default doc3.html
```

Regardless of the format, map file content is the same. For each selectable region, you specify its shape, which can be CIRCLE, RECT for rectangular, POLY

---

[1]Both CERN (origin of the Web) and NCSA (origin of Mosaic) maintain Web server software that they developed independently.

for an irregularly shaped polygon, or POINT for a single selectable point. Table 9-1 lists the required coordinates for each shape. Figure 9-1 shows an example of obtaining coordinates with a graphics program.

TABLE 9-1   IMAGE MAP SHAPES

Shape	Coordinates Required	Example
CIRCLE	x, y, r (radius)	30, 30, 15
RECT	x1, y1, x2, y2 (upper left, lower right)	10, 10, 40, 40
POLY	x1, y1, x2, y2, ... xn, yn	10, 10, 15, 5, 20, 10
POINT	x, y	30, 30

Figure 9-1
Shareware programs like LView Pro for Windows let you edit images and record coordinate zones (displayed at top) for image mapping files.

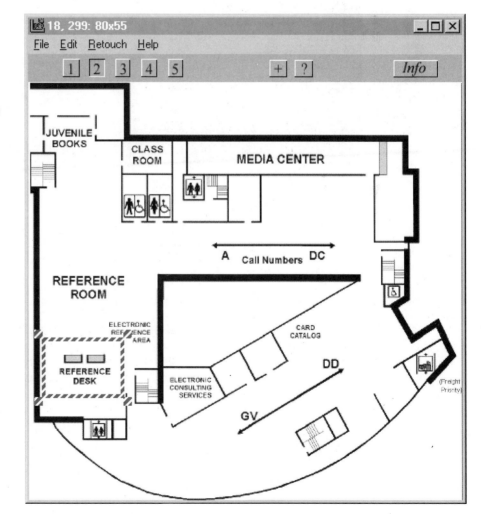

In addition to coordinate ranges, you should also include a DEFAULT entry in the mapping file that indicates where a user should be sent if they click inside the image but outside any coordinate range with an associated URL. If you do not provide a default option, an error message will be returned. DEFAULT can just point to a file that says something like "Click on a state to see the current weather" with a link back to the page containing the image map.

IMAGE MAP TOOLS

There are specialized tools for creating image maps. Tools such as MapEdit for Windows allow you to select image map regions with a mouse. When you have selected an area, the coordinates are automatically recorded. Then MapEdit prompts you for a URL for the resource that this region points to. It then allows you to save the map file in various Web server mapping formats. Such tools allow you to quickly construct complex mappings and are indispensable Web authoring tools (Figure 9-2).

Figure 9-2 Defining a coordinate zone with MapEdit for Windows

HTML 2 PROJECT STEP 7: ADDING A TOOLBAR

Let's add a toolbar to our tutorial project. This toolbar will replace the five buttons each document now has. Instead of making six requests to the Web server, Netscape can now ask for the HTML file and just one image. Open malay.htm and replace the five anchor/image tags just before the </BODY> tag with this line:

```
<A HREF="/cgi-bin/toolbar"><IMG SRC="tooltoc.gif" ISMAP></A>
```

This causes Netscape to load the image tooltoc.gif and make it an anchor. The ISMAP attribute of the image tag makes this an image map. When a user clicks on one of the "buttons" on our toolbar, the coordinates of their click are passed to the imagemap program on the local server. This program consults the toolbar map file to determine what URL should be returned:

```
#
# Created by WebMap 2.0b9
# Tuesday, September 19, 1995 at 9:46 AM
# Format: NCSA
#
rect help.htm 369,2 416,35
```

```
rect test1.htm 323,1 367,37
rect malay.htm 179,1 321,37
rect grammar.htm 97,0 176,38
rect vocab.htm 0,0 94,39
default malay.htm
```

This map file includes comments, which start with a pound sign (#). The imagemap program ignores comments, but they can be useful for documenting changes and recording the purpose of the mapping file. Each line contains the RECT geometric shape designator that indicates what shape the specified region is. Next comes the URL of the document that should be loaded if the user clicked in this region of the image. Finally, coordinate pairs are listed. In this case, upper-left- and lower-right-hand coordinates are sufficient. The DEFAULT option specifies what imagemap should return if the user clicks outside any of the specified regions. It does not require coordinates.

Each document can have a different toolbar, with the current location highlighted. They can all share the same toolbar map file, if they have the same dimensions:

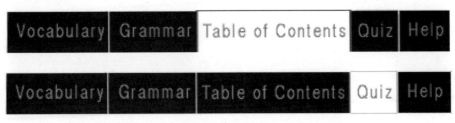

The screen printed on the following page shows malay.htm with a toolbar.

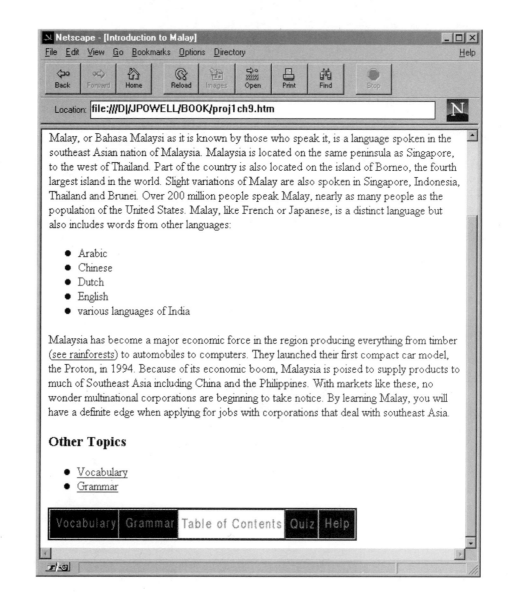

IMAGE MAP TAG USAGE SUMMARY

Tag	Permitted Context	Content Model
<IMG SRC="URL" ISMAP>	within an anchor tag	none

10

Netscape and Other Browser-Specific Extensions

CHAPTER AT A GLANCE

- Knowing when and when not to use browser-specific HTML extensions
- Using Netscape extensions to enhance your home pages
- *#RRGGBB?*
- HTML 2 Project: *Adding Netscape Extensions*
- Netscape 1.x Tag Usage and Attribute Summaries

Netscape extensions to HTML represent the first tentative steps toward addressing document appearance. These extensions were not well received by many HTML veterans, because they focus on presentation and formatting rather than structure. But the enthusiasm Web users had for Mosaic followed its developer to Netscape Navigator and the HTML extensions it supports. With more than 70% of the Web browser market, Netscape can override any agreed upon standard and revise it at will. Since Netscape is available for all major computing platforms (Mac, UNIX, and Windows), its extensions are actually platform independent. But because Netscape extensions are designed to enhance formatting, they violate the abstract distinction SGML asserts between formatting and document structure. This distinction is what makes text-only and other specialized browsers possible, and leaves the door open for HTML 3 to provide a more robust set of formatting controls in the form of style sheets. This is why Netscape extensions are viewed by some to be a less than useful contribution to the Web.

Netscape has built up a lot of good will by making many valuable contributions to the World Wide Web. Netscape Navigator 1.1 was the first browser to support tables. Some type of support for tabular data has long been promised in HTML 3. As plans for it matured, the Netscape developers grabbed a "snapshot" of the emerging standard and implemented it. As you will see in Chapter 15, Netscape selected a subset of tags that adhere very closely to the HTML 3 table standard. It was also the first Web browser to support inline JPEG images (which display images in full color, not merely 256 colors like GIF) and interlaced GIF images. Interlaced GIFs are displayed by Netscape in a low-resolution mode in the time it normally takes to display one quarter of the full graphic. Netscape has adopted other HTML 3 features such as the ID attribute (see Chapter 12), which allows any HTML tag to identify its contents as the target of a hypertext link, replacing the clumsy named-anchor markup provided in HTML 2 (while continuing to support it for backward compatibility). Such attention to supporting graphics and tag extensions that yield both performance improvements and much-sought-after presentation enhancements were the key to Mosaic's early success and have worked for Netscape as well.

In addition to having the most complete support for version 2 of HTML, Netscape chose to add functionality by supporting nonstandard but well-documented tags developed by the company. The biggest drawback to these elements is that none of them encode document structures; they are all specific markup elements. So far, few other Web browsers implement support for these extensions, although similar functionality is proposed for HTML 3, so some may become part of the HTML 3 standard. However, HTML 3 has a much more robust and flexible mechanism for supporting all of the Netscape tag extensions and many more formatting options in the form of style sheets. The two systems are likely to be blended together, with most Netscape extensions becoming redundant but easier to use for basic formatting control. Netscape extensions will at least be tolerated by the HTML 3 standard when it is completed.

Just as Netscape Navigator addresses the needs of the Web user, Netscape HTML extensions address the needs of businesses and organizations who want to have a Web presence. Netscape extensions are ideal for home pages. They allow authors to construct more attractive documents suitable for advertising, presentation, and other activities that the increasingly business-oriented Web desires. Netscape extensions are not suitable for use in articles, reports, and informational, as opposed to presentational, documents. When these tags are ignored by other browsers, it can lead to less readable documents. Reports, essays, book chapters, or articles will benefit little from these tags. Home pages are the best place to use these tags to increase impact and impress the reader. Even used here, it is best to test your home page with a non-Netscape browser prior to making it public.

The <ISINDEX> Tag

In the HTML document header, you can use the Netscape PROMPT attribute for the <ISINDEX> element to customize search options. This tag usually activates a previously inactive text input field found at the top of the document, or displays one at the top of the document. A default message "This is a searchable index. Enter search keywords:" is then displayed. With the PROMPT attribute, you may specify alternate text for the prompt by setting PROMPT equal to the desired string:

```
<ISINDEX PROMPT="Enter keywords separated by Boolean operators AND or OR">
```

This is useful for providing additional instructions that allow the user to utilize an underlying search capability more effectively.

The <BODY> Tag

Netscape supports additional attributes for various text block tags that occur in the document body. You can use Netscape attributes for the <BODY> tag to change the background color, assign a background image pattern, or change text or anchor colors. These options are particularly useful on title pages such as report covers, magazine, corporate, and personal home pages. You have the option of using an image as a document background by using the BACKGROUND attribute or a solid color with the BGCOLOR attribute:

```
<BODY BACKGROUND="clouds.GIF">
<BODY BGCOLOR="#ffff00">
```

Background images can be any image file but since the document text and graphics cannot be loaded until the background image is loaded and tiled, you should select a small image. Netscape will tile the image (display it repeatedly) so that the whole page is filled. Simple embossed logos or geometric patterns make excellent professional-looking backgrounds. More complex backgrounds must be constructed so that the pieces fit together to form an aesthetically appealing whole, or they distract the reader from the content.

#RRGGBB?

Netscape uses the RGB color definition system. In the bible of graphics formats, O'Reilly and Associates' *Encyclopedia of Graphics File Formats*, red, green, and blue are referred to as "fundamental and undecomposable." And because of the way colors mix, all other colors can be created by adding various amounts of these three colors. This color mixing system is platform independent. That's why Netscape expects color notation for

Continued on next page

Continued from previous page
backgrounds, fonts, and so on, to be specified in this way. The range allowed for each is 0 for no color to 255 for the maximum intensity and brightness of the color. For example, the triplet (0, 0, 0) is black, (255, 0, 0) is red, (255, 255, 0) combines red with green to form yellow, and so forth. Netscape expects color intensities to be specified in hexadecimal (base 16) notation. So 0 is 00, 10 is 0A, up to 255 which is FF. With this simple notation, you can represent up to 24 bits of color (more than 16 million colors!). Here are a couple of examples:

```
000000 black     ff0000 red
ffffff white     00ff00 green
```

Once you've tried a few background images and color options, you will probably soon stumble onto one that makes your text almost invisible. Dark text on a dark background can actually mean invisible text for some users as you do not always know what number of colors a remote user's system supports. If you design your document on a system with thousands of colors and the user is on a system with 256, the approximate equivalents of a dark green background might in fact be black. So Netscape also supports foreground color options for text and links. You can specify the color of text using the TEXT attribute. It works exactly like the BGCOLOR attribute. Select a color that contrasts nicely with the background image or color. Links should contrast with both the surrounding text and the background, so reserve brighter colors for the link options. Links have three states. You can set the normal link color with the LINK attribute. Links are blue by default. A link you have already selected is a visited link. The default, purple, can be customized with the VLINK attribute. Links change color when they are selected (their "active" state). The active color is set with the ALINK attribute:

```
<BODY TEXT="#rrggbb" LINK="#rrggbb" ALINK="#rrggbb" VLINK="#rrggbb">
```

The <HR> Tag

The horizontal rule has attributes to control its appearance when displayed by Netscape Navigator. The width of a horizontal rule can be specified in pixels or as a percentage of the available space. Percentage is preferable as it always comes out the way you intended, even if the user resizes the screen after they've loaded your document!

```
<HR WIDTH=25%>
<HR WIDTH=250>
```

You can control the thickness of a line with the SIZE attribute. For example,

    <HR SIZE=25>

displays a thick line that looks more like a rectangular box than a line. The horizontal rule can be centered or left or right justified using the ALIGN attribute:

    <HR ALIGN=CENTER>

You can suppress three dimensional shading for the horizontal rule by applying the NOSHADE attribute:

    <HR NOSHADE>

LISTS

Netscape provides additional configuration options for lists. The unordered and ordered lists each have new attributes. List items have attributes that allow you to override previously set formatting options mid-list. You can use a TYPE attribute with unordered lists in Netscape to specify the type of bullet displayed regardless of the indent level. The type can be set to disc, circle, or square to define a list's bullet type:

    <UL TYPE=SQUARE>

Ordered lists have a TYPE attribute which takes different values than the unordered list. You can configure ordered lists to use one of five different style options for enumerating list items: numbers, uppercase Roman numerals, lowercase roman numerals, capital letters, and lowercase letters:

    <OL TYPE=A>

In addition, ordered lists have a START attribute, which sets the starting point for a list's enumeration. You can assign a numeric value to START and Netscape automatically translates it into the corresponding roman numeral or letter if required.

List items also have a TYPE attribute useable with unordered or ordered lists. The TYPE attribute should be assigned a bullet type for an unordered list or an enumeration option for ordered lists. When encountered, the list will change at that point and all items following will be displayed with the new type. Ordered list items also have a VALUE attribute which can be used to change the current item's numbering mid-list. It too affects the current list item and all subsequent items.

    <UL TYPE=bullet>
    <LI>Apples
    <LI TYPE=square>Oranges
    </UL>

FONTS

Netscape supports resizable fonts with a <FONT> tag. Any text can be enlarged or shrunk with the font SIZE attribute. The default SIZE for displayed text, normally referred to as the base font size, is 3. Sizes from 1 to 7 are allowed, with 7 being the largest. If a size is preceded by a '+' or '-' then the current base font is increased by the size specified. The base font itself can be set with the <BASEFONT> tag. Instead of 3, a base font of 5 or 6 might be desirable for document titles:

```
<BASEFONT SIZE=4>
<FONT SIZE=+2>
```

Other font controls include the <BIG> and <SMALL> tags. These tags, which are used to tag characters and phrases, tell Netscape to display the marked text in a larger or smaller font than the current font. Perhaps the most ill-conceived Netscape extension is the <BLINK> tag. As its name implies, text marked with this tag will flash if viewed with Netscape. But beware, other Web browsers ignore this tag. Users viewing your document with something other than Netscape will miss the point!

POSITION AND TEXT FLOW

In addition to font control, text formatting and flow can be controlled with several Netscape tags. You can center text, graphics, and tables with the <CENTER> tag. This tag can be used anywhere in the body of the document to center a section of a document, but remember to use a </CENTER> end tag to mark the end of the block to be centered. Netscape also supports an ALIGN attribute for paragraphs (<P>) and the HTML 3 <DIV> element. ALIGN can be assigned the values LEFT, RIGHT, or CENTER to indicate how that block of text should be formatted:

```
<P ALIGN=CENTER>A (short) paragraph with centered text</P>
```

The line break tag <BR> has a CLEAR attribute. You can set clear to LEFT, RIGHT, or ALL to set the next line starting point to a position on the page where the margins are clear. The <NOBR> tag forces the text it marks to be displayed on one line, no matter how long.

Image positioning and text alignment in relation to images is much more precise under Netscape. There are many alignment options that you can use to control the position of the image on the page, the location of the text that follows it, or whether text flows around the image. You can set the ALIGN attribute to left or right when you want an image to float on the side margin and have text flow around it. The image will not be associated with any particular line of text, but text will wrap around it as it is reloaded or the user resizes their window. Other ALIGN options (TOP, MIDDLE, BOTTOM, TEXTTOP, ABSMIDDLE, and BASELINE) control how the text following the image will be displayed. Images can be surrounded by borders with the BORDER attribute. You can set BORDER to a numeric value to specify the thickness of the border, or simply specify BORDER, which displays a default width border around the image.

Netscape also supports some elements from the HTML 3.0 specification. In addition to <DIV>, Netscape supports the ID attribute for all HTML tags and the complete set of <TABLE> elements. Netscape continues to adopt the approach of adding formatting tags first, structural elements later. For example, it supports HTML 3 <SUB> and <SUP> (subscript and superscript) but not the full range of HTML 3 math tags. See Chapters 11 through 16 for more information about HTML 3.0.

Netscape Navigator 2.0 adds even more tags. The most important new elements are used to take advantage of new browser functionality. The <EMBED> element allows you to embed an arbitrary document type into the current HTML document:

```
<EMBED SRC="virtual_world.wrl">
<EMBED SRC="acrobat_doc.pdf">
```

When Netscape finds this tag, it attempts to load an additional piece of software, called a plug-in, to display the foreign document type alongside the HTML content. Client-side image maps are supported with the <AREA> tag. Rather than relying on the Web server to match coordinates to a URL, HTML documents that support client-side image maps include the mapping file in the document. You embed the mapping file with one or more <AREA> elements and attributes that define the hot spot shapes:

```
<MAP NAME="floorplan">
<AREA SHAPE="RECT" COORDS="10, 10, 50, 50" HREF="livingroom.html">
<AREA SHAPE="RECT" COORDS="51, 51, 20, 20" HREF="bath.html">
</MAP>
```

<AREA> attributes include SHAPE which is used to define the hot spot shape, COORDS that define coordinates for the shape, NOHREF to specify an area that does not respond to clicks, and HREF to point to the target URL. You must name and enclose a set of <AREA>'s with a <MAP> tag. This tag has one attribute, NAME, to which you assign a name to the mapping file. When you embed an image that should function as a client-side image map, you add a USEMAP attribute to the <IMG> tag, which points to this mapping data:

```
<IMG SRC="floorplans.gif" USEMAP="#floorplan">
```

Navigator 2.0 supports embedded Java applets with the <APPLET> tag. This tag supersedes the older <APP> tag originally used by Sun's HotJava browser (see the next section). The <APPLET> tag is covered in more detail in Chapters 31 through 32. To learn more about Netscape HTML extensions, access their home page at http://www.netscape.com.

OTHER BROWSER–SPECIFIC HTML EXTENSIONS

Other Web browsers support their own tag and attribute extensions. Some, such as Sun's HotJava, have extended HTML in order to provide new functionality, while others such as IBM's Web Explorer for OS/2, implemented some HTML merely to jazz up their browser. All browser-specific tags should be used sparingly if at all. Browser-specific tags often violate the central tenet of the Web—that it be platform independent. Many of the extensions listed below are extensions to browsers that run on only one type of computing platform.

OS/2's Web Explorer implements a Netscape-like user feedback mechanism in the form of an animated icon. But OS/2 provides a documented tag for replacing the default animation with one of your own. The <ANIMATE> tag can be used immediately following the document header to specify any number of image frames to be retrieved and used as a Web Explorer animation. Each image frame is specified with a <FRAME> tag. In this example, the default "superhighway" animation is replaced with a series of images of a supernova:

```
</HEAD>
<ANIMATE>
<FRAME SRC="nova_frame1.bmp">
<FRAME SRC="nova_frame2.bmp">
<FRAME SRC="nova_frame3.bmp">
</ANIMATE>
```

Note that image frames have to be in the OS/2- and Windows-native BMP graphics format. <ANIMATE> is a harmless tag that has no impact on most other browsers. It is unfortunate that Web Explorer expects this tag to occur immediately after the header end tag, since this places it outside both the document header and document body.

Microsoft's Internet Explorer supports many Netscape extensions and extends a couple, including <FONT>. It supports client-side image maps (where the browser does all of the work instead of forwarding clicks back to the server) with the <AREA> tag. It adds support for embedded sound files with a new element similar to the <IMG> element called <BGSOUND>:

```
<BGSOUND SRC="http://server.com/trumpet.wav">
```

Internet Explorer automatically downloads and plays the sound file pointed to by this attribute. Internet Explorer supports scrolling text areas called marquees with the <MARQUEE> tag. Like Netscape's <BLINK>, the user will merely see the contents of the <MARQUEE> tag as ordinary text if they are not using the Microsoft browser. To learn more about Microsoft HTML extensions, access their home page at http://www.microsoft.com.

Another browser important primarily because it was the first to support the Java programming language is HotJava. HotJava supports most Netscape extensions and adds an <APP> tag for including programs in an HTML document. An interesting feature of HotJava is that not only does it run Java applets, but it was also developed using Java!

Netscape has a large user base and despite concerns many users have about nonstandard tags, their HTML extensions play an important role in defining and extending the Web. Microsoft Internet Explorer will have an increasing impact on HTML standards as well since it is being bundled with Windows 95, purported to be the most popular software on the planet today. If you choose to use Netscape or other browser-specific elements, there are two things you should remember: identify your audience and test your documents!

HTML 2 PROJECT STEP 8: ADDING NETSCAPE EXTENSIONS

Since our "Introduction to Malay" page is a home page for the tutorial, let's apply some Netscape extensions to it. Open the malay.htm file and make the changes listed below in **bold**:

```
<HTML>
<HEAD><TITLE>Introduction to Malay</TITLE>
</HEAD>
<BODY BGCOLOR=#FFFFFF TEXT=#0000FF LINK=#FF0000>
<P><IMG SRC="images/malay_column.gif" ALIGN=LEFT>
<FONT SIZE=+4>M</FONT>alay, or Bahasa Malaysi as it is known by
those who speak it, is a language spoken in the southeast Asian
nation of Malaysia. Malaysia is located on the same peninsula as
Singapore, to the west of Thailand. Part of the country is also
located on the island of Borneo, the fourth largest island in the
world. Slight variations of Malay are also spoken in Singapore,
Indonesia, Thailand and Brunei. Over 200 million people speak
Malay, nearly as many people as the population of the United
States. Malay, like French or Japanese, is a distinct language
but also includes words from other languages:
<UL TYPE=CIRCLE>
<LI>Arabic
<LI>Chinese
<LI>Dutch
<LI>English
<LI>various languages of India
</UL>
<P>
<FONT SIZE=+2>M</FONT>alaysia has become a major economic force in
the region producing everything from timber
(<A HREF="http://server.envir.org/rainforest.html">see
rainforests</A>) to automobiles to computers. They launched their
first compact car model, the Proton, in 1994. Because of its
economic boom, Malaysia is poised to supply products to much of
Southeast Asia including China and the Philippines. With markets
like these, no wonder multinational corporations are beginning to
take notice. By learning Malay, you will have a definite edge when
applying for jobs with corporations that deal with southeast Asia.
<H3>Other Topics</H3>
```

Continued on next page

Continued from previous page

```
<UL TYPE=SQUARE>
<LI><A NAME="vocabulary" HREF="vocab.htm">Vocabulary</A>
<LI><A NAME="grammar" HREF="grammar.htm">Grammar</A>
</UL>
</BODY>
</HTML>
```

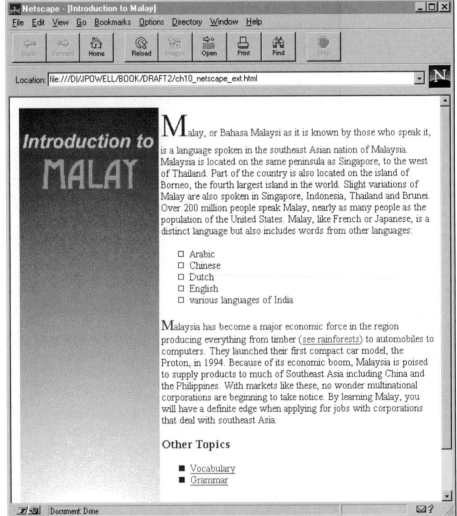

NETSCAPE 1.X TAG USAGE SUMMARY

Tag	Permitted Context	Content Model
<FONT>	document body	ASCII characters, character entities, text blocks
<BASEFONT>	document body	none
<BIG>	text blocks	ASCII characters, character entities
<SMALL>	text blocks	ASCII characters, character entities
<BLINK>	text blocks	ASCII characters, character entities, text blocks
<DIV>	see HTML 3 section	see HTML 3 section
<TABLE>	see HTML 3 section	see HTML 3 section
<CENTER>	document body	ASCII characters, character entities, text blocks
<NOBR>	document body	none
<APPLET>	document body	ASCII characters , character entities, text blocks

ATTRIBUTE SUMMARY

Tag	Attribute	Value
<ISINDEX>	PROMPT	ASCII characters, character entities
<BODY>	BACKGROUND	URL for an image
	BGCOLOR	RGB triplet in hexadecimal
	TEXT	RGB triplet in hexadecimal
	LINK	RGB triplet in hexadecimal
	ALINK	RGB triplet in hexadecimal
	VLINK	RGB triplet in hexadecimal
<HR>	WIDTH	number of pixels or percent of window width
	SIZE	number of pixels
	ALIGN	LEFT, RIGHT, CENTER
	NOSHADE	none
<UL>	TYPE	DISC, CIRCLE, SQUARE
<OL>	TYPE	1, A, a, I, i
<LI>	TYPE	any valid type for the current list
	VALUE	numeric value
<FONT>	SIZE	
<BASEFONT>	SIZE	
 	CLEAR	none
<IMG>	ALIGN	TOP, MIDDLE, BOTTOM, TEXTTOP, ABSMIDDLE, BASELINE
	BORDER	numeric value
<DIV>	ALIGN	LEFT, RIGHT, CENTER
<P>	ALIGN	LEFT, RIGHT, CENTER

11

HTML Version 3.0

CHAPTER AT A GLANCE

- Understanding the scope of HTML 3 enhancements
- Reasons for certain classes of extensions to HTML

What is HTML 3?

In 1993, discussions began on a successor to HTML 2. At that time, HTML+, as it was called, was to implement forms, tables, math tags, and some new document structures. Of course the Web was still quite young, with only a few hundred Web sites. HTML 2 was still in draft form, and would still be in draft two years later. Still, word spread quickly among enthusiastic Web authors who were happy to have such a rich publishing alternative to the then popular menu-driven gopher application. For a time everyone anticipated the next version of HTML, expecting it in a few months. Then nothing happened.

Two years later, HTML+ was still in draft. Forms markup was in such demand that it had been implemented based on draft specifications for HTML+ and became part of HTML 2 specifications (which was only then considered a final draft). HTML+, meanwhile, had been reworked by members of the World Wide Web developers list and been renamed HTML 3.

HTML 3 was simplified in some ways from the ambitious HTML+. Some proposed document structures were dropped. Style sheet support replaced a paragraph implementation that included attributes for different types of paragraphs. The group resisted efforts to include formatting tags that were applied to document structures (such as <CENTER>) in favor of recommending an ALIGN attribute. The final version is more in keeping with the SGML way: capture the document structure and mark the semantics of the document.

Various groups were not entirely thrilled with HTML as an SGML application. They felt that Web pages looked too much alike. This was often true. There were very few presentation markup options in HTML 2. For a time, there was not even support for embedded graphics. So Web pages were mainly text, often menu-like as the first wave of pages were implemented by information-system specialists who were already familiar with client/server information services such as gopher. Graphical clients for information servers were not a terribly new idea. There had been graphical gopher and WAIS (a full text search service) clients for X-Windows, Microsoft Windows, and Macintosh systems for several years. But they were not widely used. Macintosh systems were not at that time bundled with network software such as MacTCP. Microsoft Windows had some expensive proprietary solutions but Winsock, the standard for implementing TCP/IP (Internet) networking on a PC, was still evolving. So the Web and HTML arose in a world where text-based interfaces were still dominant. Figure 11-1 shows a screen capture from the text-based CERN Web browser.

Figure 11-1 CERN Web browser. Bracketed numbers represent anchors on the text-only display.

```
┌──────────────────────────────────────────────────────────────────────────┐
│ ─ │              telnet - borg.lib.vt.edu [borg:1]                  │ ▼ │ ▲ │
├──────────────────────────────────────────────────────────────────────────┤
│  File   Edit   Setup                                                  Help │
│                                                           CERN Welcome  ▲  │
│ CERN European Laboratory for     Particle Physics                          │
│                                                                            │
│                                                                            │
│      Lab[1] - News[2] -    Activities[3] - Physics[4] -   Other Subjects[5] - │
│    Search[6] -   Shrink[7] -    Expand[8]                                   │
│                                                                            │
│                                                                            │
│ About the Laboratory                                                       │
│                                                                            │
│      General:    Help[9] and   General information[10], Divisions, groups and │
│      activities[11]   (structure),   Scientific Committees[12],  Visits[13] │
│      Service,  CERN Courier[14], Safety guide[15] for experiments,  Education │
│      Services[16],  Recruitment and Vacancies[17].                         │
│                                                                            │
│      Databases:    Directories[18]   (phone & email, services & people),   │
│      Scientific Information Service[19] (library, archives or Alice),       │
│      Preprints[20].                                                        │
│                                                                            │
│      Agenda and News:    Press Releases[21],   News from the Users'        │
│      Office[22], current    Seminars[23],  CERN Schools & Conferences[24], │
│      internal Newsletters[25],  internal CERN news[26]  and Other news[27]. │
│ 1-54, Back, Up, <RETURN> for more, Quit, or Help: │                     ▼  │
│ ←│                                                                    │→   │
└──────────────────────────────────────────────────────────────────────────┘
```

Then along came Mosaic. Mosaic was just what the Internet community needed: a multipurpose graphical client. It could interact with gopher servers, and ftp archives, and launch applications to open documents it could not handle on its own. Most importantly, it supported HTML and ran on three of the most popular computing platforms: X-Windows, Microsoft Windows, and MacOS. Now users with Macs or PCs were finally able to justify the time and expense necessary to put a client machine on the Internet. Mosaic started to drive the push for networking standards for Macs and PCs. Users excited about what Mosaic could do wanted more. Forms support was added to Mosaic while HTML 3 was stilled called HTML+. Gopher sites fell out of favor and companies and organizations that had never considered a gopher site were putting up Web pages. Commercialization was not far behind.

Private industry hired away the core of developers that had made Mosaic such a success. Netscape emerged from this group and again essentially grabbed control of the HTML markup standard from the working group, adding markup elements as they saw fit. But many of the proposed features of HTML+ were not implemented because they were not flashy enough to have a large group of users requesting them. Math tags interested only a small number of the Web authors, and rigorous structural elements even fewer. But as the Web became more fragmented, Web pages started to look radically different from one system to another. Suddenly, standards didn't look so bad.

As much as they disrupted the standards process, the Netscape developers also deserve some credit for saving HTML+ from certain death. They faithfully implemented the table specification, and quietly implemented many other items from HTML 3. They hedged their bets, in case Netscape extensions backfired.

So rather than becoming the PostScript of the Web, HTML 3 is more like an "SGML Lite." It is a powerful and flexible markup language that borrows from other SGML applications (such as TEI) while striving to remain generic enough to support a wide range of data from e-mail messages to documentation to database query results. While Netscape extensions are driven by presentation and page layout issues, HTML 3 addresses document structure, navigation, and desperately needed markup support for tables and mathematical formulae. HTML 3 specifies hooks for page layout in the form of tag subclasses, and defines an

Evolution of a Tag

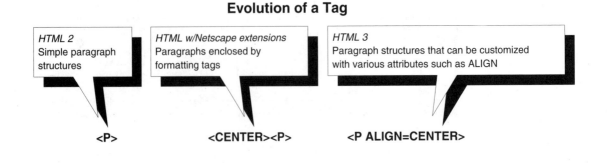

HTML 2
Simple paragraph structures

<P>

HTML w/Netscape extensions
Paragraphs enclosed by formatting tags

<CENTER><P>

HTML 3
Paragraph structures that can be customized with various attributes such as ALIGN

<P ALIGN=CENTER>

external formatting mechanism called style sheets. SGML has long relied on style sheets to control page layout for a collection of documents, but to HTML authors who've grown accustomed to enhancing their pages with specific markup extensions defined by Netscape and others, style sheets will take some getting used to.

HTML 3 continues to undergo discussion and revision. Netscape supports a number of HTML 3 tags and attributes such as the <TABLE> tag and its elements, and the ID attribute for precise hypertext authoring with less markup than required in HTML 2. The designers of HTML 3 decided early on that they needed a browser that would support HTML 3 tags and that would allow them to test their new markup as they developed it. So the W3 organization (which arose from CERN's discontinued Web development team—see http://www.w3.org for more information on W3) created the experimental Arena browser for programmers and HTML authors anxious to use and contribute ideas to HTML 3. HTML 3 math markup examples in this book use Arena renderings and Arena screen captures to illustrate HTML 3. Some other examples are presented with a Windows-based HTML 3 browser called UdiWWW (Figure 11-2). Many HTML 3 markup elements will work with Netscape 2.0 as well, and it is used whenever possible.

RELATIONSHIP OF HTML 2 TO HTML 3

The World Wide Web has become the dominant information format on the Internet in a relatively short period of time. This is due to the many features it supports over other delivery systems, such as full text, inline graphics, and platform independence. It is also due to the simplicity of the HTML markup language. HTML 3 has been designed to include many often-requested extensions without making the language more difficult to learn or adding dozens of additional tags. Many HTML 2 tags have new attributes and there are new tags for math and tables but many aspects of HTML 3 markup are similar if not identical to HTML 2.

HTML version 2.0 and HTML version 3.0 are intended to coexist indefinitely on the Internet. HTML 3 documents are expected to identify themselves as such by using a different document prologue and a different filename extension. In practice, Web browsers are expected to ignore the markup they cannot interpret and render, so it is likely that file naming conventions and prologues will be rare. Nonetheless, they are a good idea and an excellent way to clearly record which documents adhere to which standard. This text uses the extension .htm3 for HTML 3 documents.

With companies such as Netscape extending the HTML 2 tag set through support for new tags with their own browser and adding HTML 3 features piecemeal, widespread support of the HTML version 3.0 standard will occur slowly. The best strategy for now is to use HTML version 2.0 for most documents, include Netscape tags only if you believe the majority of your audience will be using Netscape and compatible browsers, and use HTML version 3.0 document structure tag sets when no equivalent exists in HTML version 2.0. Large, com-

Figure 11-2
UdiWWW HTML 3
Web browser
available from
http://www.
uni-ulm.de/
~richter/udiwww/
index.htm

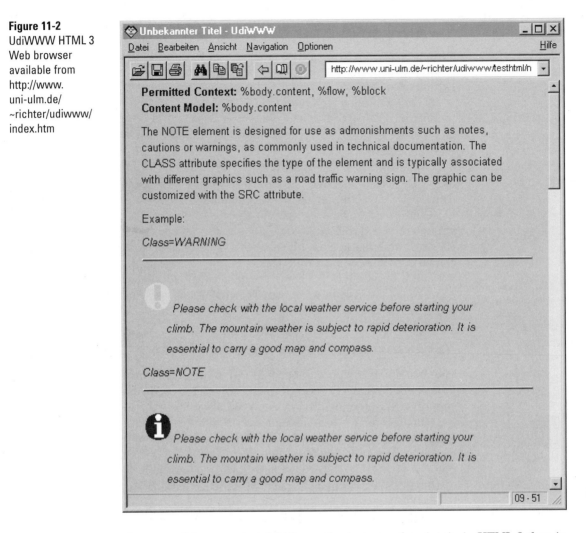

plex sets of documents might be easier to tag and maintain in HTML 3 than in HTML 2, since there are more document structure tags available. Do not use HTML 3 tags in documents that do not identify themselves as version 3.0, and make sure all documents identifying themselves as version 3.0 are fully compliant with the standard. HTML 3–compliant browsers are expected to support HTML 2 fully, so if HTML 2 continues to meet your needs stay with it.

It is very important that HTML 3 documents identify themselves as such so they can be processed correctly. HTML 3 documents should include a prologue that specifies the precise type (HTML) and version (version 3.0) of a document. Prologues were optional with HTML 2 and almost never used in practice, so Web server software usually attached one to the beginning of each HTML document it delivered, and the browser expects only the most basic prologue.

HTML 3 documents can be named differently such as with the extensions .html3 or .ht3, and should have the following prologue as the very first line of the document:

```
<!DOCTYPE HTML PUBLIC "-//IETF//DTD HTML 3.0//EN>
```

This identifies the document as an HTML document of type version 3.0 with the version defined using an SGML Document Type Declaration (DTD) of HTML 3.0 from the IETF (Internet Electronic Task Force). IETF is a group of people with representatives from education and the private sector who design and publish standards for the Internet. The DTD is a technical document written in SGML that defines the tags and attributes for HTML 3.

HTML 3 DOCUMENT STRUCTURE

HTML 3 enforces much stricter standards on document structure than HTML 2. The top-level structure <HTML><HEAD><BODY></HTML> still applies. But in a document that is fully HTML 3 compliant, text should only be found within text structures in a document. Text structures are defined as document divisions using the <DIV> tag; headings; block elements such as paragraphs, lists, forms, tables, math, and figures; and horizontal rule and address tags. Adding the following definition to a document prologue enforces strict 3.0 structure:

```
<!DOCTYPE HTML PUBLIC "-//IETF//DTD HTML 3.0//EN" [ <!ENTITY %
HTML.Recommended "INCLUDE"> ] >
```

while you can indicate old-style markup with this definition in the prologue (which is the default for backwards compatibility):

```
[ <!ENTITY & HTML.Deprecated "INCLUDE"> ]
```

When the entity HTML.Deprecated is set to INCLUDE, a less structured approach is permitted. When it is set to IGNORE, which is automatically the case when HTML.Recommended is set to INCLUDE, text outside text blocks is ignored and not displayed at all.

HTML 3 adds a few new tags for presentation control but emphasizes a reliance on style sheets for controlling presentation. Unlike Netscape's tag and attribute extensions to HTML 2, style sheets provide maximum control over the appearance of a document while maintaining HTML as a platform- and presentation-independent language. Style sheets are composed of a simple text-based language and can exist as separate documents linked to the HTML 3 document with a <LINK> tag in the document header, for example:

```
<HEAD>
<TITLE>A Document</TITLE>
<LINK REL=STYLESHEET TYPE="text/css" HREF="http://server.edu/style">
</HEAD>
```

or they can be embedded in the header portion of an HTML document with a <STYLE> tag, or included in the document body with the global STYLE attribute. HTML 3 uses a cascading style mechanism where the user's local Web browser settings for a given tag override all other settings. If a browser supports style sheets, then style sheet settings override the default renderings for a given tag, and the default renderings apply only if local customizations and style sheets are not present. This implementation provides complete backwards compatibility with HTML 2 while allowing authors to gain nearly complete control over the presentation of their documents.

Authors who wished to include various types of tabular data had three options with HTML 2. They could either create their table with some type of software supporting tables such as a word processor or spreadsheet application, then print the table, and finally scan the result and include it as an inline image. Or they could save the table as a PostScript or Acrobat document and provide a link from their HTML document. Or they could attempt to include the table in a preformatted text block. None of these were satisfactory solutions. HTML 3 provides a solution with its <TABLE> elements. Tables can be used to present data in rows and columns, present highly structured collections of text and graphics, or provide precise control over the layout of HTML form fields. Among the first HTML 3 markup elements supported by Netscape were table tags.

Another limitation of HTML 2 was a complete lack of support for mathematical data. There were no entities for Greek or common mathematical symbols and no way to structure formulae, equations, or proofs. Authors could provide formulae as inline graphics, but these are not scaled with the text and therefore easily fall out of context. Or they could link to non-HTML documents in PostScript, Acrobat, or TeX formats. HTML 3 includes a set of <MATH> elements that support superscripts, subscripts, arrays, and other options. It also defines a set of character entities for Greek letters and other mathematical symbols. Some <MATH> elements are similar to TeX control words so users of this markup language can easily migrate to it. It is simple enough that authors could hand tag formulae or word processors could generate HTML math elements from their own internal equation editors.

The continued success of the Web depends on its support of open document standards such as HTML. Acceptance and implementation of HTML 3 on the Internet will prove once again that platform-independent, structured documents are a safe, long-term global solution for electronic communication. Despite inroads made by impatient developers creating excellent browser software coupled with tag extensions of questionable value, the Web, like the Internet at large, will bypass problem areas. Nonstandard documents will be bypassed in favor of open, cross-browser and cross-platform standards such as HTML 3.

HTML 3
Overview of
Header and Body
Tags

CHAPTER AT A GLANCE

- Document structures that have been added to HTML 3 and how to apply them
- What is and is not an independent document structure in HTML 3
- HTML 3 Project: *Converting Netscape Extensions to HTML 3 Markup*
- HTML 3 Header and Body Tag Usage and Attribute Summaries

HTML 3.0 not only enforces a stricter document structure than HTML 2.0 but also includes some attributes for defining relationships between sets of hypertext documents and between structures and elements within the document. While some of the changes affect virtually every tag, they are still easy to understand. Once you learn them you may find yourself wondering why things weren't always done this way. Many new features are provided through global attributes, that is, attributes that can be applied to any HTML 3 tag.

HTML 3 documents start off with a prologue followed by an <HTML> tag. The <HTML> tag has three attributes: VERSION, URN, and ROLE. VERSION is defined as "--//W3O//DTD W3 HTML 3.0//EN" for version 3.0. URN is the Universal Resource Name for the document. URNs must be registered with a URN service. URNs are as yet an undefined standard for separating a document name from its physical location(s) on the Web. Eventually, documents might have a unique identifier on the Internet instead of a URL, and they could then be easily mirrored and accessed through a document name server much like the Domain Name Service (DNS) that helps a Web browser find a computer on the Internet today. ROLE indicates what role this document might play in a larger collection of documents, such as a table of contents.

\<HEAD\> Elements

There are three new tags in the \<HEAD\> section of the document : \<BANNER\>, \<STYLE\>, and \<RANGE\>. All attributes are optional unless otherwise noted. \<BASE\> is still present and functions as it did in version 2.0—defining a URL for the document so links in the document can refer to items relative to the defined base URL. \<ISINDEX\> has a PROMPT attribute like the one Netscape has added and an HREF that can be used to specify a URL for processing searches:

   \<ISINDEX HREF="whats-new.pl" PROMPT="Search our what's new databank"\>

\<LINK\> is used to include external style sheets as well as build navigational tool bars for HTML 3 Web browsers, point to authors, or include external documents (Figure 12-1). Each toolbar item is controlled with an REL and HREF attribute:

   \<LINK REL=ToC HREF="toc.html"\>
   \<LINK REL=copyright HREF="copyright.html"\>
   \<LINK REL=glossary HREF="glossary.html"\>

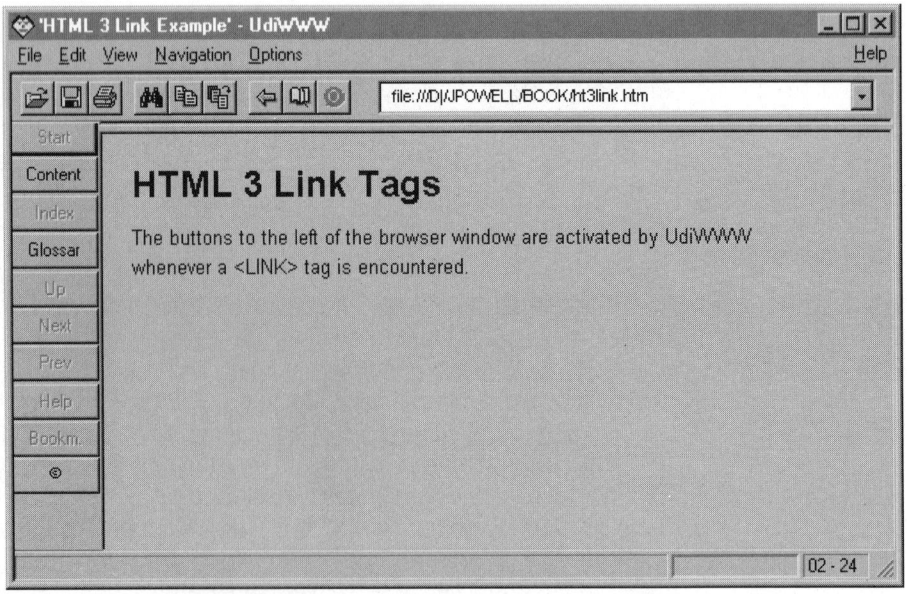

Figure 12-1 HTML 3 toolbar generated with \<LINK\>

The following relationships are reserved for this toolbar (most are self-explanatory): HOME, ToC (Table of Contents), Index, Glossary, Up, Next, Previous, Help, Bookmark, and Copyright. Each is used to assist users to follow certain paths in a set of linear or nonlinear hypertext documents. <LINK> is also used to include another document as a banner. This data is displayed above the text of the document and does not scroll with it:

<LINK REL=Banner HREF="university-logo.html">

The university-logo.html file can be updated at any time to update all documents that refer to it. Other <LINK> relationship names are proposed and will be documented by authors and browser implementers as they become accepted for widespread use.

The <META> tag is included in HTML 3 for embedding non-HTML information and markup. It has three attributes: NAME, CONTENT, and HTTP-EQUIV. NAME is used to indicate the name for a <META> property. Some example NAMEs are author, publication data, etc. CONTENT is paired with NAME and specifies the value assigned to the NAME, for example:

<META NAME="author" CONTENT="George Washington">

HTTP-EQUIV is used to relate a CONTENT value with a Web server response header. This information is passed by the Web server in the document header, outside the body of the text.

<RANGE> has a variety of potential applications such as marking a region of a document for special formatting or as an area containing a search query. Traditionally, the find function of word processors displays the search key in inverse video, but Web browsers have not had a way to indicate an occurrence of a word or string. The <RANGE> tag could be used to accomplish this. <RANGE> would rarely be inserted by an author but rather usually by software. It has four attributes: ID which names the text so that it can function as the target of a hypertext link (similar to "<A NAME=..."), CLASS to name a subclass for this range tag for style applications and other uses, FROM is assigned the value of an ID in the document that marks the start of the range, and UNTIL is assigned the value of an ID that marks the end of the range.

<RANGE CLASS="inverse_video" FROM="query_start" UNTIL="query_end">

The <STYLE> tag was discussed in some detail in Chapter 11. It has one optional attribute, TYPE, which specifies the type of style notation used in the style section:

<STYLE TYPE="text/css">

<STYLE> and <TITLE> are the only two tags in the document header that have end tags. <TITLE> is not changed from version 2.0. As you may recall, titles are used to uniquely identify the document and are usually displayed in the title bar of a Web browser. They should be descriptive as they are also used by bookmark programs as the title associated with the document URL.

<BODY> Elements

The HTML 3 document body begins with the <BODY> tag. It has five attributes, four of which are global HTML 3 attributes. These attributes are ID, LANG, STYLE, and CLASS. Hypertext links in HTML 2 could be pointed at text within the current document, but the target had to be marked with an anchor tag using the NAME attribute. This markup is confusing to create and revise. The ID attribute allows virtually any tag to be used as the target of a hypertext anchor. Assign it a value unique to this document. LANG specifies the language of the HTML document. Languages are specified using a two-character abbreviation from the ISO-639 standard, followed by an optional period and a two-letter country code from ISO-3166:

LANG=en.uk

CLASS creates a subclass of an HTML tag. These are used to relate style sheet formatting information with tags. A tag can have complex class names separated by a dot, with the most general class on the left (like Internet IP addresses):

<P CLASS=newspapers.sports>

Complex class names should relate to the semantics of the marked text so they can be used to programmatically extract information from the document(s). For example, the above subclass indicates that this paragraph is from the sports section of a newspaper. These attributes are powerful additions to HTML and can be used the same way throughout a document so they are also easy to learn and remember. The STYLE attribute specifies a formatting style for an HTML 3 element. Styles are explained in Chapter 14.

The fifth attribute of the <BODY> tag is associated only with the <BODY> tag. It is the BACKGROUND attribute. Backgrounds are supported by Netscape as well; the format of the BACKGROUND attribute in HTML 3 is the same:

<BODY BACKGROUND="/images/checkerboard.gif">

TEXT BLOCKS: MAJOR TEXT BLOCKS

Now let's look at the <BODY> tags that mark document structures. The first of these is the <BANNER> tag. This tag is used to include logos and other information, such as supplementary navigational aids, that should display while the user is reading the document whether they scroll forward or not. In fact, any structures or markup valid in the document body is also valid in the banner. You can build an entire document that is enclosed within the <BANNER> start and end tag. The banner contents almost become part of the Web browser (Figure 12-2). The <BANNER> tag has ID, LANG, and CLASS attributes as described above. <BANNER> is similar to Netscape 2 frames (see Chapter 17), although it provides only a subset of frames functionality.

```
<HTML>
<HEAD>
<TITLE>HTML 3 Banner Example</TITLE>
</HEAD>
<BODY>
<BANNER>
<H1>An HTML 3 Banner</H1>
</BANNER>
```

Figure 12-2
Banners can appear at the top of HTML 3 documents and do not scroll with the document body.

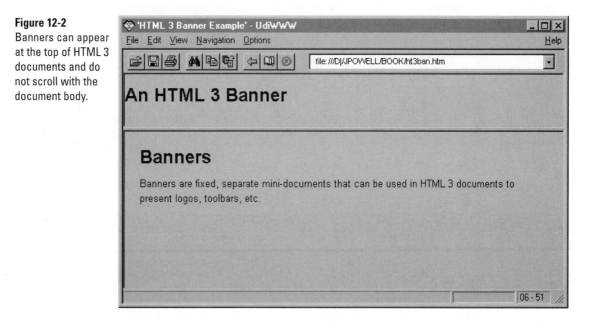

Document headings in HTML 3 divide sections of a document into a hierarchy. Headings are not in themselves document structures, but are usually associated with HTML 3 document structures such as divisions. They can occur outside of other document structures. A heading normally is displayed in a different font and set apart from document text. The text of a heading is wrapped onto multiple lines as needed by default unless a NOWRAP attribute is included. A break tag <BR> can occur in a heading if a line break is desired. Headings have CLASS, ID, and LANG attributes like virtually all HTML 3 tags. Headings are more list-like in HTML 3, essentially listing the structures within a document so they have a number of attributes to control their list behavior. SEQNUM assigns a sequence number to a heading. Each heading is normally numbered 1 for level 1 headings to 6 for level 6 headings, and numbering is reset when a higher level heading is encountered, such as when an <H1> occurs after an <H3>. SKIP is used to increment the default sequence numbering by a specified value. The DINGBAT attribute specifies an HTML 3 icon that should be displayed with the heading. SRC specifies that an image should precede the heading. SRC is assigned the URL for an image. Here is an example that implements some HTML 3 heading attributes:

```
<H1 CLASS="big" SRC= "square_bullet.gif" NOWRAP>HTML 3</H1>
```

Other HTML 3 heading attributes include MD. The MD attribute is a new HTML 3 attribute for all tags that link to URLs. It is used to enhance document security. Web browsers can use the value assigned to MD (called a checksum) to determine if a graphic or other file has been altered since the link was established. Checksums are alphanumeric strings generated from the original file contents. If the file changes or is corrupted, the checksum will not match and the linked item should not be retrieved. The CLEAR attribute moves the next line downward by the specified value assigned to it. CLEAR can be set to LEFT, RIGHT, or ALL to move the line down to the next line with clear left, right, or left and right margins. Or CLEAR can be assigned a value in pixels or en units to move the line down that amount of space.

The <DIV> tag marks document divisions. These can be sections like chapters, abstracts, appendices, etc. Division type is assigned with the CLASS attribute:

```
<DIV CLASS=Chapter.1>
```

Using multiple class names to subclass the division allows more control in the style sheet. In this example, this division is subclassed as "Chapter" and further subclassed as "1." Style specifications could address it as a Chapter and further unique style enhancements could be applied to only the first chapter. You can use other division attributes including ID, LANG, and ALIGN to specify whether the division's paragraphs should be aligned left, right, or center. Divisions have a NOWRAP attribute to turn off automatic line wrapping in the browser. Lines that should be wrapped must end with a <BR> tag when NOWRAP is specified. Divisions can also have a CLEAR attribute like headings.

Paragraphs (<P>) are similar to HTML 2 paragraphs and structure text outside of and within document divisions, forms, and other textual elements. Paragraphs have the same attributes (ID, LANG, CLASS, ALIGN, CLEAR, NOWRAP) as divisions.

LISTS

There are three list types in HTML 3. Unordered, ordered, and definition lists can be used outside of or within divisions, paragraphs, and other text elements. The HTML 2 <MENU> and <DIR> tags have been superseded by attributes to the unordered list (<UL>) tag:

```
<MENU> is now <UL PLAIN>
<DIR> is now <UL PLAIN WRAP=HORIZ>
```

Unordered and ordered lists have an optional list heading <LH> and one or more list items <LI>. List headings have the basic HTML 3 attribute set (ID, LANG,

CLASS). List items have a similar attribute set to document headings: ID, LANG, CLASS, CLEAR, SRC, MD, DINGBAT, and SKIP. Unordered lists have the following attributes: ID, LANG, CLASS, CLEAR, PLAIN (no bullets displayed with items), SRC, MD, DINGBAT, COMPACT (reduces spacing between list items), and WRAP (which determines whether the items are listed vertically down the page or horizontally, i.e., VERT, HORIZ). As in HTML 2, HTML 3 lists can be nested (Figure 12.3).

```
<UL PLAIN COMPACT>
<LH CLASS="bold">North America</LH>
<LI>Canada
<LI>United States
<LI>Mexico
</UL>
```

HTML 2 ordered lists <OL> are lists of numbered items. HTML 3 includes attributes for changing the numbering sequence (SEQNUM) or continuing a new ordered list with the next number in sequence from the last ordered list (CONTINUE). Ordered lists have an optional list header tag and multiple list item tags that have the same attributes as unordered lists. Unlike Netscape's list extensions which include attributes for both controlling sequence and numbering style, HTML 3 leaves numbering styles such as roman numerals or compound numbers to external style sheet definitions.

Figure 12-3
Unordered list example

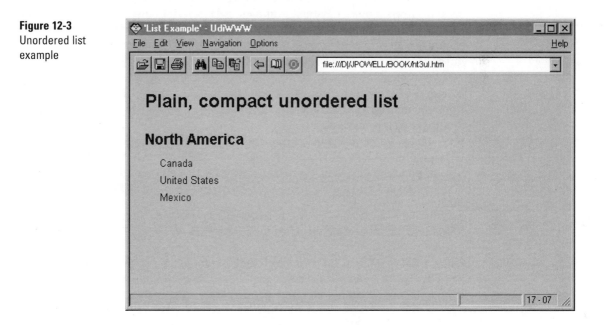

```
<OL SEQNUM=3>
<LH>Months</LH>
<LI>janvier
<LI>f&eacute;vrier
<LI>mars
<LI>avril
<LI>mai
</OL>
```

HTML 3 supports the HTML 2 definition list <DL> with little modification. Definition lists may have one list header <LH> that describes the content of the list. As in HTML 2, definition list contents consist of definition terms <DT> and definitions <DD>.

IMAGES

If you wanted to include an image in an HTML 2 document, the only tag available was <IMG>. In HTML 2, inline images were treated just like text, with large images disrupting the flow of a document since there was no mechanism to allow text to flow around a graphic. There was also no support for captions, overlays, or client-side image maps. Figures (<FIG>) provide all of these capabilities and more. Figures are large inline graphics that can have captions, function as image maps, and allow text to flow around them. The <IMG> tag is only used to insert icons and small graphics in HTML 3. Figure blocks can include captions marked with the <CAPTION> tag, photographic or artistic credit tagged with the <CREDIT> tag, client-side image mapping (the mapping file is included in the HTML document) with anchors combined with the SHAPE attribute, as well as document textual structures such as paragraphs and headings. Text included between the <FIG> start and end tag can be used to provide descriptions for images and text-based alternatives to image maps for users without graphical Web browsers.

You can add captions to figures with the <CAPTION> tag. Short text descriptions combined with phrase and typographic markup can be included in the figure caption. The ALIGN attribute can be used with a caption to specify where the caption should be placed in relation to the figure (TOP, BOTTOM, LEFT, or RIGHT):

```
<FIG SRC="andromeda.gif"><CAPTION ALIGN=BOTTOM>The
<EM>Andromeda</EM> galaxy</CAPTION></FIG>
```

Overlays are a useful addition to inline graphics. They allow a new image to be combined with a previously loaded image. For best results, this image should have been referenced by a previous document, so that it will be stored in the Web browser's cache file. This reduces the amount of time required to build documents with complex figures. It is ideal for tutorials and slide presentations that build on previous slides and graphics. Each overlay is specified with an <OVERLAY> tag within the <FIG> block. Like <FIG> and <IMG>, it has an SRC attribute for specifying the URL to the overlay image.

OTHER TEXT BLOCK ELEMENTS

You can tag warnings and other special information that you wish to draw the reader's attention to with the <NOTE> tag. This type of text block is generically referred to as an admonishment. It can be a simple note reemphasizing a previous point, or a special warning that identifies some safety precaution or other important information (Figure 12-4). Admonishments are usually displayed indented and offset from the surrounding text. The <NOTE> tag can be assigned ID, CLASS, and LANG attributes. The CLASS attribute has three special values with the <NOTE> tag: NOTE, CAUTION, and WARNING:

```
<NOTE CLASS="NOTE">This is an ordinary HTML 3 Note</NOTE>
<NOTE CLASS="CAUTION">This is a Caution Note</NOTE>
<NOTE CLASS="WARNING">This is a Warning Note</NOTE>
```

HTML 3 browsers should have a built-in graphic that they display automatically when they encounter an admonishment belonging to one of these three classes. You can also create custom classes and specify formatting with a style sheet and a custom graphic with an SRC attribute:

```
<NOTE CLASS="notice" SRC="notice.gif">
```

Other attributes for <NOTE> include the CLEAR attribute for establishing blank space around the admonishment and MD for verifying the image specified with the SRC attribute.

Many hypertext systems such as Microsoft Windows Help render footnotes as pop-up text blocks. HTML 3 includes a footnote tag <FN> for tagging footnotes so that they can be presented this way with a Web browser. Footnotes have ID, LANG, and CLASS attributes. In the case of footnotes, the ID attribute is

Figure 12-4
<NOTE> Examples

required for uniquely identifying the footnote so that it can be referenced in the body of the text. Footnote references are constructed with the anchor tag. Footnotes should contain valid HTML 3 text blocks such as paragraphs:

```
HTML 3 <A HREF="#fn1">footnotes</A> are a handy addition to HTML
<FN ID="fn1"><P>Footnotes are tagged with the &lt;FN&gt; tag</FN>
```

Text block elements common to both HTML 2 and HTML 3 include hard rule <HR>, line break <BR>, preformatted text block <PRE>, address <ADDRESS>, and blockquote which has been shortened to <BQ>. Each of these tags can serve as the target of a hypertext link if given an ID attribute, can be subclassed with the CLASS attribute, and can be made language specific with a LANG attribute.

FORMS

HTML 3 forms look very much like version 2.0. A form block is tagged with the <FORM> tag, which has attributes for specifying how the contents should be processed and where they should be sent (METHOD, ENCTYPE, and ACTION). The <FORM> tag now also has a SCRIPT attribute that can be used to specify a script for client-side processing. The SCRIPT attribute would be assigned a URL pointing to a processing script that the Web browser should automatically download and run using the contents of the form. The Java <APPLET> tag performs a similar function. The idea is that a client-side script would perform additional functionality to a Web form, such as checking the data a user inputs to determine if it falls within a predefined set of allowed values. However, no scripting language is defined in the specification.

Input fields still support a wide range of data entry functions. All the HTML 2 TYPE attribute values are still supported (TEXT, PASSWORD, CHECKBOX, RADIO, HIDDEN, SUBMIT, IMAGE, and RESET). HTML 3 adds three new TYPE attribute values. The range type allows a user to select a numeric value between two values. This type is always used in conjunction with the MIN and MAX attributes, which are assigned the lower and upper limit of the allowable range values. Ranges might be displayed by a Web browser as a sliding bar. The scribble type allows the user to draw on an image. Input fields of this type should always include an SRC attribute which is assigned the URL of an image. The file type allows the user to attach one or more files to the contents of the form. An optional ACCEPT attribute can be used to specify what types of files are allowed.

HTML 3 supports large text input fields with the <TEXTAREA> tag, like HTML 2. Two new attributes are supported, which are also valid with all other HTML 3 form elements: ERROR and DISABLED. When a client-side script has been specified, the ERROR attribute value is displayed when the script determines that the user has input incorrect data. The DISABLED attribute causes a field, such as a generated form with a preassigned value to be displayed, but not be editable.

<SELECT> menus are carried over from HTML 2 but can now be optionally presented as a graphic. Like <FIG> image maps, you can specify both text and image coordinates that correspond to a selection option, so that both graphical and text-based Web browsers are supported by a single form. The <SELECT>

image is specified, verified, and customized with the SRC, MD, WIDTH, UNITS, ALIGN, and HEIGHT attributes. Each selectable area and/or text option is tagged with an <OPTION> tag. The SHAPE attribute of the <OPTION> tag specifies what region of the graphic corresponds to which selection option. It uses the same syntax as <FIG> image maps:

```
<SELECT SRC="barchart.gif">
<OPTION SHAPE="rect 10, 10, 30, 40">Bar 1(Sales)
<OPTION SHAPE="40, 10, 30, 40">Bar 2(Profits)
</SELECT>
```

HTML 3 PROJECT: CONVERTING NETSCAPE EXTENSIONS TO HTML 3 MARKUP

Find an HTML 2 Web page with some Netscape extensions and make it an HTML 3–compliant page.

Here is the HTML 2/Netscape markup for the figure on page 125.

```
<HTML>
<HEAD>
<TITLE>Scholarly Communications Project of VPI & SU</TITLE>
</HEAD>
<CENTER>
<BODY background="/images/scpback.gif" text=ffffff>
<TABLE border=1>
<TR><TD><IMG src="/images/logobar.gif" alt="Scholarly Communications
Project"></TD>
</TABLE>
<BR>
<TABLE border=3>
<TR><TD><IMG src="/images/newlogo.gif" alt="Scholarly Communications
Project"></TD>
</TABLE>
<P><I>University Libraries, Virginia Polytechnic Institute and State University</I>
<HR size=5>
<TABLE border=3 cellspacing=3>
<TR><TD align=center><A href="/scpabout.html">About the Project
<BR></A></TD><TD align=center><A href="http://scholar3.lib.vt.edu/VA-news/VA-
news.html">Virginia News <BR></a></TD>
<TR><TD align=center><A href="/ejpage.html">Electronic Journals
<BR></A></TD><TD align=center><A href="/vtpub.html">Virginia Tech
Publications</A> <BR></TD>
<TR><TD align=center><A href="/theses/theses.html">Theses and Dissertations
<BR></A></TD><TD align=center><A href="/reports/reports.html">Publishing
Tools</A></TD>
```

Continued on next page

Continued from previous page

```
    </TABLE>
    <HR size=5>
    <TABLE border=3 cellspacing=3>
    <TR><TD align=center><FORM method=get action="http://scholar.lib.vt.edu/cgi-
    bin/scholar.sonofwais.pl">
    Database Search: <INPUT name="" SIZE=30>
    <INPUT type=reset value="Clear">
    <INPUT type=submit value="Do Search">
    </FORM></TD>
    </TABLE>
    <HR size=5>
    <TABLE border=1>
    <TR><TD><A HREF = "http://scholar.lib.vt.edu/cgi-bin/imagemap/scpmenu"><IMG
    border=0 SRC = "/images/menubar.gif" ISMAP></A></TD>
    </TABLE>
    <HR size=5>
    </CENTER>
    <A href="http://www.vt.edu"><IMG border=1 src="/images/HPButton.gif"></A>
    <P>
    <CITE>
    Scholarly Communications, <A HREF="http://vatech.lib.vt.edu/">University
    Libraries</A><BR>
    Send Suggestions or Comments to <a
    href="mailto:webmaster@scholar.lib.vt.edu">webmaster@scholar.lib.vt.edu</A><B
    R>
    Last updated: August 9, 1995
    <P>
    URL: http://scholar.lib.vt.edu/
    </CITE>
    </BODY>
    </HTML>
```

We can eliminate all of the Netscape extensions and enhance the page with some HTML 3 features such as client-side image maps. The logobar.gif image should become a document banner, since this will allow it to be displayed even when the rest of the page scrolls. Text color can be handled with a style sheet entry. We can replace each <CENTER> tag by adding an ALIGN=CENTER attribute to the paragraph tags. The tables are already HTML 3 so we don't need to modify them. The toolbar would work more quickly and serve more users if it were a client-side image map, so let's convert it to a figure with <FIG>. Here is the HTML 3 version of the page:

```
<HTML>
<HEAD>
<TITLE>HTML 3: Scholarly Communications Project of VPI & SU</TITLE>
<STYLE TYPE="text/css">
text-color: ffffff
</STYLE>
</HEAD>
<BODY background="/images/scpback.gif" >
<BANNER>
<DIV CLASS="banner.center">
<FIG src="/images/logobar.gif" align=center alt="Scholarly
Communications Project"></FIG></TD>
</DIV>
</BANNER>
<DIV CLASS="home.center">
<FIG src="/images/newlogo.gif" align=center alt="Scholarly
Communications Project"></FIG></TD>
<P align=center> <I>University Libraries, Virginia Polytechnic
Institute and State University</I>
<HR size=5>
<TABLE border=3 align=center cellspacing=3>
<TR><TD align=center><A href="/scpabout.html">About the Project
<BR></A></TD><TD align=center><A href="http://scholar3.lib.vt.edu/VA-news/VA-
news.html">Virginia News <BR></a></TD>
<TR><TD align=center><A href="/ejpage.html">Electronic Journals
<BR></A></TD><TD align=center><A href="/vtpub.html">Virginia Tech
Publications</A> <BR></TD>
<TR><TD align=center><A href="/theses/theses.html">Theses and Dissertations
<BR></A></TD><TD align=center><A href="/reports/reports.html">Publishing
Tools</A></TD>
</TABLE>
<HR size=5>
<TABLE border=3 align=center cellspacing=3>
<TR><TD align=center><FORM method=get action="http://scholar.lib.vt.edu/cgi-
bin/scholar.sonofwais.pl">
Database Search: <INPUT name="" SIZE=30> <INPUT type=reset value="Clear">
<INPUT type=submit value="Do Search">
```

```
</FORM></TD>
</TABLE>
<HR size=5>
<FIG SRC = "/images/menubar.gif" ALIGN=center IMAGEMAP>
<P>
<UL>
<LH>Pointers for Navigation</LH>
<LI><A SHAPE="rect 67,0,124,35"
HREF="http://scholar.lib.vt.edu/scholar.html3">Home Page</A>
<LI><A SHAPE="rect 126,0,198,35" HREF="http://scholar3.lib.vt.edu/VA-news/VA-
news.html">Virginia News</A>
<LI><A SHAPE="rect 200,1,275,34" HREF="ejpage.html">Journals</A>
<LI><A SHAPE="rect 277,1,398,35" HREF="vtpub.html">Virginia Tech
Publications</A>
<LI><A SHAPE="rect 401,1,458,35" HREF="/theses/theses.html">Theses and
Dissertations</A>
<LI><A SHAPE="rect 461,0,504,35" HREF="/reports/reports.html">Publishing
Tools</A>
</UL>
</FIG>
<HR size=5>
</DIV>
<A href="http://www.vt.edu"><IMG border=1 src="/images/HPButton.gif"></A>
<P>
<CITE>
Scholarly Communications, <A HREF="http://vatech.lib.vt.edu/">University
Libraries</A><BR>
Send Suggestions or Comments to <a
href="mailto:webmaster@scholar.lib.vt.edu">webmaster@scholar.lib.vt.edu</A><B
R>
Last updated: September 26, 1995
<P>
<ACRONYM>URL</ACRONYM>: http://scholar.lib.vt.edu/
<P>
<NOTE><I>HTML 3.0 Test Page</I></NOTE>
</CITE>
</BODY>
</HTML>
```

HTML 3 HEADER AND BODY TAG USAGE SUMMARY

Tag	Permitted Context	Content Model
<HTML>	around document	<HEAD>, <BODY>, <!-- -->
<HEAD>	before document body	<TITLE>, <BASE>, <ISINDEX>, <LINK>, <NEXTID>, <!-- -->
<TITLE>	within document header	ASCII characters, character entities
<BASE>	within document header	no contents
<ISINDEX>	within document header	no contents
<LINK>	within document header	no contents
<NEXTID>	within document header	no contents
<META>	within document header	no contents
<STYLE>	within document header	CSS style notation
<!-- -->	anywhere in document	ASCII characters, character entities
<BODY>	after document header	text block elements
<BANNER>	anywhere in document	text block elements
<DIV>	document body	text block elements
<H1>–<H6>	document body	ASCII characters, character entities
<P>	document body	ASCII characters, character entities, phrase and typographic elements
<UL>	document body	list items (<LI>)
<OL>	document body	list items (<LI>)
<DL>	document body	definition items (<DT>, <DD>)
<LH>	before list items	ASCII characters, character entities, typographic elements
<LI>	lists	ASCII characters, character entities, typographic elements
<DT>	definition lists	ASCII characters, character entities, typographic elements
<DD>	definition lists	ASCII characters, character entities, typographic elements
<FIG>	document body	text block elements
<OVERLAY>	inside <FIG>	no contents
<CAPTION>	inside <FIG> or <TABLE>	ASCII characters, character entities
<CREDIT>	inside <FIG>	ASCII characters, character entities
<HR>	document body	no contents
<PRE>	document body	ASCII characters, character entities, form elements
<NOTE>	document body	ASCII characters, character entities
<FN>	document body	ASCII characters, character entities
<BQ>	document body	ASCII characters, character entities

HTML 3 HEADER AND BODY TAG USAGE SUMMARY, CONT.

Tag	Permitted Context	Content Model
<ADDRESS>	document body	ASCII characters, character entities
<FORM>	document body	body tags, <INPUT>, <SELECT>, <OPTION>, <TEXTAREA>
<INPUT>	within an HTML form	no contents
<SELECT>	around list of selectable options with an HTML form	<OPTION>
<OPTION>	within a <SELECT> list	ASCII characters, character entities
<TEXTAREA>	within an HTML form	ASCII characters, character entities

ATTRIBUTE SUMMARY

(All HTML 3 body elements support the global attributes ID, CLASS, STYLE, and LANG, so they will not be repeated in this table).

Tag	Attribute	Value
<HTML>	VERSION	-//W3O//DTD W3 HTML 3.0//EN
	URN	Universal Resource Name (ASCII text)
	ROLE	ASCII text
<RANGE>	FROM, TO	ASCII text
<STYLE>	TYPE	ASCII text
<DIV>	ALIGN	LEFT, CENTER, RIGHT, JUSTIFY
	NOWRAP	none
	CLEAR	LEFT, RIGHT, ALL, pixels or en units
<H1>–<H6>	ALIGN	LEFT, CENTER, RIGHT, JUSTIFY
	CLEAR	LEFT, RIGHT, ALL, pixels or en units
	SEQNUM	numeric value
	SKIP	numeric value
	DINGBAT	icon name (ASCII text)
	SRC	URL of a graphic file
	MD	checksum (ASCII text)
	NOWRAP	none
<P>	ALIGN	LEFT, CENTER, RIGHT, JUSTIFY
	CLEAR	LEFT, RIGHT, ALL, pixels or en units
	NOWRAP	none
<UL>	CLEAR	LEFT, RIGHT, ALL, pixels or en units
	PLAIN	none

ATTRIBUTE SUMMARY, CONT.

Tag	Attribute	Value
	SRC	URL of a graphic file
	MD	checksum (ASCII text)
	DINGBAT	icon name (ASCII text)
	WRAP	VERT, HORIZ
	COMPACT	none
<LI>	CLEAR	LEFT, RIGHT, ALL, pixels or en units
	SRC	URL of a graphic file
	MD	checksum (ASCII text)
	DINGBAT	icon name (ASCII text)
	SKIP	numeric value
<OL>	CLEAR	LEFT, RIGHT, ALL, pixels or en units
	CONTINUE	none
	SEQNUM	numeric value
	COMPACT	none
<DL>	CLEAR	LEFT, RIGHT, ALL, pixels or en units
	COMPACT	none
<DT>	CLEAR	LEFT, RIGHT, ALL, pixels or en units
<DD>	CLEAR	LEFT, RIGHT, ALL, pixels or en units
<FIG>	CLEAR	LEFT, RIGHT, ALL, pixels or en units
	NOFLOW	none
	SRC	URL of a graphic file
	MD	checksum (ASCII text)
	ALIGN	LEFT, CENTER, RIGHT, JUSTIFY
	WIDTH, HEIGHT	numeric values
	UNITS	PIXELS, EN
	IMAGEMAP	URL (ASCII text)
<OVERLAY>	SRC	URL of a graphic file
	MD	checksum (ASCII text)
	UNITS	PIXELS, EN
	X, Y	numeric values
	WIDTH, HEIGHT	numeric values
	IMAGEMAP	URL (ASCII text)
<CAPTION>	ALIGN	LEFT, CENTER, RIGHT, JUSTIFY
<HR>	CLEAR	LEFT, RIGHT, ALL, pixels or en units
	SRC	URL of a graphic file
	MD	checksum (ASCII text)
<PRE>	CLEAR	LEFT, RIGHT, ALL, pixels or en units
	WIDTH	numeric value
<NOTE>	CLEAR	LEFT, RIGHT, ALL, pixels or en units
	SRC	URL of a graphic file
	MD	checksum (ASCII text)

ATTRIBUTE SUMMARY, CONT.

Tag	Attribute	Value
<BQ>	CLEAR	LEFT, RIGHT, ALL, pixels or en units
	NOWRAP	none
<ADDRESS>	CLEAR	LEFT, RIGHT, ALL, pixels or en units
	NOWRAP	none
<FORM>	ACTION	URL (ASCII text)
	METHOD	GET, POST
	ENCTYPE	MIME encoding type (ASCII text)
	SCRIPT	URL (ASCII text)
<INPUT>	TYPE	TEXT, PASSWORD, CHECKBOX, RADIO, RANGE, SCRIBBLE, FILE, HIDDEN, SUBMIT, IMAGE, RESET
	NAME	ASCII text
	VALUE	ASCII text
	DISABLED	none
	ERROR	ASCII text
	CHECKED	none
	SIZE	numeric value
	MAXLENGTH	numeric value
	MIN, MAX	numeric values
	ACCEPT	MIME content types (ASCII text)
	SRC	URL of a graphic file
	MD	checksum (ASCII text)
	ALIGN	LEFT, CENTER, RIGHT, JUSTIFY
<TEXTAREA>	NAME	ASCII text
	ROWS	numeric value
	COLS	numeric value
	DISABLED	none
	ERROR	ASCII text
	ALIGN	LEFT, CENTER, RIGHT, JUSTIFY
<SELECT>	NAME	ASCII text
	MULTIPLE	none
	DISABLED	none
	ERROR	ASCII text
	SRC	URL (ASCII text)
	MD	checksum (ASCII text)
	WIDTH, HEIGHT	numeric values
	UNITS	PIXELS, EN
	ALIGN	LEFT, CENTER, RIGHT, JUSTIFY
<OPTION>	DISABLED	none
	ERROR	ASCII text
	VALUE	ASCII text
	SELECTED	none
	SHAPE	DEFAULT, CIRCLE x,y,r, RECT x,y,w,h, POLYGON x1,y1,x2,y2,...

13

HTML 3 Text Flow, Phrase, and Typographic Elements

CHAPTER AT A GLANCE

- Changes to text flow markup in HTML 3.0
- Advantages of client-side image maps over server-side
- New phrase and typographic elements in HTML 3
- *Specific Markup vs. Style Sheets*
- HTML 3 Project: *Text Flow, Phrase, and Typographic Elements*
- HTML 3 Text Flow, Phrase, and Typographic Tag Usage and Attribute Summaries

HTML 3 includes many of the same tags as HTML 2 for phrase, character, and text flow markup. However, it is much more strict with respect to what elements it allows in various sections of a document. These elements should only occur within text block elements. This means they should occur only within paragraphs, headings, divisions, tables, and other elements. Since HTML 3 includes many more text block elements than HTML 2, it should not prove difficult to adhere to this requirement.

Text Flow

HTML 3 includes one familiar and one new text flow element. The <BR> tag allows you to force a line break between text. In addition to the HTML 3 global attribute set (ID, CLASS, STYLE, LANG), the <BR> tag has a CLEAR attribute like that found in the Netscape version of the tag. CLEAR can be set to LEFT, RIGHT, or ALL to move the next line of text down the number of lines necessary to achieve clear margins on either the left, right, or both. CLEAR can also be assigned a value in either en units or pixels:

some text <BR CLEAR="60 pixels"> more text

HTML 2 ignored all tabs and provided no mechanism for inserting tabs in a document. Even preformatted text segments were required to have spaces instead of tabs by most browsers. HTML 3 includes a <TAB> tag for establishing tab stops in a document. A tab stop is created when a <TAB ID="tab1"> is inserted between text. With tabs, the ID attribute is used to define a name for a tab stop. Any name can be assigned to the ID attribute and since this value is user definable, it should be enclosed by double quotes. This tab can later be referenced with a <TAB TO="tab1"> tag. The TO attribute specifies the tab stop in the text with which this text should align itself. Figure 13-1 is an example.

<B>specific markup</B><TAB ID="tab1">is essentially the opposite of generalized markup —
<TAB TO="tab1">markup that determines how text will look.

You can control the <TAB> tag with several other attributes. You can use the INDENT attribute to specify how far text should be indented by assigning it a numeric value in en units. You can align text with margins with the ALIGN attribute which can be assigned the values LEFT, CENTER, or RIGHT to align the text with the current left, center, or right margin. ALIGN may also be assigned

Figure 13-1
<TAB>

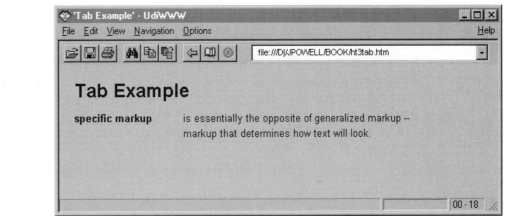

the value DECIMAL. This is often used in conjunction with the DP attribute which can be assigned a period (.) or a comma (,) indicating which of these characters is to be considered the decimal point character. When ALIGN= DECIMAL, the next character defined as a decimal point is located, then the text following it (up to the next <TAB> or line break, e.g., <BR> or <P>) is aligned with the decimal point character.

ANCHORS

Hypertext links have changed little from HTML 2 to HTML 3. They are still tagged with the anchor tag <A>. The biggest change is the elimination of the NAME attribute in favor of the universal ID attribute as the markup for a text fragment to function as the target of a hypertext link. ID is a global attribute that can be used with any other HTML tag. The NAME attribute is still available for those instances where a target has no associated HTML markup, but ID is preferable in most instances. In addition to ID and NAME, the anchor tag has LANG, CLASS, REL, REV, and HREF attributes. Most of these are carry-overs from HTML 2 and have the same function. A TITLE attribute can be paired with an HREF to provide a TITLE for targets that do not have their own HTML title, such as graphics or gopher menu items. An MD attribute can also be paired with an HREF. It is assigned a checksum that is used to verify the contents of the target document. An HTML 3 Web browser should use it to determine if the target document has been modified and if so, notify the reader.

CLIENT-SIDE IMAGE MAPS

HTML 3 includes support for client-side image maps. Client-side image maps are faster than server-side, since the map file is included in the HTML document. The SHAPE attribute can be used when the anchor occurs within a figure, <FIG>, to make the image an image map. You can assign SHAPE to any of the following types of values:

```
default
circle x, y, r
rect x, y, w, h
polygon x1, y1, x2, y2, ...
```

Each SHAPE value should be enclosed in double quotes since most include user-definable options (such as coordinate values). Multiple anchors with SHAPE attributes can be specified within a <FIG> to achieve the same effect as the ISMAP attribute for the <IMG> tag. This lets the Web browser avoid the additional overhead of contacting the Web server and passing coordinates to be mapped into an image map file. Figure 13-2 is an example.

```
<FIG SRC="eastern_us.gif">
<CAPTION>Weather for the Eastern United States - Select a State</CAPTION>
<UL>
<LI><A HREF="/cgi-bin/weather?virginia" SHAPE="polygon 10, 300, 50, 350, 100,
300">Virginia</A>
<LI><A HREF="/cgi-bin/weather?ncarolina" SHAPE="polygon 10, 300, 50, 250, 100,
300">North Carolina</A>
</UL>
</FIG>
```

In this example, users with graphical Web browsers will see a map of the eastern United States. Two triangular areas will be selectable, corresponding to two eastern states. Nongraphical browsers will display the unordered list with text-based anchors for Virginia and North Carolina. The <IMG ... ISMAP> combination from HTML 2 provided no such support for text-based browsers.

Figure 13-2 A figure with optional unordered list text revealed at right

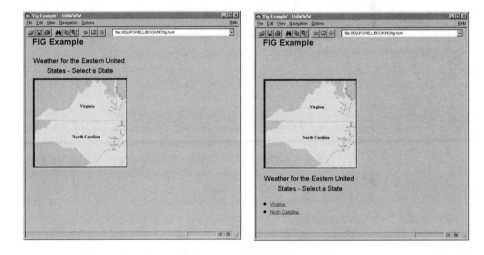

PHRASE AND TYPOGRAPHIC MARKUP

HTML 3 supports the same phrase and typographic markup as HTML 2 and adds some new elements. As you may recall, phrase markup is generalized markup used to tag content. An important point in a document might be tagged with the <EM> tag, a citation can be indicated with the <CITE> tag, and so on. Typographic markup is specific markup used to specify how a piece of text should look. An author might choose to tag key words in bold, perhaps mentioning this fact prior to the first keyword. HTML 3 continues to support this type of markup despite its style sheet mechanism for two reasons: 1) Backwards compatibility with HTML 2; 2) To provide primitive formatting controls for browsers that do not know about the style sheet mechanism.

Phrase Elements

You may remember from Chapter 5 that phrase elements are sometimes referred to as logical style elements. Logical style elements mark sections of text based on their content. Most such tags cannot be automatically inserted by software, but must be inserted by someone who is familiar with the document content, such as its original author. HTML 3 supports all HTML 2 phrase elements with one exception: the <BLOCKQUOTE> element (now shortened to <BQ>) is now a text block element instead of a phrase tag.

HTML 2 phrase elements had no attributes. HTML 3 phrase elements can have any of the three global attributes (ID, CLASS, LANG). For short quotes, HTML 3 adds the quote element, <Q>. Quoted text is displayed with double (") or single (') quotes (this can change depending on the LANG attribute value). Quotes can be nested and nested quotes are enclosed with alternating double and single quotes:

<Q>phrase elements are <Q>generalized markup</Q></Q>

"phrase elements are 'generalized markup'"

Other tags are inherited from HTML 2. The logical style elements <EM> and <STRONG> are still available when you want to indicate that a passage has increased importance over the surrounding document text.

Other phrase elements carried over from HTML 2 include <CODE>, <SAMP>, <KBD>, and <VAR> for tagging programming code and application output text. The definition tag, <DFN> is also retained in HTML 3 for tagging the definition of a term. And citations are still tagged with the <CITE> tag. Figure 13-3 illustrates several HTML 3 phrase markup elements.

Figure 13-3
<Q>, <DFN>,
<ACRONYM>, and
<ABBREV>

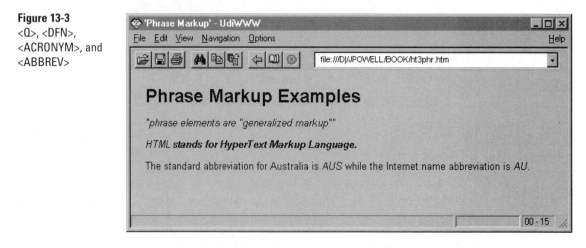

New phrase elements for HTML 3 allow authors to tag content they would have otherwise marked with typographic tags in HTML 2. The author tag, <AU>, is used to indicate the name of an author, usually the author of the current document. The name of a person in a document can be tagged with the <PERSON> tag. Acronyms can be indicated with the <ACRONYM> tag. The <ABBREV> tag contains an abbreviation:

<DFN><ACRONYM>HTML</ACRONYM> stands for HyperText Markup Language.</DFN>

The standard abbreviation for Australia is <ABBREV>AUS</ABBREV> while the Internet name abbreviation is <ABBREV>AU</ABBREV>.

The acronym and abbreviation tags are especially important for visually impaired users. HTML 3 browsers with speech capabilities would likely be designed so that they did not try to pronounce "HTML," "AUS," and "AU" as words but would instead say each letter. HTML 2 supports no such markup so a browser would have no idea it should not attempt to pronounce these as words. The <LANG> tag indicates the contents are of a different language than the surrounding text. Text marked in this way might include links to translations, or pronunciation keys.

<INS> and <DEL> mark sections of text that have been inserted or deleted from a previous version of the text. HTML 3 Web browsers might choose to display inserted text in a different style, and draw a line through deleted text. Others might provide the option of concealing deleted or inserted text with the click of a button. They provide simple editing markup for group authoring online.

Typographic Elements

HTML 3 divorces document structure from presentation by supporting style sheets. But to maintain backwards compatibility with HTML 2 and to support authoring for browsers without style sheet support, HTML 3 includes and extends its collection of typographic elements. These elements can be nested to achieve combined effects, such as nesting bold and italics to produce bold, italicized text segments. However, when a phrase markup exists for the type of text you are tagging, it is better to select that type of markup.

Five types of specific markup were carried over from HTML 2. Bold and italics tags <B> and <I> are still available in HTML 3. Typewriter text <TT> causes the enclosed text to be displayed in a fixed, typewriter-like font. The underline tag <U> marks text that should be displayed with underlining. The HTML 2 <STRIKE> tag has been shortened to <S> in HTML 3 but otherwise works the same way, causing the tagged text to be displayed with a line drawn through it. Each HTML 3 typographic element can include the global attribute set ID, CLASS, and LANG.

Four new typographic elements have been added to HTML 3. <BIG> and <SMALL> mark text that should be displayed in a larger or smaller font than the surrounding text. They do not provide attributes for controlling precisely how much larger or smaller the text should be, like Netscape's <FONT> tag. Subscripts and superscripts are supported both within mathematical equation blocks and in normal text blocks with the <SUB> and <SUP> tags.

All of the presentation options provided with HTML 3 typographic elements are also supported in the style sheet standard. Authors should at least subclass items that are tagged with typographic markup so that style sheets can be applied when available:

<B CLASS="bold">Important Notice</B>

Ideally you should strive to reduce or eliminate typographic markup in favor of logical markup combined with style sheet entries in HTML 3 documents.

SPECIFIC MARKUP VS. STYLE SHEETS

Since HTML 3 encourages the use of style sheets, you must be wondering why there are still specific markup elements. One reason is for backwards compatibility with HTML 2. Supporting specific markup elements makes converting documents from HTML 2 to HTML 3 easier. Specific markup is also much easier to support in a browser. Style sheets can be part of the HTML document or external documents. If the style sheet is external, the browser has to go out and get it. Then it has to apply its contents to the HTML document. Since style sheets can completely change the appearance of the document, this can take some time. Even as HTML 3 becomes widely supported, style sheets still may not be supported by all browsers. So specific markup can ensure important passages receive some type of typographic emphasis when displayed by any browser.

Another reason why specific markup is part of HTML 3 is that there may be instances when no generalized markup is valid for the passage you wish to emphasize. If you cannot apply some type of markup to the passage, then you cannot subclass the markup. A subclass or tag name is required for each type of markup for which you wish to specify a style (although it should at least be possible to use <EM> or <STRONG>). So there may be instances when you just have to mark a passage as bold.

The Image Element

<IMG>, unlike <FIG>, is designed to include an image in the text and treat it as though it were itself text. It is suitable for including icons and small graphics in HTML documents, while <FIG> is intended for large graphics, diagrams, and

images with captions. The HTML 3 <IMG> tag includes the global attributes ID, CLASS, and LANG. It also includes the HTML 2 attributes SRC, ALIGN, ALT and ISMAP. New attributes for <IMG> include MD for specifying a checksum. This can be used to ensure the image has not changed since the image pointed to by SRC should have the same checksum as the value of MD. WIDTH and HEIGHT can be used to scale the image to a certain size, specified in pixels or en units. The UNITS attribute can change the default WIDTH and HEIGHT units to pixels or en units (half-point size). The ALIGN attribute has two new values: LEFT and RIGHT to cause text to flow around the image and to specify the direction it should flow. Here is an example utilizing some of the new <IMG> attributes:

```
<IMG SRC="company_logo.gif" MD="md5:jkdi43jd9MMkj9" UNITS=en
WIDTH="400" ALT="Company Logo">
```

HTML 3 PROJECT 1: TEXT FLOW, PHRASE, AND TYPOGRAPHIC ELEMENTS

Congress has sold some tour contracts for national park areas to private companies. You have been asked to design an electronic brochure for the ACME LavaLand tours company, which has purchased the contract for the Mount St. Helens National Volcanic Monument and the Mount Adams Wilderness Area in Washington state. LavaLand wants to bring in more hikers and climbers to make the venture profitable.

```
<HTML>
<HEAD><TITLE>LavaLand</TITLE></HEAD>
<LINK REL=STYLESHEET type="text/css" HREF="lavaland.css">
<BODY>
<BANNER>
<FIG SRC="welcome.gif" ALIGN=center IMAGEMAP>
<P>
<UL>
<LH>Tour LavaLand Online<LH>
<LI><A SHAPE="rect 30, 300, 100, 35" HREF="about.html">About LavaLand
Tours</A>
<LI><A SHAPE="rect 130, 300, 80, 35" HREF="#tour">See the Mountains</A>
<LI><A SHAPE="rect 210, 300, 60, 35" HREF="rates.html">Rates</A>
</UL>
</FIG>
</BANNER>
<H1 CLASS="large_heading">Welcome to LavaLand Tours!</H1>
<DIV CLASS="introduction">
<P CLASS="introductory">We are your exclusive source for tours of and
information about Mt. St. Helens and Mount Adams, two jewels of the Cascade
mountain range.
```

Continued on next page

Continued from previous page

```
<P CLASS="introductory">The 1980 eruption of Mt. St. Helens and the 1996
eruption of Mt. Adams have captured the imagination of millions of people around
the world.
<P CLASS="introductory">Come experience nature's fury in the scenic pacific
northwest. We offer day and week passes for camping, hiking and climbing. Or you
can experience the stark beauty of the blast zones from the comfort of your own
car along the LavaLand toll highway.
</DIV>
<DIV CLASS="options">
<P CLASS="option">
<I CLASS="largeitalics">Join us now in a virtual tour of these monuments to
</I><A HREF="#tour"><STRONG CLASS="extrabold"> nature's
power</STRONG></A>
<P CLASS="option">
<A HREF="selloff.html"><STRONG CLASS="extrabold">Order a piece of the
mountains!</STRONG></A>
<P CLASS="option">
<A HREF="schedule.html"><STRONG CLASS="colorbold">Schedule a
Tour</STRONG></A>
</DIV>
<HR ALIGN=CENTER>
<DIV CLASS="tours">
<H2 CLASS="tourheading"><IMG SRC="volcano.gif" ALIGN=CENTER>Nature's
Power - a virtual tour</H2>
<FIG SRC="summit.gif" ALIGN=RIGHT></FIG>
<P CLASS="tour">
<B CLASS="title">Spirit Lake and Mt. Ranier as seen from the summit of Mt. St.
Helens</B>
<P>
<I CLASS="description">The May 18, 1980 eruption of Mt. St. Helens blew away
1300 feet of material from the mountain's summit. The current summit is 8364 feet
and an enjoyable climb for any would-be mountain climber.</I>
</BODY>
</HTML>
```

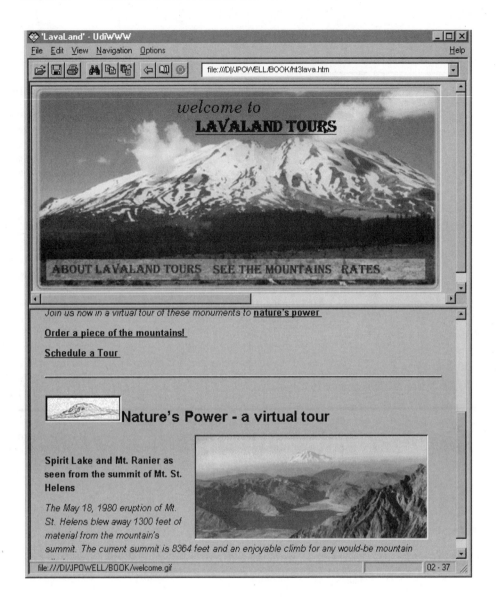

HTML 3 TEXT FLOW, PHRASE, AND TYPOGRAPHIC TAG USAGE SUMMARY

Tag	Permitted Context	Content Model
 	text blocks	none
<TAB>	text blocks	none
<A>	document body outside text blocks	ASCII characters, character entities
<EM>	text blocks, sentences and phrases	ASCII characters, character entities

HTML 3 TEXT FLOW, PHRASE, AND TYPOGRAPHIC TAG USAGE SUMMARY, CONT.

Tag	Permitted Context	Content Model
<CITE>	text blocks	ASCII characters, character entities
<STRONG>	text blocks, sentences and phrases	ASCII characters, character entities
<CODE>	text blocks, sentences and phrases	ASCII characters, character entities
<SAMP>	text blocks, sentences and phrases	ASCII characters, character entities
<KBD>	text blocks, sentences and phrases	ASCII characters, character entities
<VAR>	text blocks, sentences and phrases	ASCII characters, character entities
<DFN>	text blocks, sentences and phrases	ASCII characters, character entities
<Q>	text blocks, sentences and phrases	ASCII characters, character entities
<LANG>	text blocks, sentences and phrases	ASCII characters, character entities
<AU>	text blocks, sentences and phrases	ASCII characters, character entities
<PERSON>	text blocks, sentences and phrases	ASCII characters, character entities
<ACRONYM>	text blocks, sentences and phrases	ASCII characters, character entities
<ABBREV>	text blocks, sentences and phrases	ASCII characters, character entities
<INS>	text blocks, sentences and phrases	ASCII characters, character entities
<DEL>	text blocks, sentences and phrases	ASCII characters, character entities
<B>	text blocks, sentences and phrases	ASCII characters, character entities
<I>	text blocks, sentences and phrases	ASCII characters, character entities
<TT>	text blocks, sentences and phrases	ASCII characters, character entities
<U>	text blocks, sentences and phrases	ASCII characters, character entities
<S>	text blocks, sentences and phrases	ASCII characters, character entities
<BIG>	text blocks, sentences and phrases	ASCII characters, character entities
<SMALL>	text blocks, sentences and phrases	ASCII characters, character entities
<SUB>	text blocks, math blocks	ASCII characters, character entities
<SUP>	text blocks, math blocks	ASCII characters, character entities
<IMG>	document body	none

ATTRIBUTE SUMMARY

(All HTML 3 phrase and typographic elements support the global attributes ID, CLASS, STYLE, and LANG, so they will not be repeated in this table).

Tag	Attribute	Value
<TAB>	TO	name
	ALIGN	LEFT, CENTER, RIGHT, DECIMAL
	DP	. (period), , (comma)
<IMG>	SRC	URL of a graphic file
	MD	checksum (ASCII text)
	WIDTH, HEIGHT	numeric values
	UNITS	PIXELS, EN
	ALIGN	LEFT, RIGHT, TOP, MIDDLE, BOTTOM
	ALT	ASCII text
	ISMAP	none

14

HTML 3
Style Sheets

CHAPTER AT A GLANCE

- Why style sheets are superior to HTML formatting tags
- Cascading style sheets (CSS)
- Applying CSS level 1 style properties to any HTML 3 tag
- HTML 3 Project: *Creating a CSS Style Sheet*
- Style Properties Summary

HTML is at a crossroads. Under pressure from HTML authors and vendors such as Netscape and Microsoft, some dialects of HTML include formatting tags. But HTML was not intended to be a formatting language. Like other SGML markup languages, HTML's purpose is to capture structure, utilizing an external mechanism to control presentation (a style sheet). This mechanism has been built into Web browsers in the form of default and user-configurable renderings for various headings and other markup. But many developers have lost sight of this and that is why Netscape Navigator supports tags like <FONT> and <CENTER>. Since Internet standards are developed by committees, they evolve slowly. But finally a standard is emerging for applying an external presentation mechanism to HTML. That mechanism is called cascading style sheets (CSS).

The HTML 3 cascading style sheet mechanism acknowledges and maintains support for user-configurable presentation options, browser options, and author-specified formatting. All such options are merged by the browser rather than ignored, thus achieving the cascading effect to which the standard's name refers. Style sheets can be incorporated into HTML documents or placed on the web as separate, addressable documents that can be linked to by others. Different style sheets can be applied to the same document to achieve dramatically different effects. For example, a publisher might provide a large-print edition style sheet that, when applied to an issue of their electronic magazine, instantly enlarges all typefaces in the document. There would be no need for multiple versions of each issue, one incorporating different <FONT> and <BASE-FONT> markup to enlarge type, another for readers without visual impairments. Style sheets could be revised and all documents referring to them would instantly use the new presentation specifications. CSS provides unparalleled flexibility for formatting that would be impossible with specific markup extensions to HTML.

CSS supports an inheritance of formatting styles through a cascading style mechanism, and it also supports style inheritance when styles are applied to document structures (see Figure 14-1 for an illustration of this cascading style mechanism). Every element within a document section inherits the specified style properties. Style properties are formatting specifications such as typeface, font size, and color. A style specified for the <BODY> tag will be applied to all HTML elements within the body of the document, unless other style properties are specified for a particular element. Style properties specified within the <STYLE> element in the document header take precedence over other formatting options and are only overridden by style options selected by the reader with their own Web browser.

Style sheets are composed of a simple text-based language used to relate HTML tags to style sheet formatting options, which are in turn paired with user-specified values. They can exist as separate files linked to the HTML 3 document using a <LINK> tag in the document header, for example:

```
<HEAD>
<TITLE>A Document</TITLE>
<LINK REL=STYLESHEET TYPE="text/css" HREF="http://server.edu/style">
</HEAD>
```

or be embedded in the header portion of an HTML document with a <STYLE> tag. HTML 3 uses a cascading style mechanism where the user's local Web browser settings for a given tag override all other settings. If a browser supports style sheets, then style sheet settings override the default renderings for a given tag, and the default renderings apply only if local customizations and style sheets are not present. This implementation provides complete backwards compatibility with HTML 2 while allowing authors to gain much greater control over the presentation of their documents.

Figure 14-1
Hierarchy of Style
Sheet inheritance.
User options over-
ride all others.

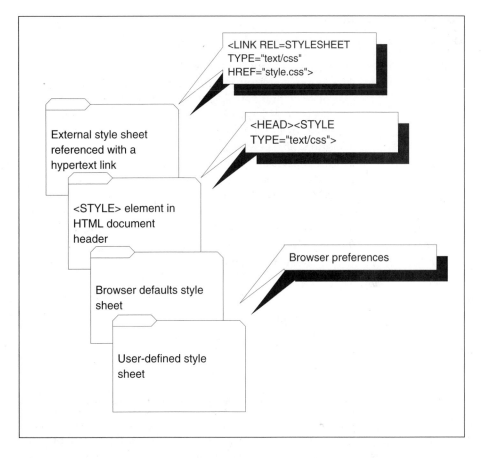

Style sheets are usually created by the document author. They relate HTML tags with style properties in such a way that the local software can decide exactly how to display the information using these properties as hints. This allows browsers with certain limitations such as small screen size, limited font set, or lack of graphics support to ignore or substitute the requested rendering with an approximation. For example, if the style sheet says to use a 12-point Palatino font for the text in the body of a document and Palatino is not an option on the remote system, then the Web browser can substitute Times-Roman at the specified font size. Another nice feature of style sheets is the ability to use multiple style sheets. You may find a style sheet on the Web that does almost everything you want (font style and sizes for various tags) but you can change one or two options, such as select an especially large font size for level 1 headings, and otherwise hand over control of the presentation to the other style sheet.

Selectors and Properties

Style sheet syntax is simple. Each tag and/or class that an author wishes to specify presentation information for is listed in the style sheet followed by a pair of curly brackets ({}). In CSS, element and class names are also referred to as selectors. A subclassed element should be listed with a period dividing the tag name from the subclass name. The selector is followed by the type of presentation, also referred to as a property (align, color, margin, font, or indent), followed by colon (:) and an appropriate value for the presentation type. Property names are indicated by class and specific type by placing a dash between the property and its specific type name, for example, font-size for font size, font-family for typeface, margin-right for right margin, etc. (a complete list of level 1 CSS style property names and example values is provided at the end of this chapter).

Here is a style example that sets font, color, and alignment options for a level 1 heading:

```
H1 {
    text-align: center
    color: #ffggee
    font-family: times
    font-size: 36pt
}
```

HTML elements are specified first on the line in upper- or lowercase. Brackets ("<>") should not be used around selectors since style sheets can be embedded in an HTML document and this might confuse some browsers into thinking they have encountered the document body. Multiple selectors can be listed on one line separated by commas:

```
h1, h2, h3 {text-align: center}
```

Style sheet selectors can include a class name, to specify that the properties be applied to only one class of HTML elements:

```
h1.big {font-size: 48pt}
```

Selectors can also be grouped on one line:

```
h1 {text-align: center; color: #ffggee; font-family: times; font-size: 36pt}
```

to specify multiple properties for one selector or selector class. Style sheets can become quite complex, so it is helpful to include comments. A comment can occur on a line by itself or following a style sheet entry. It should be surrounded by slash asterisk pairs:

```
h1.big {font-size: 48pt} /* 48 pt is big enough */
```

At this point you can add more entries to control more aspects of the page presentation, or insert a URL pointing to another style sheet to be used. If the style information is embedded in the HTML 3 document header, it should be within the <STYLE> start and end tag. Styles can be specified in the document body with the STYLE attribute:

```
<P STYLE="font-family: times">
```

Styles can also be in separate documents; this is especially useful if the style will be used by many documents, although it can slightly slow down document display. Locally defined styles take precedence over items redefined in an external style sheet.

Styles can be applied more specifically than with every occurrence of a given tag. You can define a class for a tag within an HTML document using the CLASS attribute, and then refer to that class in a style sheet. Each tag of that class within the document will be presented using the style you have defined for that class:

```
<STYLE>
H1.banner {font-size: 48pt}
</STYLE>
</HEAD>
<H1 CLASS="banner">Got your attention!</H1>
```

Level 1 headings not of the banner class will not be displayed using the banner style. If you want to make global definitions, use the HTML tag to indicate all document contents should default to this style:

```
HTML {font-family: helvetica}
```

If a style is specified for an HTML element, all subclassed elements of that type will also assume the style unless a separate style is defined for the subclass. For example, if a division style is established that sets font-family to times-roman, and this division includes several paragraphs, those paragraphs will use the Times-Roman font. Thus cascading takes place even between style sheet elements, using the topmost structure's style:

```
DIV {font-family: times-roman}
```

unless there is a style property for the embedded element:

```
P {font-family: helvetica}
```

in which case Helvetica would be used within paragraphs even if they appear inside divisions that have their font-family defined to be times-roman.

Perhaps the most powerful feature of styles is the ability to specify context-sensitive styles. You can list tag pairs without commas to specify context. For example, if the document is a scientific article and the first paragraph is always an abstract, the following style entry would assign a font family of Helvetica to this paragraph:

```
H1 P {font-family: helvetica}
```

Styles are a new, somewhat complex, and still evolving addition to HTML 3. They are a potential worksaver when used instead of specific markup to control document formatting. Organizations and multiple authors could all use the same style sheet to achieve a good deal of uniformity between documents without encoding style information into their texts. Style sheets could be copied and then tailored to suit local needs much like Web page sources are captured and perused to discover the tricks used to achieve special effects in previous versions of HTML. Style sheets will do for publishing content to the Web what Netscape extensions have done for the home page: make documents much more professional, attractive, customizable, and easy to read from one type of computer system to another.

This chapter only covers CSS Level 1. Level 2 is currently under development. It will include support for specifying style properties for different output devices such as ultrahigh color, high-resolution displays, and low-resolution output such as paper, speech, or Braille rendering. Plans are to support text block border styles, page style properties, list, table, and math styles.

HTML 3 PROJECT 2: CREATING A CSS STYLE SHEET

In the last chapter we created a page for the fictional LavaLand Tours company. The markup for this page included a number of hooks for style sheet entries, in the form of element subclasses. Some subclasses are named for the type of content their class element marks (e.g., <DIV CLASS="introduction">), to make them reusable. Others are simply named for a type of formatting (e.g., <I CLASS= "largeitalics">). Now we are going to use these element classes to create a CSS style sheet that will be applied to the LavaLand home page.

lavaland.css:

```
/* This style sheet was designed for the Lavaland Tour company */
/* electronic brochure, introduced in Chapter 13. */
HTML {color: #000000} /* Set a default text color */

/* Division styles */
DIV.introduction {font-family: times-roman}
DIV.options {font-family: times-roman /* font style shorthand */
DIV.tours {font-family: helvetica}

/* Heading styles */
H1.large_heading {font-size: 24pt}
H2.tourheading {font-size: 24pt; font-style: italics}
/* Paragraph styles */
P.introductory {font: 12pt times-roman /* font style shorthand */
P.option {font-style: bold; font-size: 16pt}
P.tour {font-size: 12pt}
```

```
/* Phrase and typographic element styles */
I.largeitalics {font-size: 16pt; font-family: italics}
I.description {font-style: italics}
STRONG.extrabold {font-weight: extra-bold}
STRONG.colorbold {color: #ff0000} /* red text */
```

STYLE PROPERTIES SUMMARY

Property	Description	Values
font-size	typeface size	font size in points e.g., 12pt, percent or: xx-small	x-small	small	medium	large	x-large	
font-family	typeface	font family names such as times-roman
font-weight	density	extra-light, light, demi-light, medium, normal, demi-bold, bold, extra-bold, -3, -2, -1, 0, 1, 2, 3
font-style	style of typeface	italic, italics, roman, oblique, upright, small-caps, normal
line-height	distance between baselines	length (number) or percent e.g., 25%
font	shorthand for size [leading] [weight][style]	valid settings for these properties e.g. 16pt helvetica bold
color	modifies color of various elements	color name or RGB value e.g., #rrggbb
background	background image	URL such as "http://server/images/bricks.gif"
bg-blend-direction	blends two background colors	Shorthand for ompass directions e.g., N	NW	W	SW	S	SE	E	NE
bg-style	background image layout	repeat	repeat-x	repeat-y	no-repeat	scroll	fixed
bg-position	initial position of background image	percentage e.g., 50%
word-spacing	space between words	percentage e.g., 50%
letter-spacing	spacing between letters	length (number)
text-decoration	text formatting options	underline, overline, line-through, box, blink
vertical-align	vertical position of an element	percent or baseline	sub	super	top	text-top	middle	bottom	text-bottom
text-transform	transformation of first character of a word or entire word(s)	capitalize, uppercase, lowercase, none
text-align	local text alignment	left, right, center, or justify
text-indent	indent text	length or percent

STYLE PROPERTIES SUMMARY, CONT.

Property	Description	Values
padding	space between borders and contents	length, percent (can specify up to four values corresponding to top, right, bottom, and left)
margin-left	size of left margin	in em units e.g. 3 em (an em is half the size of the letter 'M')
margin-right	size of right margin	in em units e.g., 3 em
margin-top	size of top margin	in em units, e.g., 4 em
margin-bottom	size of bottom margin	in em units, e.g., 4 em
margin	shorthand for margin-top, right, bottom, left, respectively	in em units, e.g., 4em, 3 em, 4 em, 3 em
display	turns display of element on or off	block, inline, none
width	width of an element	number or percent
height	height of an element	number, auto, from-canvas
float	image positioning	left, right, none
clear	does element allow images to float with it?	none, left, right, both
pack	packing of element boxes	tight or loose
border-style, border-style-internal	border styles for margins, tables, etc.	none | dotted | single | double | thin-thick | thick-thin | beveled | raised (can specify up to four values corresponding to top, right, bottom, and left)
border-width, border-width-internal	border width	number or thin | medium | thick (can specify up to four values corresponding to top, right, bottom, and left)
border-color, border-color-internal	border color	color name or RGB value e.g., #rrggbb
list-style	list item styles	disc | circle | square | decimal |lower-roman | upper-roman | lower-alpha |upper-alpha | none or URL of bullet image
magnification	enlargement value for elements	number
white-space	whether extra white space inside a block should be ignored or retained	normal or pre (for preformatted style)

15

HTML 3
Table Primer

CHAPTER AT A GLANCE

- Using tables to present spreadsheet and database output
- Nesting tables
- Presenting structured text and HTML forms with tables
- *Netscape Tables*
- HTML 3 Project: *Creating an HTML 3 Table*
- HTML 3 Table Tag Usage and Attribute Summaries

Table support was one of the most requested features by users of HTML 2. It provides a structured alternative to the preformatted text tag. <PRE> produces text that is often difficult to read, minimally structured, and unattractive. HTML 3 tables are highly structured text blocks. They are row oriented, that is they are constructed of rows of cells rather than columns of cells. Tables constructed of rows rather than columns of cells require less markup. Multiple rows placed on top of one another build columns of cells.

Tables are text block structures whose permitted context is the document body, that is, anywhere between the <BODY> start and end tags of an HTML 3 document. The content model for a table is a <CAPTION> followed by one or more table rows. Tables start with a table start tag <TABLE> which has a BORDER attribute for turning on and specifying a few bordering styles. While HTML 3 encourages you to use a style sheet entry to control border formatting, some browsers, such as Netscape Navigator, allow you to assign the BORDER attribute a value. This value is used to specify a thickness for the table cells and edges. Tables have the standard suite of HTML 3 global attributes including ID, LANG, STYLE, and CLASS for making tables anchors, specifying table language, and subclassing tables, respectively. Tables also have a CLEAR attribute for margin control and NOFLOW to prevent text surrounding the table from flowing around it. You can use the ALIGN attribute to specify the horizontal alignment of a table by assigning it one of these values:

BLEEDLEFT	flush left with browser window's left border
LEFT	flush left with left text margin in browser
CENTER	center the table and disable text flow (the default)
RIGHT	flush right with the right text margin in the browser
BLEEDRIGHT	flush right with the browser window's right border
JUSTIFY	resize the table so that it extends to both margins

You can specify table size in a variety of ways: table width, row width, and individual column widths. Table attributes accept width values in three units: en, which is equivalent to half a typographic character's point size; relative, which means sizing is left up to the Web browser software using your values for cell and table alignment as hints; and pixels on the display, a tedious, error-prone measurement based on the size of the table item as an image. Units are set table-wide with the UNITS attribute:

<TABLE UNITS="en">

The WIDTH and COLSPEC attributes are assigned values in the units type assigned to UNITS. WIDTH controls table width. COLSPEC allows you to control column width individually. You control individual column widths by assigning to COLSPEC multiple pairs of values, one pair per column. The value pairs are L for left, C for center, or R for right justification of column contents, D for decimal place, and a numeric value for column width:

<TABLE UNITS=en COLSPEC="L30 C10 R20">

The DP attribute sets the decimal point marker. The default is a period (.) but it can be assigned a comma (,). Finally, you can tell the browser exactly how many columns your table has (rather than let it figure it out after it has retrieved the entire table) by assigning the value to a COLS attribute. This will let the Web browser get a head start building a table if the connection happens to be slow.

NETSCAPE TABLES

Netscape partially supports the HTML 3 specification for tables and adds some formatting attributes not found in the current version of HTML 3. Among these are several additional <TABLE> tag attributes. In addition to a WIDTH attribute for explicitly setting the table width, Netscape allows a HEIGHT attribute. This attribute controls the overall height of the table. Netscape supports user definable BORDER values so you can not only ensure your table is bordered but also define exactly how wide this border should be. Netscape's CELLPADDING and CELLSPACING attributes set default sizes for table header and data cells. CELLSPACING is assigned a value that determines how far apart cells are spaced both horizontally and vertically. CELLPADDING determines how much horizontal and vertical space is between a cell's contents and the cell borders. Netscape has proposed that these attributes be accepted as part of any final table standard.

NETSCAPE TABLE ELEMENTS

Tag	Description
TABLE	Surrounds table content
TH	Table header tag
TR	Table row tag
TD	Table data cell tag
CAPTION	Caption describing table content

You may place a caption on a table using the <CAPTION> tag. Captions are useful for providing a brief description of the table contents. If you are including a caption, it should immediately follow the <TABLE> tag and occur before the first table row <TR>. A caption can contain text, that is ASCII text tagged with text and character markup. Captions can have ID, LANG, and CLASS attributes for functioning as the targets of anchors, specifying caption language, and subclassing the caption so that it can be referenced from a style sheet for special formatting:

```
<TABLE>
<CAPTION CLASS="bottom" ALIGN=bottom>Figure 1: <I>1995
Profits</I></CAPTION>
```

Captions also have an ALIGN attribute which specifies where the caption will be displayed in relation to the table. You can specify that your caption appear on top, to the left or right, or on the bottom of your table.

TABLE-WIDE ELEMENTS

There are several table elements that Web browsers apply on a table-wide basis. They should occur before the table header or first table row. You can group columns with the <COLGROUP> element. Column groupings let you simplify markup for sets of columns by allowing you to specify characteristics once for the group. You can specify additional options on a column by column basis with the <COL> element:

```
<TABLE>
<COLGROUP CLASS="totals">
<COL WIDTH="2*">
<COL WIDTH="1*">
</COLGROUP>
```

The WIDTH is used to specify the new relative column width. The default column width is 1, so WIDTH=2 causes the specified columns to be twice as wide as a column would be if the Web browser had automatically selected a size for it.

```
<COL WIDTH=3>
```

This <COL> example sets the relative width of a column to be three times the default width.

HEADERS, BODIES, AND FOOTERS

Tables can have headers and bodies, just like HTML documents. These are useful for specifying different borders and content alignment options for the header and body cells. A browser might choose to redisplay the header contents when displaying or printing a long table, such as at the start of each page. There is also an element for those table footers that appear after the table body. Table headers are tagged with the <THEAD> tag. This tag should follow the <TABLE>, <COLGROUP>, and <CAPTION> tags if present. <THEAD> attributes include ID, LANG, CLASS, STYLE, and BORDER, as well as the <TABLE> formatting attributes such as ALIGN and VALIGN. You can place multiple rows in the table header but there should only be one header per table. The table body tag, <TBODY>, follows the table header and has the same attributes. The table footer <TFOOT> follows the table body, has the same attribute set, and should only occur once per table. You can omit table headers, bodies, and footers from a table if they are not needed, but they do provide valuable information to the Web browser and the user.

CELLS

As stated earlier, the bulk of the information in a table is stored in rows and columns. The intersections of rows and columns are known as cells. The heading, body, and footer of an HTML table are constructed of rows of cells. Vertical rows of cells form columns. You can use special cells called table headings to start off each row and to head each column. Table rows start with the table row tag <TR>. Table rows have the standard set of HTML 3 attributes: ID, LANG, and CLASS and several formatting attributes that are applied to the contents of the row. Data within the table rows is aligned with the ALIGN attribute. ALIGN can be set to LEFT, CENTER, RIGHT, JUSTIFY, DECIMAL, and a recently proposed CHAR value, which is similar to but more flexible than DECIMAL. Here is an empty table row:

```
<TR ALIGN=center></TR>
```

You have encountered most of the valid ALIGN values before and they function the same ways in table rows. DECIMAL alignment causes the first occurrence of a decimal point on each line to align vertically with the decimal points above and below it. DP is used to specify the decimal point character. VALIGN sets the vertical alignment for items in the row. It can be assigned TOP, MIDDLE, BOTTOM, or BASELINE. TOP, MIDDLE, and BOTTOM alignment position the cell contents to the corresponding vertical position in the cell. BASELINE simply makes sure they all share the same typographic baseline. NOWRAP is also available as an attribute to the table row tag (<TR>), and forces table row data to consume horizontal space rather than wrap to several lines within a narrow cell. The CHAR attribute is used when ALIGN=char. It is assigned the value of the character that cell contents should align on:

```
<TR ALIGN=char CHAR=":">
```

In this example cells would align their contents so that the colons lined up vertically.

HEADINGS

Table headings <TH> are a special type of table cell used to tag rows or columns. The first row of a two-dimensional table consists of a row of table heading cells marking the columns. Then each row that follows starts off with a table heading cell. An example of this type of table would be a budget table. A household budget table covering six months might have six columns headed by six table heading cells, one per month. Then each row would start off with the name of a creditor. Table data cells would contain monthly bills and perhaps the table would end with a row of totals by month:

```
<TR ALIGN=center>
<TH>January</TH>
<TH>February</TH>
<TH>March</TH>
<TH>First Quarter Totals</TH></TR>
```

Since table headings are just specialized table cells, they support the same attributes as data cells. Every table cell has three common HTML attributes

(ID, LANG, and CLASS), plus a number of layout attributes. You can force table cells to take up more than one row or column with the COLSPAN and ROWSPAN attributes. A table heading might indicate quarterly information, so COLSPAN=3 would be used to make the heading span three columns. ROWSPAN might in turn be used to block off the remainder of a row; for example, if you paid off a bill and owed nothing further, you could use ROWSPAN to fill out the remaining cells for that row. Tables can have subheadings and table cells can themselves contain entire tables!

Table data cells are tagged with the table data tag <TD>:

```
<TR><TD>$2000</TD><TD>$2500</TD><TD>$2275</TD><TD
ALIGN=RIGHT>$6775</TD></TR>
```

The table data cell tag has a matching end tag but the next occurrence of a table data start tag or table row tag implies the end tag of a cell item, so you can safely omit them. The row, heading, and data cell tags can be combined in a number of ways to produce a variety of table styles. Here is a simple table combining the tags covered so far:

```
<TABLE BORDER=all>
<CAPTION>Budget</CAPTION>
<THEAD>
<TR><TH>January</TH><TH>February</TH><TH>March</TH><TH>Total</TH>
</TR>
</THEAD>
<TBODY>
<TR><TD>$2000</TD><TD>$2500</TD><TD>$2275</TD><TD
ALIGN=RIGHT>$6775</TD></TR>
</TBODY>
</TABLE>
```

The Web browser automatically aligns table headings with table data cells. If a data cell is missing anywhere in the table, the browser will create an empty heading or data cell to pad the row so that it is as wide as the widest row. You can change the layout of the table so that table heading cells appear in the left-most column instead of the first row:

```
<TABLE BORDER=all>
<CAPTION ALIGN=bottom>Budget</CAPTION>
<TR><TH>January</TH><TD>$2000</TD></TR>
<TR><TH>February</TH><TD>$2500</TD></TR>
<TR><TH>March</TH><TD>$2275</TD></TR>
<TR><TH>Total</TH><TD ALIGN=RIGHT>$6775</TD></TR>
</TABLE>
```

```
┌─────────────────────────────────────────────────────────────────┐
│ —           Netscape - [Table, headings example]        ▼  ▲     │
├─────────────────────────────────────────────────────────────────┤
│ File  Edit  View  Go  Bookmarks  Options  Directory  Window  Help│
├─────────────────────────────────────────────────────────────────┤
│  ⇦o   o⇨    ⌂     ®     ⬚     ⇛o    ⬚     ⬚     ○                 │
│ Back Forward Home Reload Images Open  Print  Find  Stop           │
├─────────────────────────────────────────────────────────────────┤
│ Location: file:///D|/JPOWELL/book/CH11-16/table2.htm       ↓  N  │
├─────────────────────────────────────────────────────────────────┤
│                                                                   │
│     January  $2000                                                │
│     February $2500                                                │
│       March  $2275                                                │
│       Total  $6775                                                │
│          Budget                                                   │
│                                                                   │
└─────────────────────────────────────────────────────────────────┘
```

Table headings can be nested to group related rows or columns. As mentioned earlier, the ROWSPAN attribute for a table heading or data cell causes the specified cell to fill multiple rows. The cell need only be specified where it should start:

```
<TABLE BORDER=all>
<CAPTION ALIGN=bottom>Budget</CAPTION>
<TR><TH ROWSPAN=4>First
Quarter</TH><TH>January</TH><TD>$2000</TD></TR>
<TR><TH>February</TH><TD>$2500</TD></TR>
<TR><TH>March</TH><TD>$2275</TD></TR>
<TR><TH>Total</TH><TD ALIGN=RIGHT>$6775</TD></TR>
</TABLE>
```

Headings or data cells that span columns are placed in their own row or in an existing row if they do not fill all columns.

```
<TABLE BORDER=all>
<CAPTION>Budget</CAPTION>
<THEAD>
<TR><TH COLSPAN=4>First Quarter</TH></TR>
<TR><TH>January</TH><TH>February</TH><TH>March</TH><TH>Total</TH>
</TR>
<TBODY>
```

Continued on next page

Continued from previous page
```
<TR><TD>$2000</TD><TD>$2500</TD><TD>$2275</TD><TD
ALIGN=RIGHT>$6775</TD></TR>
</TABLE>
```

```
┌─────────────────────────────────────────────────────────────────────┐
│ ═    Netscape - [Table, COLSPAN example]              ▼  ▲ │
├─────────────────────────────────────────────────────────────────────┤
│ File   Edit   View   Go   Bookmarks   Options   Directory   Window   Help │
├─────────────────────────────────────────────────────────────────────┤
│  ⇦      ⇨      ⌂       ⟲       ⊞       ⇉       🖶       🔍       ⬤      │
│ Back  Forward Home   Reload  Images   Open    Print   Find    Stop     │
├─────────────────────────────────────────────────────────────────────┤
│ Location: file:///D|/JPOWELL/book/CH11-16/table1.htm           ± │ N │
├─────────────────────────────────────────────────────────────────────┤
│                                                                       │
│            Budget                                                     │
│                                                                       │
│         ┌──────────────────────────────────────┐                     │
│         │           First Quarter              │                     │
│         ├─────────┬──────────┬────────┬────────┤                     │
│         │ January │ February │ March  │ Total  │                     │
│         ├─────────┼──────────┼────────┼────────┤                     │
│         │ $2000   │ $2500    │ $2275  │ $6775  │                     │
│         └─────────┴──────────┴────────┴────────┘                     │
│                                                                       │
├─────────────────────────────────────────────────────────────────────┤
│ 🖭-©  Document: Done                                                   │
└─────────────────────────────────────────────────────────────────────┘
```

FORMATTING TABLE CELLS

There are several attributes you can use to control the format of cell data. Remember that table cell data can be graphics or text including one or more paragraphs. You can use ALIGN to control the horizontal alignment of the cell data where accepted values are LEFT, RIGHT, CENTER, JUSTIFY, and DECIMAL which applies to the first occurring decimal point in the cell data and forces vertical alignment with neighboring decimal points. DP specifies the character to be used for a decimal point in the data cell, overriding any table-wide setting. VALIGN controls vertical alignment within a table cell. VALIGN can align cell data with the top, middle, or bottom of the cell or with the baseline of the surrounding text. ALIGN and VALIGN are particularly useful in mixed-content tables where some cell items are graphics and some are text. NOWRAP prevents the Web browser from wrapping data contained within a cell, but makes the table wider. AXIS and AXES are used to define abbreviations or alternate names for cells that are used mainly when the table is rendered by a speech synthesizer for users who are visually impaired or otherwise have reason to desire vocal rendering instead of a visual display. AXIS defines a table header cell's alternate name. AXES is a comma-separated list of axes that identify row and column headers for this cell. Usually this would be a pair of items but if the table contains subheadings or nested tables, it could be quite a long list.

```
<TABLE BORDER=all>
<CAPTION>Budget</CAPTION>
<THEAD>
<TR><TH>Last
Quarter<TH>January</TH><TH>February</TH><TH>March</TH><TH>Total</TH>
</TR>
<TBODY>
<TR><TD>
<TABLE BORDER=all>
<CAPTION>Budget</CAPTION>
<THEAD>
<TR><TH>January</TH><TH>February</TH><TH>March</TH><TH>Total</TH>
</TR>
<TBODY>
<TR><TD AXES="Last Quarter, January">$2000</TD><TD AXES="Last Quarter,
February">$2500</TD><TD AXES="Last Quarter, March">$2275</TD><TD
ALIGN=RIGHT AXES="Last Quarter, Total">$6775</TD></TR>
</TABLE></TD>
<TD>$2000</TD><TD>$2500</TD><TD>$2275</TD><TD
ALIGN=RIGHT>$6775</TD></TR>
</TABLE>
```

Netscape - [file:///D|/JPOWELL/book/CH11-16/tabnest.htm]

File   Edit   View   Go   Bookmarks   Options   Directory   Window   Help

Back   Forward   Home   Reload   Images   Open   Print   Find   Stop

Location: file:///D|/JPOWELL/book/CH11-16/tabnest.htm

Budget

Last Quarter				January	February	March	Total
Budget							
January	**February**	**March**	**Total**	$2000	$2500	$2275	$6775
$2000	$2500	$2275	$6775				

As with other HTML elements, it is essential to know what tags and attributes are available for a certain type of content before you start tagging. In the case of tables it is also helpful to know a bit about the way Web browsers process tables. Tables are automatically sized by Web browsers when they are rendered, unless a COLS attribute is present; in this case the width is predetermined. The table is always as wide as its longest row, and missing cells will be added as blank cells. You can add blank cells by inserting multiple table header or table cell tags with no contents. The contents of a table header cell are centered by default, while the contents of data cells are left justified. Tables can be borderless providing very fine text alignment for texts with columns and aligning rows of data input fields. Web browsers try to display tables within the available space by wrapping table cell contents, unless the author has specifically disallowed this behavior. In the case of wide tables, a portion of the table is displayed and the user is provided a scroll bar to pan across the table.

Table appearance can be further controlled through the use of style sheets. You can subclass tables, rows, and even individual cells to achieve unique formatting effects. For input forms contained within borderless tables, this might be useful for highlighting nonoptional sections of the form with brighter colors or larger fonts. With other tables, it might be used to gray out unused cells in a row or column. Table headers could also be subclassed to provide special emphasis for rows or columns of totals.

HTML 3 PROJECT 3: CREATING AN HTML 3 TABLE

Here is an Excel spreadsheet containing average temperature for several Australian cities. Convert this spreadsheet into an HTML 3 table.

degrees C	Summer			Fall			Winter			Spring		
	Jan	Feb	Mar	Apr	May	Jun	Jul	Aug	Sep	Oct	Nov	Dec
Sydney	25	25	24	21	19	16	16	17	19	21	23	25
Perth	30	30	28	25	21	17	16	17	19	20	24	27
Alice Springs	36	35	32	27	23	20	20	23	27	31	34	35
Townsville	30	30	30	29	28	25	24	25	26	28	29	30
Average	30	30	29	26	23	20	19	21	23	25	28	29

```
<HTML>
<HEAD>
<TITLE>Average Temperatures for Australian Cities</TITLE>
</HEAD>

<TABLE BORDER=all>
<CAPTION ALIGN=TOP>Average Monthly Temperatures for Selected Australian
Cities</CAPTION>
<THEAD>
   <TR>
      <TH>degrees C</TH>
      <TH COLSPAN=3>Summer</TH>
      <TH COLSPAN=3>Fall</TH>
      <TH COLSPAN=3>Winter</TH>
      <TH COLSPAN=3>Spring</TH>
   </TR>
   <TR>\
<TH></TH><TH>Jan</TH><TH>Feb</TH><TH>Mar</TH><TH>Apr</TH>
      <TH>May</TH><TH>Jun</TH><TH>Jul</TH><TH>Aug</TH><TH>Sep</TH>
      <TH>Oct</TH><TH>Nov</TH><TH>Dec</TH>
   </TR>
</THEAD>
<TBODY>
   <TR>
      <TH>Sydney</TH><TD>25</TD><TD>25</TD><TD>24</TD><TD>21</TD>
      <TD>19</TD><TD>16</TD><TD>16</TD><TD>17</TD><TD>19</TD>
      <TD>21</TD><TD>23</TD><TD>25</TD>
   </TR>
   <TR>
      <TH>Perth</TH><TD>30</TD><TD>30</TD><TD>28</TD><TD>25</TD>
      <TD>21</TD><TD>17</TD><TD>16</TD><TD>17</TD><TD>19</TD>
      <TD>20</TD><TD>24</TD><TD>27</TD>
   </TR>
   <TR>
      <TH>AliceSprings</TH><TD>36</TD><TD>35</TD><TD>32</TD>
      <TD>27</TD><TD>23</TD><TD>20</TD><TD>20</TD><TD>23</TD>
      <TD>27</TD><TD>31</TD><TD>34</TD><TD>35</TD>
   </TR>
   <TR>
      <TH>Townsville</TH><TD>30</TD><TD>30</TD><TD>30</TD>
      <TD>29</TD><TD>28</TD><TD>25</TD><TD>24</TD><TD>25</TD>
      <TD>26</TD><TD>28</TD><TD>29</TD><TD>30</TD>
   </TR>
   <TR>
      <TH><EM>Average</EM></TH><TD>30</TD><TD>30</TD><TD>29</TD>
      <TD>26</TD><TD>23</TD><TD>20</TD><TD>19</TD><TD>21</TD>
```

Continued on next page

Continued from previous page

```
        <TD>23</TD><TD>25</TD><TD>28</TD><TD>29</TD>
    </TR>
    <TR>
        <TD COLSPAN=13 ALIGN=LEFT><IMG SRC="temps.gif"></TD>
    </TR>
</TBODY>
</TABLE>
</BODY>
</HTML>
```

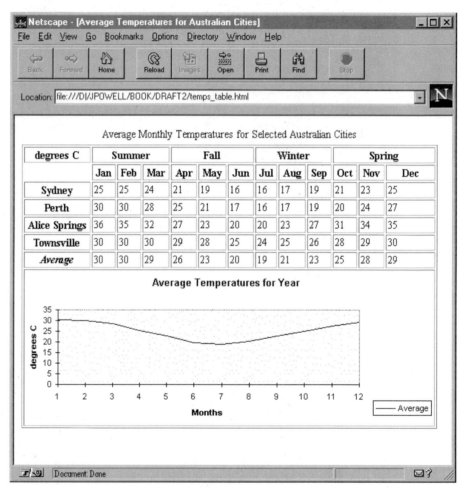

HTML 3 TABLE TAG USAGE SUMMARY

Tag	Permitted Context	Content Model
<TABLE>	document body	<CAPTION>, table rows <TR>
<CAPTION>	inside <TABLE>, before header or first table row	ASCII text
<TR>	inside <TABLE>, <THEAD>, or <TBODY>	<TH>, <TD>
<THEAD>	inside <TABLE>	<TR>, <TH>
<TBODY>	inside <TABLE>	<TR>, <TD>
<TFOOT>	inside <TABLE>	<TR>, <TH>
<TH>	inside <TR>	ASCII characters, character entities
<TD>	inside <TR>	ASCII characters, character entities
<COLGROUP>	inside <TABLE>	<COL>
<COL>	inside <COLGROUP>	none

ATTRIBUTE SUMMARY

(Most HTML 3 table elements support the global attributes ED, CLASS, STYLE, and LANG, so they will not be repeated in this table.)

Tag	Attribute	Value
<TABLE>	CLEAR	LEFT, RIGHT, ALL, pixels or en units
	NOFLOW	none
	ALIGN	BLEEDLEFT, LEFT, CENTER, RIGHT, BLEEDRIGHT, JUSTIFY
	UNITS	EN, RELATIVE, PIXELS
	COLSPEC	column widths (numeric values) and alignment specifications (ASCII text)
	DP	. (period), , (comma)
	WIDTH	numeric value
	BORDER	none
	NOWRAP	none
	COLS	numeric value
	CELLSPACING	numeric value
	CELLPADDING	numeric value
	FRAME	VOID, ABOVE, BELOW, HSIDES, LHS, RHS, VSIDES, BOX, BORDER
	RULES	NONE, GROUPS, ROWS, COLS, ALL
<THEAD>	ALIGN	LEFT, CENTER, RIGHT, JUSTIFY, CHAR
	CHAR	quoted ASCII character
	CHAROFF	numeric value or percentage
	VALIGN	TOP, MIDDLE, BOTTOM, BASELINE

ATTRIBUTE SUMMARY, CONT.

Tag	Attribute	Value
<TBODY>	ALIGN	LEFT, CENTER, RIGHT, JUSTIFY, CHAR
	CHAR	quoted ASCII character
	CHAROFF	numeric value or percentage
	VALIGN	TOP, MIDDLE, BOTTOM, BASELINE
<TFOOT>	ALIGN	LEFT, CENTER, RIGHT, JUSTIFY, CHAR
	CHAR	quoted ASCII character
	CHAROFF	numeric value or percentage
	VALIGN	TOP, MIDDLE, BOTTOM, BASELINE
<CAPTION>	ALIGN	TOP, BOTTOM, LEFT, RIGHT
<TR>	ALIGN	LEFT, CENTER, RIGHT, JUSTIFY, CHAR
	CHAR	quoted ASCII character
	CHAROFF	numeric value or percentage
	VALIGN	TOP, MIDDLE, BOTTOM, BASELINE
<TH>	AXIS	ASCII text
	AXES	ASCII text
	NOWRAP	none
	ROWSPAN	numeric value
	COLSPAN	numeric value
	ALIGN	LEFT, CENTER, RIGHT, JUSTIFY, CHAR
	CHAR	quoted ASCII character
	CHAROFF	numeric value or percentage
	VALIGN	TOP, MIDDLE, BOTTOM, BASELINE
<TD>	AXIS	ASCII text
	AXES	ASCII text
	NOWRAP	none
	ROWSPAN	numeric value
	COLSPAN	numeric value
	ALIGN	LEFT, CENTER, RIGHT, JUSTIFY, CHAR
	CHAR	quoted ASCII character
	CHAROFF	numeric value or percentage
	VALIGN	TOP, MIDDLE, BOTTOM, BASELINE
<COLGROUP>	SPAN	numeric value
	WIDTH	numeric value
	ALIGN	LEFT, CENTER, RIGHT, JUSTIFY, CHAR
	CHAR	quoted ASCII character
	CHAROFF	numeric value or percentage
	VALIGN	TOP, MIDDLE, BOTTOM, BASELINE
<COL>	SPAN	numeric value
	WIDTH	numeric value
	ALIGN	LEFT, CENTER, RIGHT, JUSTIFY, CHAR
	CHAR	quoted ASCII character
	CHAROFF	numeric value or percentage
	VALIGN	TOP, MIDDLE, BOTTOM, BASELINE

16

Overview of
HTML Math

CHAPTER AT A GLANCE

- Structure of HTML 3 math blocks
- How to use math elements and attributes
- Table 16-1: *Frequently Used Math Entities*
- HTML 3 Project: *Math Markup*
- Math Tag Usage and Attribute Summaries

Before HTML 3, authors had little choice but to include mathematical formulae as bitmapped graphics or external files in other formats such as TeX. HTML 3 incorporates a simple set of markup tags for including math symbols and formulae within a Web document. Authors familiar with HTML 2 will find the new markup for math easy to learn, as will authors who are familiar with TeX. Some of its tags were derived from TeX control words, others from SGML applications such as the AAP (American Association of Publishers) document type declaration for mathematical markup in electronic publishing.

HTML math is a combination of tags and character entities. Most HTML math tags are only permitted between the <MATH> start and end tags. A few can be used in contexts other than mathematical formulae. For example, <SUB> and

<SUP> for subscripts and superscripts are also allowed in text blocks within the document body. But even these tags have additional attributes within a math block.

HTML math is designed to be brief and simple. It uses SGML short reference definitions to achieve brevity without adding complexity. Short references are characters or strings of characters that can be used to represent tags in certain document contexts. For example, underscore normally represents an underscore character in the body of an HTML document. But between an HTML <MATH> start and end tag, it indicates that the character(s) that follow are to be treated as subscript characters. The underscore ("_") is said to be the shortref of the <SUB> tag. As you would expect, there is also a shortref for superscripts. A caret ("^") may be used instead of the <SUP> tag. Other shortrefs are covered below.

The <MATH> tag for enclosing formulae or expressions has three attributes. You can assign the block an ID attribute so that it can be the target of a hypertext link. The CLASS attribute is used to subclass a particular math block. The BOX attribute has no value but when present causes the Web browser to draw a rectangular box around the block.

Math blocks can contain simple or complex formulae. There are a number of HTML 3 math elements that can be used to construct and structure equations.

<BOX>

Not to be confused with the <MATH> box attribute, the <BOX> element is used for a variety of purposes within math blocks. Basically, <BOX> functions like parentheses in complex expressions, to clarify and group terms. It is also used in conjunction with other elements to delimit expressions and apply *stretchy* symbols to expressions. Stretchy symbols are symbols such as integral signs that are automatically stretched to match the height of the integrand, in instances where it is taller than one line of text. Figure 16-1 shows some examples of the <BOX> element and *stretchy* symbols in use. The <BOX> start and end tag can be used but the short reference notation {} simplifies the markup, making it easier to read and maintain. Of course, this means you must use character entities for left and right curly brackets inside a math block ({, }).

Here is an example of a math block using the <BOX> element and the short reference elements:

```
<MATH><BOX>dy<OVER>dx</BOX>=<BOX>dy<OVER>dx</BOX>
<BOX>du<OVER>dx</BOX></MATH>
```

or with the <BOX> short reference {}:

```
<MATH>{dy<OVER>dx}={dy<OVER>dx}{du<OVER>dx}</MATH>
```

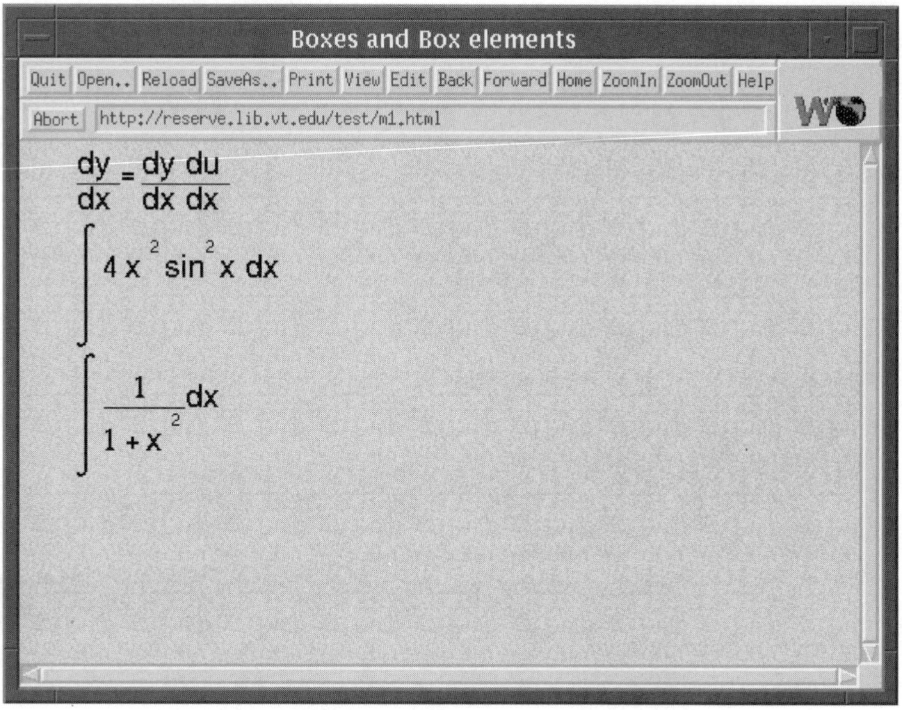

Figure 16-1 Arena
displaying mathe-
matical markup

As you can see, the <BOX> tag allows you to group complex fractions or other
equations into logical groups. Without the box tag, the equation would have
been incorrectly displayed as "dy du/dx". By reducing HTML math elements
from bracketed tags to single character representations, short references make
HTML math blocks easier to read and maintain.

<LEFT>, <RIGHT>, <OVER>, <ATOP>, AND <CHOOSE>

The <LEFT> and <RIGHT> elements are used to indicate that a stretchy expression delimiter should be inserted in the math box. Unlike other HTML tags, the
tagged character is placed before the <LEFT> tag, and after the <RIGHT> tag, and
there is no end tag for either. The stretchy delimiter can be an integral sign, sum,
parentheses, etc.

```
<MATH>{&int;<LEFT>4x^2^ sin^2^ x dx}</MATH>
<MATH>{&int;<LEFT>{1<OVER>1 + x^2^} dx}</MATH>
```

Simple fractions can be represented with the forward slash character (/)
dividing the numerator from the denominator. More complex fractions involving expressions should be tagged with the <OVER> tag. It should be placed
between the numerator and denominator just like the slash character.

```
<MATH>1/2</MATH>
<MATH>1<OVER>x^2^ -1</MATH>
```

To place one expression or term over another without a dividing line, use the <ATOP> tag. <CHOOSE> works like <ATOP> except it places rounded brackets around each expression.

```
<MATH>{A B <ATOP> C D}</MATH>
<MATH>{A B <CHOOSE> C D}</MATH>
```

<SUB> AND <SUP>

The subscript <SUB> and superscript <SUP> tags can be used to tag sub- and superscripts both within math blocks and in the text of an HTML 3 document.

```
<P>
e=mc<SUP>2</SUP> was discovered by Albert Einstein.
<MATH>x=x<SUB>1</SUB>+x<SUB>2</SUB></MATH>
```

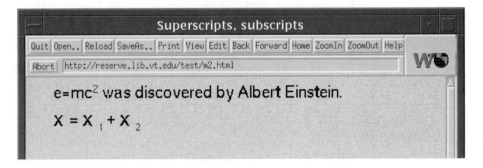

When, within the context of an HTML math block, sub- and superscript tags exchange their ID, LANG, and CLASS attributes for an ALIGN attribute. The ALIGN attribute can be assigned LEFT to position the sub- or superscript to the left of the variable name, CENTER to position it above or below, and RIGHT to position it to the right of the variable.

```
<MATH>
X<SUB ALIGN=RIGHT>a</SUB><SUP ALIGN=RIGHT>b</SUP>Y
</MATH>
```

As mentioned before, you can use short references for <SUB> and <SUP> within math blocks. The short reference for <SUB> is the underscore character (_) and the short reference for <SUP> is the caret or exponent symbol (^):

```
<MATH>X_a_ ^b^Y</MATH>
```

The subscript and superscript short references must surround the exponent or subscript expression, just like start and end tags. Be sure to insert a blank space between separate terms with subscripts or superscripts; another option is to use the <BOX> tag or its short reference to clarify the markup:

{H_2 } {O_2 }

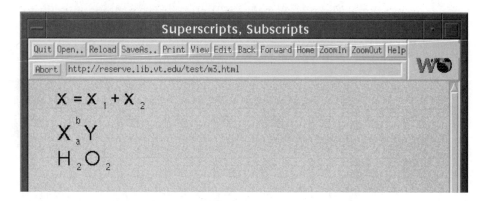

<ABOVE> AND <BELOW>

The <ABOVE> tag is used to draw a line or some other type of accent above an expression. The SYM attribute is assigned an entity name for the type of line or accent that should be used. Valid symbol entity names are line (the default), cub (for curly bracket), larr (left arrow), rarr (right arrow), equals, tilde, and hat. Do not use the ampersand and semicolon with the entity name as you normally would with other character entities—"&line;" is incorrect.

1<ABOVE SYM=line>1 + X^2</ABOVE>

The <BELOW> tag is used to draw a line or accent below an expression. It has a SYM attribute just like <ABOVE>.

<BELOW SYM=line>1</BELOW>1 + X^2

<VEC>, <ABOVE>, <BELOW>, <BAR>, <DOT>, <DDOT>, <HAT>, AND <TILDE>

There is also a set of accents for terms, which are drawn over the contents of the element. The vector element <VEC> draws a right arrow over a term (like the rarr entity used with the <ABOVE> and <BELOW> expression elements). The bar element <BAR> draws a line above a term. <DOT> and <DDOT> are used to draw single and double dots above a term. <HAT> and <TILDE> draw the named character above a term.

<VEC>B</VEC> x <VEC>V</VEC>
<TILDE>X</TILDE>

<SQRT> AND <ROOT>

The square root element <SQRT> is used to draw a square root symbol around a term or an expression:

```
<SQRT>1 + X^2^</SQRT>
```

The root element <ROOT> is used to express an arbitrary root of an expression. The radix is separated from the radicand by the <OF> tag.

```
<ROOT>X<OF>1 - X^2^</ROOT>
```

<ARRAY>, <ROW>, AND <ITEM>

The array element <ARRAY> is used to tag arrays and matrices. Array markup is somewhat similar to table markup. An array consists of one or more rows tagged with the <ROW> tag. Each cell is marked with an <ITEM> tag. Both the item and row end tags can usually be safely omitted since the next item or row start tag implies the end of the previous one. The <ARRAY> element simply provides consistent spacing between items, and does not provide all of the functionality of a table such as headings, borders, captions, etc.

<ARRAY> and <ITEM> do have a few formatting attributes for controlling appearance and content alignment. The <ARRAY> element has an ALIGN attribute for specifying the alignment (TOP, MIDDLE, BOTTOM) of multiple expressions in a row. COLDEF allows you to specify column alignment and column divider characters. Alignment is specified as left, right, or center but for COLDEF you only provide the first letter of the alignment type for each column. Here is the COLDEF attribute for a four-column array:

```
<ARRAY COLDEF="RCCL">
```

In this example, the first column is right justified, the next two are centered, and the final column is left justified. You can specify one of three possible column separators "+," "-," or "=," this character should be inserted between the centering attribute values:

```
<ARRAY COLDEF="R+C+C+L">
```

The entire array can be contained by a delimiter character if you include left and right delimiter attributes LDELIM and RDELIM. These attributes can be assigned one of three possible characters: '|' and '{' for LDELIM or '}' for RDELIM. Finally, there is a LABELS attribute that indicates that the first row and first column of each subsequent row should be treated as a label and displayed offset from the remaining array elements.

There is an ALIGN attribute for the <ITEM> tag that controls the horizontal alignment of array cell contents. The contents of a cell can span multiple rows and/or columns by including a COLSPAN or ROWSPAN attribute. Each can be assigned an integer value for the number of rows or columns the current item cell should fill.

```
<ARRAY LABELS>
<ROW><ITEM><ITEM COLSPAN=5>Key Values</ROW>
<ROW><ITEM>1.<ITEM COLSPAN=5>a_1_ &lt; b_1_, or
<ROW><ITEM>2.<ITEM>a_1_ = b_1_ and <ITEM COLSPAN=4>a_2_ &lt; b_2_, or
<ROW><ITEM COLSPAN=6 ALIGN=CENTER>&vdots;
<ROW><ITEM><ITEM>a_1_ = b_1_, <ITEM> a_2_ = b_2_, <ITEM>&cdots;
,<ITEM>a_{k-1}, and <ITEM>a_k_ &lt; b_k_.
</ARRAY>
```

<TEXT>

The <TEXT> element is used to include a short block of text within a math block. The contents of this element are displayed just like text would be displayed within any other text block in an HTML 3 document. Without this tag, some Web browsers might not correctly space the contents of a block of text.

```
<MATH BOX>
<TEXT>Find dy/dx for </TEXT>{y= (ax + b)<OVER>(cx + d)}
</MATH>
```

<B>, <T>, AND <BT>

Variables are normally displayed in italics in math blocks but you can specify alternate formatting with several math elements. You can tag a term with the bold tag <B> to bold the term. If you prefer not to have a term in italics, you can use the <T> tag to have it displayed in a normal, upright font. If you desire both effects, there is a combined tag <BT> that is short for <B><T>. These three tags also support the CLASS attribute if you wish to subclass them and apply additional formatting information with a style sheet entry.

As you may have noticed from some of these examples, HTML 3 includes a number of new character entities for math. The characters are covered in detail in Chapter 18, Special Characters, and in Appendix A. Here is a table of some of the most common entities:

TABLE 16-1   FREQUENTLY USED MATH ENTITIES

Character	Meaning	Entity Equivalent
{ }	Curly brackets	{ }
< >	less than, greater than	< >
≤ ≥	less than or equal to greater than or equal to	≤ ≥
∫	integral	&int;
Σ	sum	&sum;
π	pi	&pi;

HTML 3 math entities are only valid within HTML math blocks.

HTML 3 PROJECT 4: MATH MARKUP

Your calculus professor has given you three problems to solve for homework. For extra credit, you can markup your homework with HTML and send your professor a URL instead of handing in the assignment on paper.

Here is the markup:

```
<HTML>
<HEAD><TITLE>Homework</TITLE></HEAD>
<BODY>
<H1>Homework assignment</H1>
<H2>John Doe</H2>
<P>
1. Find <MATH>dy/dx</MATH> for <MATH>y = {<SQRT>4+2x</SQRT>}</MATH>
<P>
<B>Solution is: </B>
<MATH>y' = {(4 + 2x)}^1/2^</MATH>
<P>
2. Find the area under a curve <MATH>{y = cos x} from {x = -&pi;/2} to {x =
&pi;/2}</MATH>
<P>
<B>Solution is:</B>
Area <MATH>= {_-&pi;/2_&int;^&pi;2^} {cos x dx} = {sin x |^&pi;/2^_-&pi;/2_} = {1 -
(-1) = 2}</MATH>
<P>
3. Evaluate <MATH>_d{_1_}_&int;^d_2_^ {(ax^2^ + bx + c)} dx </MATH>
<P>
<B>Solution is: </B>
<MATH>{(a/3) (d_2_^3^ - d_1_^3^)} + {(b/2)(d_2_^2^ - d_1_^2^)} + {c(d_2_ -
```

```
d_1_)}</MATH>
<P>
</BODY>
</HTML>
```

The results should look like this:

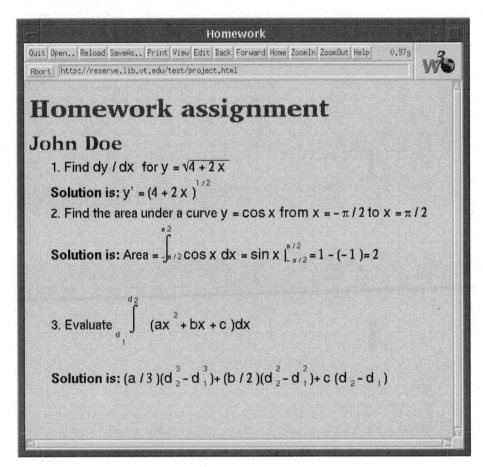

MATH TAG USAGE SUMMARY

Tag	Permitted Context	Content Model
<MATH>	within document body	ASCII characters, character entities, math elements
<BOX> or {}	within <MATH> blocks	ASCII characters, character entities, <OVER>, <LEFT>, <RIGHT>, <ATOP>, <CHOOSE>

MATH TAG USAGE SUMMARY, CONT.

Tag	Permitted Context	Content Model
<CHOOSE>	within <BOX>	ASCII characters, character entities
<OVER>	within <BOX>	ASCII characters, character entities
<RIGHT>	within <BOX>	ASCII characters, character entities
<LEFT>	within <BOX>	ASCII characters, character entities
<ATOP>	within <BOX>	ASCII characters, character entities
<SUB> or _	within <MATH> blocks	ASCII characters, character entities
<SUP> or ^	within <MATH> blocks	ASCII characters, character entities
<ABOVE>	within <MATH> blocks	ASCII characters, character entities
<BELOW>	within <MATH> blocks	ASCII characters, character entities
<VEC>	within <MATH> blocks	ASCII characters, character entities
<BAR>	within <MATH> blocks	ASCII characters, character entities
<DOT>	within <MATH> blocks	ASCII characters, character entities
<DDOT>	within <MATH> blocks	ASCII characters, character entities
<HAT>	within <MATH> blocks	ASCII characters, character entities
<TILDE>	within <MATH> blocks	ASCII characters, character entities
<SQRT>	within <MATH> blocks	ASCII characters, character entities
<ROOT>	within <MATH> blocks	ASCII characters, character entities, <OF>
<OF>	within <ROOT>	none
<ARRAY>	within <MATH> blocks	<ROW>
<ROW>	within <ARRAY>	<ITEM>
<ITEM>	within <ROW>	ASCII characters, character entities
<TEXT>	within <MATH> blocks	ASCII characters, character entities
<B>, <T>, <BT>	within <MATH> blocks	ASCII characters, character entities

ATTRIBUTE SUMMARY

(Most HTML 3 math elements do not support the global attributes ID, CLASS, STYLE, and LANG, so these attributes are listed with those elements that do support them.)

Tag	Attribute	Value
<MATH>	ID	ASCII text
	CLASS	ASCII text
	BOX	none
<BOX>	SIZE	NORMAL, MEDIUM, LARGE, HUGE
<SUB>, <SUP>	ALIGN	LEFT, CENTER, RIGHT
<ABOVE>, <BELOW>	SYM	CUB, LINE, LARR, RARR, HAT, TILDE
<ARRAY>	ALIGN	TOP, MIDDLE, BOTTOM
	COLDEF	ASCII text string
	LDELIM, RDELIM	ASCII character
	LABELS	none

ATTRIBUTE SUMMARY, CONT.

Tag	Attribute	Value
<ITEM>	ALIGN	LEFT, CENTER, RIGHT
	COLSPAN	numeric value
	ROWSPAN	numeric value
<B>, <T>, <BT>	CLASS	ASCII text

17

Document
Frames Tutorial

CHAPTER AT A GLANCE

- Introducing Netscape document frames
- Markup for redirecting hypertext targeted documents to specific frames
- Implications of frames for constructing more traditional hypertext systems
- *Building Reusable Frame Contents*
- HTML 3 Project: *Frames Markup*
- Frame and Related Tag Usage and Attribute Summaries

HTML documents are becoming less and less like the printed documents we are familiar with and more active and interactive. HTML documents have long been able to incorporate dynamic data such as images updated every few minutes from a weather satellite. But in order to effect change on the textual content of a Web document, the entire document text would have to be replaced or generated upon request. HTML 3 includes an element that allows several documents to be combined into one when displayed for a reader: <BANNER>. Netscape supports a more flexible alternative that will undoubtedly influence the implementation of the HTML 3 <BANNER> element, and perhaps replace it. Netscape refers to their multipart page-presentation system as frames.

A frame document has a different structure than any other HTML document type covered in this book. Instead of the header-body structure, a frame super-document has the structure header-frameset. A frameset lists the documents that should be combined to create a frames document. It also describes where and how much of the available Web browser screen each of these documents is allowed. Framesets are contained by the <FRAMESET> element. The document frameset can contain <FRAME> and <NOFRAME> elements, as well as nested <FRAMESET> elements. The <FRAME> tag is used to specify each document that should be loaded and included as part of the master frame document. Each <FRAME> tag must have an SRC attribute assigned the URL of the document to be loaded. The <NOFRAMES> element tags text to be displayed by Web browsers that do not support frames. One drawback is that frame documents are not, technically, valid HTML documents since they lack a <BODY> tag. Like <BANNER>, frames can be used to present corporate logos or navigational aids. But frames can be combined with other frames to create complex and useful presentations not possible with banners.

Frame Elements in Netscape

Before exploring design possibilities, let's look at Netscape's frame elements and attributes. Some attributes may be familiar since tables use some of the same attributes to present data. Indeed, frames are to documents what tables are to data. Both provide a highly structured presentation, with table cells roughly equivalent to individual document frames. Both can also contain themselves, allowing for extremely complex and sophisticated data presentation. The <FRAMESET> tag has both a ROWS and COLS attribute. You can use these individually to split a document into rows or columns, or combine them to achieve a table-like effect. These attributes accept a comma-separated list of values that indicate the amount of the Web browser's available window space they should receive. The best way to specify this value is as a percentage. To do this, provide a number between 1 and 100 followed by a percent sign (%) for each frame. Of course, the percentages must add up to 100, or the browser will adjust the frames to fill or fit the unspecified area. Instead of percentages, you can use a relative size value, which is a numeric value followed by an asterisk (*), or just an asterisk to tell the browser to give the frame whatever space remains. Here is an example that assigns three-quarters of the window to the first frame and the remaining quarter to the second frame:

```
<FRAMESET COLS="3*, *">
```

The clumsiest and least accurate way to specify frame sizes is by simply providing a numeric value for each frame. Any numeric value that is not followed by a percent sign or an asterisk is accepted by the browser as a value in pixels.

But no two Web browser windows are likely to be the same size so the pixel values will probably be too large or too small. In this case, the browser will override the values you specify to make things fit. Of course, these value types can be mixed as well. For example, this frameset devotes 25% to the first frame row, 200 pixels to the second, and the remaining space to a third frame row, then splits the window up into two columns for a total of six frames:

```
<FRAMESET ROWS="25%, 200, *" COLS="60%, 40%">
```

Make sure you have a size specification for each frame that follows, or the document will not load properly (and may not load at all).

Frame contents are defined with the <FRAME> tag. This tag does not mark text, so it doesn't have an end tag. Instead, it functions much like the <IMG> tag, specifying external content (usually an HTML document) that should be embedded in the current document. A <FRAME> tag should have an SRC attribute to which the URL of a document is assigned. The document at this location can be any ordinary HTML document. If it contains a background image or color specifications, these will be used within the frame. Each frame can have a NAME attribute that is assigned an alphanumeric identifier. Netscape anchor tags have a TARGET attribute that can be assigned the name of a frame or window. If a TARGET attribute is provided with an anchor, the contents pointed to by the anchor will replace the contents of that frame if it is present in the current document. So you could open a home page that served as a table of contents, select a link from that contents page, and have it display itself in a different frame so that the contents page stayed visible:

```
<!— portion of view.html, a frame document —>
<FRAMESET COLS="30%, 70%">
<FRAME SRC="contents.html">
<FRAME SRC="section1.html" NAME="sections">
</FRAMESET>
...
<!— portion of contents.html —>
<UL>
<LH>Contents</LH>
<LI><A HREF="section1.html" TARGET="sections">Section 1</A>
<LI><A HREF="section2.html" TARGET="sections">Section 2</A>
...
```

Otherwise, the default behavior is to replace the contents of a frame with the target of one of its anchors. In this way users can navigate in one frame while leaving the contents of other frames untouched. Any Netscape HTML element that functions as an anchor can have a TARGET attribute. Here is a form that targets a frame called "results":

```
<FORM METHOD="GET" TARGET="results" ACTION="/cgi-bin/do_results">
Input search term: <INPUT NAME="search_term" TYPE="TEXT" SIZE=20
<INPUT TYPE="SUBMIT"></FORM>
```

You can set targets for all anchors in a given document using a body <BASE> tag. This should not be confused with the header <BASE> tag, which specifies the base URL of a document. The body <BASE> tag occurs between the <BODY> start and end tags and has one attribute, called TARGET. When TARGET is assigned a value, every anchor in this document that does not already have a TARGET attribute will use this global TARGET value:

```
<HTML>
<HEAD><TITLE>Frames demo</TITLE>
<BASE HREF="http://server/">
<BODY>
<BASE TARGET="pages">
...
```

This makes updating a collection of documents to function with a particular frame layout simply a matter of adding one tag to each HTML document in the set. It is unfortunate that the tag is called <BASE>, because of the potential for confusion. Another way to specify a global target for an individual frame without editing the documents that it points to is to add a TARGET attribute to the <FRAME> tag that includes that document:

```
<FRAMESET COLS="30%, 70%">
<FRAME SRC="contents.html" TARGET="sections">
```

SPECIAL-PURPOSE TARGETS

Some target names are reserved for special purposes. Each of the reserved names begins with an underscore. You can use these reserved names with <FRAME> or anchor TARGET attributes or with the <BASE> TARGET attribute. Each specifies a document or frame relative to the current frame, rather than specifically naming a frame. The _top target causes the anchors to load their contents over the entire window. So if the target of one of the frames in a multiframe document is assigned _top, any anchor in that frame will cause the entire window to be replaced when it is selected and loaded. This clears the frames and resets the browser to a nonframes mode. If the target is _parent, the frameset containing the frame will be replaced. _self replaces the contents of the current frame, which is the default behavior. If the target is _blank, then a new window is opened for the target document. Table 17-1 summarizes these reserved frame targets.

TABLE 17-1   RESERVED FRAME TARGET TYPES

Target	Meaning	Uses
_top	Replace the entire window with the target's contents	Good for getting rid of a frame
_self	Replace this frame with the target's contents	(default behavior)
_parent	Replace the frameset that contains this frame, but not all the frames	Used to clear out an embedded frameset
_blank	Open a new window and display the target's content in it	Preserves existing windows and framesets

Here is an example where a table of contents frame targets a wider frame (right) where the selected document is displayed, and a third frame (bottom) ties this document into a larger collection, allowing the items to which it points to overwrite the entire window:

```
<HTML>
<HEAD><TITLE>Frames</TITLE></HEAD>
<FRAMESET ROWS="85%, 15%">
```

```
<FRAMESET COLS="40%, 60%">
<FRAME SRC="contents.htm" NAME="overview" TARGET="pages">
<FRAME SRC="chapter1.htm" NAME="pages">
</FRAMESET>
<FRAMESET COLS="*">
<FRAME SRC="toolbar.htm" TARGET="_top">
</FRAMESET>
</FRAMESET>
</HTML>
```

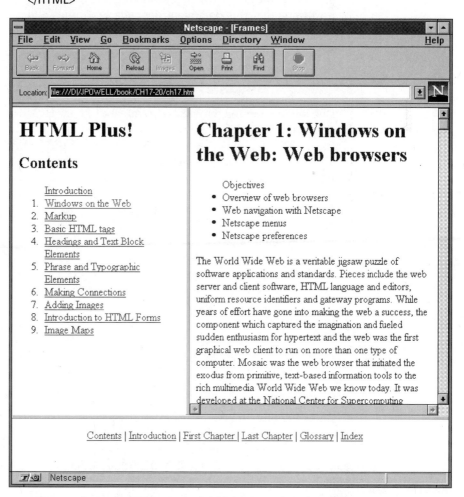

The remaining <FRAME> attributes let you control other frame layout options. Each frame has a dividing line called a margin. The MARGINWIDTH and MARGINHEIGHT attributes let you control the size of this divider. Any value you assign to the margin attributes is automatically assumed to be in pixels. You can activate or deactivate scrolling within a frame with the SCROLLING attribute. If it is assigned NO, then no scroll bars are available and the user has to resize the window to see more of that frame. If set to YES the frame will have scroll bars whether its contents fit the frame or not. If set to AUTO (the default), then scroll bars are provided only if the contents are too large for the frame. Finally, each frame is resizable by default. But if the NORESIZE attribute is specified, then the frame and any neighbors bordering it will not be resizable.

You can also make frames documents backwards-compatible with browsers that do not support frames by enclosing alternate content with the <NOFRAMES> start and end tags. You can put any element valid in the document body (and can include the <BODY> tag, although this structure makes little sense) inside the <NOFRAMES> tag. Typically this would include an alternate version of the page, or a warning that this document depends on frames and a pointer to an alternate document. It is a good idea to include a <NOFRAMES> element with alternate content in every frames document.

BUILDING REUSABLE FRAME CONTENTS

Documents pointed to by frames can be ordinary HTML documents. They need not include any frames-aware markup to be embedded in a frame. The default behavior for any anchor in a document embedded in a frame is to load the target document over itself, which is usually just fine. When it is not the desired behavior, you can alter this in the document containing the <FRAMESET> definitions, rather than by adding a <BASE TARGET> tag or TARGET attribute to anchors within the plain HTML document. Otherwise, you lock the document into expecting a particular frame, when it might be useful in a different frames document with different frames. You might want to avoid using any background or text coloring in the document as well, since it could very well clash with the background and color scheme of other documents it is paired with later. Clearly identify the function of the document, if it is not obvious from its content (most people would understand a back arrow, but make sure it is clear where it would go back to). Finally, use full URLs with each anchor in the document, or use a header <BASE> tag to configure a base URL for the document, so there's no opportunity for confusion.

Implementing frames is tricky and requires considerable planning. Since frames are similar to tables in that they split the document window up into separate cells, it might be helpful to sketch out a simple table with the content of each document you wish to use in the frames document represented. Since individual frames can be addressed using the TARGET attribute with an anchor, this also has some implications for design. Users cannot return to the previous contents of a frame using the Netscape back button, but can right click to access a "back" option. This is clumsy enough to make it worthwhile to link the documents that are to appear in a given frame together with a hypertext link. Or implement a navigational bar as one of your frames. Otherwise, new users might find themselves accidentally selecting the back button and getting lost and frustrated.

While frames provide all sorts of possible formatting options such as multi-column documents, multiple backgrounds, and colors, the real strength of frames lies in the way in which complex hypertext systems can be presented in multiple views simultaneously. For example, a table of contents might be available in one window, with an abstract of a selected chapter in a second, the chapter itself displayed in the third, and a toolbar to quickly access the glossary, index, last, and first chapters available in a fourth frame. Or multiple language versions of a document might be presented side by side. Banners, toolbars, and navigational aids suddenly become reusable since they can be referenced by many different documents. This in turn reduces maintenance since the toolbar need only be updated once because it is referenced by other frames-based documents, instead of being incorporated into them. There are many other uses for frames including tutorials, hypertext online manuals, database interfaces, footnotes and footers, and glossaries, to name a few.

HTML 3 PROJECT 5: FRAMES MARKUP

Use the Web page from Chapter 12 (http://scholar.lib.vt.edu/) or locate a suitable page on the Web with a similar layout (banner, content, and navigation bar) to create a frames-based document with reusable components. Separate the banner and navigation bar from the document body, and place each in its own HTML document. Don't use the <BASE TARGET> or TARGET attribute in either document; instead, assign all targets in the frames document. The final document should look like the one printed on the following page.

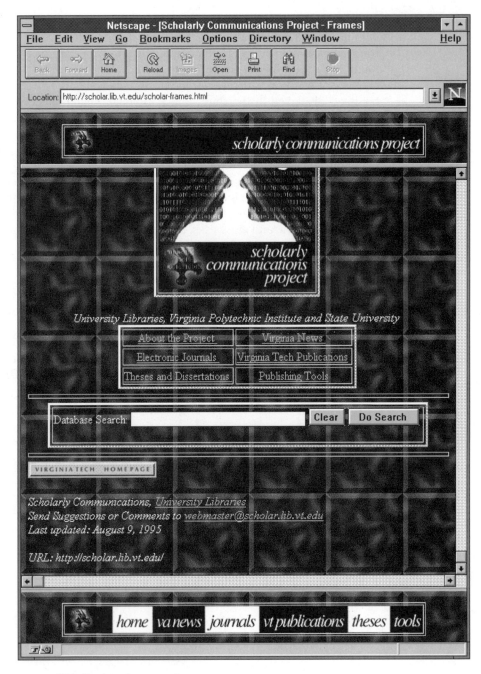

The frames document:

```
<HTML>
<HEAD><TITLE>Scholarly Communications Project - Frames</TITLE></HEAD>
<FRAMESET ROWS="10%, 80%, 10%">
<FRAME SRC="fbscholar.html" NORESIZE SCROLLING=no>
```

```
<FRAME SRC="fscholar.html" name="main">
<FRAME SRC="fmscholar.html" NORESIZE SCROLLING=no TARGET="main">
</FRAMESET>
</HTML>
```

The banner document:

```
<HTML>
<HEAD>
<TITLE>Scholarly Communications Project of VPI & SU</TITLE>
</HEAD>
<CENTER>
<BODY background="/images/scpback.gif" text=ffffff link=b1c89e vlink=c8c8c8>
<TABLE border=1>
<TR><TD><IMG src="/images/logobar.gif" alt="Scholarly Communications
Project"></TD>
</TABLE>
<BR>
</CENTER>
</BODY>
</HTML>
```

The main contents:

```
<HTML>
<HEAD>
<TITLE>Scholarly Communications Project of VPI & SU</TITLE>
</HEAD>
<CENTER>
<BODY background="/images/scpback.gif" text=ffffff link=b1c89e vlink=c8c8c8>
<BR>
<TABLE border=3>
<TR><TD><IMG src="/images/newlogo.gif" alt="Scholarly Communications
Project"></
TD>
</TABLE>
<P><I>University Libraries, Virginia Polytechnic Institute and State University</I>
<TABLE border=3 cellspacing=3>
<TR><TD align=center><A href="/scpabout.html">About the Project
<BR></A></TD><TD align=center><A href="http://scholar3.lib.vt.edu/VA-news/VA-
news.html">Virginia News <BR></a></TD>
<TR><TD align=center><A href="/ejpage.html">Electronic Journals
<BR></A></TD><TD align=center><A href="/vtpub.html">Virginia Tech
Publications</A> <BR></TD>
<TR><TD align=center><A href="/theses/theses.html">Theses and Dissertations
<BR></A></TD><TD align=center><A href="/reports/reports.html">Publishing
```

Continued on next page

Continued from previous page

```
Tools</A></TD>
</TABLE>
<HR size=5>
<TABLE border=3 cellspacing=3>
<TR><TD align=center><FORM method=get action="http://scholar.lib.vt.edu/cgi-
bin/scholar.sonofwais.pl">
Database Search: <INPUT name="" SIZE=30>
<INPUT type=reset value="Clear">
<INPUT type=submit value="Do Search">
</FORM></TD>
</TABLE>
<HR size=5>
</CENTER>
<A href="http://www.vt.edu"><IMG border=1 src="/images/HPButton.gif"></A>
<P>
<CITE>
Scholarly Communications, <A HREF="http://vatech.lib.vt.edu/">University
Libraries</A><BR>
Send Suggestions or Comments to <a
href="mailto:webmaster@scholar.lib.vt.edu">webmaster@scholar.lib.vt.edu</A><B
R>
Last updated: August 9, 1995
<P>
URL: http://scholar.lib.vt.edu/
</CITE>
</BODY>
</HTML>
```

The navigation bar:

```
<HTML>
<HEAD>
<TITLE>Scholarly Communications Project of VPI & SU</TITLE>
</HEAD>
<BODY background="/images/scpback.gif" text=ffffff link=b1c89e vlink=c8c8c8>
<CENTER>
<TABLE border=1 align=center>
<TR><TD><A HREF = "http://scholar.lib.vt.edu/cgi-bin/imagemap/scpmenu"><IMG
border=0 SRC = "/images/menubar.gif" ISMAP USEMAP="#toolbar"></A></TD>
</TABLE>
</CENTER>
<MAP NAME="toolbar">
<AREA SHAPE="rect" COORDS="461,0, 504, 35" HREF="/reports/reports.html">
```

```
<AREA SHAPE="rect" COORDS="401,1, 458, 35" HREF="/theses/theses.html">
<AREA SHAPE="rect" COORDS="277,1, 398, 35" HREF="/vtpub.html">
<AREA SHAPE="rect" COORDS="200,1, 275, 34" HREF="/ejpage.html">
<AREA SHAPE="rect" COORDS="126,0, 198, 35" HREF="http://scholar3.lib.vt.edu/">
<AREA SHAPE="rect" COORDS="0,0, 124, 35"
HREF="http://scholar.lib.vt.edu/fscholar.html">
</MAP>
</BODY>
</HTML>
```

FRAME AND RELATED TAG USAGE SUMMARY

Tag	Permitted Context	Content Model
<FRAMESET>	around document	<FRAMESET>, <FRAME>, <NOFRAMES>
<FRAME>	within <FRAMESET>	none
<NOFRAMES>	within <FRAMESET>	HTML body tags
<BASE>	document body	none

ATTRIBUTE SUMMARY

Tag	Attribute	Value
<FRAMESET>	ROWS	value in pixels
		value in percent
		relative value (*)
	COLS	value in pixels
		value in percent
		relative value (*)
<FRAME>	SRC	URL of a document
	NAME	alphanumeric string (note: _blank, _self, _parent, _top are reserved for special purposes)
	MARGINWIDTH	value in pixels
	MARGINHEIGHT	value in pixels
	SCROLLING	yes, no, auto
	NORESIZE	none
<A>	TARGET	alphanumeric string
<BASE>	TARGET	alphanumeric string

18

Special Characters and Multilingual Documents

CHAPTER AT A GLANCE

- Multilingual character support in today's Web
- Table 18-1: *charset Code Values*
- Table 18-2: *ISO-639:1988 Language Codes*
- Character sets and the implications of Unicode
- Localization issues on the horizon and how they might be resolved

The World Wide Web should be renamed the "English Wide Web." Everything from browser menus, to the markup elements, right down to the normally invisible hypertext transfer protocol commands are in English. In order for the Web to become a truly global phenomenon, it will have to become multilingual. Some standards are emerging that will make this possible soon. Providing international character sets and document localization are issues that must be resolved if the Web is to ever become truly worldwide.

The HTML Character Sets

HTML uses a small character set in order to maintain compatibility across different computer systems. This character set is often referred to as ASCII, which stands for the American Standard Code for Information Interchange. Web browsers support a subset of ASCII called ISO 8859-1. ASCII includes 128 letters, numbers, and symbols. Basically these are the characters you see on a typical computer keyboard. Many other characters are available for use in HTML documents, as you've seen from previous chapters. An extended character set called ISO Latin-1 is supported by HTML that includes character entities such as &Aagrave; for "À." If 8-bit ASCII encoding is used, then 128 more ASCII characters from 129–255 can be accessed with numeric entities, such as Ÿ for "Ÿ". Some Web browsers provide still more characters by supporting character entities. For example, the HTML 3 browser Arena supports entities such as π and ∫ to represent Greek symbols and mathematical operators and symbols in math blocks.

Still, ASCII and character entities cannot support every language spoken on earth. The character entity set supported by most Web browsers is a finite collection of character codes tailored to western European languages. Numeric entities can produce unexpected results on computers where English is not the default language. With numeric entities, you can't always be sure what others will see.

Instead of using character entities, you might choose to use images of characters. You could create graphics of the characters you need and insert them into your documents with the <IMG> tag. After all, the contents of the image tag are treated as a character. The trick is to select a size that will fit the surrounding text. The graphic should also have a transparent background and match the font of the surrounding characters. With Netscape extensions, you can use the <FONT> tag to control the font size, and use WIDTH and HEIGHT attributes with the <IMG> tag to control the size of the graphic when displayed by Netscape. There are even repositories of GIF character images with transparent backgrounds available on the Web for this purpose. But this approach is time-consuming and requires that the Web browser retrieve each character image as a separate file in order to construct the full document. Users are unlikely to return to such a document very often.

Neither of these solutions comes close to resolving the fundamental issue of presenting documents with non-English characters. The number of character entities any one browser would have to support would be astronomical. Then consider how many different types of browsers are in use today, including several text-based browsers used by millions of sighted and sight-impaired people around the world. What would they see or hear if they happen to be an English-speaking individual accessing a non-English document using a non-English character set? What about other localization issues such as representations of numbers, dates, phone numbers, weights, and other forms of information that are represented in different ways from culture to culture? And don't forget to factor in the authoring process!

MULTINATIONAL CHARACTER SETS

Web browsers are usually dependent upon the operating system to provide fonts for displaying text, and this is no different whether the system is configured for English, Japanese, or any other language. So if a user wishes to view documents in anything other than the language she normally uses to interact with her computer, then she will have to retrieve (or purchase) and install a set of fonts for that language. The key then for an author producing documents for an international market is to create the document in her native language and provide additional information through the Web server or in the body of the document that identifies the character set used to create it. Then, if possible, the author should provide pointers to fonts for this language. Another alternative is to place multiple versions of the pages online, using widely spoken languages such as French or English in an effort to target a larger audience.

Character sets are mapped to fonts by the operating system when the contents of a document are displayed. So while you might think of the two as synonymous, try accessing a Web site in Russian or Japanese using a system that only has English language fonts installed. The contents of the document might be encoded in ASCII, but without the correct fonts, you will see gibberish. Figure 18-1 shows a multilingual Web authoring package displaying a Russian document with Cyrillic font.

Figure 18-1
Accent Soft's Multilingual Publisher lets you author documents in up to 30 languages (http://www.accentsoft.com).

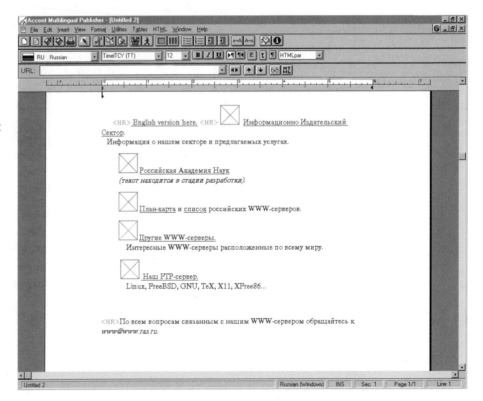

There is not yet one solution that works for all languages. The primary burden falls on the author to make things as easy as possible for his audience. If you plan to publish multilingual documents, you will have to locate editing and testing tools that provide prompts and controls in your native language, or become familiar with a language for which such tools exist. You should look for the following capabilities:

- an HTML editor with prompts and controls in your native language
- a Web browser that you can use to display and test your documents
- a complete font set (ideally a royalty-free font you can distribute)
- a Web server that can correctly deliver your HTML documents and accept data from a client in the language such as that returned by a Web client processing a form

One solution that fits these requirements is a suite of commercial applications for Microsoft Windows systems called Internet with an Accent. Included with this package are Multilingual Mosaic (Figure 18-2), a Web browser bundled with fonts for dozens of languages, and Multilingual Publisher, which is a WYSIWYG HTML editor that provides language and other essential functions such as floating keyboard character mapping panels (Figure 18-3).

Of course if you just need to work in your native language you might be able to get away with creating simple text documents using 8-bit character set encoding. These documents may contain up to 128 non-English characters by utilizing the second half of the ASCII character set (129–255). These codes are mapped to different characters by the operating system, if the user's Web browser is able to handle 8-bit ASCII. This works for some languages such as Russian (using the Cyrillic alphabet) and other European languages. However, Japanese and other languages with very large character sets rely primarily on two bytes to encode a character (16-bit encoding). So 8-bit encoding will not always work.

Figure 18-2
Russian Academy
of Sciences page
displayed with
Multilingual
Mosaic

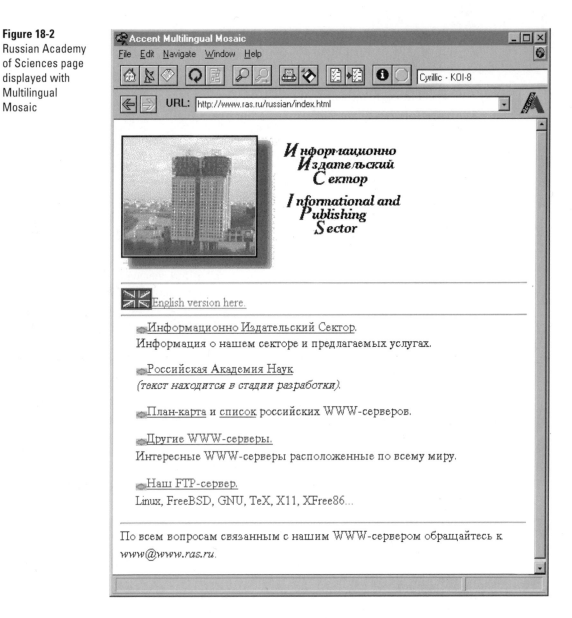

Figure 18-3
Multilingual
Publisher's Cyrillic
keyboard mapping
panel

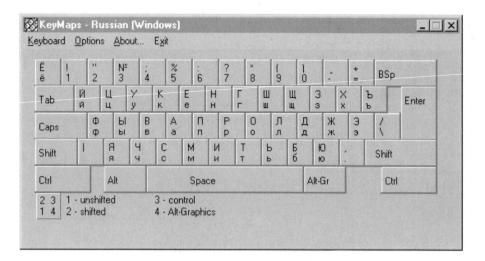

An HTML document can identify the character set it uses by passing a value called charset with the document; charset can be assigned any of the following values:

TABLE 18-1   charset CODE VALUES

Character Set Code	Contents
US-ASCII	US English/ASCII character set
ISO-8859-1	Latin/Western European languages (Albanian, Catalan, Danish, Dutch, English, Faeroese, Finnish, French, German, Galician, Irish, Icelandic, Italian, Norwegian, Portuguese, Spanish, Swedish)
ISO-8859-2	Latin/Central European language (Czech, German, Hungarian, Polish, Romanian, Croatian, Slovak, Slovene)
ISO-8859-3	Latin/Esperanto, Galician, Maltese, Turkish
ISO-8859-4	Latin/Estonian, Latvian, Lithuanian
ISO-8859-5	Latin/Cyrillic alphabet (Bulgarian, Byelorussian, Macedonian, Russian, Serbian, Ukrainian)
ISO-8859-6	Latin/Arabic alphabet
ISO-8859-7	Latin/Greek alphabet
ISO-8859-8	Latin/Hebrew alphabet
ISO-8859-9	Latin/Turkish
ISO-2022-JP	Japanese
ISO-2022-JP-2	Japanese
ISO-2022-KR	Korean
UNICODE-1-1	Universal
UNICODE-1-1-UTF-7	Universal
UNICODE-1-1-UTF-8	Universal

These character-set codes should be specified in the document using the <META> tag in the document header:

```
<META HTTP-EQUIV="Content-Type" CONTENT="text/html; charset="ISO-2022-
    JP">
```

8-bit character sets and matching fonts can solve many character-encoding problems, if the browser knows how to use this information. But the user's system must include a suitable Web browser and have the required fonts installed.

HTML 3 Internationalization

HTML 3 tackles document globalization with many new extensions. Virtually every HTML 3 tag supports a LANG attribute. This attribute is assigned a two-character code representing the language of the element contents. Table 18-2 lists codes that are part of ISO standard 639:1988.

TABLE 18-2   ISO-639:1988 LANGUAGE CODES

Code	Language	Code	Language	Code	Language
aa	Afar	ie	Interlingue	rn	Kirundi
ab	Abkhazian	ik	Inupiak	ro	Romanian
af	Afrikaans	in	Indonesian	ru	Russian
am	Amharic	is	Icelandic	rw	Kinyarwanda
ar	Arabic	it	Italian	sa	Sanskrit
as	Assamese	iw	Hebrew	sd	Sindhi
ay	Aymara	ja	Japanese	sg	Sangro
az	Azerbaijani	ji	Yiddish	sh	Serbo-Croatian
ba	Bashkir	jw	Javanese	si	Singhalese
be	Byelorussian	ka	Georgian	sk	Slovak
bg	Bulgarian	kk	Kazakh	sl	Slovenian
bh	Bihari	kl	Greenlandic	sm	Samoan
bi	Bislama	km	Cambodian	sn	Shona
bn	Bengali; Bangla	kn	Kannada	so	Somali
bo	Tibetan	ko	Korean	sq	Albanian
br	Breton	ks	Kashmiri	sr	Serbian
ca	Catalan	ku	Kurdish	ss	Siswati
co	Corsican	ky	Kirghiz	st	Sesotho
cs	Czech	la	Latin	su	Sudanese
cy	Welsh	ln	Lingala	sv	Swedish
da	Danish	lo	Laothian	sw	Swahili
de	German	lt	Lithuanian	ta	Tamil
dz	Bhutani	lv	Latvian, Lettish	te	Telugu
el	Greek	mg	Malagasy	tg	Tajik
en	English	mi	Maori	th	Thai
eo	Esperanto	mk	Macedonian	ti	Tigrinya
es	Spanish	ml	Malayalam	tk	Turkmen
et	Estonian	mn	Mongolian	tl	Tagalog

TABLE 18-2   ISO-639:1988 LANGUAGE CODES, CONT.

Code	Language	Code	Language	Code	Language
eu	Basque	mo	Moldavian	tn	Setswana
fa	Persian	mr	Marathi	to	Tonga
fi	Finnish	ms	Malay	tr	Turkish
fj	Fiji	mt	Maltese	ts	Tsonga
fo	Faeroese	my	Burmese	tt	Tatar
fr	French	na	Nauru	tw	Twi
fy	Frisian	ne	Nepali	uk	Ukrainian
ga	Irish	nl	Dutch	ur	Urdu
gd	Scots Gaelic	no	Norwegian	uz	Uzbek
gl	Galician	oc	Occitan	vi	Vietnamese
gn	Guarani	om	(Afan) Oromo	vo	Volapuk
gu	Gujarati	or	Oriya	wo	Wolof
ha	Hausa	pa	Punjabi	xh	Xhosa
hi	Hindi	pl	Polish	yo	Yoruba
hr	Croatian	ps	Pashto, Pushto	zh	Chinese
hu	Hungarian	pt	Portuguese	zu	Zulu
hy	Armenian	qu	Quechua		
ia	Interlingua	rm	Rhaeto-Romance		

A second global attribute related to multilingual document publishing is proposed for HTML 3. The DIR attribute specifies the direction that text should be displayed. This attribute would also apply to almost every HTML 3 element.

Since HTML 3 is a draft specification that is still under development, an intermediate version of HTML that addresses internationalization is in the works. HTML 2.1 includes the HTML 3 LANG attribute for tags. Like HTML 3, it also redefines the base character set for HTML to be UCS-2 (Unicode) instead of ISO 8859-1. UCS-2 is identical to ISO 10646 which is a superset of all ISO standard character sets. It is a 16-bit encoding scheme that supports up to 65535 different characters (for comparison, ASCII is an 8-bit system supporting 256 characters). Unicode supports most of the languages currently spoken in the world today. Other changes include bidirectional character entities, an ALIGN attribute for most tags (since justification is more of an issue in some languages than it is in English), and a <SPAN> element, which is placed around text that would not otherwise be tagged, but requires some type of justification. If this revision is successful, these changes will certainly become part of the HTML 3 specification as well.

Localization

What about localization issues? There are aspects of human communications other than language that differ from culture to culture, such as the way we specify dates, times, weights,zx and other measures. Gavin Nicol suggested some new HTML elements in his Web article entitled "The Multilingual World Wide Web" that would allow authors to at least identify the geographic region of the document and tag the content that would be variable in different localities. His tags are not yet in use but these or similar elements will undoubtedly be added to future versions of HTML and perhaps appear soon as international commerce starts to proliferate on the Web.

Nicol proposes a <LOCALE> element for the HTML document header. Here, the author would specify the originating location of the document. Precise values would have to be determined by a standards group but the tag usage might resemble the following:

```
<HEAD>
<TITLE>Multilingual HTML</TITLE>
<!— Locale for this document is Australia —>
<LOCALE>AU</LOCALE>
```

A multinational Web browser, if it also knew the locale of the person reading the document, might apply some localization rules to the contents of the <BODY> elements proposed. Those elements include <DATE>, <TIME>, <WEIGHT> (such as grams, kilograms, or pounds), <NUMBER> for a non-punctuated numeric value, and <CURRENCY>. An advanced browser might facilitate communications by not only reformatting the contents of these elements, but also by providing automatic conversion to a format familiar to the reader. A weight in pounds might be converted to kilograms by a Web browser in use in Britain, a currency might be converted from British Pounds Sterling to Yen for a reader in Japan (although this would be a risky proposition, due to fluctuating exchange rates!). But these are just proposed elements, not part of any standard. The final solution could look quite different from this, but it would have to solve some of the same problems.

The Web is not the only form of electronic communication that has had to cope with the problem of internationalization. Electronic mail systems have had to deal with these problems as well, and have done so in a piecemeal fashion with MIME extensions and ISO character sets. So far, the Web has inherited much of this patchwork, but piecemeal solutions will not hold the Web together. Unicode and HTML 3 together will go a long way toward making the World Wide Web truly global.

Contributing
to the Web

The Home Page

CHAPTER AT A GLANCE

- The difference between *designer* and *resource* pages
- Considerations for using graphics, and browser-specific markup
- Table 19-1: *Netscape and HTML 2/3 Element Equivalents*
- Ways of identifying the author

The World Wide Web ties together a wide variety of information resources in such a way that all public pages on the Web are essentially part of one large, dynamic document. With such an arrangement, it's easy to imagine how resources and sites can be difficult to find. Early on, Web authors developed a strategy of publishing one page in particular that is linked to other resources at their site. This page is called the home page. A home page can be a document about a subject, a product, a company, an idea, or about nothing at all. The main goal of the home page is to get the user's attention. Home pages can include logos, descriptions, hypertext links, and perhaps a search option. In hypertext theory, this page might be called the top level node. In HyperCard this is the home card. Whatever you call it, it is the most important piece of your publication as it is often the first document readers will see.

Essentially, there are two types of home pages on the Web: *designer pages* and *resource pages*. This chapter focuses on issues related to designer pages: Web documents whose purpose is to advertise, welcome, sell, or entertain. Designer pages sit atop a collection of disparate documents, providing links to resources at a Web site. Resource pages are views into a hypertext that covers a specific topic with the goal of educating the reader. While both types of pages share common problems, such as network bandwidth and use of HTML standard markup versus browser-specific tags, most issues related to creating resource pages are discussed in Chapter 20.

When you are building any Web page, there are two facts about the nature of the Web that you should keep in mind at all times. First, it is a hypermedia system. *Hypermedia* means multimedia hypertext. On the Web both text and graphics can serve as links. Target documents can be any type of document including sound, motion video, graphics, and of course HTML. This provides both infinite potential for linking to your own and other resources, and a variety of ways to construct links. Secondly, the Web is based on a structure-oriented language. Presentation issues take a back seat on the Web. Certainly there are some workarounds, but the real goal of any Web document should be communication, and structure dictates what a document is, not what it looks like. Viewed in that light, the lack of formatting elements actually enhances communication by maintaining a high level of platform independence for documents, rather than putting a damper on creativity as some would maintain. You cannot change these two characteristics of the Web, but let them be your guide, not your prison.

The first step to creating your own home page is planning. What is this page the introduction to? Will it be the main access point for a number of resources or more of a title page for one resource? Home pages can include search forms, tables, graphical image maps, essays, tables of contents, or any other structure you dream up. But don't pick a structure yet. Decide what the home page is the home of and start writing. Write an essay or create an outline. Just create a first draft without considering length or formatting issues. Say what you need to say. There are those who maintain that there is an optimal length for a Web page; if you let content be your guide you will always find the optimal length for your document, and come to realize that arbitrary rules such as "no more than 60 lines or three screens" are illogical.

If you find that you have created a substantial essay, say over 1000 words, you should construct a table of contents to it. You can make this table of contents the core of your home page, or you may choose to simply place it at the top of your document and make the whole essay a home page. But you aren't ready to create the home page yet.

Next, do some research. You probably have already found it necessary to do some as you developed your content. If you didn't, do some now. Find some related resources, some items that are complementary to your topic, and make a list. Readers like to explore at their own pace, and some may need more background material while others just want the latest information on a topic.

Developing a list of related resources allows you to build a bidirectional link to the Web (publishing your home page is the first direction).

Now, write your content. Expand your plan or use it as an outline. You may even have written enough during the planning stage that you are simply rewriting and revising this material. If so then this is the time to correct grammar and spelling errors. Make your prose concise. Readers tend to get impatient, especially when staring at a computer monitor. Use a hook to entice them to keep reading. The title should be catchy, descriptive, and unique. The first sentence should challenge the reader. It should be clear what this site is all about by the third or fourth sentence. If the page includes a list, make sure there is some recognizable order to the items. If the items need not occur in any particular order, then sort them alphabetically.

Now is the time to consider graphics. Graphics on a home page can be more than just a logo. You can use icons to group sets of related hypertext links or represent hypermedia links (such as using a frame or two from an animation, or a speaker icon to indicate audio). With image maps, you can build a graphical navigation tool describing your site's structure. But remember, there are users with different needs that you should keep in mind. Some users have slow network connections, and are going to be frustrated by a page overloaded with graphics. So consider carefully before using graphics that merely make a page more attractive such as background images and large logos. Use image types that can be interlaced, such as GIF or PNG. This allows the user to see a rendering of the image even before it is all loaded. They can then choose to allow the image to continue downloading or cease transfer. Other users might be using Web browsers that don't support graphics at all. Always include a description with each graphic using the ALT attribute for an <IMG> or the <CAPTION> element of the <FIG> tag. And provide a text-based alternative to any image maps.

Once you've rewritten your content draft and started incorporating useful images, it is time to construct a first draft of your page. Insert the tags for your images as empty tags in this draft, for example, <IMG SRC="logo.png" ALT="My Logo">. Read the text and eliminate any graphics that don't clarify a point or provide additional information. Let your table of contents bubble to the top; repeat visitors don't want to scroll down to the bottom of a long page to access a specific section. Reduce your home page to a brief description, outline, and a few graphics if you can. Your outline should be a condensed version of your site in any case, and if it is well constructed, it will lead readers where they and you want them to go (which is to the information they need, not necessarily always what you want them to see). Remember, anything you cut can still be used in a document linked to the home page.

Now plug in your graphics and navigational aids. Treat your home page as if it were a new piece of software you just installed. Make sure it is consistent and easy to navigate. Are you able to find everything you are looking for? Or are some items hidden or opaque due to a poorly worded link? Have others try out your still-private page. Does it make the impression you had hoped for? Consider their feedback and debug your page accordingly. It is, after all, like a software application and you want it to be useful and bug-free.

Steps in creating a home page:

- Plan your Web page(s)
- Write down your plan
- Research the Web for related information
- Rewrite and refine your text
- Plan any graphics carefully
- Test thoroughly
- Refine formatting and layout

Next, consider formatting. Although your options are limited, a home page should be as attractive as you can make it since it is the first impression a reader has of your resources. There are some specific markup elements that you can use such as bold and italics, the break tag <BR>, and the ALIGN attribute of the <IMG> tag that are supported by virtually every browser in use and are part of the official specifications of the two latest versions of HTML. Adding Netscape extensions is another option. Some 70% of the people navigating the Web are using a version of the Netscape browser. Some Netscape extensions are even supported by other browsers (Microsoft Internet Explorer, OmniWeb, etc.). But these tag extensions are not currently part of any browser-neutral standard. If you choose to use them, first investigate HTML 3 alternatives. For example, the <CENTER> element is Netscape only while the paragraph ALIGN attribute <P ALIGN=center> is part of the HTML 3 specification and is already widely supported. Table 19-1 lists some other Netscape extensions and HTML 2 or HTML 3 alternatives.

TABLE 19-1   NETSCAPE AND HTML 2/3 ELEMENT EQUIVALENTS

Netscape	HTML2/3
<CENTER><tag>	<tag ALIGN=center>
<BODY BGCOLOR=#0000ff TEXT=#ff0000>	<BODY BACKGROUND="blue.gif">
<NOBR>	
<FONT>	<BIG>, <SMALL>
<MAP>	<FIG> or <IMG ... ISMAP>

If you do choose to use Netscape extensions, test your Web page on a text-based browser such as Lynx, and on a graphical browser that does not support Netscape extensions, such as NCSA Mosaic. Are you satisfied with the way your home page looks on these browsers? Many users will see them this way.

You are almost finished with your home page. All that remains are some finishing touches that, although not required, will be useful to your audience. Keywords can help users locate your document in the maze of Web pages on the Internet. You can add keywords to the document header with a <META> element:

```
<META NAME="keywords" CONTENT="history, civil rights">
```

While the contents of the <META> element will not be displayed, Web search systems and some browsers will use them.

Next, make sure you identify yourself as the author of the document. You can do this in two ways (and probably should use both methods): by adding a <LINK> tag to the document header:

```
<LINK REV="made" HREF="mailto:author@email.address">
```

or by adding your name in an <ADDRESS> block at the bottom of the document:

```
<ADDRESS>
author name<BR>
author@email.address
</ADDRESS>
```

If you choose to place your name elsewhere, just remember that the <ADDRESS> block should be the last text block in an HTML document, so you will have to use a different element to tag your name. If this is an HTML 3 document, use the <AU> author tag. Structural tags are always preferable to random placement with nice formatting. What if the next big development in Web browsers includes a way to display a hypertext document's author and title before the full document is loaded?

There is no tag created specifically for notifying the user of the last time the page was updated. Some Web servers will send the last-modified date in a <META> element with your document. But this information is buried under a menu option in Netscape and not available at all through some Web browsers. So it should be part of your home page's content. Place it at the top or bottom of the document and offset it from the content both with vertical space and with some specific markup element such as italics.

Any other content you wish to use as a document header or footer is up to you. Develop your own style and use it consistently. A footer example appears at the top of the following page.

If your page is not only a published entity unto itself but also part of a group project or a corporation's Web presence, then you might wish to add a link on some or all of your pages back to the parent home page. But resist inappropriate requests such as large buttons that slow down your document loading, or complex footers that link to many different sites. You may need to work with the designer of the other page(s) to determine an appropriate "depth" to which an organization-wide header or footer would be required and useful. Basically, any table-of-contents page that sits atop of a set of pages and has sufficiently unique content as to be pointed to by others might be a candidate for such a footer. End nodes with no links except one that takes you back to a higher level in the hierarchy don't need to be burdened with excessive additional text or links.

```
┌──────────────────────────────────────────────────────────────────────────┐
│ ─           Netscape - [Virginia Tech University Libraries: Help]    ▼ ▲  │
├──────────────────────────────────────────────────────────────────────────┤
│ File   Edit   View   Go   Bookmarks   Options   Directory   Window   Help │
├──────────────────────────────────────────────────────────────────────────┤
│  ⇦o    o⇨    ⌂      ⊛      📇      ⇔o      🖨      🔍      ●               │
│  Back  Forward Home  Reload  Images  Open    Print   Find    Stop          │
├──────────────────────────────────────────────────────────────────────────┤
│ Location: http://www.lib.vt.edu/test/Help/Help.html                  ⬍ N  │
├──────────────────────────────────────────────────────────────────────────┤
│   Select this item if you want to learn more about the services available through the University │
│     Libraries.                                                             │
│   Hot Topics                                                               │
│       Select this item if you want to see the latest information, plus any information of a time-critial or │
│       time-sensitive nature.                                               │
│   Library Instruction Page                                                 │
│       Content in development.                                              │
│                                                                            │
│   ─────────────────────────────────────────────────────────────          │
│                                                                            │
│   University Libraries, Virginia Polytechnic Institute and State University │
│   Send Suggestions or Comments to webmaster@www.lib.vt.edu                 │
│   Last updated: October 20, 1995                                           │
│   URL: http://www.lib.vt.edu/Help/Help.html                               │
└──────────────────────────────────────────────────────────────────────────┘
```

The finishing touches:

- Add keywords and author information

- Add footers

- Review graphics for size and format

- Use content as links

- Select simple filenames when possible

Graphics also might need a bit of touching up. Keep in mind that all logos and icons should be GIF format, if possible. GIF is still the most widely supported graphics format on the Web. Most logos and small icons can be reduced to 256 colors, which not only makes it possible to save them as GIF images, but also makes them smaller. If you create a PNG or GIF image that should have a transparent background, make sure the color(s) you intend to be transparent are in fact displayed that way. If the item is a logo, where some surrounding area is transparent, you may want to select a gray (gray is #eeeeee in RGB) before making the area transparent. If you do this, the few browsers that cannot handle transparent images may still display the image the way you intend if the user has configured it to use gray as the window background color. If you have a number of images on your page that you cannot bear to part with, consider creating thumbnail versions that point to the full-size images. Software such as Adobe Photoshop can easily scale an image to a thumbnail size of generally less than 100 pixels on a side. The smaller the image, the smaller the file and the quicker it will load.

Hypertext links should be reviewed as well, before publication. Anchor styles are as varied as pages, but there are some basic practices that will improve your page. Avoid links that say "click here," or any other phrase that specifies the action rather than describes the content pointed to. People who use hypertext systems know that certain words or phrases are links. Browsers give clues in the form of underlined, colored, or framed text for anchors. So instead of such action-oriented phrases, use part of the description or annotation for the target of the link as the text of the hypertext link:

instead of:

click here to find out more about ecotourism.

use

more information about ecotourism is available.

or make the word a link in context:

Ecotourism motivates third world countries to preserve endangered forest.

Don't include any punctuation in the link (such as the period at the end of a line) unless it is an essential part of the text. Most browsers underline links, and underlining tends to obscure this punctuation. Place punctuation after the anchor end tag </A>.

Finally, save your home page with a filename of a reasonable length. If possible, arrange with your Web server software administrator to have a default name established for home pages. This might be default.html or index.html. When a default page is configured, the user need only specify the server name and directory of your home page and the server will send them the appropriate document. Don't use special characters such as ~, #, forward or backward slashes, or spaces in the filename. These can be at the least difficult to type and in some cases make your home page inaccessible to some users since the URL might not be acceptable to the user's Web browser.

Remember that once you get past the bells and whistles, a home page is still a document, just like a letter, article, or book. It is a writing project, and half the battle of writing is organization. Plan, organize, and rewrite your page. Don't just throw something together and excuse its incompleteness and dead-end links with the phrase "under construction." Everyone realizes the Web is a collection of living documents, constantly changing. When a page is ready to publish, some of the content to which it points should be ready also. The Web is one giant Web page that is always under construction. Construct your piece of it well.

20

Building Hypertext Content on the Web

CHAPTER AT A GLANCE

- Hypertext views and how to create them with HTML
- Presentation styles for hypertexts
- Types of links available for HTML hypertexts

Hypertext systems are constructed of links and nodes. Links are segments of text that the user can select. Graphics can also serve as hypertext links. Graphical links are often referred to as buttons. Buttons use icons or thumbnail images to represent the data to which they point, but otherwise are functionally identical to text-based links. On the Web links are created with HTML anchor tags. Nodes are the targets of hypertext links. Nodes on the World Wide Web can be any document type that can be stored on a computer. Many nodes are HTML documents, or document fragments (specific locations within HTML documents). Other node types include image files, motion video, sound, text files, gateway scripts that interact with database engines, and even telnet sessions.

So far we've focused on creating node documents. But node documents can themselves be collections of links and this can occur recursively, so that many documents link to many other documents until finally a linkless fragment is reached. These complex interconnected documents can be human or machine generated. The links between them are different depending on who or what created them. Machine-generated links tend to be navigational aids such as previous and next buttons when browsing a set of database records returned by a gateway, automatically generated contents and index documents, and history lists that keep track of where you've been. Human-created links include navigational aids, but humans also build links emphasizing different paths through the hypertext such as definitions, overviews, footnotes, commentaries, and links to other resources on the Web covering similar topics.

Many useful documents on the Web are flat text end nodes. But a flat document is pointed to by the Web rather than serving as an integral part of it. Readers are better served by a hypertext version of a document than a flat, paper-like version. Not only can hypertext provide beginners with additional information, it can also provide more-knowledgeable readers with clues to the essential portions of the document they should read for an understanding of the topic. Hypertext also allows linkage to nontextual data such as images, motion graphics, and audio files. There are ways to structure hypertexts so that the reader gets some idea of the size of a collection of information, without having to quote it in bytes.

The structures presented below could be applied to home pages as well as content pages. But home pages are more like billboards or customized license plates than overviews or structural representations of hypertext. These structures are better suited for information that adheres to the three golden rules of hypertext (Shneiderman, 1989):

- a large collection of information that is organized into many fragments
- some fragments relate to each other
- the user needs only one or a few fragments at a time

The collection of information should ideally cover a finite topic (unless you are planning to create a hypertext encyclopedia). Each fragment could consist of a chapter not unlike a book chapter, an article, a paragraph, a footnote, a chart or graph, an image, a reference, or a multimedia entity such as an audio or video clip. Each fragment should be addressable with a hypertext link. This means the item should have a URL of its own or be a named anchor within a document that has a URL (using the <A NAME> or <tag ID> elements).

This is not an exhaustive list of all the possible structures. It does cover many of the hypertext styles in use in other hypertext systems such as HyperCard or Microsoft Windows Help. Some of these complex, specialized systems cannot be readily simulated with HTML. But the Web is flexible enough that many of the structures presented here can be replicated, granted with a little more work than would be required with other hypertext systems. But the benefits of publishing structured collections of addressable information fragments to a worldwide network far outweigh the minor sacrifices required to port a hypertext from some other, more author-friendly system. After all, no other hypertext system currently in existence can connect you to millions of documents on millions of computers, serve as an interface to hundreds of library catalogs, access thousands of relational and full-text databases, large collections of multimedia journals, newspapers and other publications, and even let you peer into a salt water aquarium in California or check in on the inhabitants of an office in Finland.

Application Structures

MENU

A menu is a set of links presented as a list of options, one per line. A variation on this would be an annotated menu, with descriptive text accompanying, but not necessarily part of, each link. HTML unordered <UL> and ordered <OL> lists can be used to create menus (avoid <MENU> or <DIR> since they will go away in HTML 3). Annotated menus can be created with unordered or ordered lists combined with descriptive paragraphs for each list item, or with a definition list <DL>. With definition lists, the defined term <DT> would serve as the hypertext link and the definition <DD> as the annotation.

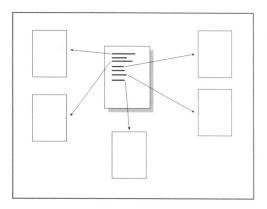

FISHEYE VIEW

A fisheye view is a specialized menu structure. An overview of a collection of documents is visible, with the nearest fragments displayed in the most detail, and other fragments compressed. This is like an outline or table-of-contents structure, but only the current (nearest) chapter is expanded to its full complexity. Other chapters are merely represented by their numeric designation and title. Icons and hypertext links are used to inform the reader that chapters can be expanded in the hierarchical view. In order to create this structure, multiple versions of the hierarchy have to be maintained to achieve the selective expanding effect:

HTML fragment from expand_ch3.html:

```
<UL>
<LI><A HREF="expand_ch1.html">Chapter 1</A>
<LI><A HREF="expand_ch2.html">Chapter 2</A>
<LI>Chapter 3
<UL>
 <LI>header tags
 <LI>the body tag
</UL>
</UL>
```

HTML fragment from expand_ch1.html:

```
<UL>
<LI>Chapter 1
<UL>
 <LI>Web browsers
 <LI>Netscape
</UL>
<LI><A HREF="expand_ch2.html">Chapter 2</A>
<LI><A HREF="expand_ch3.html">Chapter 3</A>
</UL>
```

For large, complex structures (especially those that change frequently) a better solution would be to use a script to generate the views.

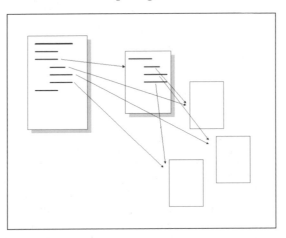

HIERARCHICAL VIEW

A hierarchical view is similar to a fisheye view. However, a detailed outline-like overview is provided for the entire fragment collection, with the structure of both the entire collection and each subsection immediately visible. Each item listed in the hierarchy is instantly accessible from a hypertext link associated with the listing. The main difference from a fisheye view is that all subsections of the structure are fully expanded in the document. This type of structure is created with nested lists.

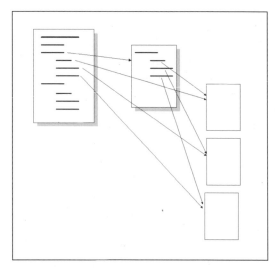

NETWORKS

Networks, sometimes referred to as webs, are highly interconnected fragments of text. The structure is based purely on semantic relationships and is often not discernible from any other level. The best practice for managing such a structure is containment, or framing the fragments. The author is responsible for imposing a boundary between a collection of linked fragments and external collections of fragments. The boundary should be based on a commonality among the fragments that is not strongly shared by external documents. An example of a framed document set would be a collection of documents on the mineral content of Martian soil that is a subset of a larger collection of materials on the soil composition of terrestrial planets. Networks can be represented by graphical diagrams with related topics displayed as interconnecting lines and proximity to one another, and unrelated topics displayed disconnected and far from one another. The number of links between a set of nodes often makes this impractical. Think of networks on the Web as collections of HTML documents with anchors embedded within the text of paragraphs that refer the documents to each other.

INDEX

It could be said that an index is a special case of a menu, but indexes require more and different types of planning. An index of a collection of fragments defining terms might be organized in alphabetical order. Indexes might often include cross links and "see-also" references, while these would not usually be required in menu structures. Another important issue related to indexes is that each fragment should be addressable since you or other authors may wish to refer a reader to a specific term in the index from another document. Indexes can be constructed with lists, each item both a named anchor (using <A NAME=> or the HTML 3 ID attribute) that could be targeted by other links and a hypertext link to the actual definition of the term.

Presentation Styles

Hypertext styles are applied to the elements of a collection of hypertexts. Rather than providing an overall view of a set of related fragments, hypertext styles are methods of presentation that visually and semantically tie a set of fragments together. They include sequences of document nodes, use of graphics, and the general look and feel of hypertext links and navigation aids.

TUTORIAL

A tutorial style presents information in a known to unknown manner. The reader is presented with obvious hints leading them on a particular path. Each subsequent node builds on the knowledge the reader obtained from previous fragments. A tutorial need not be single-threaded, that is there can be more than one path for a reader. Different paths might address the needs of different classes of readers; beginners might follow a different path than people with some experience in the subject being discussed. Hierarchical structures presented at the beginning of the tutorial as well as textual hints periodically reminding readers of different paths guide differently skilled readers down the correct path for them.

SLIDE SHOW

A slide show is a sequential method of presenting a topic. There are generally few, if any, links in the body of the slide. Instead, nodes presenting a specific topic are presented followed by a few nonobtrusive graphical navigation aids such as back and forward buttons.

TABLE OF CONTENTS

A table of contents in hypertext is virtually identical to that found in a book. Each node that presents a discrete concept is represented by a link. Items pointed to by the table of contents usually have a similar appearance and share some navigational aids in common such as buttons to move sequentially through the hypertext or to access the table of contents, a glossary, or an index. But these fragments also link to one another as needed, unlike a slide show, so many paths are available to the reader. A table of contents is an excellent way to tell the reader how much material, or how many nodes, are contained within the hypertext.

INTERACTIVE TOUR

An interactive tour might resemble a slide show, but it utilizes multimedia such as audio and video clips to present a topic. It also frequently invites the reader to interact with the system. The reader can provide input, such as a list of interests, and the system either constructs a unique course through the hypertext or presents one of several HTML documents already existing that closely matches the user's interests. This consists of a set of hypertext links pointing to relevant nodes, with multimedia nodes consistently represented by graphical links. The recommended course through the hypertext would also be indicated with some type of hypertext links.

CHRONOLOGICAL PRESENTATION

A hypertext might present a collection of information nodes in chronological order. Chronological presentations might be presented like a story, or a sequence of events that happened over a course of days, months, or years as in an historical narrative. Nodes can also be organized according to the natural sequence of events in a system, such as the life cycle of a plant or animal.

GEOGRAPHICAL PRESENTATION

Information can be presented simulating a real or virtual geographical organization. A hypertext zoo might provide hypertext links that present animal exhibits in the same order that a tourist would encounter them if they actually went to the zoo in person. Virtual geographies might represent a hypertext using a user-clickable diagram (image map) or a three-dimensional walk-in database represented by a series of image nodes or by linking to a virtual reality node (such as VRML).

TYPES OF LINKS

Link types are directly determined by the structure and style of a hypertext. For example, links in a table of contents would likely be text-based since that is what constitutes the bulk of material in such a document. Many reusable navigational aids are graphical because the user only has to learn once how they work. Footnotes, cross-references, quotes, sticky notes, indexes, and commentaries are all examples of link types that can be represented with HTML anchors targeting other nodes or fragments. HTML 3 includes markup elements such as <NOTE>, <Q>, and <FN> for tagging these types of links.

Web documents endure only when the information they provide is arranged in a structured, easily navigable fashion. The way to attract and retain interest in a hypertext has more to do with its structure and content than with whether it uses some novel markup technique to outdo other sites. Presentation issues such as logos, icons, and the use of color should be considered as part of the authoring process. A slick collection of documents that has few nodes with any real content, or has no obvious structure or path will ultimately fail. To build a successful Web site, construct your hypertext around content-rich nodes, use graphics consistently and sparingly, and test your structure.

21

Touring
Hypertexts

CHAPTER AT A GLANCE

- Differences between instructional hypertexts and home pages
- How to incorporate Netscape markup without sacrificing platform independence

Hypertexts are more than just links and HTML markup. As Chapter 20 demonstrated, there are a number of ways in which collections of documents can be organized within a hypertext system. The linear mode of communication that books and magazine articles are locked into by virtue of their presentation medium is optional on the Web. Hierarchies and networks dominate the landscape where they are used to tie home pages, tutorials, manuals, and many other collections of documents together.

We will consider two separate hypertext examples in some detail. The first example is a slide show designed to introduce users to HTML. It was the precursor to this text and is still in use today. As new versions and dialects of HTML arise, it can easily be expanded to discuss and demonstrate these new sets of elements. We'll look at several separate pages from this document that illustrate its dual nature as a hierarchical structure for advanced users and a linear slide show for instructing individuals new to HTML markup.

The second example illustrates an organization's home page, in this case the home page of the University Libraries of Virginia Tech. This page includes an innovative fish-eye view providing the user with a myriad of navigation options, while maintaining a hierarchical structure that is easy to learn and navigate. Rather than instructing users on a specific topic, it guides them to hundreds of Internet resources, as well as presenting information, database interfaces, and request forms for accessing various library services.

Example 1: An Instructional Hypertext

Figure 21-1 shows an instructional hypertext, an online HTML tutorial.

Figure 21-1 The first page of an online HTML training document

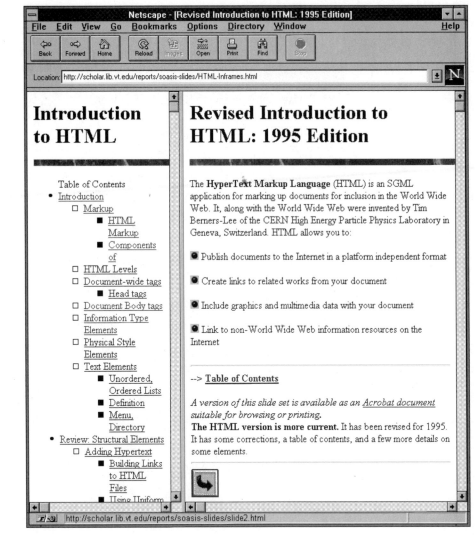

Source for the page displayed in Figure 21-1:

```
<HTML>
<HEAD>
<TITLE>Revised Introduction to HTML: 1995 Edition</TITLE>
<LINK REV="made" HREF="mailto:jpowell@vt.edu">
</HEAD>
<FRAMESET COLS="35%, 65%">
<FRAME SRC="slides-contents.html" NAME="contents" TARGET="pages">
<FRAME SRC="slide1.html" NAME="pages">
</FRAMESET>
<NOFRAMES>
<!— HTML course for Spinning the World Wide Web, Cincinati, Ohio September 19-2
0, 1994 SOASIS —>
<!— keywords: HTML, html, hypertext, Hypertext Markup Language —>
<!— keywords: markup, hmtl version 2, html version 3, netscape —>
<!— keywords: hypermedia, graphics, jpeg, gif, world wide web, www —->
<BODY>
<H1>Revised Introduction to HTML: 1995 Edition
</H1>
<IMG SRC="BlueMarbleLine.gif"><P>
The <B>HyperText Markup Language</B> (HTML) is an SGML application for marking u
p documents for inclusion in the World Wide Web. It, along with the World Wide
Web were invented by Tim Berners-Lee of the CERN High Energy Particle Physics La
boratory in Geneva, Switzerland. HTML allows you to:
<P>
<IMG SRC="blueball.gif" align="bottom">
Publish documents to the Internet in a platform independent format<P>
<P>
<IMG SRC="blueball.gif" align="bottom">
Create links to related works from your document<P>
<P>
<IMG SRC="blueball.gif" align="bottom">
Include graphics and multimedia data with your document<P>
<P>
<IMG SRC="blueball.gif" align="bottom">
Link to non-World Wide Web information resources on the Internet<P>
<P>
<HR>
<B>—&gt; <A HREF="slides-contents.html">Table of Contents</A></B>
<P>
```

```
<I>A version of this slide set is available as an <A HREF="http://scholar.lib.vt
.edu/reports/html-int.pdf">Acrobat document</A> suitable for browsing or printin
g.</I><BR> <B>The HTML version is more current.</B> It has been revised for 19
95. It has some corrections, a table of contents, and a few more details on some
 elements.
<HR>
<A HREF="slide2.html"><IMG SRC="forward.gif" ALT="Next Slide"></A>
<ADDRESS><A HREF="mailto:jpowell@scholar.lib.vt.edu>James Powell</A><BR>
Scholarly Communications Project, University Libraries<BR>
Virginia Polytechnic Institute and State University<BR>
jpowell@scholar.lib.vt.edu</ADDRESS>
</NOFRAMES>
</HTML>
```

The home page (Figure 21-1) is presented in different ways to different users. Users with a Netscape 2.0 or compatible browser see a document with two frames. The left frame contains an outline of the slide set. This outline is a hierarchical view of the hypertext. Indentation indicates that a topic is a subtopic of the item above it in the list. The right-hand side of the screen contains the first slide in the series. The slides were designed to fit one browser screen whenever possible. Some slides are longer due to the nature of the topic covered but even the longest slide is no more than two screen lengths. Users can force more of the slide to fit on the screen by reducing the size of the hierarchical view frame.

The contents of the outline frame are brief titles for the slides. The level of indentation was kept to a minimum both because there was no need for additional depth in this particular hierarchy and to keep the titles from being indented so far that they wrap excessively and become unreadable. A few slides contain links to external documents, such as pages that further illustrate a particular markup element. These documents are not listed in the hierarchical view.

In addition to the hierarchical view presented in the left frame, arrows are provided at the bottom of each screen for users who are truly new to the topic and wish to follow the slide set in a linear fashion. The user can navigate through the slide set by selecting the right arrow icon, or access pages directly from the outline by selecting the topic from the list. The contents of the right frame are replaced each time a new slide is loaded, but the outline frame remains constant. The first slide uses a right-angled arrow to indicate that it is the starting point. This is not necessary but it helps users differentiate it from other slides.

Users without frames-capable browsers see the first slide from the slide show (Figure 21-2). The contents of this slide have been pasted into the frames-based version between the <NOFRAMES> element to achieve this effect. This makes extra work for the maintainer since any changes to the introductory slide must be replicated in the frames document as well. But it would be unaccept-

Figure 21-2 The HTML document as displayed by a browser without frame support

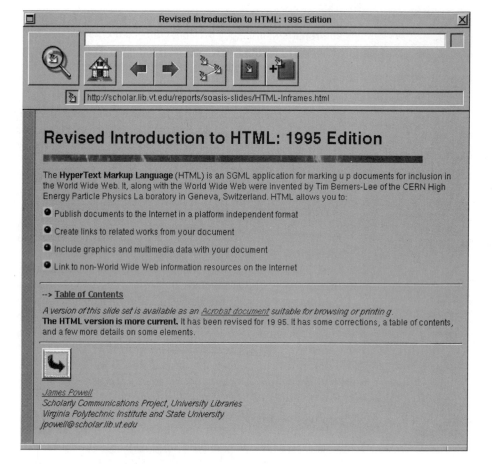

able to present an empty, unviewable document or a document encouraging the user to switch browsers. Frames tremendously enhance navigation of this hypertext but are not indispensable. This leaves the choice of browsers up to the user and imposes only a small penalty if they choose some other browser.

Each slide in the set describes a basic concept in HTML (Figure 21-3). Character markup is used sparingly. Each page ends with a graphical navigation icon that leads to the next page in the set. One drawback of the frames-based version is that titles are invisible to the user. A framed document keeps the title of the starting document when a user navigates through a set of documents within a frame. So each slide also contains the title as a level 1 header within the body of the document.

The document occasionally points to external resources (Figure 21-4) but this was kept to a minimum in order to reduce maintenance requirements. This page contains the source for an HTML form and points to the actual live form in order to demonstrate how the markup elements translate into results.

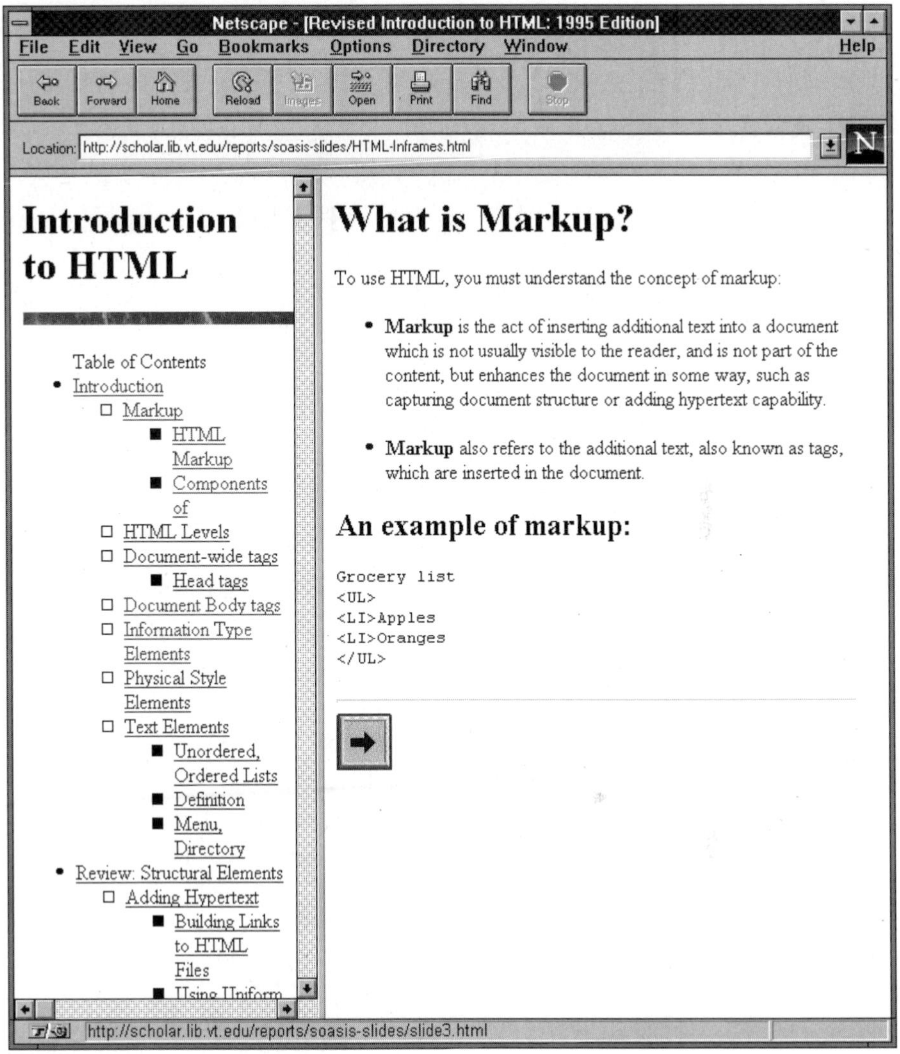

Figure 21-3
Another slide in the
set. Notice how the
right frame
changes but the
left frame still dis-
plays the document
outline.

Figure 21-4 A slide with a hypertext link to an external resource demonstrating forms

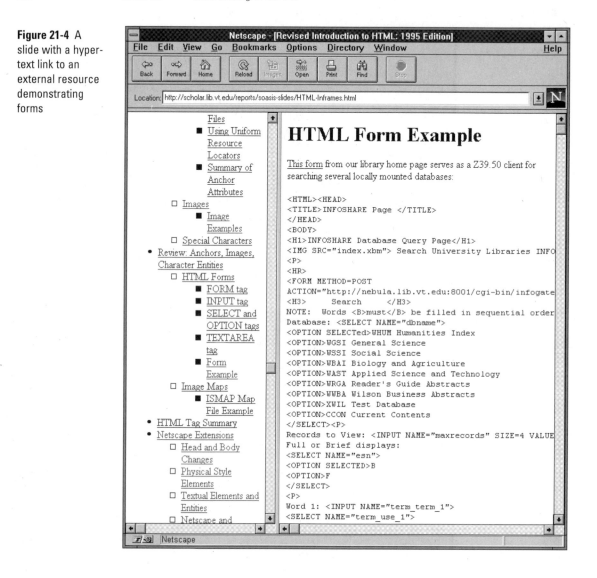

While this hypertext is enhanced with Netscape frames extensions, the slides are otherwise devoid of Netscape-specific markup. The only exceptions to this rule are the handful of slides that cover Netscape HTML extensions (Figure 21-5). By necessity, these slides both describe these markup elements and utilize them in examples. Each document containing Netscape extensions includes "Netscape" as part of its title to warn users immediately of their content. Netscape extensions in general are not recommended for a general audience where as many as 35 percent of the readers will be using a browser other than Navigator. They would be appropriate if the audience were members of an organization that has standardized on the Netscape Navigator browser.

Content does not have to be static. Several of the slides refer to Netscape-specific element attributes that require an RGB color value. These slides include links to a page that is not exclusively a member of this hypertext, the RGB Color

Figure 21-5
Netscape markup is used sparingly. Here it is used to demonstrate Netscape extensions.

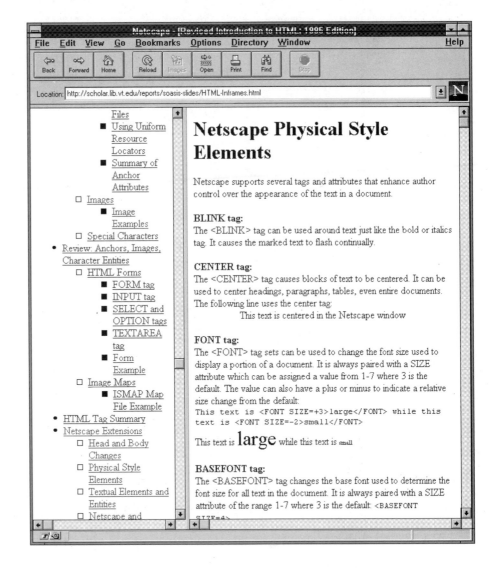

Guide (Figure 21-6). This page points to a CGI (Common Gateway Interface) script, which generates a demonstration page using the color selected by the user. A table of preset colors is present plus the user is given the option to enter an RGB sequence at the bottom of the screen, assuming they will have read the

Figure 21-6 Live content in the form of a CGI-based color picker

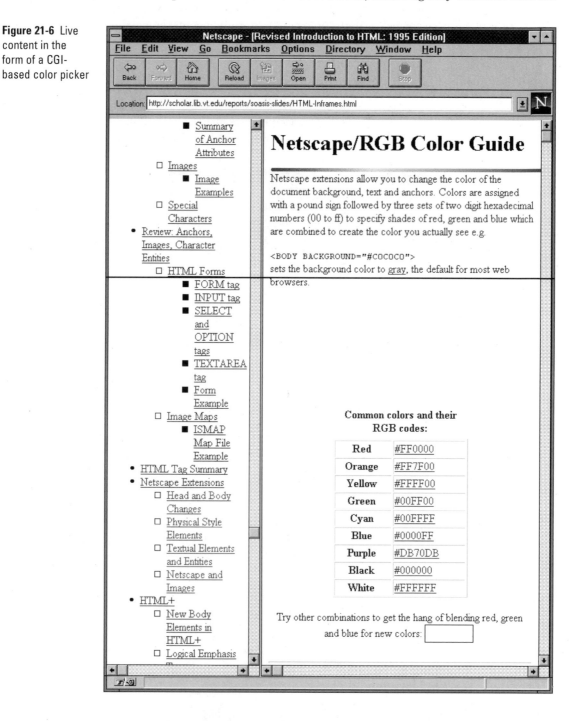

slide and mastered this simple color coding scheme. In this way the hypertext not only instructs the user but functions as a test bed for developing their own HTML documents.

Another way in which the document not only trains but serves as a reference document for developers is through its hypertext references page (Figure 21-7). Each document used to develop this training guide is noted on this page. Each annotation includes both a hypertext link to the original document and the URL to the document as part of the text.

Realizing that some users prefer to print or capture a local copy of a document for future reference, the hypertext includes a link on the introductory page to an Acrobat version of the entire slide set (Figure 21-8). Since Acrobat is also a hypertext document system, it includes a hypertext table of contents. The title page of the Acrobat file also includes a URL-based hypertext link pointing to this HTML hypertext so the user can check for revised versions. Acrobat supports navigating URL links via its WebLink plug-in (see Chapter 35).

Figure 21-7
References serve as a jump point for further study.

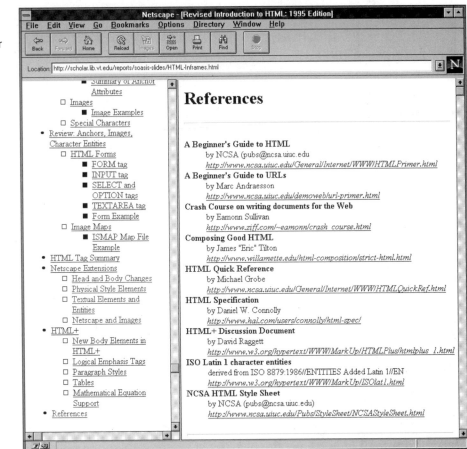

Figure 21-8 An
Acrobat version of
the document is
available for those
wishing a local
copy for further
review or printing.

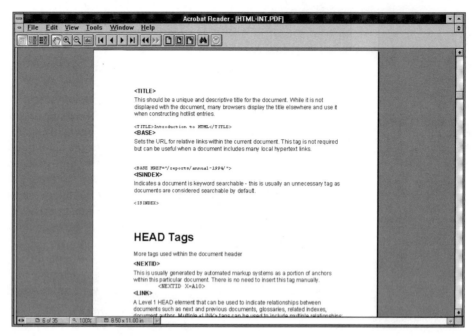

Example 2: An Organization's Home Pages

Figure 21-9 shows an example of a set of highly structured hierarchical home pages for an organization.

Figure 21-9 Home page of the Univeristy Libraries of Virginia Tech

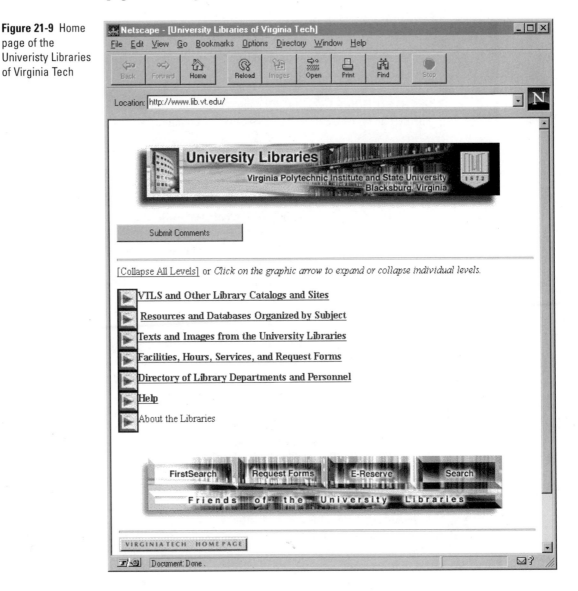

Source for the page displayed in Figure 21-9:

```
<HTML>
   <HEAD><TITLE>University Libraries of Virginia Tech</TITLE>
<BASE HREF = http://www.lib.vt.edu/homepage.html>
</HEAD>
<BODY bgcolor="#FFFFFF">
<CENTER>
<IMG SRC="/images/logo-bar3b.gif" alt="University Libraries Logo Bar">
</CENTER>
<BR>
<FORM ACTION = "/cgi-bin/ulComments.cgi" METHOD = "POST">
<INPUT TYPE = SUBMIT VALUE = "Submit Comments"></FORM>
<HR>
<A NAME = "top"></A>
<A HREF = "/cgi-bin/exp3?file=HOMEPAGE">[Collapse All Levels]</A> <!—<A
HREF = "/cgi-bin/exp3?all">[Expand All Levels]</A>—> or <EM>Click on the
graphic arrow to expand or collapse individual levels.</EM><BR>
<DL><DT><A HREF = "/cgi-bin/exp3?file=HOMEPAGE&levels=1#top"><IMG SRC =
"/images/expand.gif" ALT = "Click to expand header" ALIGN = MIDDLE></A><A
HREF = "/VTLS/VTLS.html"><B>VTLS and Other Library Catalogs and
Sites</B></A><BR><DT><A HREF = "/cgi-
bin/exp3?file=HOMEPAGE&levels=2#top"><IMG SRC = "/images/expand.gif" ALT =
"Click to expand header" ALIGN = MIDDLE></A> <A NAME = "Resources"><A
HREF = "/Resources/Resources.html"><B>Resources and Databases Organized by
Subject</B></A></A><BR><DT><A HREF = "/cgi-
bin/exp3?file=HOMEPAGE&levels=3#top"><IMG SRC = "/images/expand.gif" ALT =
"Click to expand header" ALIGN = MIDDLE></A><A HREF =
"/Texts_And_Images/Texts_And_Images.html"><B>Texts and Images from the
University Libraries</B></A><BR><DT><A HREF = "/cgi-
bin/exp3?file=HOMEPAGE&levels=4#top"><IMG SRC = "/images/expand.gif" ALT =
"Click to expand header" ALIGN = MIDDLE></A><A HREF =
"/Facilities/Facilities.html"><B>Facilities, Hours, Services, and Request
Forms</B></A><BR><DT><A HREF = "/cgi-
bin/exp3?file=HOMEPAGE&levels=5#top"><IMG SRC = "/images/expand.gif" ALT =
"Click to expand header" ALIGN = MIDDLE></A><A HREF =
"/Directory/Directory.html"><B>Directory of Library Departments and
Personnel</B></A><BR><DT><A HREF = "/cgi-
bin/exp3?file=HOMEPAGE&levels=6#top"><IMG SRC = "/images/expand.gif" ALT =
"Click to expand header" ALIGN = MIDDLE></A><A HREF =
"/Help/Help.html"><B>Help</B></A><BR><DT><A HREF = "/cgi-
bin/exp3?file=HOMEPAGE&levels=7#top"><IMG SRC = "/images/expand.gif" ALT =
"Click to expand header" ALIGN = MIDDLE></A>About the Libraries<BR><BR>
<CENTER>
<A HREF = "/cgi-bin/imagemap/Maps/Home.map">
<IMG SRC="/images/newmenubar.gif" ISMAP BORDER=0></A>
```

```
</CENTER>
<HR>
<A HREF="http://www.vt.edu"><IMG size=0 SRC="/images/HPButton.gif" border=0
alt="Go to Virginia Tech Home Page"></A>
<P>
University Libraries, Virginia Tech<BR>
Send Suggestions or Comments to <a
href="mailto:webmaster@www.lib.vt.edu">webmaster@www.lib.vt.edu</A><BR>
Last updated: Jan 30, 1996
URL: <CITE>http://www.lib.vt.edu/</CITE><BR>
</BODY>
</HTML>

<!—$Id: homepage.html,v 1.42 1996/02/16 19:33:42 balin Exp $—>
</BODY></HTML>
```

The library home page (Figure 21-9) is an entry point for campus-based users as well as users accessing library services over the Internet from around the world. Among the issues considered in its design were structure, content, length, size and number of images, enhanced navigation, and appearance. Unlike the instructional page above, we decided early on that some Netscape elements for improving the appearance would be allowed on the home page since it was desirable to make a good impression on new users. Whenever possible, we elected to use HTML 3 markup to achieve a particular "look" when both HTML 3 and Netscape extensions would provide a similar effect and be rendered by Netscape and other browsers. The pages were also extensively tested on non-Netscape browsers to ensure that the document structure and usability were not impacted when Netscape/HTML 3 elements were ignored. Among the browsers utilized for testing were Mosaic 2.0, OmniWeb 1.0, and Lynx.

The page starts off with a set of links to the second level of pages (Figure 21-10) that provide access to many of the library's electronic resources and holdings. In order to maintain page brevity, we elected to implement a fish-eye view of the page. Each topic could be expanded before visiting. The expanded page presents an alternate version of the home page with annotations displayed for the topic the user selected for expansion. Each topic listing actually consists of two hypertext links. The first link, the right pointing arrow, expands the topic. The title of the category targets the actual second-level page containing the category resource listing.

The second-level pages are structured documents grouping resources by categories. These categories are presented as links on the library home page when a topic is expanded. This provides yet another way for the user to access a resource quickly once they have learned the site's overall structure. If a user is confused by these options, they can simply select the [*Collapse All Levels*] link to revert the home page to its initial state. Finally, the home page includes a set

Figure 21-10
More of the home page demonstrating the fish-eye view feature that a user may access by selecting the arrow buttons next to a section title.

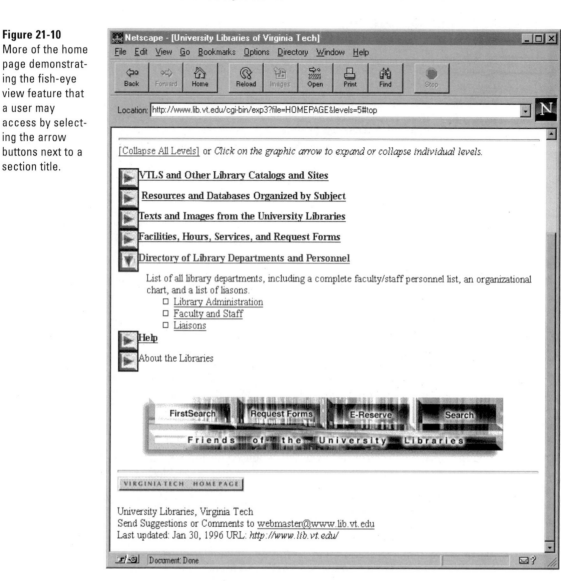

of quick-access buttons to selected resources and services that were considered important enough to be promoted to the top level of the hierarchy. Some buttons will remain on the page while others might rotate as a new resource takes its permanent home elsewhere in the hypertext.

Before we consider the second-level page, let's consider briefly the mechanism for presenting the fish-eye view. Rather than use a set of alternate home pages to implement the selected expansion option, a script was developed that loads and parses the fully expanded library page and automatically conceals the annotations. Each expansion button passes its state (expanded or contracted) to the processing script when selected, so the script can return a page matching the previous state and display the new state for the selected category. This option is not for every implementation. It requires a server that can serve a CGI script as a home or default page. Many Web servers cannot do this. It also places additional demands on the server since the processing script has to be run each time the home page is requested. A set of alternate home pages would have been quicker but the script solution eliminated the time-consuming mainte-nance that would have introduced, since these pages could change frequently.

Each category listed on the main page has its own page (Figure 21-11). These second-level pages include a link back to the home page as well as quick access to other category pages at this level. Each category has a tab item directly under the page's logo bar. The current page is the tab raised to the top level. Other tabs can be selected to access other pages since the entire tab bar is an image map.

Figure 21-11
A second-level page featuring an image map tab bar for quick access to other pages at this level

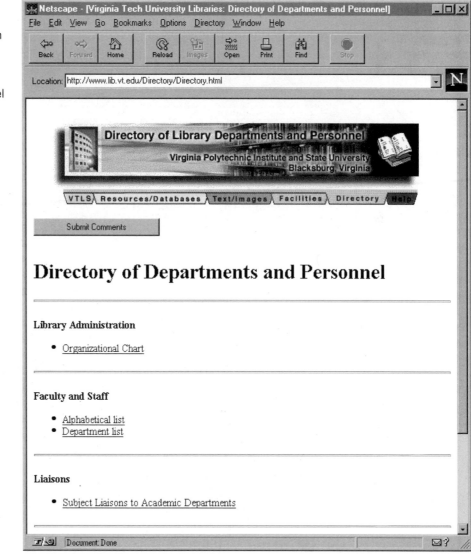

Quick access to other pages at the same level allows the user to change course if they fail to find the resource they are looking for on the current page.

Finally, users sometimes enter URLs incorrectly when attempting to access a page from memory or from a printed e-mail message. So when a user requests a nonexistent URL on the server, a specially designed page is returned that will assist most users in getting back on course. The page consists of four frames. The top frame, or banner, notifies the user that there was an error in the URL they requested. It contains a ticker-tape-style Java applet. The left frame describes the page they have been presented, a graphical hierarchical view of the library home pages. The right frame contains this graphical structure as an image map for quick access to major portions of the hypertext. The bottom frame, or ledge, informs the user of the URL of the page as well as the organization and individual responsible for its maintenance (Figure 21-12).

Figure 21-12 A page returned when an error occurs. This document makes excellent use of frames and ledges.

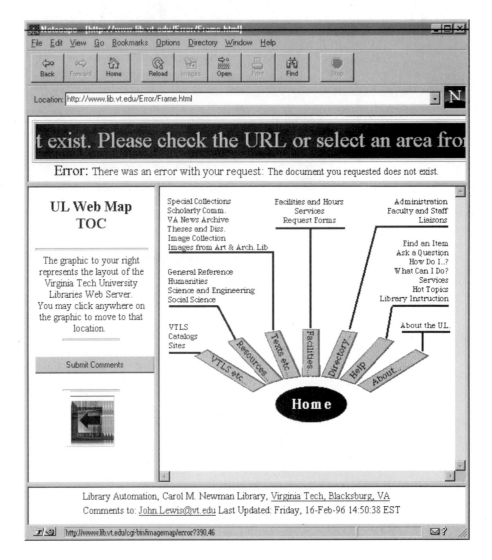

Source for the page displayed in Figure 21-12:

```
<FRAMESET ROWS = "100,*,60">
<FRAME SRC = "ULWebMap.frame.header.html" scrolling = "no" MARGINHEIGHT
= 5 MARGINWIDTH = 5>
<FRAMESET COLS = "200, *">
        <FRAME SRC = "ULWebMap.frame.TOC.html" scrolling = "no">
        <FRAME SRC = "ULWebMap.frame.gif.html" SCROLLING = "yes"
MARGINHEIGHT = 1 MARGINWIDTH = 1>
</FRAMESET>
<FRAME SRC = "ULWebMap.frame.footer.html" MARGINHEIGHT = 1
MARGINWIDTH = 1>
</FRAMESET>
```

These hypertexts are but two examples of the endless combination of structures and pages possible with HTML. They can be adapted to your own needs or you may prefer to brew your own structure, navigational aids, and style from scratch. The key is consistency and in knowing where your boundaries lie when you start a project.

22

Considerations for Users with Special Needs

CHAPTER AT A GLANCE

- Investigation of the problems faced by visually and hearing-impaired users
- Which HTML tags to avoid and which tags will enhance Web pages for these users
- *Forms for the Blind*

The Web empowers and amplifies the abilities of most users. Authors gain huge audiences that might not otherwise be accessible to them without significant work and expense. Readers have access to large collections of hyperlinked text and multimedia data. Unfortunately, some of the same features of the Web that empower most of its users amplify the problems of physically handicapped users. Imagine if you were blind, being read a page that contains nothing more than the word *image*, or deaf, accessing a link that retrieves a video segment with a soundtrack and no transcript or closed captioning provided. Some users miss critical information locked in the document that is plainly accessible to sighted or hearing users.

Certain browsers are more usable than others by certain groups of users. Those who rely on Braille or text-to-speech software generally have better results with nongraphical Web interfaces such as CERN's text-based Web browser or the Lynx text browser from the University of Kansas. Graphical Web browsers are a recent development and most provide little direct support for visually or hearing-impaired users. But there are simple markup practices that can make a big difference for these types of users as well.

Designing more accessible Web pages not only increases the likelihood that a physically disabled user will be able to use your page, but also enhances the page for other users. For example, many of the markup practices discussed in this chapter will also enhance the access of users with slow data connections. A user who has decided to turn off automatic image loading is presented with a generic icon devoid of information each time a graphic is encountered, unless the author provided descriptive text for the images. A user without audio hardware or without a filter that will allow their browser to play back an audio clip will hear silence, and have nothing but the anchor that took them to the file to tell them what they might have missed.

Users with visual impairments might not be able to see anything at all. But many more users will have limited vision than will be completely blind. And they may prefer large font sizes for document text over spoken rendering. So let's first consider issues related to presenting documents to users with limited vision, and then how HTML 2, browser-specific, and HTML 3 markup will enhance and limit readability.

Documents for Users with Limited Vision

TEXT SIZE

Users who need to enlarge the fonts in a document from the Web need a document whose markup focuses on the document structure rather than its appearance. Preformatted text blocks <PRE> should be kept to a minimum since they are usually rendered in thin monospaced fonts that don't always contrast sharply enough with the background to be readily readable even by users with 20/20 vision. Paragraphs should be tagged with the paragraph tag <P> rather than separated by simply inserting a break tag <BR>. Paragraph tags insert vertical spacing between text blocks that prevent large text from appearing to overlap on the screen. Paragraph tags should also be used whenever possible instead of preformatted text blocks to present forms input data; otherwise users might find it difficult to read the descriptive text that tells them what type of data they need to provide for a field. Excessive use of varied type styles can be especially challenging since some typefaces, such as italics, can decrease the readability of a font for some users. If the passage is tagged with the <EM> tag instead of the <I> tag, then the user can select a rendering for emphasized text that suits their needs, and it will automatically be applied to every emphasized passage:

Wrong:

Select <I>preferences</I> from the Netscape menu

Right:

Select <EM>preferences</EM> from the Netscape menu

While it may seem that Netscape markup extensions might be just the thing to enhance the readability of a Web document, they may actually cause more problems than they solve. While relative font adjustments specified with Netscape tags such as <FONT> and <BASEFONT> might seem appropriately enabling since they will be applied properly by Netscape configured with large fonts for document text, users not relying on Netscape to view documents will see no change in the text that was to be emphasized. Microsoft Internet Explorer's <FONT> tag, which allows you to specify typefaces, is not helpful either. Netscape and Mosaic ignore this markup since they run on computer platforms that may lack the Microsoft TrueType fonts. A basic rule to remember for creating Web documents that will be accessible to visually impaired users is that specific markup in general and browser-specific markup in particular is useless and sometimes distracting noise for many users and should be avoided.

HTML 3 contains a few tags not present in HTML 2 that, when used properly, can enhance the accessibility of a page for a visually impaired user. Acronyms and abbreviations can at first appear to be words to alternate rendering systems such as speech synthesizers. In HTML 3 you can tag these visually ambiguous items with <ACRONYM> and <ABBREV>. While these are primarily intended to remind a browser rendering the document to speech not to attempt to pronounce the text as a word, they could also be rendered in a specific font using a style sheet entry. Your best tools for constructing documents for visually impaired users with HTML 3 are style sheets. You can easily provide an alternate style sheet for a user to download that provides a large-type view of your pages:

```
<STYLE TYPE="text/css">
/*large type style sheet*/
HTML {
    color: #000000;
    font-size: 18pt;
    font-family: helvetica;
}
H1 { font-size: 24pt }
```

Since style sheets are applied in a cascade, the user may already have a suitable style sheet stored locally that they can apply to override your styles as needed.

GENERAL FORMATTING ISSUES

Remember to tag your document structures. Don't use heading levels out of order when you name document sections. Use paragraph and list markup liberally, even if it does not achieve quite the visual effect you intended. Avoid using Netscape and HTML 3 colors or background images that reduce the contrast between the document text and its background.

IMAGES

Always provide an ALT attribute for images. The ALT attribute should provide a brief description of the image (no more than 1024 characters). If the image is the target of a link, let the user know that the document is an image and describe it briefly. If you use icons, make sure they are large (64 pixels or wider) and that the image has sufficient color contrast. Always provide a text-based navigation page as an alternative to any image maps you might use. This applies to both HTML 2's <IMG ... ISMAP> and Netscape's <IMG ... USEMAP>:

```
<A HREF="/cgi-bin/world_weather">
<IMG SRC="/images/world_map.gif" ISMAP ALT="Graphical World Map - text
alternative is available: "></A>
<A HREF="country_list.html">Listing of countries, in alphabetical order</A>
```

If using HTML 3, use a <FIG> tag instead of <IMG> and provide a caption as well as descriptive text for each <A ... SHAPE> tag:

Instead of Netscape's client-side image map <AREA>,

```
<A HREF="/cgi-bin/world_weather">
<IMG SRC="/images/world_map.gif USEMAP="#countries"></A>
<MAP NAME="countries">
<AREA SHAPE="rect" COORDS="10, 10, 100, 100" HREF="bulgaria.html">
</MAP>
```

use the HTML 3 <FIG> image map markup with alternate text:

```
<FIG SRC="/images/world_map.gif" IMAGEMAP>
<CAPTION>World Map</CAPTION>
<UL>
<LH>Here is a list of countries</LH>
<LI><A SHAPE="rect 10, 10, 100, 100" HREF="bulgaria.html">Bulgaria</A>
</UL>
</FIG>
```

VIDEO CLIPS AND OTHER DATA

Video clips should include a soundtrack whenever possible. You should include a link to a document describing the video if there is no soundtrack. Always let the user know what type of document is at the other end of the anchor. Graphical interfaces are challenging enough without the additional clutter of unexpected helper applications popping up to display marginally accessible or inaccessible data. If you are including a formatted document, consider converting the document to Acrobat's PDF (Portable Document Format). Acrobat includes a magnification tool for enlarging document text and graphics, and there is a version of the Acrobat reader suitable for use with speech systems as well.

Documents for Users with No Vision

TEXT AND GENERAL FORMATTING ISSUES

Text is the essence of content on the Web. Take care to mark structure and leave formatting to the browser. Most blind users will rely on speech rendering. Future Web browsers will undoubtedly be able to use spoken emphasis to illustrate many of the nuances of your document if you tag the content semantically rather than to achieve a certain appearance. Browser-specific tags are out of the question with two possible exceptions: Mosaic's <SND> tag and Microsoft Internet Explorer's similar <BGSOUND>. These browsers have the ability to automatically play a sound file when a <SND> (for Mosaic 2.0 or higher) or <BGSOUND> (for Internet Explorer) tag is included in the document. This inline sound file might be a spoken version of the Web page the user has just accessed. The user will still need to refer to the page itself to access links, but will instantly have access to the content of the page if they are using this tag/browser combination. It is unfortunate that there is not a more widely accepted standard for inline sound files. This "Web-on-cassette" style could provide a unique and enjoyable alternative to digitized speech.

IMAGES

Always provide an ALT attribute describing the image. Always include a text-based alternative for any image maps. Use HTML 3 <FIG>, <ACRONYM>, and <ABBREV> elements when authoring in that version of HTML so graphics and abbreviations are rendered in a form suitable for blind users.

VIDEO CLIPS AND OTHER DATA

Always warn the reader and provide descriptive text for graphical data. Video clips should include a soundtrack or description.

OTHER ALTERNATIVES FOR VISUALLY IMPAIRED USERS

Just as there are automated HTML validation services, there are automated conversion services for presenting standard HTML documents in other formats. The International Committee for Accessible Document Design (ICADD) has developed SGML applications specially designed for visually impaired users (Figure 22-1 shows the submission form for the HTML to ICADD Gateway). The ICADD Document Type Declarations define markup for large print, for Braille, and for voice synthesizers. While you could learn the markup language and duplicate your documents in both HTML and ICADD, there is a free transformation service online that uses a CGI script to convert standard HTML 2 documents into ICADD documents or to a Braille-output file format suitable for sending directly to Braille printers or Braille "displays." Here are a few lines of ICADD-tagged output as returned by the gateway:

<Para><XRef IDRef="http://scholar.lib.vt.edu/ejournals/JTE/jte.html"><It>Journal of Technology Education</It> </Para>
<BQ> Another
print journal that is also published electronically is the
<It>JTE</It>, edited Dr. Mark Sanders (Technology Education, Virginia Tech). Because he has been electronically preparing the journal

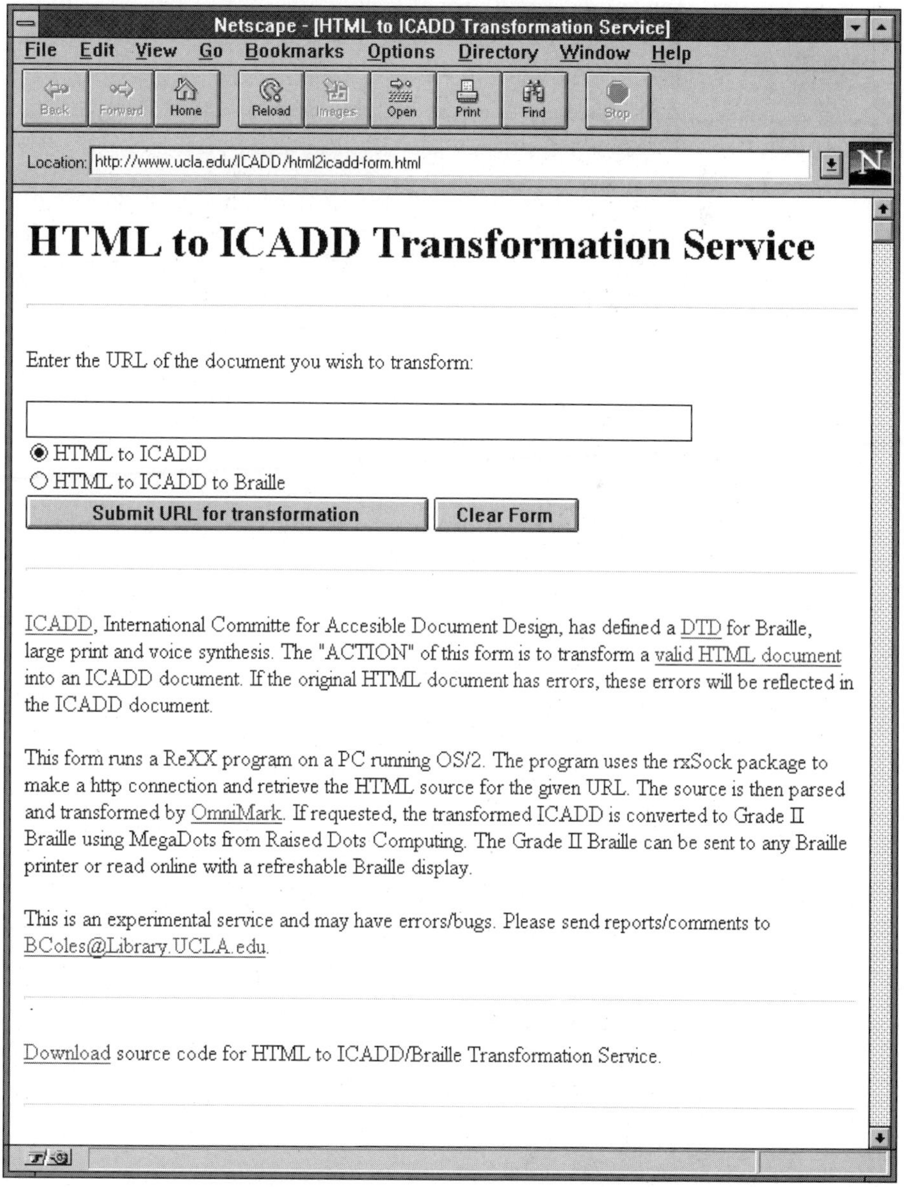

Figure 22-1 The HTML to ICADD Transformation Service at http://www.ucla.edu/ICADD/html2icadd-form.html

The service specifically requires HTML 2–compliant documents, which means that some of the markup options we've covered in this chapter would be only partially converted. Unrecognized tags will be replaced in the ICADD document with a comment like this:

```
<!— Document uses proprietary procedural markup, eg Netscape —>
```

So if you plan to point users to this service or retrieve the freely available source and provide it locally, make sure you review your documents to ensure that they are HTML 2, and do not include Netscape or HTML 3 tags. Future versions of the software will probably support HTML 3 but since the majority of Netscape extensions are intended for controlling page layout, it is unlikely that they can or will ever be supported by this service.

FORMS FOR THE BLIND

Forms pose a special challenge for blind users. They cannot see the input fields, and graphical forms elements such as pull-down menus are essentially inaccessible. But HTML 3 supports a new input type within HTML forms called file. This input type allows the user to attach a file to the form before submitting it to the gateway for processing. One option for authors trying to reach visually impaired users with forms would be to provide such a field as an alternative to entering text into the form fields:

```
Or you may submit a spoken response to this form: <INPUT
NAME="speech" TYPE=file>
```

A blind user could speak and record his answers and return a digitized audio file. Netscape 2.0 already supports this new input type.

Documents for Users with Limited or No Hearing

HTML documents in general pose less of a problem to hearing-impaired users than for users with limited vision. However, audio-only and video segments with audio are becoming increasingly common on the Web as increasing numbers of multimedia-ready computers are sold. Audio is treated as an inline object by some browsers, such as Mosaic and Internet Explorer. While this may prove beneficial to blind users, deaf users have no idea this information has been presented when inline audio is included in a document. So if you decide to use inline audio for a page, mention this in the document text, using the description as a hypertext link to a transcript of the audio if it is anything other than a reading of the current page:

```
<BODY>
<SND SRC="/welcome.au"><A HREF="welcome.html">An audio welcome
message from the president of the company</A>
...
```

With the advent of QuickTime and MPEG-2, synchronized audio tracks are often included with video clips. For sighted, hearing users, this is like an embedded television with all of the potential that medium provides for communication. For blind or deaf users, the problems associated with video clips are identical to those associated with television. Whenever possible, video clips intended for large audiences that might include hearing-impaired users should contain a text closed caption. Another option would be to place a transcript of the audio on the page containing the link to the video segment.

While it is reasonable to expect new developments in client and graphical user interfaces to reduce access problems for individuals with special needs, the Web changes quickly. Client technology imposes new limits for some users with every new release. If you intend to reach a large audience, or are specifically designing documents for users with various handicaps, you have seen that there are some simple markup alternatives that can unambiguously improve accessibility for all users. As HTML and the Web continue to evolve, standards will emerge to further enhance its usability for all users.

23

Making Your Documents Public

CHAPTER AT A GLANCE

- Finding out what's left of copyright on the Web
- Discovering how Web servers work
- Publicizing your resource with indexing sites
- Table 23-1: *World Wide Web Indexing Services*

Publishing on the Web is different than any other publishing mechanism ever created. Not only are your documents instantly accessible to millions of people once they are on the Web, but they can be pointed to, examined at the markup level, and readily borrowed from. You will see little more than a cryptic log entry recorded by the Web server software identifying the Internet address of the person who retrieved the file and the file they retrieved. There's no way to know whether they read the file, captured it for later review, or immediately abandoned it and went on to another document or Web site. One of the early dreams of a worldwide hypertext information system was the notion of transclusion. Ted Nelson, the hypertext theorist who coined the term *hypertext*, viewed transclusion as the mechanism for dealing with copyright on a system much like the World Wide Web. Each time a document or document fragment is accessed by a user, they are charged by the byte for the access. So even a few words would have great earning potential for an author if oft quoted by, or transcluded by, other authors. Unlike today's Web, any passage in any document could be transcluded in Nelson's web. The actual contents of the fragment would not be copied, only targeted by a link. No such mechanism is in place on today's Web, and we are probably some years away from a widely accepted mechanism for this type of hyperlinking.

Copyright on the Web

The Web has a "Wild West" mentality about copyright. On the one hand are the Congress and lawyers who try to pigeonhole the Web into print media or more bizarre still, consider it a broadcast mechanism similar to cable television. On the other hand are groups such as the League for Programming Freedom and the Free Software Foundation that give software away in order to enhance the interoperability of computer systems. Many contributors participate to reject the notion that fundamental intellectual properties such as hypertext links or compression algorithms are copyrightable objects. You have to figure out for yourself which direction you lean and protect your documents as well as you can if you consider it a priority.

If you are publishing a unique resource you should place a copyright notice on the resource home page and all related pages. It should be plainly visible but not overly obtrusive. Many browsers support the copyright entity © which is displayed as a copyright symbol (©). Even without the copyright notice you do retain the copyright of materials you publish on the Web, but adding a notice provides a little extra measure of protection, particularly in a new, uncertain environment like the Web.

Web security: Protecting Your Documents

There are several mechanisms for protecting documents built into most Web servers. The simplest way to protect files is by restricting their availability to a single computer or group of computers by Internet address. Most Web servers will let you specify IP addresses or names and ranges of addresses and computer names that can view a document, and deny access to other computers. Still more restrictive is the use of userid and password access. You can set up one or more users who are allowed access to the files by password. When a user accesses the URL of a password-protected document, the Web browser prompts them for a userid and password. After the user completes the login process correctly, the document they requested is returned. This configuration has the advantage of being accessible to anyone in the world if necessary. The two mechanisms can be combined so that only a few computers can be used to access the documents and then only by users who know the password. Communicating the necessary access information could be done by e-mail or by phone.

However, most documents published on the Web have no such restrictions. Most Web authors are trying to reach as many people as they can, so they want to make sure their documents are included in indexing services and subject-oriented link collections.

Web Servers

The next step is to decide how and where you would like to serve the documents. Many organizations have facilities in place to serve documents to the Web. If these facilities do not impose restrictions that prevent your audience from accessing your documents, then they are the best way to get your documents onto the net fast. Make sure the server is a permanent site, is backed up frequently to prevent loss of data, and is kept online 24 hours a day. Otherwise, you might want to consider running your own server, if your organization and network structure allow it.

Steps in Publishing on the Web

1. Copyright notice
2. Restrictions
3. Finding or setting up a server
4. Configuring the server
5. Registering your pages

Web servers use the Hypertext Transfer Protocol (HTTP) to respond to requests for documents and data made by Web clients, which also speak the same protocol. A typical document request as formulated by a Web client might look like the following:

```
GET /docs/contents.html
```

Additional information such as the type of client making the request is passed in hidden environment variables. The latest version of HTTP, version 1.0, provides for the exchange of quite a bit more data between the client and server. But this information generally has no role in the immediate job at hand: understanding the request, locating the document, and sending it back with the proper Content-type header. Once a client makes a request, it sends no additional data to the server. It waits for some type of response from the Web server. The server responds with the appropriate document or an error code. Then the connection between the client and server is broken. Each additional request requires a new connection; this is known as a *stateless connection*. Stateless connections place less of a burden on the computer running the Web server, since it does not have to keep track of multiple open connections. The program can be launched when a document request is detected, respond to the request, and then exit. Because Web servers are so simple, they can run on a variety of computer platforms including UNIX, Macintosh systems, and PCs running Windows NT or Windows 95.

BUILDING A SIMPLE WEB SERVER

To demonstrate just how simple a Web server can be, let's build a simple one. Our server will have a preset document directory and default document, and be able to respond to GET requests for HTML documents. If it fails to find the document, it will return an HTTP error code indicating that the document was not found. If the request is anything other than the GET request, it will respond with an internal server error. This server, written in Perl, is designed to run on UNIX systems as an inetd service. The UNIX inetd program watches network ports, which are internal addresses associated with specific network services provided by the computer. When a request is detected at a specific port, such as a request for a document at the standard HTTP server port 80, inetd looks at its configuration file where actual programs are associated with port numbers and launches the appropriate program, funneling data from the network to the program as though it were being typed in at the command line (from stdin). Output from the server is delivered back to the appropriate port and returns to the application client. We do not need to worry about network functionality for our server since it is all taken care of by the UNIX operating system.

The first task then is to accept the input from the client:

```
$buffer=<STDIN>;
```

This Perl code looks for data delivered on the application's standard input, represented by <STDIN>, until an end-of-line character is detected signaling the end of the data stream. One line of data from standard input is placed in $buffer.

Next, we need to determine if there is a GET command in this request, and decide what to do next:

```
$where_isGet=index($buffer, 'GET');
if ($where_isGet>=0) {
    &process_request();
} else
{
    &request_error;
}
```

The Perl index() operator looks for the string GET in the variable $buffer. If the GET command is found in the buffer, then its position in the string is assigned to $where_isGet. The command can occur at position 0 (the first position in the file) or elsewhere. If it is not found, $where_isGet is assigned the value -1. If found, the function &process_request() is called, otherwise the program executes the &request_error() function and exits.

So let's now look at the &process_request function:

```perl
sub process_request {
    local ($document)="";
    local($line_end)=length($buffer);
    for ($count=$where_isGet+4; $count<=$line_end; $count++) {
        $character=substr($buffer, $count, 1);
        if ($character eq '\n') {
            $count=$line_end;
        } else {
            $document=$document.$character;
        }
    }
    open (document, "$dir$document") || &not_found;
    print "Content-type: text/html\n\n";
    while (<document>) {
        print $_;
    }
    close (document);
}
```

This function first builds the name of the document the client has requested by putting each character after the command GET (and after the space separating the command from the document name) into the variable $document. When an end-of-line character (\n) is detected, then the function knows it has reached the end of the document name since this character cannot be part of a filename. So it then attempts to open the file. If it finds it, it sends its contents back to the waiting client, preceded by an HTML "Content-type" header. Content-type headers tell the client what kind of data is being returned, for example, image file (image/gif), text (text/plain), or HTML (text/html). Content-type is discussed in more detail in Chapters 26 and 27. For now, just remember it tells the Web client whether it should try to display the document or launch a helper application. If the server cannot open the requested file, it responds with an error and exits:

```perl
sub not_found {
    print "HTTP/0.9 404 File not found\n";
    exit 0;
}
```

Here's the full source for this simple, Perl-based Web server:

```perl
#!/usr/local/bin/perl
# Simplest Web server possible!
# Respond to GET requests with requested document or an error
# $dir is the location of our published Web documents
$dir="/home/WWW/";
$buffer=<STDIN>;
$where_isGet=index($buffer, 'GET');
if ($where_isGet>=0) {
    &process_request();
```

```
} else
{
  &request_error;
}
exit 0;
sub process_request {
# look for a GET request
# return the requested document if found
    local ($document)="";
    local($line_end)=length($buffer);
    for ($count=$where_isGet+4; $count<=$line_end; $count++) {
        $character=substr($buffer, $count, 1);
        if ($character eq '\n') {
            $count=$line_end;
        } else {
            $document=$document.$character;
        }
    }
    open (document, "$dir$document") || &not_found;
    print "Content-type: text/html\n\n";
    while (<document>) {
        print $_;
    }
    close (document);
}
sub not_found {
# return a message telling the client the document was not found
    print "HTTP/0.9 404 File not found\n";
    exit 0;
}
sub request_error {
# return a message telling the client the request was not recognized
    print "HTTP/0.9 400 Bad Request: Unknown Method\n";
    exit 0;
}
```

This server has many limitations but it demonstrates just how simple the communications between a client and a server can be. Improvements to this server include responses to other commands besides GET, sending the appropriate Content-type header if the document is not an HTML document, and implementing security support such as restriction by Internet address and by password. Luckily there are many servers available that already implement these and many other functions.

There are some configuration options available with all Web servers due to their shared goal of distributing data to Web clients. Each Web server has a documents directory, where documents that are to be published to the Web must reside. A default filename for the home document can be configured.

Multimedia content types that your server knows about are added to a file usually entitled mime.types. Access restrictions can be enabled or disabled. Finally, access logging can be configured and some servers allow you to log optional information such as the client type. Most servers maintain these configuration options in human-readable text files that can be hand edited, or updated through some tool provided with the server software.

The most popular Web server for the Macintosh system is Webstar. Once known as MacHttpd, Webstar is now a full-fledged commercial Web server available for Macintosh systems. It can be run in the foreground, so that it has a window displaying connection activity, or run as a background application with no interface.

For Windows 95 and Windows NT systems, O'Reilly and Associates WebSite is an excellent publishing utility that includes an editor and Web server application (Figure 23-1).

WebSite is bundled with all the tools necessary to create and publish Web documents. In addition to the Web server and server administration tools, WebSite includes Wizards, an automatic home page builder, WebView for managing hierarchies of Web pages, Image Map Editor for setting up image map files, and WebIndex for building a searchable index of your HTML documents. WebSite is a commercial application.

Most UNIX sites prefer to use one of the two public domain Web servers that have been tested and available on the Internet for several years now. CERN's httpd and NCSA's httpd both rely on text-based configuration files for setting security, content types, and the server home and script directories. NCSA's server is controlled by modifying one of its configuration files stored in the conf subdirectory of the server home directory. The file srm.conf includes options for the Web server document root directory and default index filename for directories in the Web server's root; httpd.conf includes options for how the server is run (standalone or launched on connect by inetd) and server administrator; and mime.types, which should only be modified when serving a new document type that does not yet have a Content-type/file extension entry. NCSA and CERN

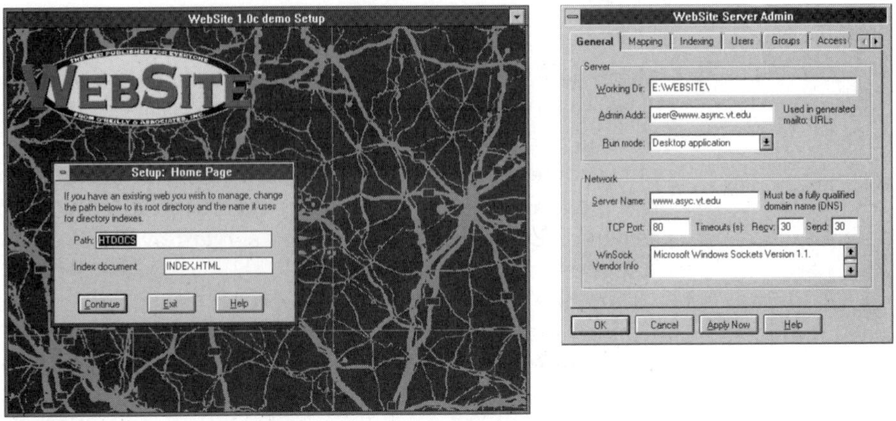

Figure 23-1
WebSite setup and
Server Admin
control panel

httpd will both run on virtually any UNIX system. You will need the assistance of your UNIX system's administrator to install and configure the software.

Netscape's NetSite Web server for UNIX includes a set of HTML Web forms for server administration. NetSite includes security features not found in other Web servers such as those necessary to perform secure monetary transactions over the Web using Netscape's HTTPS (Hypertext Transfer Protocol Secure) protocol. While it is more expensive than the other commercial and freeware servers described here, if you need a robust server with remote administration and secure transaction features, this is the best one for the job.

Advertising Your Documents

The final step in the Web publishing process is to register your new resource with indexing services. There are several types of indexing services. One type simply requests the base URL for your site, and keywords which should be associated with the site. Your URL and keyword list are indexed at the site for users to find. Another type accepts the URL of your site and adds it to a list of sites to be explored. When your site is explored by this indexing service, the full text of each document on your server that is publicly available is retrieved and indexed. A third type of site places humans, usually librarians, between your site and the index. When you register, you are actually placing a request with the site to have them visit, evaluate, and catalog your site. Of the three types, the third is often the most consistently useful for end users. Here are some Web indexing sites that you might want to register your site with:

TABLE 23-1   WORLD WIDE WEB INDEXING SERVICES

Indexing Service	URL	Cataloging Source
Alta Vista	http://altavista.digital.com	Robot-searched
EINet Galaxy	http://galaxy.einet.net/cgi-bin/annotate?Other	Robot-searched & Human-evaluated
Harvest	http://harvest.cs.colorado.edu/Harvest/brokers/register-with-CU-gatherers.html	Robot-searched
Infoseek	http://www2.infoseek.com/doc/help/AddingSites.html	Robot-searched
JumpStation	http://js.stir.ac.uk/jsbin/submit	Robot-searched
Lycos	http://lycos.cs.cmu.edu/lycos-register.html	Robot-searched
NetCenter	http://www.netcenter.com/netcentr/whats-new/whats-new.html	User-supplied
New Rider's WWW Yellow Pages	http://www.mcp.com/newriders/wwwyp/submit.html	Human-evaluated
NIKOS	http://www.rns.com/www_index/new_site.html	Robot-searched
Open Text Web Index	http://www.opentext.com:8080/omw-submit.html	Robot-searched

Starting Point	http://www.stpt.com/util/submit.html	Human-evaluated
WebCrawler	http://webcrawler.com/WebCrawler/ SubmitURLS.html	Robot-searched
Whole Internet Catalog	http://gnn.com/gnn/forms/comments.html	Human-evaluated
World Wide Web Worm	http://www.cs.colorado.edu/home/mcbryan/ WWWWadd.html	Robot-searched
Yahoo	http://www.yahoo.com/bin/add?	User-supplied

There are also a few metaindex sites that allow you to simultaneously register with a number of indexing services. One such site is "Submit It!" at http://www.submit-it.com/. Once you complete their initial registration form, a script at their site reformats your input into suitable formats for a variety of other registration services. Such sites are a great time saver, and help you reach more readers.

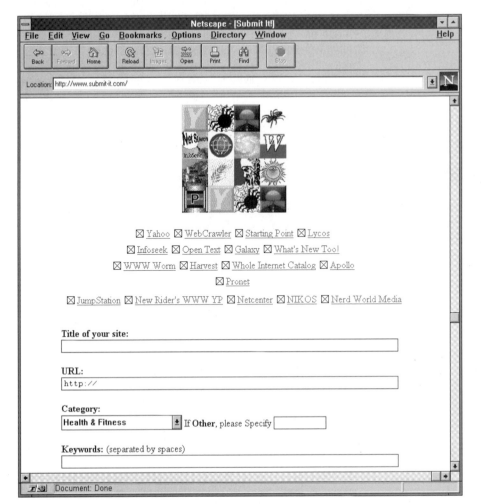

24

Publishing HTML on CD-ROM

CHAPTER AT A GLANCE

- Using CD-ROMs to publish an HTML project
- Filesystem and file naming restrictions
- Constructing URLs for use on a CD-ROM project
- Choosing data formats for cross-platform compatibility

Using HTML as your document format of choice for a CD-ROM project makes a lot of sense. Most CD-ROMs utilize some type of hypertext system to provide access to their contents. CD-ROMs can contain up to 640MB of data and are often used today to create multimedia educational and entertainment packages. They evolved from audio CDs, developed in the early 1980s. CD-ROMs (Compact Disc Read Only Memory) store digital information instead of audio data. They also include error correction data. The CD-ROM standard is sometimes referred to as the "Yellow Book" standard, because the specifications for the CD-ROM standard were published in a yellow book. Yellow Book is the only CD standard suitable for storing HTML and multimedia data on compact disc. Future standards (so-called multifocus, or blue light disks) will allow the storage of several gigabytes of data on the same 5-inch optical disks that are limited to 640MB today.

HTML/CD-ROM projects might include complete training manuals or text-books utilizing hundreds or thousands of hypertext documents and fragments to provide introductory material, in-depth coverage, research, advanced topics, and reference materials. Since HTML and Web browsers work together to support the delivery of multimedia data, such a project could incorporate graphics, audio, and motion video segments for training and further coverage of a topic. And while CD-ROMs are inexpensive enough to replace as needed for updates, HTML is a network document delivery language, meaning that topics that change frequently could be covered lightly on the disk and include hypertext links allowing a user with an Internet connection to access a remote archive containing the latest information on certain topics. HTML/CD-ROM projects could almost be considered self-updating!

CD-ROM Filesystems

The CD-ROM specification only describes how digital data should be stored on a compact disc, not how files should be stored. HTML determines the format of most of the textual content of the disk. So there remains the issue of cross-platform filesystem compatibility for what is essentially a portable hard drive. There are several filesystem structures used on CD-ROMs. A few are proprietary, that is, the filesystem structure was modeled after that used by a particular operating system and can only be accessed by computers running that environment. Vendors may choose a proprietary filesystem because it stores additional information needed to enhance the performance of read access to the disk, or for extra-long filenames. Proprietary formats are often used to distribute software and operating system updates, where cross-platform compatibility is not an issue.

Apple uses a proprietary CD-ROM filesystem structure called HFS (Hierarchical File System) for delivering software and operating system updates to customers. It supports all of the features of the Macintosh filesystem such as 31-character filenames that can include any characters, not just alphanumeric characters, and custom icons for software and documents. There are accepted standards for placing HFS and non-HFS filesystems on the same CD-ROM. Hybrid disks can contain two separate partitions, one HFS and one some other filesystem. However, this means the data has to be duplicated in each partition, which essentially reduces the capacity of a CD-ROM from over 600MB to around 300MB. A global hybrid merges HFS with another standard, ISO-9660, so that the disk appears to be an HFS disk to a Macintosh, and an ISO disk to other platforms. This is achieved by embedding two tables of contents on the disk. A small amount of additional disk space is consumed but files do not have to be duplicated.

The best choice for publishing HTML on CD-ROM is the ISO-9660 (International Standards Organization format 9660) filesystem. This standard imposes stringent filenaming limitations on the contents of the disk as well as some other limitations not present in many modern filesystems, but results in a disk that is readable on almost every computer platform available today. There are two variations on the ISO-9660 format. The most restrictive version, ISO-9660 Level 1, has the following limitations:

- Filenames can only contain capital letters A–Z, numbers 0–9 or underscore (_) characters
- Filenames are limited to 8-character names, a dot (.) and a 3-character extension
- The filesystem can be no more than eight directories deep

A second version of the ISO-9660 standard, Level 2, supports 32-character filenames (Figure 24-1).

The only operating system in widespread use today that does not support filenames longer than 8.3 characters is the DOS/Windows 3.1 environment. If you choose to support users of this environment, you will have to stick to the most restrictive standard. Otherwise, you can simply let your users know that your disk requires Windows NT or Windows 95 if they are going to use it in a PC environment.

CD writing software that supports both ISO-9660 levels can usually be configured to automatically truncate filenames. However, if the disk were created on a Macintosh or Windows operating system supporting longer filenames, this could result in broken links. And of course, since CD-ROM is a write once medium, the broken links could not be repaired. So it is better to shorten the file and directory names while preparing the data for the CD, if you intend to create an ISO-9660 Level 1 disk.

Finally, there is the multimode option. HFS or ISO-9660 disks can be created with both a digital data filesystem and a digital audio partition. Audio tracks would be playable on ordinary audio CD equipment, while the filesystem would be accessible on Macintosh or other systems (if ISO-9660 compliant). Most audio file formats used by computers today do not match the quality available with the CD audio format. Multimode disks are used when the quality of audio

Figure 24-1
Recordable CD (RCD) backup software ISO-9660 Level selection panel

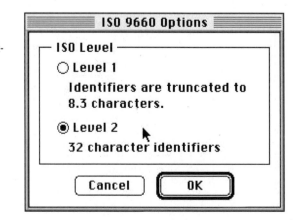

tracks is a major concern. But remember, this data is not accessible from the filesystem, and could not be targeted by a hypertext link like a computer audio file.

STRUCTURING YOUR FILESYSTEM/NAMING YOUR FILES

Before writing a disk, you will need to create an image of the CD-ROM on your hard drive. The first step is to establish a temporary root for the CD image. Any folder will do but is important that at least as much disk space be available as will be consumed on the CD by HTML and multimedia data. CD writing programs function best when files reside on a single defragmented partition on the disk. Figure 24-2 shows a typical CD-ROM writing program's filesystem layout window. You may need to purchase a defragmenting utility, which examines files and makes sure all of their contents are on contiguous sectors on your hard disk. You should defragment the drive after you have created your disk image but before you write a CD. The next step is to create the directory tree in which files will be stored. This step determines the path information that will be recorded in hypertext links.

Ordinarily a large HTML project might rely heavily on the HTML <BASE> header tag to simplify the creation and maintenance of hypertext links. <BASE> allows you to establish a URL prefix that is used by all relative links in the document body. For example, this <BASE> tag sets a root URL path pointing to a directory two levels deep on a server called "server.com":

<BASE HREF="http://server.com/trees/conifers/">

Later, an anchor within the text is assigned a value pointing to a file in a subdirectory beneath this base:

Figure 24-2
Constructing a filesystem on a CD-ROM

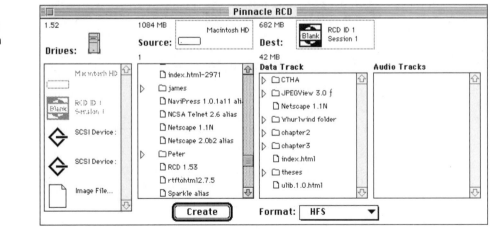

```
<A HREF="sequoia/sempervirens.html">Coastal Redwood</A>
```

which is expanded as:

```
"http://server.com/trees/conifers/sequoia/sempervirens.html"
```

But an absolute path has a high probability of being incorrect once a CD-ROM is mounted. This is due to the variety of ways computer systems mount CDs. Some systems such as DOS and Windows treat the CD as a hard drive. This means a <BASE> like this one:

```
<BASE HREF="/trees/conifers">
```

will not work if the document is contained on a CD-ROM because the drive letter assigned to the filesystem is missing. Unfortunately, this drive letter can be most any letter of the alphabet (probably not A: or C: since they represent the floppy and hard drive on most DOS systems). So if a <BASE> tag is used at all on these types of systems, it will have to specify a relative path:

```
<BASE HREF="trees/conifers">
```

This path is relative to the drive from which the Web browser was launched. If the user runs Netscape from the C: drive with the CD-ROM specified as its working directory, then this <BASE> tag will point to the desired files. DOS users may also have noticed that the slashes are forward rather than backward. All Web browsers expect paths to use forward slashes, so even if you create your disk on a PC that uses backward slashes to indicate directory names, the anchors will have to use forward slashes, which are the "UNIX way" of referring to directories.

UNIX systems may point the way to the correct tilt of directory slashes, but they are no smarter about mounting CDs to avoid breaking hypertext links than DOS systems. UNIX mounts the CD-ROM as a directory under the root directory. So instead of addressing the CD with a drive letter, it will have a directory name like /CD or /mnt. Macintosh systems mount disks in the same way, using the disk label as a folder name under which the root filesystem of the disk is accessible.

For multiplatform CD-ROMs, anchors are more reliable if no <BASE> tag is used at all. Instead use relative paths to all files. Whenever possible, refer to the files in the same directory by filename with no path information. Otherwise, specify a path relative to the directory in which the current document is stored. For example, consider the following structure:

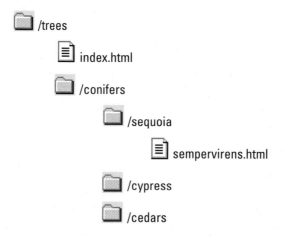

The root directory of this disk contains one subdirectory called trees. Under it are an index.html file and a subdirectory, conifers. Under conifers, there are three subdirectories: sequoia, cypress, and cedars. If the file sempervirens.html under sequoia points back to the /trees/index.html file, its anchor should look like this:

<A HREF="../../index.html">Return to Trees Page</A>

Each "../" means move back one directory level. So this path translates to trees/conifers/index.html from the sequoia subdirectory. A path like this should yield an anchor that will work on Macs, PCs, and UNIX systems.

Steps in Building an HTML CD-ROM
- Gather your files into one directory/folder on your hard disk
- Determine whether you will use ISO-9660 Level 1 or 2
- Adjust your filenames to match the selected level
- Check your paths and use relative URLs whenever possible
- Test your links
- Consider DOS/UNIX/Macintosh filesystem variations
- Add viewers or information about viewers
- Defragment your drive
- Write the CD

If you have selected an especially restrictive filesystem such as ISO-9660 Level 1, you will have to be diligent about making sure anchor filenames match real filenames. Longer filenames are generally easier to remember, since they can be words or phrases. Reducing filenames from 32 to 8 characters not only strips away much of the meaning held by the names, but makes them difficult to recall. Another very important detail to remember about Level 1 filenames is that they allow only capital letters. This is not a problem for DOS or Macintosh systems that ignore case, but UNIX systems are case sensitive. For example the following anchors would point to two different files on a UNIX system:

```
<A HREF="filovir.htm">Filoviruses</A>
<A HREF="FILOVIR.HTM">Filoviruses</A>
```

Only the second anchor is a valid ISO-9660 Level 1 filename. Macs and PCs will view both links as pointing to the same file.

Remember that you can also use full URLs to point to network-accessible resources. These might include updates or supplemental material, or information available on the Internet for which you were unable to obtain permission to place on the disk. While it might be a copyright violation to use someone's Web pages on a CD-ROM without obtaining permission, there is no problem with including an anchor that points to the page. But there is a slight risk: if the file moves or the server is renamed, then the links will be broken. And a broken link on a CD-ROM is broken forever.

Data Formats for Multiplatform HTML CD-ROMs

You should consult Chapter 30 about general issues for including multimedia data in HTML documents. There are some special issues to consider when including multimedia with HTML documents on a CD-ROM. Perhaps the most important consideration is whether to provide viewers for data formats that cannot be embedded in HTML documents and viewed with a Web browser. Image formats such as GIF and JPEG are pretty safe bets for inline graphics formats. But data such as audio or video are generally not viewed inline, so you may need to provide viewers or pointers to viewers for this type of data for each computing platform you intend to support. You may wish to provide a viewers subdirectory off the CD root directory with a subdirectory for Macintosh, Windows, and other systems on which you wish people to be able to use your disk. Be careful selecting and including viewers on a CD-ROM. Check the license agreement even if the software calls itself freeware. You may be required to obtain permission or even pay a fee to include the software.

Some data formats such as video or proprietary page description languages might lack viewers for every possible platform. You may have to leave some users to rely on their own network tracking skills to locate viewers for less common systems such as NEXTSTEP or UnixWare. Try to provide a README.html or similar document that includes some URLs pointing to system-specific resource sites, especially if you choose not to provide any viewers with your disk. If you decide to support only one or two platforms, you can place a copy of the Web browser you prefer users to use (subject to restrictions imposed by the browser license) along with your documents, with viewers preinstalled and configured on the CD-ROM.

One final consideration for including multimedia data on a CD is the filename extensions used for the data. DOS and Windows systems rely exclusively on the file extension to determine the file type of locally stored multimedia data. Macintosh systems also refer to the resource fork (if one exists) of a file to determine its content. This makes creating fully functional multimedia HTML document collections for Macs more difficult. In fact, if you are serious about supporting Macintosh systems as well as PCs, it is better to create the disk on a Mac using an ISO-9660 Level 2 filesystem or even create a Mac-specific partition or hybrid ISO/HFS partition to ensure that the resource fork is available to the Mac operating system. UNIX systems throw another wrench into the equation since they very often expect a specific file extension in *lowercase letters only.* This means multimedia data stored on ISO-9660 Level 1 disks might not be recognized since the file extension will be recorded in uppercase letters. The user may be able to reconfigure their Web browser's MIME types to support both lower- and uppercase extensions. But you will have to be aware of the problem so you can let them know in your installation or readme notes.

CD-ROMs are superior to all but the fastest network connections for delivering multimedia data. You can use full-color images and high-quality video and audio clips with less worry over their accessibility, since the problems of slow network connections and overloaded servers are eliminated. HTML as a CD-ROM authoring format has the advantage of near-global platform support while being very inexpensive to create and only slightly more difficult to plan and develop than setting up an Internet-based Web resource. The key to a successful HTML CD-ROM is testing. If you've tried your disk out on the systems for which it is intended and provide sufficient documentation for resolving most common problems, then the disk will be a success.

25

HTML Editors

CHAPTER AT A GLANCE

- Purpose of an HTML editor
- Overview of HTML editor features
- Examples of editor types
- Table 25-1: *Types of HTML Editors*

Until now, you've created HTML documents by hand, that is, used a simple text editor to type in the tags as well as the text. This should have given you a better understanding of the intended role of HTML markup—to encode the structure of your documents and make them accessible on a wide variety of computer platforms. Now that you are familiar with HTML 2 and HTML 3 tags, you are ready to turn over some of the markup chores to a class of software broadly referred to as HTML editors. Editors can be as simple as text editors with menu options for inserting HTML tags, word processor–like document-editing applications, or sophisticated document management systems. We will look at each class and consider an example. You will most likely use a combination of tools depending on the size of your project.

The goal of this chapter is to illustrate the features available in major classes of HTML editors so you can determine which tools are suitable for your markup project. There are dozens of editors for Macintosh and Windows-based systems;

new entries, particularly commercial editors, are introduced frequently. Freeware editors usually have certain limitations such as small maximum file size and no preview option. Commercial editors generally have no file size restriction and many can act as full-fledged Web browsers. When selecting a commercial editor, you may want to locate a cross-platform editor that is supported on both Macintosh and Windows systems, if your organization has both types of systems. Such editors look virtually identical on both platforms.

HTML Tag Editors

The simplest and most readily available tools for creating Web documents are HTML tag editors. An HTML tag editor consists of a basic text editor with a toolbar and/or set of pull-down menus each of which inserts a specific tag into the document. These tools are especially useful for authors who only create HTML documents occasionally and may have forgotten what tags are available. Another useful feature typically found with these tools are attribute prompts. When a tag that requires an attribute is selected, such as <IMG SRC=""> or <A HREF="">, the editor will display a panel requesting a value for the required attribute. This can improve the accuracy of markup.

These types of editors are often free and available for virtually any computer platform in use today. They can be difficult to locate, but you can check major indexing services such as Yahoo or software archives you normally rely on for other freeware utilities for your particular system. You should download a few if more than one editor is available so you can compare features. Limitations such as 32K file size can take a while to encounter, and may not be mentioned in the documentation. Also freeware editors might be maintained irregularly or not at all. The editor may support HTML tags that have been deprecated, that is, are not supported anymore (<XMP> is an example of a deprecated tag). Features to look for include a *multiple document interface*, which allows you to edit more than one document at a time, *save as UNIX*, which allows you to prepare files to be served on Web servers running the UNIX operating system, and *user-configurable tag bars* that allow you to create a custom floating bar containing the tags you use most often.

One example of an HTML tag editor is HotDog. This software is available for Windows-based PC systems. While it is not free, it can be downloaded and "test-driven" before purchase. The program features a toolbar reminiscent of the button bars found in many Windows applications. Buttons provide quick access to markup elements such as anchors, lists, inline images, headings, and typographic tags. Larger buttons control program features such as activating floating tag and character bars, automatic forms and table markup, preview and publishing options. Typical of this class of HTML tool, HotDog requires that you install and configure a Web browser for preview mode. It has no internal mechanism for rendering HTML documents.

HotDog can be used to create HTML 2, Netscape, or HTML 3 compliant documents (Figure 25-1). Unfortunately, you must have some knowledge of the

Figure 25-1
HotDog HTML
editor for
Windows

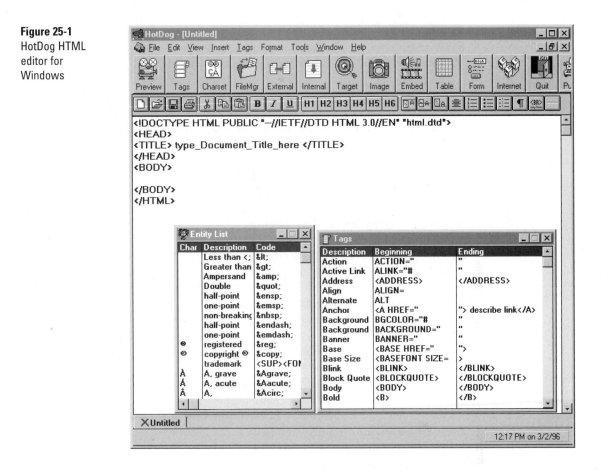

appropriate elements of each version of HTML. HotDog will allow you to insert any element in any document. This is another feature typical of the editor class of HTML tools. They have no mechanism for defining the level of HTML to be used (providing access only to appropriate tags) or validation for finished documents.

Despite these minor limitations, HTML editors are essential tools for creating Web documents. You will have to use some type of text-editing package to create HTML documents. Using an HTML-aware editor saves keying tags and reduces the amount of time you might have to spend reviewing HTML reference material while creating documents.

CONVERTERS

Converters are perhaps the biggest work savers in the HTML-editor tool class. Converters transform the native codes of a word processor or other text formatting system into HTML tags. Converters can save hours of tedious text markup. Converters make assumptions about the structure of a document based on the formatting characteristics specified in the document's original format. For example, if the document started out as a Microsoft Word file, heading styles or large type fonts might indicate that the text so tagged should be converted to one of the six HTML heading levels available.

The simplest HTML converters are filter applications that essentially have no user interface. The rtftohtml filter converts RTF (Microsoft's Rich Text Format) files, to which many word processors will export from their native document format, into HTML. On the Macintosh, the user simply drags the icon of the RTF file she wishes to convert to HTML onto the rtftohtml program icon. The filter processes the file, creating an HTML output file, and sometimes a listing of errors. Errors are RTF structures it failed to map to HTML. There are some slight variations in RTF output by various programs, and occasionally rtftohtml will encounter a code it does not recognize. The filter also extracts embedded images and inserts anchor tags pointing to the images in external files, creates external files and anchors within the main document for footnotes, and translates special characters to their corresponding character entity.

Rtftohtml can be customized so that it maps certain RTF tags to certain HTML markup elements. The html-trans file has four tables controlling the markup of certain types of data found in the original RTF file. The .Ptag table allows you to control the style of the paragraphs output by rtftohtml. You can specify the start tag, end tag, or even have the software build a table of contents from certain paragraphs. The .TTag table describes how text should be tagged. The .Pmatch table matches .Ptag entries with the styles used in the RTF file. The .Tmatch table matches a .TTag entry to an RTF style. These tables are cryptic but do allow you a great deal of control over the HTML output by rtftohtml. If you are going to be converting a lot of documents, it is worth the time and effort required to modify the html-trans file to suit your needs.

Internet Assistant for Microsoft Word (Figure 25-2) is a combination converter/editor with a sophisticated user interface. Users can almost instantly export a Word document to HTML using the same procedure they would normally perform to save the document as text or RTF. Internet Assistant also converts Word into a Web browser. Word interprets and renders HTML tags, embeds graphics, and supports hypertext link navigation over the Web just as a real Web browser would. It also has a toolbar for inserting markup into an HTML document. Documents can be edited in a preview, WYSIWYG mode, or in HTML mode where tags are both displayed and rendered.

Internet Assistant itself is freely distributed by Microsoft from their home page http://www.microsoft.com. However, you must already own a copy of Microsoft Word 6 or 7, and it only works with the Windows versions of the word processor.

WYSIWYG WEB PAGE EDITORS

Another class of HTML editors are WYSIWYG editors. These programs conceal HTML markup. Some do not allow you to even view the raw HTML. Instead they present tags, attributes, and entities as toolbar or pull-down menu items. They

Figure 25-2
Internet Assistant
for Microsoft
Word for
Windows

CH25.DOC

let you import text and provide automatic formatting tools such as table generators. Such tools also let you drag and drop images and text just like WYSIWYG word processors.

Netscape Navigator Gold   Netscape Navigator Gold (Figure 25-3) is a version of the popular Navigator browser that lets you download and edit existing pages or create new documents. Instead of presenting HTML tags along with the content, the Web page is displayed just as it would appear in Netscape Navigator. In fact, you cannot directly edit the HTML source code within Navigator Gold. Instead, you enter or drag text and images into the editor window to insert them into your documents. Navigator Gold places heavy emphasis on format and appearance of a page and it supports all of Netscape's HTML extensions. Any changes you make to a document are instantly visible. You can easily modify elements with context-sensitive inspector panels that let you specify information such as the address of a document for a hypertext link, text and link colors for the document, or image size and ALT attribute values for graphics. Navigator Gold lets you create attractive home pages with minimal knowledge of HTML.

Figure 25-3
Netscape
Navigator Gold

TABLE 25-1   **TYPES OF HTML EDITORS**

Editor Type	Example Editors	Available Platforms
HTML tag editors	HotDog	Windows
Translators & Converters	rtf2html	Windows, Macintosh, UNIX
		Windows
	Internet Assistant for Microsoft Word	
WYSIWYG editors	Netscape Navigator Gold	Windows
	Adobe Pagemill	Macintosh
Structured Web page editors	HoTMetaL	Windows, Macintosh, UNIX
	InContext Spider	Macintosh
Web Document management systems	NaviPress	Windows, Macintosh, UNIX

Adobe Pagemill Adobe Pagemill (Figure 25-4) is another example of a WYSIWYG Web page editor. Like Navigator Gold, Pagemill is designed to help users unfamiliar with HTML to develop attractive Web pages. Pagemill lets you modify elements with floating property panels. You can change document-wide settings, or modify the attributes for links, images, or other content once it is inserted into the document. Like Netscape's editor, Pagemill lets you edit in preview mode, so you always know exactly how your document will look when it is published. You can insert graphics into Pagemill by simply dragging the graphics file's icon into the editor window. Pagemill also lets you edit graphics and create image maps.

STRUCTURED WEB PAGE EDITORS

Some HTML editors not only provide access to the HTML tag set, but also work to ensure that you use tags in the appropriate context within a document, that is, they validate markup. Structured Web page editors focus on the logical structure of a document rather than its appearance. These types of editors might switch modes so that a <TITLE> tag is unavailable from a toolbar or pull-down menu when the text insertion point is no longer within the document header. While some users prefer to have more control over markup, these types of editors provide automatic validation by not allowing you to insert tags or attributes where they do not belong.

HoTMetaL Pro HoTMetaL Pro (Figure 25-5) is one example of such a package. HoTMetaL uses a rules file to determine when a certain HTML tag is allowed. Tags can only be inserted when they are legally elements of other tags. This ensures that you are creating valid HTML documents. It also includes templates and an attribute inspector for modifying HTML tags.

Figure 25-4
Adobe Pagemill

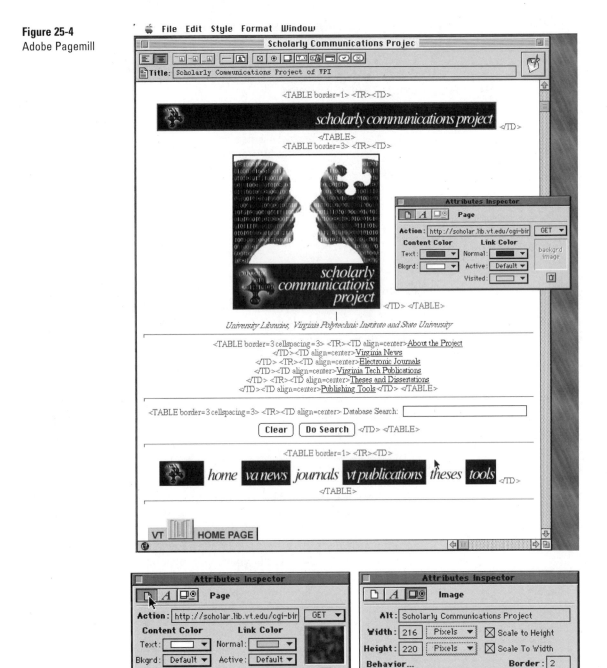

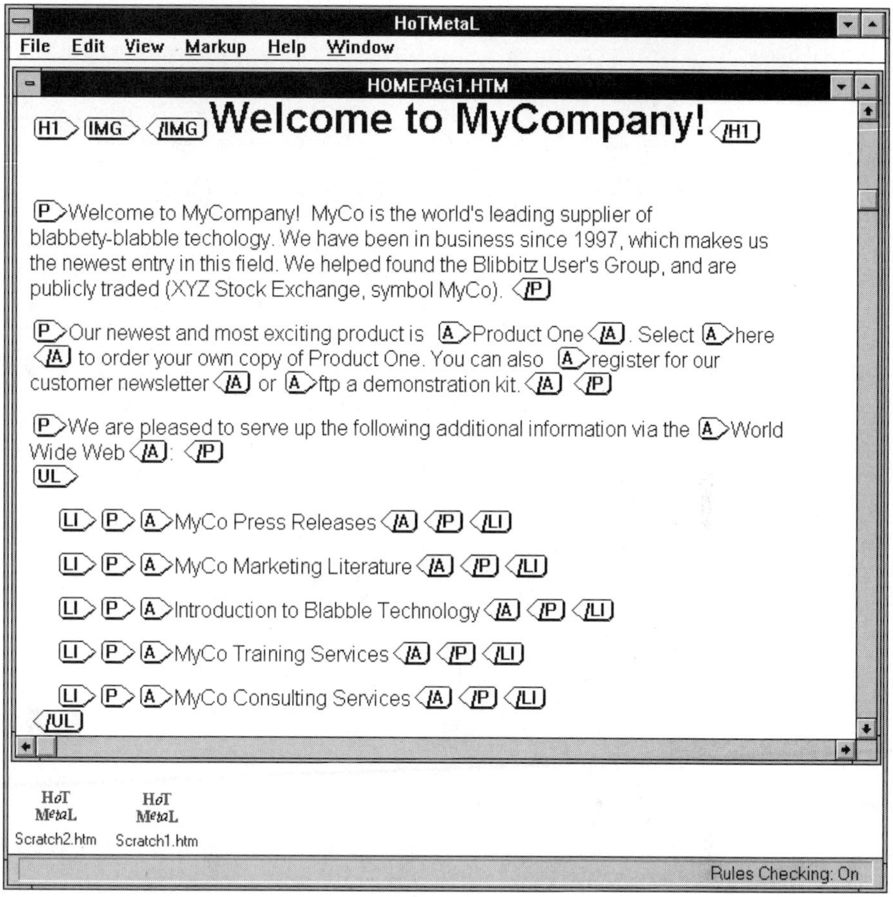

Figure 25-5
SoftQuad
HoTMetaL Pro

Figure 25-5
SoftQuad
HoTMetaL Pro

InContext Spider InContext Spider (Figure 25-6) is another example of a structured Web page editor. It presents the open page in a split view. The left side of the window is the logical editor. The logical editor displays the overall structure of your document by presenting nested boxes representing major elements within the document. You can modify the overall structure of your document in the logical display, but not the content. The content editor allows you to edit the contents of a particular document structure. When you select content in the content editor, the corresponding element in the logical display is highlighted as well. InContext Spider includes an extensive toolbar and a unique Web manager feature that lets you quickly assemble a Web page from a bookmark list or other set of hypertext links. It also includes a set of starter templates for building resumes, home pages, and other types of documents.

Figure 25-6
InContext Spider

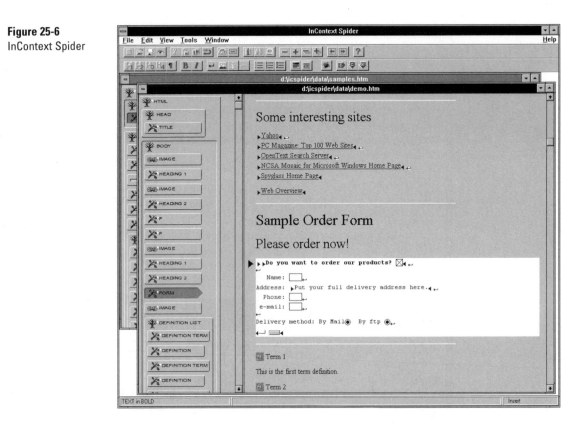

HTML DOCUMENT MANAGEMENT SYSTEMS

As authors have worked to place more and more content on the Web, they have sought tools that will not only allow them to easily create and manipulate one HTML document, but to manage a collection.

NaviPress (Figure 25-7) is one of the latest cross-platform document editing tools. It is a true WYSIWYG HTML editor that doubles as an HTML browser, and is available for Macintosh, Windows, and some UNIX platforms. NaviPress can be used to construct or edit HTML documents, put finished documents on a Web server (must be a NaviPress server), and even create and manage a set of HTML documents. The latter feature, managing a set of hypertexts, is a new but increasingly common feature among high-end commercial HTML tools. NaviPress refers to a collection of Web documents as a *miniweb*. It provides a simple point-and-click interface for establishing connections between HTML documents, in addition to editing each document's contents.

Each of these types of editors is designed for users with different skills and publishing goals. Simple HTML tag editors are often preferred by veteran HTML authors because they allow you to insert and view tags at all times, while relying on external browsers to provide a preview function. Translators and con-

Figure 25-7
NaviPress

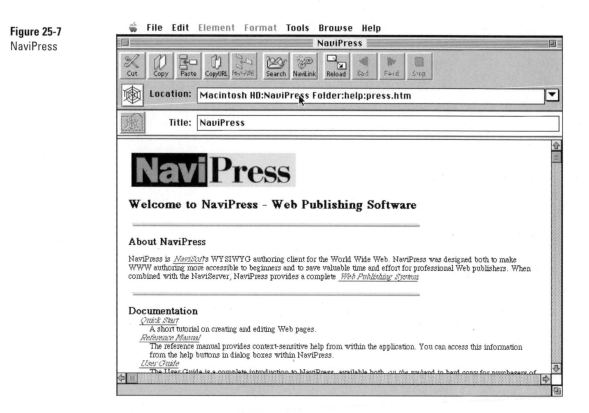

verters let you quickly publish large collections of existing electronic documents by mapping formatting or structural characteristics of a set of documents to HTML markup. WYSIWYG editors allow novice users to create eye-catching home pages with minimal knowledge of HTML. Structured Web page editors let users create platform-independent documents while enforcing high markup standards to ensure standards compatibility. Document management systems let publishers create and maintain large collections of hypertexts by providing both document-editing and hypertext-linking facilities. If you select a tool that matches your needs, HTML editors can save you both time and money.

Dynamic and Interactive Documents

26

Processing
Forms Data

CHAPTER AT A GLANCE

- Review of HTML form tags
- Overview of forms processing: the Common Gateway Interface
- Table 26-1: *Some Common MIME Types*
- Building valid documents in response to form submissions

HTML forms have made it possible for Web clients to function as interfaces into a world of data outside of the Web. Users can navigate non-HTML data such as relational databases through gateways consisting of HTML forms and gateway scripts. HTML forms markup contains enough types of input fields that many database interfaces can be readily duplicated as Web pages. HTML forms can provide primitive error checking by restricting the values allowed in certain fields to a pull-down list of options. While many systems establish a two-way connection between a client and an information server, referred to as a stateful connection, this is often not necessary for meaningful, responsive interaction with an information server. Any service that accepts a search value or set of input values, processes this data, and responds with a set of search results or an acknowledgment of receipt can be accessed through a Web form.

The World Wide Web is a stateless system. A Web browser establishes a connection with a server only long enough to request a document and receive it or an error message. This reduces the workload, particularly for the server system, which may be asked to deliver several files after it delivers the first HTML file. Each inline graphic must also be retrieved from the server, which requires a connection. So quickly delivering a file and breaking the connection with the client is in the server's best interests. But it does not always serve the client's best interests. Documents containing many inline graphics can take some time to load when each image requires that a new network connection be established. And systems that require stateful connections cannot be accessed by Web browsers.

Gateway scripts accept and process data from Web forms. Processing can be as simple as packaging the data as a mail message and sending it on to another site or as complex as building an SQL (Structured Query Language) query from the form content, passing it on to a relational database server such as Oracle, accepting the database reply, reformatting the result set into an HTML document, and delivering the results back to the Web client. While this processing is taking place, the Web client maintains the connection because it knows it must receive a Web document in response to its submission. It has no idea that an intermediate system might have established a stateful connection on its behalf in order to gather the data that will constitute the returned Web document. So gateway scripts need to be clever and efficient at their task in order to maintain the illusion of a simple request/reply protocol.

Review of Form Tags

Forms can include six different types of user input fields. Plain text input fields present users with a single line input field that scrolls horizontally when filled: <INPUT TYPE=TEXT>. These fields can be used to request user name, userid, search strings, or other information that will typically be less than 80 characters in length. Other variations on input fields include password input fields, hidden fields with values preassigned, and visible input fields with preassigned values. For longer free text entry, text area input fields <TEXTAREA> present a multirow, multicolumn region that can scroll both horizontally and vertically. Radio buttons present users with a list of choices from which they are to select only one, while checkboxes present a list of options that can each be independently selected (checked) or not. Both radio buttons <INPUT TYPE= RADIO> and checkboxes <INPUT TYPE=CHECKBOX> have preset values. Selection lists <SELECT> and <OPTION> also present users with a predefined set of options, of which they may select one or more items if the document author has configured the selection list to allow multiple selections. Submit buttons cause the contents of the form to be sent to a script, but in one special case, they also act as input devices. Image map input fields <INPUT TYPE=IMAGE> submit not only the form content but also the coordinates of the user's last mouse click.

Here is a pair of HTML form examples. The screen on the left has a pair of <INPUT TYPE=TEXT> fields and Reset and Submit buttons. But the form on the right looks like an ordinary list of hypertext links:

It is not. The second form was generated by a script that was the target of the first form. Each link on the page includes a URL to another script. Paired with that URL is an escaped name/value pair. When the user selects a link, the script sees this data and thinks the user entered the data accompanying the URL in a text entry field, when it actually looked like this:

<LI><A HREF="/cgi-bin/ER_course?query=Ande3869">Anderson,Mark</A>

The file has no <FORM> tag, but the data is encoded in such a way that any script that can handle GET method data can handle the data encoded in this URL. Building forms dynamically is but one of the many ways by which complex interactions between a Web client and a database system (in this case, an Oracle database) can be handled with forms and scripts.

PROCESSING HTML FORMS

Delivered with the contents of these fields are the names of the fields as specified by the form author. It is these pairs of field names and field contents that form scripts must process and respond to. The value assigned to the METHOD attribute of the <FORM> tag determines how the contents are processed by the gateway. This value can be GET or POST. The difference between these two values is due mainly to the platforms on which the Web was originally developed. Forms processing like the Web itself was initially developed on systems running the UNIX operating system. Scripts were originally UNIX shell scripts, C applications, or Perl scripts. The server expected to deliver data to a script in one of two ways used by scripts to communicate with one another before the Web ever came into being: they could either assign a set of name/value pairs to a single variable and pass this variable to the script's memory space, or pass the values on the command line. These two methods of data interchange used by UNIX applications correspond to the GET and POST methods used by forms today. If the method value was GET, then the script expects to find all of the data contained in the form in a variable called $QUERY_STRING. If the method was POST, then the data will be on the command line just as if a user had entered the script name and the forms content as a line of text following it in a terminal window. Since there is a limit (which varies from system to system) on the amount of data that can be stored in an environment variable, POST is safer for long forms, especially those with <TEXTAREA> fields. The length of the data being sent is placed in a variable called $CONTENT_LENGTH.

Web browsers must perform some additional processing in order to safely and unambiguously deliver data in this manner, and that is to "escape" the name/value pairs. The contents of the form are converted from an arbitrary collection of strings to one large string with no spaces and no special characters, just alphanumerics. Then this string is passed in an encoded block of data or as a URL to the processing script, again depending on the method type.

GET:
```
SERVER_SOFTWARE = NCSA/1.5b6
SERVER_NAME = hoohoo.ncsa.uiuc.edu
GATEWAY_INTERFACE = CGI/1.1
SERVER_PROTOCOL = HTTP/1.0
SERVER_PORT = 80
REQUEST_METHOD = GET
HTTP_ACCEPT = image/gif, image/x-xbitmap, image/jpeg, image/pjpeg, */*
HTTP_USER_AGENT = Mozilla/2.0b1 (Windows; I; 32bit)
HTTP_REFERER = http://scholar.lib.vt.edu/jpowell/form2.html
PATH_INFO =
PATH_TRANSLATED =
SCRIPT_NAME = /cgi-bin/test-cgi
QUERY_STRING =
database=inst_course&title=Ereserve+Instructor+List&field=last&query=Anderson
REMOTE_HOST = paisley.async.vt.edu
REMOTE_ADDR = 128.173.18.79
REMOTE_USER =
AUTH_TYPE =
CONTENT_TYPE =
CONTENT_LENGTH =
ANNOTATION_SERVER =
```

POST:
```
SERVER_SOFTWARE = NCSA/1.5b6
SERVER_NAME = hoohoo.ncsa.uiuc.edu
GATEWAY_INTERFACE = CGI/1.1
SERVER_PROTOCOL = HTTP/1.0
SERVER_PORT = 80
REQUEST_METHOD = POST
HTTP_ACCEPT = image/gif, image/x-xbitmap, image/jpeg, image/pjpeg, */*
```

Continued on next page

Continued from previous page

```
HTTP_USER_AGENT = Mozilla/2.0b1 (Windows; I; 32bit)
HTTP_REFERER = http://scholar.lib.vt.edu/jpowell/form1.html
PATH_INFO =
PATH_TRANSLATED =
SCRIPT_NAME = /cgi-bin/test-cgi
QUERY_STRING =
REMOTE_HOST = paisley.async.vt.edu
REMOTE_ADDR = 128.173.18.79
REMOTE_USER =
AUTH_TYPE =
CONTENT_TYPE = application/x-www-form-urlencoded
CONTENT_LENGTH = 77
ANNOTATION_SERVER =
database=inst_course&title=Ereserve+Instructor+List&field=last&query=Anderson
```

At this point you may be wondering why the client workstation doesn't just download the script with the form and run it locally. One reason this is not done is because there is no single accepted language for creating scripts. Perl is widely used but scripts are also written in Applescript, Visual Basic, C, and other languages. Some of these languages are compiled, that is, the program is converted to machine language suitable for only one type of computer platform. And of course, none of these languages have any mechanism for verifying that their programs have not been modified. So they would be an easy target for distributing viruses and other rogue programs. The Java language will change all of this, since it is platform independent, and secure. But for now, scripts still need to reside on and be run by a Web server.

Forms processing scripts are called CGI (Common Gateway Interface) scripts. They must reside in the Web server's cgi-bin directory and be executable by the computer running the Web server. Scripts can perform any number of tasks such as grabbing the latest weather satellite photographs, accessing data in a spread sheet, or submitting a search request to a database. They then reformat the requested data so that it is returned as an HTML document (or some other document type a Web browser can display or call a helper application to open). Their main activity is to act as an intermediary between a Web client, a Web server, and some set of data not necessarily available on the Web server system. That is why they are called gateways.

When a gateway application returns data to the Web browser, it must first clearly identify the document type being returned. In most instances, this will be an HTML document. But gateways are also used to return text files, GIF images, and file types that require helper applications such as VRML (Virtual Reality Modeling Language) documents. Whatever the document type, the gateway must specify it as the first line of data returned to the browser. This is called the content type or MIME (Multipurpose Internet Mail Extensions) type of the document. MIME was originally developed so that multimedia data could be included in mail messages. Here are a few MIME types commonly generated by gateway scripts (see Chapter 30 for a discussion of MIME types):

TABLE 26-1   SOME COMMON MIME TYPES GENERATED BY CGI SCRIPTS

Document type	Viewer	MIME type	File extension
HTML	Web browsers	text/html	.html, .htm, .htm3, .html3
ASCII text	Web browsers	text/plain	.txt, .text
Graphic	Web browsers	image/gif	.gif
VRML	VRML browser	x-world/x-vrml	.wrl

The document type can be any valid MIME type that the Web server executing the gateway application knows about. If you return a search result set as an HTML document, generated by the gateway script, you would need to return the data like this:

```
Content-type: text/html

<HTML>
<HEAD><TITLE>...
```

The first line must be Content-type: some mime type. This must be followed by a blank line, and only then can the actual document be sent back to the browser. A few browsers do cheat and try to assume the document is an HTML document, but most rely on this mechanism alone to tell them what type of document they are about to receive.

These are the key points to remember when planning a gateway:

- Provide a unique name attribute for each form-input field or option
- Use GET if the form is short, POST if the user reply might exceed 255 characters
- Unescape the data delivered from the browser so that spaces and special characters are unencoded
- Process the data or request as quickly as possible so the browser does not timeout
- Return a Content-type header with a MIME type registered with the Web server serving the CGI script, followed by a blank line
- Return the document and quit

CGI SCRIPT EXAMPLES

Now let's look at a couple of examples. The first form is probably the simplest form you will ever see. It is nothing more than a submit button that requests the status of the computer running the Web server. No data is passed to the CGI script, it is just asked to run:

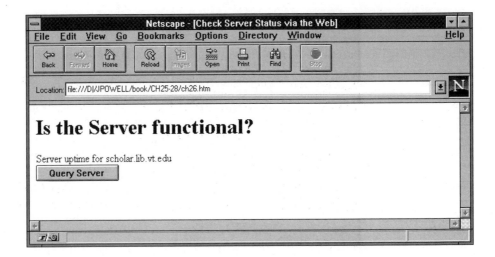

The gateway script is a Bourne shell script, a UNIX batch language similar to DOS .BAT files. Each line in the file could be typed at the UNIX command prompt and processed immediately, just like the DIR or COPY commands in DOS.

```
#!/bin/sh

UPTIME='which uptime'

echo Content-type: text/html
echo
echo "<H1>Uptime for server</H1>"
echo "<HR>"
echo "<H3>Uptime</H3>"
echo "<PRE>"
if [ -x $UPTIME ]; then
        $UPTIME
else
        echo Cannot find uptime command on this system.
fi
echo "</PRE>"
echo "<H3>Current Connections:</H3>"
echo "<PRE>"
netstat
echo "</PRE>"
echo "<HR>"
```

The script returns a simple HTML file (text/html) that is little more than the output of a pair of UNIX system commands: uptime (how long has the server been running?) and netstat (who is logged on?):

```
┌──────────────────────────────────────────────────────────────────────────┐
│ ─          Netscape - [http://scholar.lib.vt.edu/cgi-bin/uptime?]    ▼ ▲  │
├──────────────────────────────────────────────────────────────────────────┤
│ File   Edit   View   Go   Bookmarks   Options   Directory   Window   Help │
├──────────────────────────────────────────────────────────────────────────┤
│  ⇦      ⇨      ⌂      ⊚      ⊞      ⇄      ⎙      🔍      ●               │
│ Back  Forward  Home  Reload  Images  Open   Print   Find    Stop           │
├──────────────────────────────────────────────────────────────────────────┤
│  ⟋  Location: http://scholar.lib.vt.edu/cgi-bin/uptime?            ▼  N   │
├──────────────────────────────────────────────────────────────────────────┤
```

Uptime

```
    2:11am  up 13 days, 11:31,  1 user,  load average: 2.00, 1.76, 1.50
```

Current Connections:

```
Active Internet connections
Proto Recv-Q Send-Q  Local Address          Foreign Address          (state)
tcp        0      0  borg.4728              borg.711                 TIME_WAIT
tcp        0      0  localhost.4727         localhost.714            TIME_WAIT
tcp        0      0  localhost.4726         localhost.sunrpc         TIME_WAIT
tcp        0      0  borg.http              access.rrinc.com.3260    ESTABLISHED
tcp        0      0  borg.4725              europa03.netdepo.1336    TIME_WAIT
tcp        0      0  borg.4724              borg.711                 TIME_WAIT
tcp        0      0  localhost.4723         localhost.714            TIME_WAIT
tcp        0      0  localhost.4722         localhost.sunrpc         TIME_WAIT
tcp        0      0  borg.http              202.218.214.19.1576      TIME_WAIT
tcp        0      0  borg.4721              borg.711                 TIME_WAIT
tcp        0      0  localhost.4720         localhost.714            TIME_WAIT
tcp        0      0  localhost.4719         localhost.sunrpc         TIME_WAIT
```

```
 ⌐⊠  Document: Done                                                      ⊠
```

Our second example is a color picker for designing Netscape documents. It provides two possible input methods: some colors are hard coded into hypertext links that point to the CGI script, and there is also a text-input field for inputting other RGB color values.

```
<HTML><HEAD><TITLE>Netscape/RGB Color Guide
</TITLE></HEAD>
<!— Created with HTML-Editor for Nextstep —>
<BODY>
<FORM METHOD=POST ACTION="/cgi-bin/ColorPicker.pl">
<H1>Netscape/RGB Color Guide</H1>
<IMG SRC="/images/rainban.gif"><BR>
Netscape extensions allow you to change the color of the document background,
text and anchors.  Colors are assigned with a pound sign followed by three
sets of two digit hexadecimal numbers (00 to ff) to specify shades of red,
green and blue which are combined to create the color you actually see e.g.
<P><TT>&lt;BODY BACKGROUND="#C0C0C0"&gt;</TT><BR>
sets the background color to <A HREF="/cgi-
bin/ColorPicker.pl?color=c0c0c0">gray</A>, the default for most Web browsers.
<center>
```

Continued on next page

Continued from previous page

```
<TABLE BORDER WIDTH=200>
<caption><B>Common colors and their RGB codes:</B><BR></caption>
<tr><th>Red </th><td>
<A HREF="/cgi-bin/ColorPicker.pl?color=ff0000">#FF0000</A></td><br></tr>
<tr><th>Orange </th><td>
<A HREF="/cgi-bin/ColorPicker.pl?color=ff7f00">#FF7F00</A></td><br></tr>
<tr><th>Yellow </th><td>
<A HREF="/cgi-bin/ColorPicker.pl?color=ffff00">#FFFF00</A></td><br></tr>
<tr><th>Green </th><td>
<A HREF="/cgi-bin/ColorPicker.pl?color=00ff00">#00FF00</A></td><br></tr>
<tr><th>Cyan </th><td>
<A HREF="/cgi-bin/ColorPicker.pl?color=00ffff">#00FFFF</A></td><br></tr>
<tr><th>Blue </th><td>
<A HREF="/cgi-bin/ColorPicker.pl?color=0000ff">#0000FF</A></td><br></tr>
<tr><th>Purple </th><td>
<A HREF="/cgi-bin/ColorPicker.pl?color=db70db">#DB70DB</A></td><br></tr>
<tr><th>Black </th><td>
<A HREF="/cgi-bin/ColorPicker.pl?color=000000">#000000</A></td><br></tr>
<tr><th>White </th><td>
<A HREF="/cgi-bin/ColorPicker.pl?color=ffffff">#FFFFFF</A></td><br></tr>
</table><BR>
Try other combinations to get the hang of blending red, green and blue for new
colors: <INPUT NAME="color" size=8>
</FORM>
</center>
<HR>
<A HREF="slides-contents.html">&lt;&lt;</A>
</BODY>
</HTML>
```

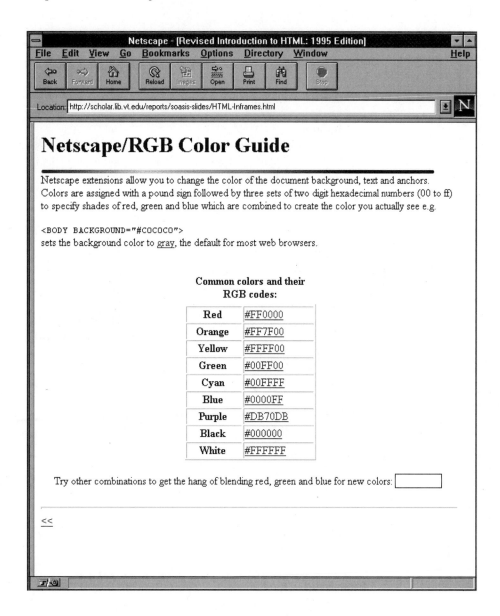

The script, written in Perl, first checks to make sure a value was provided for the single required form name/value pair: color. If no value was provided, then the script executes the blank_response function, notifying the user of an error with a short HTML document, and quits. Otherwise, it builds an HTML file assigning the given color to the <BODY BGCOLOR=> attribute of the document it returns. Here's the source for ColorPicker.pl:

```perl
#!/usr/local/bin/perl
# Program   ColorPicker.pl
# Summary: Accepts 6 digit hex number and returns colorized doc
# Programmer:       James Powell
# Date:       10 Aug 95
#
# Description:
# This application accepts a 6 digit hexadecimal value corresponding
# to RGB color codes rrggbb. It returns a Netscape-compliant
# document with the selected color set as its background.
#
#
#----------------------- CONFIGURATION SECTION -----------------------
# name of the Web server
$servername = "scholar";
@required_fields=("color");
#----------------------- END OF CONFIGURATION SECTION ---------------

# ReadParse puts the form data delivered by the Web server into the
# %in associative array. &ReadParse is a function in the external
# Perl library cgi-lib.pl, available on the Web
#
require("/usr/local/etc/httpd/cgi-bin/cgi-lib.pl");
&ReadParse();

# First return the content type of the document being generated
print "Content-type: text/html\n\n";
foreach $item(@required_fields) {
    &blank_response unless $in{$item};
}

print "<HTML>\n";
print "<HEAD>\n";
print "<TITLE>BGCOLOR=$in{'color'}</TITLE>\n";
print "</HEAD>\n<BODY BGCOLOR=$in{'color'}>\n";
print "<center>\n";
print "<table border><tr><td><IMG
    SRC=\"/images/logobar.gif\"></td></tr>\n";
print "</table>\n";
print "<H1>This is what $in{'color'} looks like...</H1>\n";
print "<TABLE BORDER><TR><TD><IMG SRC=\"/images/scp-
    logo.gif\"></TD></tr>\n";
print "</TABLE>\n<P>";
print "Service provided by <A
    HREF=\"http://scholar.lib.vt.edu/\">Scholarly Communications
    Project</A></center><P>";
```

```
print "<A HREF=\"/reports/soasis-slides/colors.html\"><B>Return to
    Color Guide</B></A><P>\n";
print "<A HREF=\"/reports/soasis-slides/slides-
    contents.html\">&lt;&lt; Go to Table of Contents</A> for
    <I>Introduction to HTML</I>\n";

&successmsg();
# Blurt out the footer stuff for the HTML return document.
print "<hr><address>$servername<br>";
print '/bin/date +"%d %b %y, %I:%M %p';
print "</address></body>\n</HTML>\n";

exit;

# subroutine blank_response
# let user know what they forgot
#
sub blank_response
{
    print "<H2>We're sorry, your call cannot be completed as
        dialed.</H2>";
    print "You must first dial a color before continuing, this is a
        recording\n";
    print "<HR></BODY></HTML>\n";
    exit;
}
```

It returns an HTML document (text/html), generated on the fly (meaning that the CGI script creates it). This document uses the selected RGB color value as the value assigned to the Netscape <BODY BGCOLOR=> attribute:

```
<HTML><HEAD>
<TITLE>BGCOLOR=ff0000</TITLE>
</HEAD>
<BODY BGCOLOR=ff0000>
<center>
<table border><tr><td><IMG SRC="/images/logobar.gif"></td></tr>
</table>
<H1>This is what ff0000 looks like...</H1>
<TABLE BORDER><TR><TD><IMG SRC="/images/scp-logo.gif"></TD></tr>
</TABLE>
<P>Service provided by <A HREF="http://scholar.lib.vt.edu/">Scholarly
Communications Project</A></center><P><A HREF="/reports/soasis-
slides/colors.html"><B>Return to Color Guide</B></A><P>
<A HREF="/reports/soasis-slides/slides-contents.html">&lt;&lt; Go to Table of
Contents</A> for <I>Introduction to HTML</I>
```

Continued on next page

Continued from previous page

```
<hr><address>scholar<br>Tue Oct 24 21:40:15 EDT 1995
</address></body>
</HTML>
```

As you can see, CGI gateways are an extremely flexible and powerful tool. They can be used to generate HTML and other document types on the fly, and even as interfaces to software applications and database systems. In the next chapter, we will explore the Perl scripting language. We will construct a simple Web-based VRML (Virtual Reality Modeling Language) editor to demonstrate features of the language. CGI scripts can be adapted to interact with systems not yet even conceived; VRML and Netscape were developed some time after HTML forms and CGI scripts were initially implemented on the Web!

Very Gentle Introduction to Perl

CHAPTER AT A GLANCE

- Introduction to Perl: data structures, control structures, input/output, functions
- Table 27-1: *Perl Comparison Operators*
- Developing Perl applications
- Perl functions for processing forms data and returning HTML documents
- Project: *A Simple VRML Editor*

Many new Internet trends started out on computers running the UNIX operating system. This complex environment has many problems and associated resources for resolving these problems, which are not available or even needed under less complex operating systems. UNIX machines generally function as servers, that is, they support multiple users accessing resources simultaneously. The job of maintaining or administering a UNIX system is far more difficult than managing the files and resources on a single-user system such as a Macintosh or Windows-based PC. A good deal of that management task involves text processing: moving groups of files, changing passwords, and managing server applications often involving text-based configuration or data files. And since UNIX first evolved as a system to nurture and cater to the needs of software developers, many tools have been developed on this platform to serve both developers and administrators. One such tool is Perl, or the Practical Extraction and Reporting Language.

Perl is an interpreted language. This means that each line of the program is read and processed at the time the program is executed. Other languages such as C or Pascal are first compiled into machine language, the native language of the computer. Compilers can often catch errors while building the executable, while programs written in interpreted languages such as Perl must be run in order to determine whether or not they have errors. Interpreted languages also tend to be somewhat slower than compiled languages since there are actually two programs running: the Perl script and the Perl interpreter.

Most Perl programs start with a line declaring the location of the Perl interpreter. On UNIX systems, this line often looks like this:

```
#!/usr/local/bin/perl
```

Pound signs occurring anywhere else in a Perl script tell the interpreter that the data following the symbol is a comment and should be ignored. Comments help other programmers understand what your program is doing, as well as identifying the overall purpose, the author, and other information about your script. You should use comments liberally to explain statements, variables, and functions. They have no impact on the speed of your program and consume only minimal additional disk space.

STATEMENTS

Every line in a Perl program that instructs the computer to actually perform a task is called a statement. Statements should always end with semicolons (;). Perl statements consist of data structures, functions, variable assignments, and other operations used to process data. When all operations are completed, a Perl script should end with an exit statement declaring whether or not the program completed successfully:

```
exit (1); # true, successful completion
```

or

```
exit (0); # false, something went wrong
```

Here is the basic structure of a Perl script:

```
#!/usr/local/bin/perl
# Name: a_program
# Author: Jane Doe
# Usage: type the program name followed by one or more numbers,
#    e.g. a_program 2 3
...
# Perl statements
...
exit (0);
```

Statements can perform any number of tasks in a script. Assignment statements place data such as numbers or strings into variables. Collections of related values can be stored in arrays or associative arrays. While statements are normally processed in the order in which they are listed in the program, control structures can be used to skip or repeat statements as needed. Frequently used statements can be grouped into miniprograms called functions, and assigned a name so they can be referred to without repeating a block of statements over and over again. And most importantly, the statements can request data from the user and display the result of all this work using input/output statements.

So let's find out how to construct Perl statements.

DATA STRUCTURES

Perl has several data structures. Data structures are variables that store certain types of data. Unlike many programming languages, you don't need to declare the type of a data structure before you use it in Perl. Perl figures out the type when you first assign a value to a variable. Some data structures do have a specific syntax, however, which is synonymous with declaring the type. But first let's look at the most basic data structure: scalar data. A scalar is one value assigned to one variable. That value can be a number, a character, or a string of characters. Scalar variables begin with a dollar sign ($) and are named with alphanumeric characters. Scalar variable names can also include underscore characters (_). Scalar values include any type of numeric data or strings of alphanumeric data. Strings must be surrounded by single or double quotes when assigned to a scalar variable. These quotes do not become part of the value stored in the scalar. Here are some examples of scalar variables being assigned values:

```
$zip_code = 24060;
$name = "John Doe";
```

OPERATORS

Perl includes a number of operators that can be used to modify or evaluate the value of a scalar variable. Mathematical operators such as +, -, and = can be used on numeric scalar values:

```
$total = $amount_of_purchase * 4.5;
```

Perl also has C-like increment/decrement operators for numeric scalars that add or subtract one from a value:

```
$count++;
```

is equivalent to

```
$count=$count+1;
```

and

    $count+=1;

String operators such as period (.) can be used to merge, or concatenate two strings together:

    $name=$first_name.$last_name;

The chop() operator removes the last character in a line. The statements

    $name="John Doe";
    chop($name);

cause the last character in $name to be removed so that $name now contains "John Do".

Comparison operators are used to compare the values of two scalar variables. For example, you might want to create a list of people with the last name "Doe," so you would use a comparison operator to compare each scalar variable to a string value to decide if the current name is identical to the name you are looking for:

    $last_name eq "Doe"

Perl uses different comparison operators for strings and numeric values. If a numeric value is compared to a string using a string comparison operator, then the numeric value is treated as though it were a string during that operation, which might yield unexpected results. Table 27-1 lists the various Perl comparison operators and the string and numeric equivalents.

TABLE 27-1   PERL COMPARISON OPERATORS

Comparison Operator	String	Numeric
Equal to	eq	==
Not equal to	ne	!=
Less than	lt	<
Greater than	gt	>
Less than or equal to	le	<=
Greater than or equal to	ge	>=

Statements utilizing scalar operators are also referred to as expressions. The value of an expression (such as "2+2") is used by other types of Perl language structures to decide whether or not to perform a particular statement. There are other types of scalar operators in Perl such as binary assignment operators. But the operators we have covered so far (math, string, and comparison) are the most commonly used operators in this or any other programming language.

ARRAYS

Perl also supports several types of arrays. Arrays contain sets of data. A simple array might contain a list of post office boxes or street names. Array names begin with the at sign (@) to tell Perl this is a set of data and not just one scalar value. The values to be placed in the array are comma-separated and enclosed in parentheses:

```
@streets = ("Jones", "Taylor", "Mason", "Powell");
```

Individual items stored in an array can be addressed by replacing the @ sign with a $ sign and then specifying the item number desired (Perl numbers array items starting with 0) in square brackets:

```
$streets[2]="Mason";
```

To get two or more values from the array, use the array name with a comma-separated list of item numbers in square brackets ([ ]):

```
@streets[2,3]; # Mason and Powell
```

While this might seem confusing, remember that the contents of an array are simply multiple scalar values. So when you only want one, use a scalar version of the name, specified with the $ sign just like other scalar variables, followed of course by the index value in brackets.

An associative array contains pairs of data. Names and phone numbers might be stored in an associative array, so that if you know a name, you can get at the person's phone number, and vice versa, provided the values are stored in alternating order within the array. Associative arrays are ideal for storing the name/value pairs from Web forms. Associative array names start with a percent (%) sign:

```
%phone_list = ("Jane Doe", "555-1244", "John Doe", "555-9987");
```

What makes associative arrays especially powerful are the various ways in which the data can be accessed. For example, to access John Doe's phone number, simply use his name as an item specifier, or key, to access the other half of the value pair:

```
$phone_list("John Doe"); # is equivalent to 555-9987
```

Keys are the odd-numbered items within the array. You can access each pair of items in the associate array with the foreach control structure (discussed below) and the keys operator:

```
foreach $names (keys %phone_list) {
# put a name in $names and process statements between curly brackets
# repeat until you reach the end of the list
    $name=$names; # Jane Doe first time through, John Doe next
    $phone_number=$phone_list($names); # 555-1244, then 555-9987
}
```

Other useful operators include values( ) which accesses the even-numbered items in an associative array, and each( ) which returns a pair consisting of one key (odd-numbered item) and its associated value (even-numbered item).

CONTROL STRUCTURES

Statements can be grouped into blocks of statements with curly braces ({ }). Statements are grouped when they work together to accomplish a task. Control structures cause statements and blocks of statements to be repeated a certain number of times or to be selectively executed or skipped. Without control structures, a Perl script would be limited to performing each statement only once, in sequence.

All control statements use expressions to selectively process a statement or block of statements. The if/else statement pair selectively processes a statement or statement block one time:

```perl
if ($name="John Doe")
{
    $wife="Jane Doe";
} else
{
    # do something else
}
```

if/else statements can be strung together to check for a number of possible values using elsif:

```perl
if ($street="Mason")
{
    $turn="left";
} elsif ($street="Powell")
{
    $turn="right";
} else
{
    $turn="Lost!";
}
```

The while and until structures repeat a set of statements until a certain condition is met. while performs an action while the expression is true, until performs a statement block until an expression becomes true:

```perl
while ($name ne "Jane Doe") {
    # perform some statements
}

until ($name eq "Jane Doe") {
    # perform some statements
}
```

The for structure performs an action a specified number of times. It includes an assignment statement, a conditional expression, and an increment statement:

```
for ($count=0; $count<10; $count++) {
    # do something ten times
}
```

Finally, as demonstrated previously, foreach works its way through a set of values stored in an associative array.

INPUT/OUTPUT AND FILE I/O

There would be little point to all this work if we could not interact with the program and get results from it. Perl treats all input and output as though it were interacting with files. If the output file is not declared, then output is sent wherever the program's standard output is directed. If you are running the program from a command line, this means it is displayed in the window from which the program was started. If the Perl program is a CGI script, then the standard output is grabbed by the Web server and returned to the Web browser. Data delivered to the program from this location will be found in a "file" called <STDIN>, or standard input.

One of the most confusing aspects of Perl is the special variables it uses. File input and output usually involves one of these special variables, $_, which contains the current line retrieved from an input source. Consider this statement block that reads several lines from stdin and sends each back to stdout:

```
while (<STDIN>) { # when the end of the data
                # is reached, this returns false
    print $_; # send the current line from standard in,
                # stored in $_ to standard out
}
```

This statement block has the effect of echoing data typed in back to the screen, if stdin and stdout are both in the same window. Files can be accessed for input by specifying them on the command line with the script name. The data in the file is accessed using while(<>) instead of <STDIN>. <> is a shortcut to explicitly opening a file and assigning a variable name called a file handle to it, in order to retrieve data:

```
open (phone_list, "phone_list.txt");
while (<phone_list>) {
    # each line is placed, one per loop in $_
}
```

Perl output is performed with the print and printf statements. The print statement sends a quoted string or set of strings to a file or to stdout. If a file is specified, it must be opened using single or double greater than signs which mean open and replace contents, or open and append to contents, respectively:

```
open (phone_list, ">phone_list.txt"); # notice >, this means open and
                                       # replace the contents
print "hello, world"; # print one string to standard out
print ("hello, ", "world"); print a pair of strings to standard out
print phone_list "hello, world"; # print a string to the file opened
                                 # with the filehandle phone_list
```

The printf statement allows you to perform formatted output, just like the C programming language statement of the same name.

FUNCTIONS

Functions, also referred to as subroutines, are blocks of statements that can be referred to by name as needed in the main program. The statement block is declared with sub followed by the name and the statements to be executed:

```
sub counter {
    for ($count=0; $count<10; $count++) {
        # count to ten
    }
}
```

Functions can be declared anywhere in the program but it is best to group them at the beginning or end of the program, to avoid confusion and make them easier to keep track of. When a function is needed, simply refer to it by name using a statement like this, beginning with an ampersand (&):

```
&counter; # counts to ten
```

Functions can access variables declared in the main program, but sometimes you may wish to pass values to the function as arguments. Arguments are listed after the function name in parentheses when it is called:

```
&counter($start, $end);
```

Arguments are also accessed from another strangely named array called @_. The function counter can find these two arguments in $_[0] and $_[1]:

```
sub counter {
    for ($counter=$_[0]; $count<$_[1]; $count++)
        # count from the value assigned to start, $_[0], to the value
        # assigned to $end, $_[1]
    }
}
```

Functions can have their own "private" variables. They must be declared at the beginning of the function using the local() operator:

```
sub counter {
    local($counter); # $counter is only visible inside the function's statement block
```

Functions can return values. The value of the last expression in the function is returned to the main program. So a scalar can be assigned to a function name to access it:

```
$counted_to = &counter($start, $end); # would be assigned the
                                # value of $_[1] ($end)
```

Finally, functions can be stored in separate files. You might want to do this if you have a set of functions that perform a specific task (such as tagging text with HTML tags) that you will want to use in more than one Perl program. You can call these functions just like functions you declare in your script, but first you must tell your script to use the function library:

```
require "/usr/local/sources/cgi-lib.pl"; # might contain a few or dozens of functions
```

DATA TRANSFORMATION

Data transformation involves the process of extracting and converting single characters and character strings into other characters or strings. Character replacement is performed with the transliteration (tr), and substitute (s) operators. Substitution replaces one character (following the first forward slash) with another (following the second forward slash):

```
$phone="540-555-5010";
$phone=~ s/-/./;
```

The first line assigns a phone number to the scalar variable $phone. The second line tells the substitute operator to process the $phone variable, indicated by the tilde (~), substituting periods (.) for each dash (-) it finds.

The transliteration operator performs the same function on a range of letters. Here all capital letters are replaced with lowercase letters in a string:

```
$name="JANE DOE";
$name=~ tr/A-Z/a-z/;
```

Ever more complex search-and-replace strings can be constructed with regular expressions. An entire book could be devoted to the topic of regular expressions. Basically, they are a set of pattern-matching commands that can be combined with strings of characters to locate specific strings or match character patterns. They can be used with assignment statements, conditional structures, and character transformation operators to examine and modify the contents of a string. The transliteration and substitution examples above both use regular expressions to identify a character /-/./ or a range of characters /A-Z/a-z/. Regular expressions are most commonly used in CGI scripts to "unescape" form content as in the following form-parsing function:

```perl
# cgi-lib.pl is an external module containing one function called
# "ReadParse" which extracts field name-value pairs from a form and
# unescapes them returning the data in an associative array called
# "in"
sub ReadParse {
# Retrieve GET or POST form data
    if ($ENV{'REQUEST_METHOD'} eq "GET") {
        $buffer=$ENV{'QUERY_STRING'};
    } else {
        $content_length=$ENV{'CONTENT_LENGTH'};
        for ($count=0; $count<$length; $count++) {
            $buffer.=getc;
    }
    }

    # Split the name-value pairs
    @formdata = split(/&/, $buffer);

    foreach $pair (@formdata)
    {
        ($name, $value) = split(/=/, $pair);

        # Unescape data in value
        # convert plus signs back to spaces
        $value =~ tr/+/ /;
        # convert hexadecimal representations back to ASCII characters
        $value =~ s/%([a-fA-F0-9][a-fA-F0-9])/pack("C", hex($1))/eg;
        # now put the name-value pair into the associative array
        $in{$name} = $value;
    }
}
return 1;
```

In Chapter 8, the forms project was a simple quiz on the Malay language. We can use a CGI script written in Perl to "grade" the responses to the test questions. Here's the Perl source for the grading program (score-test); note the use of cgi-lib.pl to extract name/value pairs from the form data:

```perl
#!/usr/local/bin/perl
require ("/usr/local/etc/httpd/cgi-bin/cgi-lib.pl");
&ReadParse;

print "Content-type: text/html\n\n";
print "<HTML>\n<HEAD><TITLE>Your Score</TITLE></HEAD>\n";
print "<BODY>\n<H1>Test 1 Score</H1>\n";

$score=0;
$no_questions=7;
```

```
if ($in{'q1'} eq "Malaysia") { $score+=1; }
if ($in{'q2a'} eq "English") { $score+=1; }
if (!$in{'q2b'}) { $score+=1; }
if ($in{'q2c'} eq "Dutch") { $score+=1; }
if (!$in{'q2d'}) { $score+=1; }
$q3=$in{'q3'};
$q3=~ tr/A-Z/a-z/;
if (($q3 eq "beras") || ($q3 eq "nasi")) { $score+=1; }
if ($in{'q4'} eq "ayam-ayam") { $score+=1; }
$score=100/7 * $score;
print "<EM>Your score was $score</EM>\n<HR>\n</BODY>\n</HTML>\n";

exit 0;
```

Regular expressions are a powerful feature of Perl. If you find that you need to perform a lot of string or character pattern matching, you may want to consult a text devoted exclusively to Perl.

Perl has data transformation operators for locating and extracting substrings from alphanumeric strings of characters. The index() and rindex() operators locate the left-most and right-most occurrence of a string, respectively, and return a numeric value that corresponds to the position of the first letter of that string, its index value:

```
$names="Jane Doe John Doe";
$leftmost=index($names, "Doe"); # returns 5
$rightmost=rindex($names, "Doe"); # returns 14
```

If the string is not found, index returns -1. It does not return 0 (which is normally the value used for "false"), since it is possible for the substring to start in the first position in the string, which is 0. Substrings can be extracted from a string using the substr() operator, by providing the string variable name, and the start point and length of the string you wish to extract:

```
$names="Jane Doe John Doe";
$leftmost=index($names, "Doe");
$last=substr($names, $leftmost, 3);
```

There are more operators and language structures, but we've covered most of the Perl language features you will use when writing CGI scripts.

PROJECT: A SIMPLE VRML EDITOR

While Perl is fairly easy to learn, particularly for individuals with some programming experience, it is also quite powerful. To demonstrate the potential of Perl combined with Web forms, here is a simple VRML (Virtual Reality Modeling Language) editor. VRML is a text-based language for describing three-dimensional objects and worlds. These documents are delivered by Web servers to VRML-capable browsers. VRML is discussed in some detail in Chapters 33 and

34. This editor allows users to create basic shapes: spheres, cones, or cubes in various sizes by selecting options and providing dimensions using this HTML form:

```
<HEAD><TITLE>Simple VRML Editor</TITLE></HEAD>
<BODY>
<H1><IMG SRC="vrmlogo.gif" alt="VRML">
Editor</H1>
<P>
This form allows you to specify shapes and shape dimensions
for objects that are to be rendered by a Virtual Reality
Modeling Language Browser. The shapes are automatically
positioned apart from one another, so they do not overlap,
unless you turn on overlap mode.
<HR>
<FORM METHOD=GET ACTION="/cgi-bin/VRML-Editor">
<TABLE>
<TR><TD COLSPAN=2>Overlap Mode? <INPUT NAME="Overlap" TYPE=RADIO
VALUE="On"> On <INPUT NAME="Overlap"
TYPE=RADIO VALUE="Off" CHECKED> Off</TD></TR>
```

```
<TR><TD COLSPAN=2>Distance between objects (only applies if Overlap mode is
Off): <INPUT NAME="transform"
SIZE="4"></TD></TR>
<TR><TD>Select shape 1: <SELECT NAME="shape1"><option
selected>Cone<option>Sphere<option>Cylinder
</SELECT></TD><TD>Dimensions of Object -&gt; Radius <INPUT NAME="radius1"
SIZE="4"> Height (if applicable):
<INPUT NAME="height1" SIZE="4"></TD></TR>
<TR><TD>Select shape 2: <SELECT NAME="shape2"><option>Cone<option
selected>Sphere<option>Cylinder
</SELECT></TD><TD>Dimensions of Object -&gt; Radius <INPUT NAME="radius2"
SIZE="4"> Height (if applicable):
<INPUT NAME="height2" SIZE="4"></TD></TR>
<TR><TD>Select shape 3: <SELECT
NAME="shape3"><option>Cone<option>Sphere<option selected>Cylinder
</SELECT></TD><TD>Dimensions of Object -&gt; Radius <INPUT NAME="radius3"
SIZE="4"> Height (if applicable):
<INPUT NAME="height3" SIZE="4"></TD></TR>
</TABLE>
<P>
<INPUT TYPE=RESET VALUE="Start Over"> <INPUT TYPE=SUBMIT VALUE="Draw
It!">
</FORM>
</BODY>
</HTML>
```

The script has to deal with several input fields from an HTML form, so it calls cgi-lib.pl (from earlier in this chapter) to unescape the data and convert it into name/value pairs. It creates VRML code for up to three 3-D shapes (See Chapters 33–34 for more information about VRML).

```perl
#!/usr/local/bin/perl
# VRML-Editor
# A simple forms-based VRML editor implemented with HTML and Perl

# cgi-lib.pl from Chapter 27
require("/usr/local/sources/cgi-lib.pl");
# function from cgi-lib.pl to unescape and extract name-value pairs
# from form data
&ReadParse;

# Now return a VRML document
print "Content-type: x-world/x-vrml\n\n";
print "#VRML V1.0 ascii\n\n";
# access settings for each object
for ($count=1; $count<4; $count++) {
    $radius = $in{"radius$count"};
    if ($radius>0) {
```

Continued on next page

Continued from previous page

```
            # generate VRML for a separator node to contain the shape
            print "DEF shape$count Separator \{\n";
            # add a transform node if overlap mode is off
            if (($in{'Overlap'} ne "On") && ($count>1)) {
                transform($in{'transform'}+($radius*4));
        }
        # now build the specified shape
        print "  Material \{emissiveColor 1 1 1 \}\n";
        print "   $in{\"shape$count\"} ";
        if ($in{"shape$count"} eq "Sphere") {
            print "\{ radius $radius \}\n\}\n";
        } else {
                print "\{ radius $radius height $in{\"height$count\"}\}\n\}\n";
            }
        }
    }
    exit 0;

    sub transform {
    # apply a tranform node to each shape
    # move the shapes four radii plus distance specified by user
        local($distance)=pop(@_);
        print "Transform \{ translation $distance $distance $distance \}\n";
    }
```

A VRML document (MIME type x-world/x-vrml) is generated and returned by the CGI script. When the Web browser sees the VRML Content-type, it passes the data on to a VRML browser:

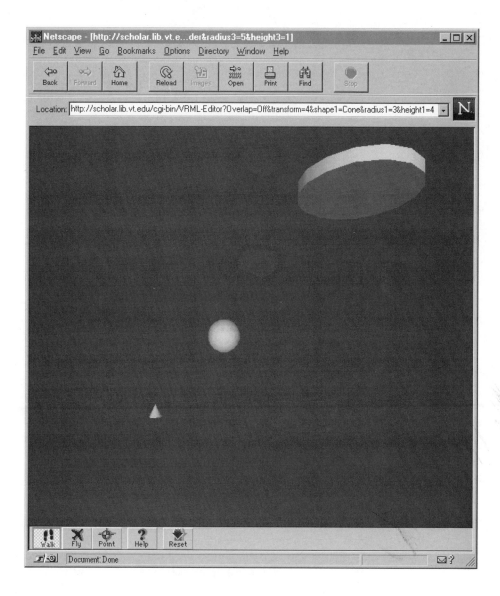

28

Search Systems and HTML

CHAPTER AT A GLANCE

- How to make your documents searchable
- How some of the tools used to index the Web work
- *ABC's of Search Types*

Hypertext systems are designed to facilitate quick access to their content. But as the number of documents and document fragments increases and the number of ways to get at the information grows to suit various users, it becomes more difficult to reach a particular piece of information quickly. It is also difficult to anticipate and accommodate the needs of every type of user. This is where a search capability can help. A search option allows a user to navigate by providing a word or phrase that should be part of the content of any targeted document. The search engine looks for files that contain the word or phrase specified and returns a list of documents.

Small collections of documents can be searched with a very simple search engine. Below we build just such a search option. It includes a Web form for the user to provide a search string and a CGI script that checks each file in a directory for this string. However, as the number of documents increases, this type of search system rapidly becomes unusable. The problem is that every document must be opened and every line examined. A computer can perform this task on ten or a hundred small documents and respond within a reasonable period of time, depending on the type of computer and number of users and programs being run concurrently. But try searching thousands of documents of varying lengths stored in dozens of directories, and the task becomes virtually impossible. Multiply it by ten or a hundred users and you will find that it could take days for a user to receive a list of documents matching their query—literally days. Yet we are able to search so-called meta indexes that index large chunks of the Web and receive a list of matching documents in a matter of seconds. How is this possible?

The key is indexing. Virtually all of the meta index systems (systems that index documents on more than one server) on the Web are built around an index. The index is built by a tool that opens and extracts portions of the document for storage in a central file together with a pointer to the document from which this data was extracted. An index might contain every word in a document, but more likely it will only contain words it deems significant or a summary of each document. An indexing program determines if a word is significant by length, number of occurrences, or other criteria. Many meta indexes on the Web simply record the contents of the <TITLE> element of an HTML document together with its URL. Others look for keywords as well, such as those embedded in a <META> or comment tag:

<META NAME="keywords" CONTENT="html, markup">

Ultimately, everything depends on content. The HTML document should include sufficient information for a user to locate it. Keywords, synonyms, and a descriptive title are essential components of an HTML document destined to be indexed.

So there are really two issues to consider when you are preparing a site that might be indexed or you yourself might index. What should be added to or included in each HTML document to enhance its searchability? And how many documents on how many computer systems will need to be included in the index? It is not necessary to dissect the indexing algorithm to learn how to select a search system and prepare documents for it. Instead you need to figure out who your audience is and determine what issues are critical to them. If performance is critical then you will want to find a system that can quickly locate matching documents, perhaps at the expense of reducing the number of ways people can search. If users want Boolean, word stem, or proximity searching capabilities, then they will probably get these features instead of rapid responses to searches. You can compensate to a certain degree by planning for the type of search system you need and budget for more powerful equipment and faster network connections if needed. It is never too early to begin considering the search options, even if you do not believe it is necessary at the onset.

Search systems for the Web consist of several components (Figure 28-1). First, a collection of texts is indexed with an indexing program. It is at this point that you can narrow down the list of possible search engines to suit your needs. While most any search engine can be extended to index documents from multiple sites, most are designed to index documents stored on the same computer on which the search software is installed. Tools such as freeWAIS for UNIX and WebSite for Windows-based systems are designed to index local collections of files. The Harvest system includes facilities for selecting and indexing the contents of many Web servers. The path and server name are recorded with the document name as each is indexed, so the result set will include full URLs to each document that matched a user's search. In both types of systems, the index

Figure 28-1
Components of a search system

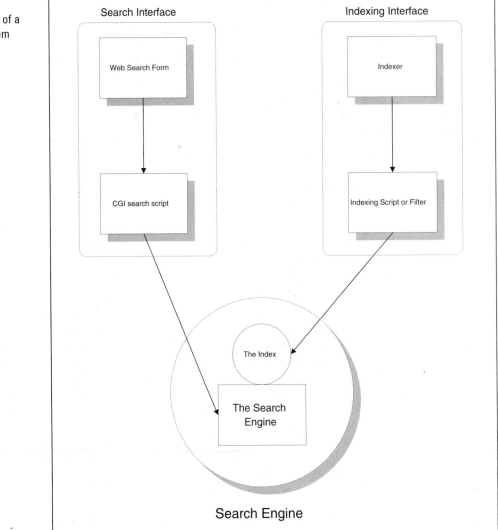

is stored on one computer, so you should make sure sufficient hard drive space is available on the system indexing and responding to searches.

WWW_SEARCH: A LOCAL SOLUTION

Meta indexes certainly have a major role to play on the Web. But there are many instances in which they are overkill. Ideally, most complex hypertext document collections should incorporate a local search option to help new and expert users quickly locate content without navigating through possibly several layers of hypertext links. Depending on the size of the archive, even search systems that index documents can provide more features (and be correspondingly more complex and difficult to maintain) for this scenario. Perhaps only a few users will utilize the search option. In this case, it might be easier to implement a simple search service that reviews each document in the archive every time a user performs a search. There are no indexes to maintain, no indexing programs to configure, and the index never has to be rebuilt since it is always as current as the archive contents themselves.

```perl
#!/usr/local/bin/perl
# WWW_Search - simple search script for a small collection of Web
#   documents in a single directory
# cgi-lib.pl from Chapter 27
require("/usr/local/etc/httpd/cgi-bin/cgi-lib.pl");

# configuration section
$docs="/home/WWW/";
$url="http://server/";
# ReadParse - function from Chapter 27 to extract name-value pairs
#   from form content
&ReadParse;

# Use UNIX grep command to search contents of the files
# place the list of files that match into /tmp/results
system ("cd $docs");
system ("grep $in{'query'} * > /tmp/results");

# Now return the list as an HTML document
print "Content-type: text/html\n\n";
print "<HTML><HEAD><TITLE>Results</TITLE></HEAD>\n<BASE HREF=$url>\n";
print "<BODY>\n";
open (results, "/tmp/results");
while (<results>) {
    ($filename, $context) = split(/:/, $_);
    print "<LI><A HREF=\"$filename\">$filename:$context</A>\n";
}
print "</UL>\n</BODY>\n</HTML>";
exit 0;
```

WWW_Search has no Indexing Interface or Search Engine (see Figure 28-1). All of the work is handled by the CGI search script. The Web Search Form is correspondingly simple:

```
<HTML>
<HEAD><TITLE>Search Docs</TITLE></HEAD>
<BODY>
<FORM METHOD=GET ACTION="/cgi-bin/WWW_Search">
Search for: <INPUT NAME="query" SIZE=20><BR>
<INPUT TYPE=RESET VALUE="Clear"><INPUT TYPE=SUBMIT VALUE="Search">
</FORM>
</BODY>
</HTML>
```

The search script presents the results as a set of hypertext links, as would be found in a real, static document. WWW_Search is a fast, simple solution for indexing a small set of documents contained in a single directory, but it does not scale to support searching hundreds or thousands of documents. Other search systems are suitable for providing this capability.

Indexing and Search Options

WWW_Search is limited to documents stored in one directory on a single server. We will now look at two other indexing options from the dozens of possibilities. The first, freeWAIS, can be used to index documents stored on a single server. The second, Harvest, can be used to index documents on a number of servers using a list of hosts and directories as a guide. It is important to realize that these search systems are constructed from a number of components. The freeWAIS solution described here uses an HTML form with a CGI script to perform searches and display results, a Perl script to build a list of documents to be indexed, and the waisindex program to build the index. Harvest uses an application called the Gatherer to retrieve documents, an indexing system called GLIMPSE (GLobal IMPlicit SEarch) to index the documents, and an application called the Broker to handle search requests. Harvest even allows you to swap the default search engine for another, such as WAIS, if desired.

There are many other issues to consider when selecting a search engine for a hypertext project. Cost is a consideration. Several powerful search engines are freely available for UNIX. Solutions for Macintosh and Windows-based servers are usually only available as commercial software. Search engines are generally not built in nor included with Web servers, but if this is a requirement then there are a few exceptions. One is WebSite for Windows, which includes indexing and retrieval software bundled with Web server software.

WAIS

The types of searches allowed are another issue. Many free search systems are built around the WAIS (Wide Area Information Server) engine. WAIS constructs an index of the complete contents of a document. When a user performs a search for a word or phrase, each document that matches a portion of or the entire search request is ranked, and documents are returned in the order in which they are ranked. Some find this disconcerting since documents that ranked high simply because they contained one word that matched the query several times might rank higher than documents that contain the entire phrase. So even most WAIS engines now include support for other search options. Boolean searching allows the user to specifically request that documents in the result set contain both terms (word1 AND word2), either term (word1 OR word2), or one term when a second does not occur (word1 NOT word2). WAIS engines simply perform their normal search and relevance ranking, and then perform a Boolean search on the result set. Word stemming is another popular feature. Word stem searches allow you to locate a set of documents that contain words with the same prefix or the same root. You could perform a word search for terms related to biology by searching for "bio*". This might return documents containing the words *biology, biologist, biochemistry,* etc. Other types of searches are possible including adjacency and proximity searching (searches where two or more words must occur next to or near one another in order for the document to match the query), but these features are only available in the most sophisticated (and often expensive) search engines.

HARVEST

The Harvest system uses a tool called the Gatherer to retrieve documents from Web servers. The Gatherer retrieves documents from servers using their native protocols. If the server is a gopher then Gatherer requests the document the same way a gopher client would; if it is a Web server then Gatherer issues a GET command with the document name to the server in order to retrieve the specified document. Gatherer also knows how to extract useful information from a variety of file formats. It understands HTML documents, and it can identify and extract textual data from image and binary files, as well as many other types of file formats. Gatherer is actually itself a collection of tools that retrieve files from servers listed in a configuration file, and extracts summary data for indexing. Gatherer can work over a network, making Harvest a meta index tool since it can index multiple servers.

Essence is the Gatherer component responsible for extracting indexing information from a document. It applies a program called a summarizer to data to extract and generate a content summary. For example, if Essence encounters a compressed HTML file, it will recognize it as such by its Content-type or file-name extension, uncompress it, and pass it on to the summarizer, which will extract title and keyword information. The SGML summarizer can recognize tags and use them to generate summaries, unlike WAIS, which actually indexes tags as though they were document content. Each summarizer can be customized to extract as much or as little information as desired. In the case of HTML, you can specify the particular elements whose content should be extracted and included in the index.

INDEXING INTERFACE

The interface to the indexing program varies from system to system. In the case of freeWAIS, indexes are constructed using a command-line program called waisindex, which allows you to index a variety of data types, using command line options. A list of files has to be provided on the command line as well:

```
waisindex -t html /home/WWW/*.html
```

waisindex can index a variety of data types including images and multimedia data. Depending on the content type specified with the -t option, it will index only the filename or the full contents if the type specified is a text-based format.

The Harvest Gatherer is configured through text-based configuration files. Indexing is automatic or can be launched manually. Once configured, Gatherer will retrieve and index new files as they are added to archives that it has been instructed to watch.

ABC'S OF SEARCH TYPES

Search types are a nebulous entity. They might (and indeed should) be described in the Web search form for a particular search service. But sometimes no mention is made of the types of searches that can be performed. This is in part due to the fact that many people do not understand some of the basic strategies available for searching indexes. And of course it does depend on the search engine, which is the component that actually determines what types of searches can be performed. If it does not understand a truncated search (where an asterisk replaces part of a search key) then it will perform a literal search for a string such as "bio*", rather than searching for words starting with *bio* such as *biology*, *biologist*, etc. You should understand at least the basic search strategies in order to select a search engine and use search services more effectively.

The simplest search is to provide a single word that should occur in any results. But this is often not sufficient for most users. So search engines support various methods of combining words to form more complex queries. WAIS engines will accept a search formed as a question or phrase such as:

show me all documents on the history of cartography

The engine will look for *history* and *cartography* and present a results set that contains one or both of these words. More exact searching is possible with Boolean searches. Booleans allow you to specify exactly which words should or should not occur in the results set, for example:

cartography AND *history*

Still more complex searches can be managed automatically by some systems, which might consult a thesaurus to locate synonyms for the item. FreeWAIS allows you construct a custom thesaurus for an index.

SEARCH INTERFACE

FreeWAIS comes with a simple text-based query program called waisq. In order to access HTML documents from a Web server using WAIS, waisq can be called from a script. The script in turn is called from some type of HTML form that must at least include one <INPUT NAME="query" TYPE=TEXT> form field so that the search string can be entered (see Figures 28-2 and 28-3 for examples of WAIS and Harvest search forms). The script formats the contents of the Web form into a waisq search, retrieves the results, and creates a list of hypertext links representing each item that matched the search string. The user can then select an item to see the document.

WAIS sorts documents according to relevance, that is, it uses an algorithm to attempt to determine which document was most likely what you were looking for, then displays them in descending order according to this rating. WAIS works best when a user can select documents from the result set and tell the server to find more documents like these. But it is difficult to implement such an interface on the Web, so most WAIS search systems either display the numeric rating or replace it with a graphical representation of the rating, and provide no option to feed selected documents back into the search engine to refine the search. However, recent versions of WAIS now support Boolean and other sophisticated query types.

Serving Requests and Presenting Results

Search requests are handled by a CGI script with WAIS. WAIS has no direct connection to the Web, nor can it typically be accessed from a URL like a gopher, telnet, or ftp archive. The WAIS CGI script should reside on the same server as the index, although it is also possible to access a WAISSERVER through a script, but this is more complex and is typically undesirable. WAIS includes the path for the document with the indexed document information so that a URL can be constructed if the server name is known. This is how a CGI script builds a hypertext result list in response to a WAIS search. The CGI script to process the result list can be written in Perl or some other programming language.

Figure 28-2
A search form for
a WAIS database

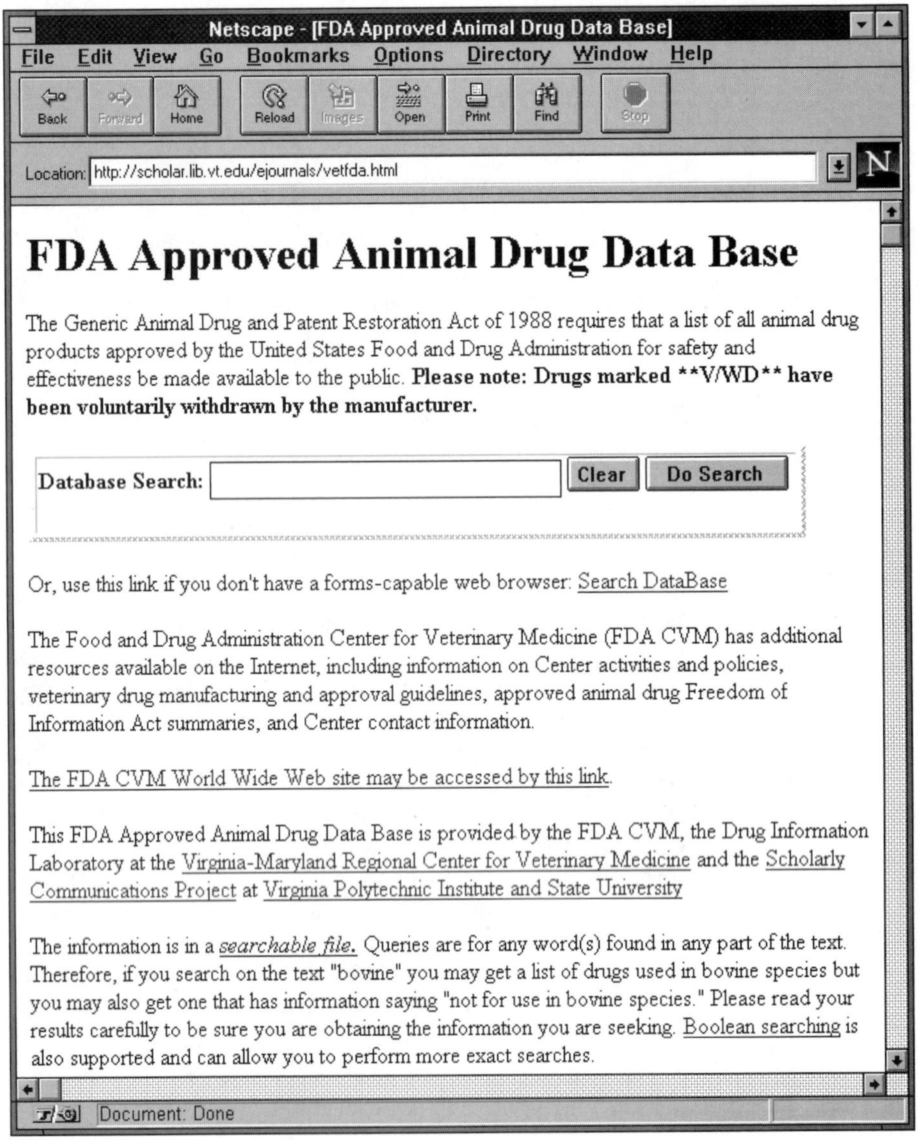

Netscape - [FDA Approved Animal Drug Data Base]

File   Edit   View   Go   Bookmarks   Options   Directory   Window   Help

Back   Forward   Home   Reload   Images   Open   Print   Find   Stop

Location: http://scholar.lib.vt.edu/ejournals/vetfda.html

FDA Approved Animal Drug Data Base

The Generic Animal Drug and Patent Restoration Act of 1988 requires that a list of all animal drug products approved by the United States Food and Drug Administration for safety and effectiveness be made available to the public. **Please note: Drugs marked **V/WD** have been voluntarily withdrawn by the manufacturer.**

Database Search: [   ]   Clear   Do Search

Or, use this link if you don't have a forms-capable web browser: Search DataBase

The Food and Drug Administration Center for Veterinary Medicine (FDA CVM) has additional resources available on the Internet, including information on Center activities and policies, veterinary drug manufacturing and approval guidelines, approved animal drug Freedom of Information Act summaries, and Center contact information.

The FDA CVM World Wide Web site may be accessed by this link.

This FDA Approved Animal Drug Data Base is provided by the FDA CVM, the Drug Information Laboratory at the Virginia-Maryland Regional Center for Veterinary Medicine and the Scholarly Communications Project at Virginia Polytechnic Institute and State University

The information is in a *searchable file.* Queries are for any word(s) found in any part of the text. Therefore, if you search on the text "bovine" you may get a list of drugs used in bovine species but you may also get one that has information saying "not for use in bovine species." Please read your results carefully to be sure you are obtaining the information you are seeking. Boolean searching is also supported and can allow you to perform more exact searches.

Document: Done

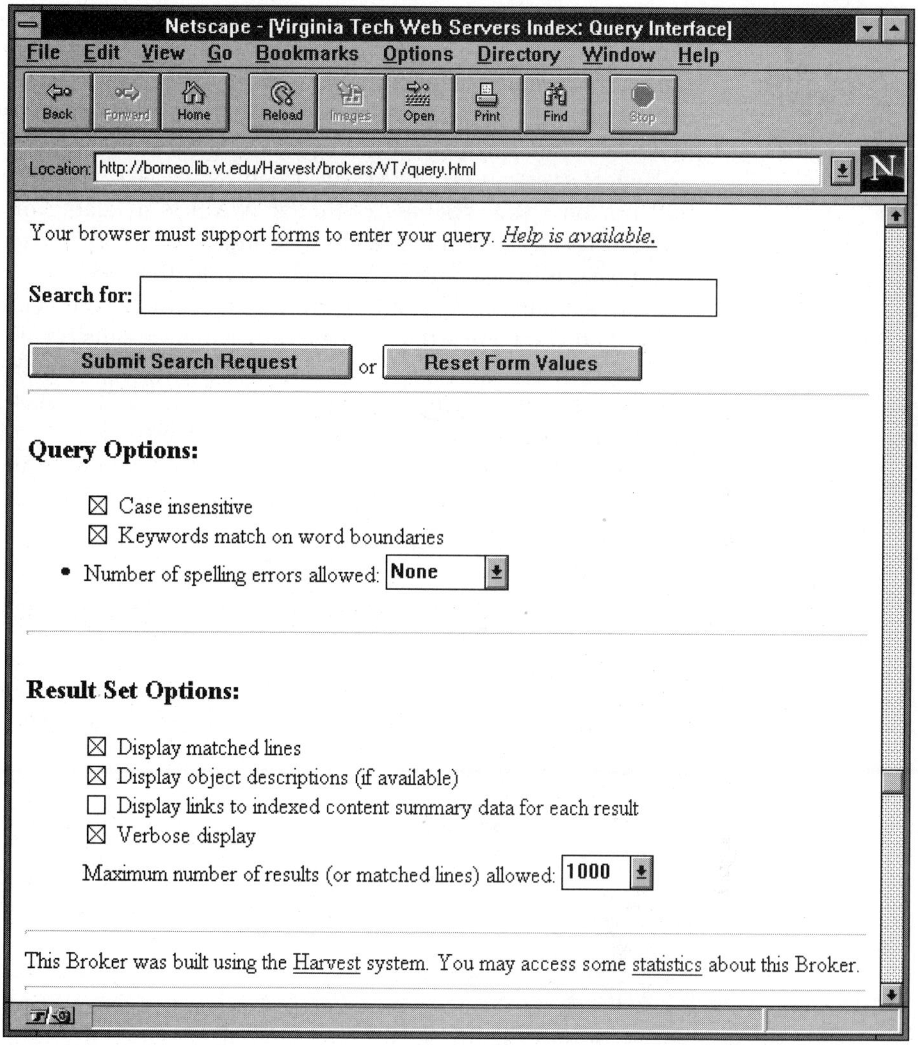

Figure 28-3
A search form for
Harvest

```
┌─────────────────────────────────────────────────────────────────────────┐
│ ─   Netscape - [Virginia Tech Web Servers Index: Query Interface]  ▼  ▲  │
├─────────────────────────────────────────────────────────────────────────┤
│ File   Edit   View   Go   Bookmarks   Options   Directory   Window   Help │
├─────────────────────────────────────────────────────────────────────────┤
│  Back  Forward  Home   Reload  Images  Open   Print   Find   Stop         │
├─────────────────────────────────────────────────────────────────────────┤
│ Location: http://borneo.lib.vt.edu/Harvest/brokers/VT/query.html          │
└─────────────────────────────────────────────────────────────────────────┘
```

Your browser must support <u>forms</u> to enter your query. *Help is available.*

Search for: [   ]

[**Submit Search Request**   ] or [**Reset Form Values**   ]

Query Options:

☒ Case insensitive
☒ Keywords match on word boundaries
● Number of spelling errors allowed: [**None** ▼]

Result Set Options:

☒ Display matched lines
☒ Display object descriptions (if available)
☐ Display links to indexed content summary data for each result
☒ Verbose display

Maximum number of results (or matched lines) allowed: [**1000** ▼]

This Broker was built using the <u>Harvest</u> system. You may access some <u>statistics</u> about this Broker.

The Harvest Broker is responsible for processing search requests for Harvest. It communicates with the GLIMPSE search engine, which actually uses the search string to locate matching documents. These documents are then presented as a set of hypertext links (Figure 28-4). Harvest can use the WAIS search engine instead of GLIMPSE to index and retrieve documents as well.

Both Harvest and freeWAIS are freely available on the Internet. Both require and run on UNIX systems (although WAIS is available in some form under Windows NT). A set of scripts used to index and search WAIS databases, called *sonofwais*, is also available on the Internet without cost. Harvest and freeWAIS can be customized to some degree. For example, the search form, indexing script, and CGI scripts that process and display results for WAIS can all be modified to suit the developer's and user's needs. Each component of the Harvest system can be customized, and some, such as the search engine, can be replaced if desired. freeWAIS provides a powerful search solution for medium to large collections of data. Harvest is an excellent system for indexing data stored on many different servers on the Internet. Your needs will determine which system is right for your Web site.

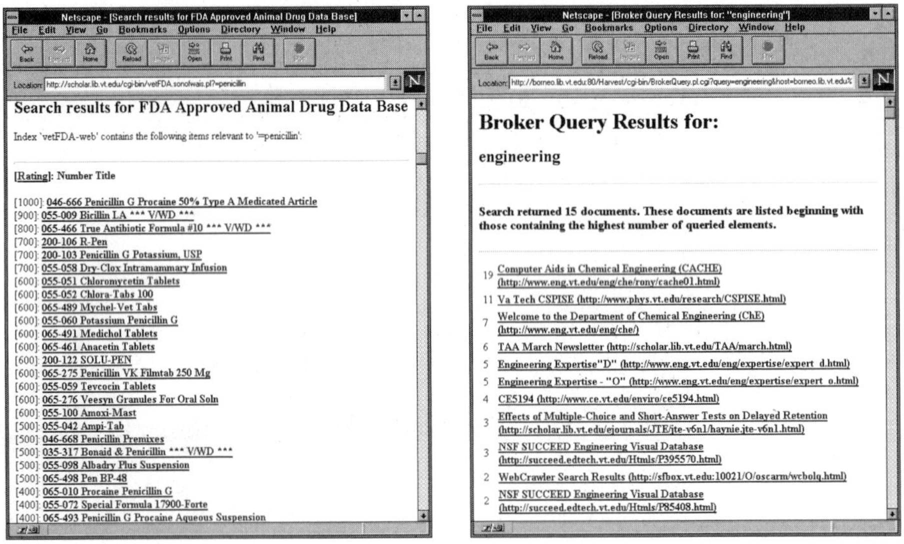

Figure 28-4 Search results from WAIS (note rankings) and Harvest

CHAPTER

29

HTML on the Fly

CHAPTER AT A GLANCE

- Unseen content that makes a Web browser accept and re-request a document as a Web document even if it doesn't really exist
- How CGI gateways can interact with stateful systems
- *Netscape Client-Pull Document Updating*
- Netscape server-push and client-pull animation

Even before the advent of Java and active local content, there have been mechanisms for producing HTML content from non-HTML information systems. This has been one of the most popular uses for CGI scripts, referred to as gateways, and has led to rapid growth and migration of content to the Web. In other cases, documents intended for the Web are stored in non-HTML format to take advantage of some characteristic of another environment. For example, a collection of documents with a uniform structure might be stored in an Oracle database. The documents can be easily tagged and presented as HTML documents upon request since the structure of the database record is known. The developer simply applies a markup template to database fields, prepends a Content-type header, and sends the newly created HTML document back to the client. This is particularly useful for managing large collections of dynamic, well-structured information.

There are other reasons to generate content dynamically as well. Frequently changing information such as weather forecasts and related data such as satellite and radar images tracking storms, or financial or news services might wish to highlight the most up-to-date information on their Web site and relegate the previous day's or hour's information to a less prominent position. CGI scripts can be used to build a page from components that are ever-changing.

Netscape invented a new type of dynamic document with its *push-pull* animation mechanism. By utilizing a new Content-type header and a CGI script, they have made it possible for authors to include inline animations that can be viewed by users of the Netscape Navigator browser. This allows the content to change in the browser window without requiring the user to manually reload the document.

Database Gateways

CGI gateways are an excellent way to publish both pre-existing databases and collections of information that can be more easily maintained and updated through the use of relational database systems. We will consider the Electronic Reserve system of Virginia Tech as a case study of a relational database published on the Web. Traditionally the library reserve service is provided for faculty who wish to temporarily make additional print material available for a course. Rather than have each student purchase a book for a few chapters or reprints of dozens of articles, the library places these materials in a special storage area and makes them available for short loan periods to students who request them. Heavily used materials are often checked out making them difficult to obtain. Course packets authored by the professor are among the most popular materials. Since many of these materials are created with desktop publishing software, they can easily be converted to an electronic format for distribution over the Internet. So professors register classes at the beginning of each semester and place course materials, sample tests, test scores, and lecture slides online as the semester progresses.

On a large university campus, an electronic reserve system must scale to support hundreds of courses. It would be very difficult for a small reserve staff to maintain hundreds of HTML documents to support such a project. So instructor and course information are stored in an Oracle database. Oracle allows relationships to be established between a single instructor and multiple courses, and between a single course and multiple course packet records. Duplication is minimal and the data can easily be managed by a small staff. No HTML tags are stored in the database. Yet the entire system is published via the Web so students can use freely available software to search and view course materials. When students submit a search for an instructor or course from an HTML form, this search is handled by a CGI gateway, which interacts with an Oracle database:

```
┌─────────────────────────────────────────────────────────────────────┐
│ ─        Netscape - [Search Ereserve Instructor Database]       ▼ ▲  │
├─────────────────────────────────────────────────────────────────────┤
│ File  Edit  View  Go  Bookmarks  Options  Directory  Window    Help │
├─────────────────────────────────────────────────────────────────────┤
│  ⇦o    o⇨    ⌂     ⊛     ⊞     ⇄o    ⊟     ⊞     ●                   │
│ Back Forward Home  Reload Images Open  Print  Find  Stop            │
├─────────────────────────────────────────────────────────────────────┤
│ Location: http://reserve.lib.vt.edu/Instructors.html         ▣  N   │
├─────────────────────────────────────────────────────────────────────┤
```

Electronic Reserve - University Libraries

Search by Instructor

Instructions

Enter instructor last name like this (capitalize first letter of name):

Last name: `Jones`

or leave last name blank and just click search to see all professors who have materials online.

Search

You may enter a partial last name.

Last name: `                          `

`[ Clear ]` `[ Search ]`

The results of the search are presented as a set of matching instructor names, which are displayed as hypertext links. These links could point to a Web home page for the professor, but in most cases they actually consist of a preformatted search that will retrieve a list of courses registered by this professor. The courses are stored in an Oracle table and related to the professor with a linker table, which contains a record for each course consisting of fields for the professor's instructor ID, the course department, and number:

```
<HTML><HEAD><TITLE>Instructor List - University Libraries
Ereserve</TITLE></HEAD>
<BODY>
<h1>Instructor List - University Libraries Ereserve</h1>
<h2>Electronic Reserve - Instructor List</h2><HR>
<LI><A HREF="/cgi-bin/ER_course?query=Ande3869">Anderson,Mark     </A>
<LI><A HREF="/cgi-bin/ER_course?query=Bonh6595">Bonham,T.W.       </A>
...
```

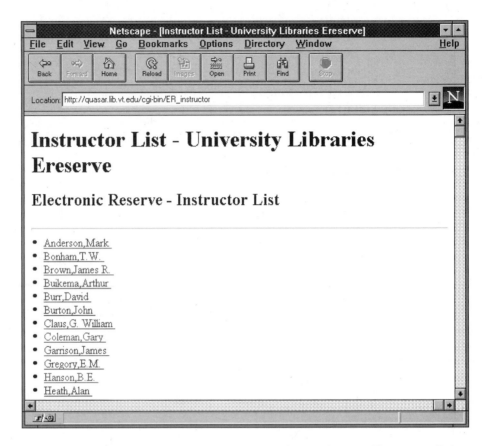

The course list looks just like the list of professors: a set of hypertext links, one per course. When a student selects one of these links, data is retrieved from several different Oracle tables to generate a Web page for the course. The professor's name, phone number, e-mail address, and other information are retrieved from the instructor table; course name, department, number, and other data are retrieved from the course table; and then materials on reserve for that course are retrieved from yet another table of reserve items. The resulting display is indistinguishable from a manually constructed Web page, but only exists while the student is reading it:

```
<HTML><HEAD><TITLE>Course Materials - University Libraries
Ereserve</TITLE></HEAD>
<BODY>
<h1>Course Materials - University Libraries Ereserve</h1>
<H2>Engineering Economy, ISE 2014</H2>
<B>Instructor:</B> Gary Coleman<BR>
Department: ISE Postal Code: 0118<BR>Phone: 231-0000<BR>
Reserved for <I>FS 95</I><BR>
<HR>
```

```
<H3>Items on Reserve</H3>
<UL>
<LI><A
HREF="http://reserve.lib.vt.edu/materials_FS/ISE/ISE2014/test1_obj.pdf"><B>Stude
nt Objectives for Test 1 (test review)
</B></A> by Coleman
<LI><A HREF="http://reserve.lib.vt.edu/materials_FS/ISE/ISE2014/ch1.pdf
"><B>Instructors Overheads for Ch. 1, Introduction
</B></A> by Coleman
...
```

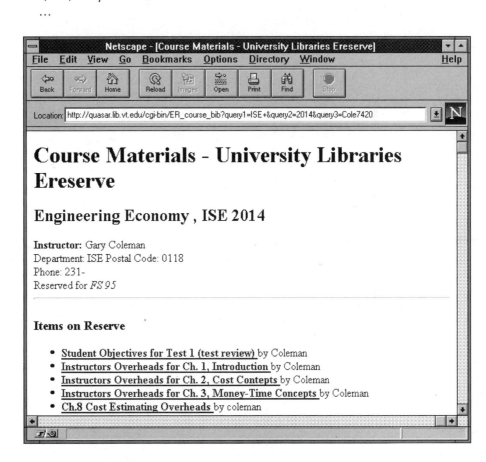

Of the HTML documents we've looked at so far, the only page that actually exists as a URL-addressable Web document is the search form. So how was this achieved? The first step is to pass the search request, whether submitted from an HTML form or as the argument passed with a hypertext link (such as `<A HREF="/cgi-bin/ER_course?query=Ande3869">`), to a gateway, which converts it to an SQL (Structured Query Language) query of the form:

```
select * from er_ic_link where instr_id='Ande3869';
```

SQL is the programming language supplied with Oracle, which allows developers to create complex database searches. In this example, the database name, er_ic_link, and query field, instr_id, are hard coded into the gateway ER_course. This script only needs a value for query in order to perform a database search. The search string is passed to a function called data_query, which formulates an SQL query and executes it:

```
sub data_query {
    # construct an sql query for Oracle
    local($temp_file)=pop(@_);
    local($commandstring)=pop(@_);
    $com_buf="set PAGESIZE 0\;\n";
    $com_buf=$com_buf."set HEADING OFF\;\n";
    $com_buf=$com_buf."set NEWPAGE 0\;\n";
    $com_buf=$com_buf."set SPACE 0\;\n";
    $com_buf=$com_buf."set FEEBACK OFF\;\n";
    $com_buf=$com_buf."set TERMOUT OFF\;\n";
    $com_buf=$com_buf."set LINESIZE 650\;\n";
    $com_buf=$com_buf."spool $temp_file.results\;\n";
    $com_buf=$com_buf.$commandstring;
    $com_buf=$com_buf."spool off\;\n";
    $com_buf=$com_buf."quit\n";
    open(er_search,">$temp_file");
    print (er_search $com_buf);
    close (er_search);
    system("sqlplus -s $authenticate \@$temp_file");
}
```

The SQL query is written to a temporary file. The search string $commandstring is an SQL select statement constructed by the main Perl program and passed to the &data_query function as an argument. The command string is a search in this case. The function call looks something like this:

```
&data_query( "select * from er_ic_link where instr_id=\'Ande3869\';", "960101-
    temp");
```

but could be a line submitting a new record ("insert into er_bib values ...") or some other SQL statement or set of statements. Finally, Perl asks the operating system to run the sqlplus command interpreter using the userid and password stored in the variable $authenticate, with the newly created SQL script as an argument. The results are stored in the file called $temp_file.results ($temp_file is a variable containing a string that is used here in place of the variable name at execution time).

Once Oracle returns the query results, the script parses the output using the size of the database fields to separate values. These values are extracted sequentially to build an HTML representation of each record returned. The resulting HTML file is returned with a Content-type header of text/html so that it looks like an ordinary Web document. Here is the function used to generate the Content-type header, HTML document header, and a portion of the HTML document body:

```
sub do_header {
    # Return Content-type and header for the HTML document.
    local($title)=pop(@_);
    print "Content-type: text/html\n\n";
    print "<HTML><HEAD><TITLE>$title</TITLE></HEAD>\n<BODY>\n";
    print "<h1>$title</h1>\n\n";
}
```

For more complex displays such as the course materials list, another gateway performs multiple searches in order to construct the page, but the basic concept is the same.

DYNAMIC INFORMATION PAGES

Another type of dynamically generated Web document is one that is generated from frequently changing data. Pages can be generated on request. But depending on how often the data changes, it is usually more efficient to generate the page once and archive it for a short period of time. The example below is a Web page that publishes the scripts of nightly local news broadcasts for a television station. These new scripts are full text and of variable length, so they are not well suited for relational database systems. Instead they are converted from plain text to HTML documents that are immediately available to users. All previous scripts are archived and the entire system is presented as an HTML table representing the calendar month in which the scripts were broadcast.

The result is a dynamic information resource, updated daily. Such a document could be updated much more frequently, even every second, so the user could simply reload the document and see new data. However, such an arrangement would push CGI gateway technology to its limits.

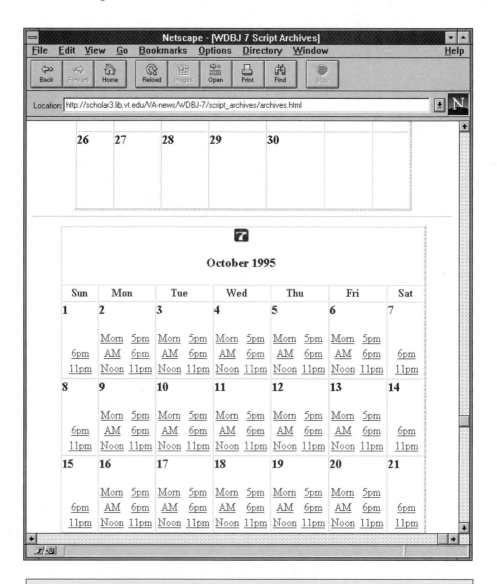

NETSCAPE CLIENT-PULL DOCUMENT UPDATING

Netscape is capable of automatically reloading a document after a brief pause. This capability provides a much cleaner mode of access to database systems, bulletin boards, and other resources where a user might submit information that is processed and then incorporated into a Web page. The user has the opportunity to view the newly updated page without selecting the back or reload buttons. Instead, the page is updated and reloaded in response to the user's submission, behaving like most other client application interfaces. The key to implementing this behavior is an

HTTP response header called Refresh. This can be returned in a <META> tag along with a value representing the number of seconds (0 or more) the client should wait before it attempts to reload the document:

<META HTTP-EQUIV="Refresh" CONTENT=2>

This tag tells the client to reload, or pull the document from the server again after the specified period of time. Unless this <META> tag is included with the returned document, the client won't request the document again. So the best way to use this capability is to return it as part of a script-generated HTML document, which is essentially a stub with an HTML header and the <META> tag. You can specify a document to be reloaded by including the URL as part of the value assigned to the CONTENT attribute:

<META HTTP-EQUIV="Refresh" CONTENT="2; http://server/stocks.html">

To provide real-time access to data without overburdening the server, you would need a client-side script that retrieves data from a remote site in real time and displays it inside the Web browser window. This is one of the potential uses for the Java programming language. Instead of passive systems that require the user to reload a document to view changes, Java lets Web documents become live windows into dynamic data resources. Java represents the first secure, cross-platform distributed programming language capable of providing just this type of service. Java-enabled Web browsers are more than ordinary Web buzzing with too much caffeine—they could evolve into a distributed desktop environment for accessing applications and information with nary a Windows 95 task list or Macintosh Finder in sight! Chapters 31–32 cover Java in more detail.

NETSCAPE INLINE ANIMATIONS WITH SERVER-PUSH

Netscape Navigator supports simple inline animations through the use of a Content-type/subtype (multipart/x-mixed-replace) that tells the Web browser to accept multiple inline image files and display each as it is received. While the process is at the mercy of network bandwidth, it is a useful method for generating certain types of dynamic content such as presenting a series of satellite photographs tracking Earth's weather, or illustrating simple processes. The key to push-pull animations, as Netscape refers to them, is a simple CGI script that can be implemented in any programming language. Here it is implemented in Perl:

```
#!/usr/local/bin/perl
# Usage: <IMG SRC="/cgi-bin/animate?image_list.txt">
$|=1;
print "HTTP/1.0 200 Okay\n";
print "Content-Type: multipart/x-mixed-replace;boundary=<HR>\n";
print "\n—<HR>\n";
open(animation,@ARGV[0]);
while (<animation>) {
    chop $_;
    print "Content-Type: image/gif\n\n";
    open(a_frame,$_);
    print (<a_frame>);
    close(a_frame);
    print "\n—<HR>\n";
}
close(animation);
```

The script first sends the appropriate server message ("HTTP/1.0 200 Okay") and then returns the push-pull animation Content-type header. Next the script opens the text file named on the CGI script's command line, which should contain a list of image files, one per line, representing the frames of the animation. You should provide the full path of each image, since the CGI script is not aware of the Web server's home directory:

```
/home/WWW/animations/disk/disk1.gif
/home/WWW/animations/disk/disk2.gif
/home/WWW/animations/disk/disk3.gif
...
```

Finally, you must create an HTML file that includes the animation inline. Notice the use of the <IMG> tag. The images pointed to by the script should be of an image format that Netscape can display inline. The SRC attribute points to the CGI script with the name of the image list as an argument:

```
<HTML>
<HEAD><TITLE>Netscape Inline Animation</TITLE></HEAD>
<BODY>
<H1>Push-Pull Animation</H1>
<IMG SRC="/cgi-bin/animate?/home/WWW/spin_disk.txt">
</BODY>
</HTML>
```

While Netscape developed this strategy for dynamic document content, there's nothing stopping other browsers from implementing this feature. It can also be used to dynamically generate entire HTML document sets on the fly. With some slight modifications, the script used above to create an inline animation can do the trick. First modify the boundary portion of the multipart content header so we can use the end of the HTML document as a boundary:

```
print "Content-Type: multipart/x-mixed-replace;boundary=</HTML>\n";
```

Now replace the portion of the document that delivers the image files with some code that generates an HTML document (replace contents of the above script starting with "open(animation,@ARGV[0]);"):

```
print "\n—</HTML>\n";
for ($count=1; $count<100; $count++) {
    print "Content-Type: text/html\n\n";
    print "<HTML>\<HEAD><TITLE>Document #$count</TITLE></HEAD>\n";
    print "<BODY>\n<H1>Watch me go!</H1>\n";
    print "$count\n</BODY>";
    print "\n—</HTML>\n";
}
```

To access the automatically generated HTML documents, just point Netscape at the CGI script. Netscape will keep retrieving documents until the script stops sending them. This is a simple method for generating near-live content. By utilizing well-documented Content-type headers and simple Perl scripts, rapidly changing data can be presented in a Web browser window.

Each of these mechanisms allows you to deliver content without human intervention, and without performing extensive markup over and over again. By converting the data to HTML, millions of users can access the content without resorting to proprietary third-party software. With dynamic Web gateways, you can convert a static document browser into a near-real-time information retrieval tool.

30

Hypermedia
with HTML

CHAPTER AT A GLANCE

- Multipurpose Internet Mail Extensions (MIME)
- Table 30-1: *MIME Types Registered with IANA*
- How MIME extends the Web
- Identifying the most widely supported media types

Few hypertext systems deliver only text. Text cannot always convey the same amount of information in a reasonable amount of space, nor make the same impact on the reader as images, sound, or motion video. So like many hypertext information systems before it, the Web is a hypermedia system. HTML document links target images, motion video, and audio files, in addition to other HTML documents. The Web utilizes an open-ended standard for transmitting multimedia data called MIME (Multipurpose Internet Mail Extensions). MIME was originally developed to allow multipart and/or multimedia or compressed content to be included within electronic mail messages. MIME is used by mail programs to encode attachments so that they will not be rendered unreadable as they are transmitted over the Internet. Most mail programs expect to transmit only ASCII text, so MIME ensures that when a multimedia data format is binary, it is encoded in an ASCII format before transmission. MIME is also used to encode documents that include non-ASCII characters, such as multinational characters. Since the Web needs to support currently defined and new multimedia data types as well as multilingual documents, MIME is as essential to the Web as the URL.

On the Web, MIME type files are maintained at both the server and the client end. At the server end, MIME types tell the server software what Content-type header to prepend to the data stream. Content-types are associated with one or more filename extensions in a mime.types file. Each line in the file defines a type and subtype. Types group formats with something in common. For example, many binary data types have the file/MIME type application. This is because one specific application is usually used to open these types of documents. The subtype specifies the actual file type being sent, for example, rtf for Rich Text Format, or pdf for Acrobat's Portable Document Format

```
application/pdf        pdf
```

Filename extensions are simply the last portion of the filename to which a file of this type is saved. Most systems don't require any particular extension, but Web servers, and Web clients to a lesser degree, rely on them to identify the type of content in the file.

Web browsers also have a MIME types configuration file that they use to match the Content-type of an incoming file with an application that can read it. Web browsers come preconfigured for a few types such as text/plain, text/html, and image/gif, which they can open themselves. But the user is expected to retrieve and install viewers for other types. Then they must configure a new MIME type entry for the file type, or specify a viewer, often referred to as a helper application.

Helper applications are launched when the incoming file includes a Content-type header matching the File type/subtype in the left-hand column of Figure 30-1, the Helper configuration panel for Netscape Navigator. This is how Web browsers support an open-ended list of hypermedia data formats.

Embedded Multimedia

Web browsers support several data formats other than HTML as embedded or inline items. Graphics in GIF, JPEG, or PNG format are retrieved and displayed alongside the text of the document. They are requested by the client and delivered separately with a Content-type corresponding to their contents, for example, image/gif for a GIF image. Since Web browsers can read and decode GIF images they do not launch an external viewer.

Web browsers are being developed with other mechanisms for supporting multimedia data. Netscape Navigator supports plug-ins that allow otherwise unfamiliar data formats to be processed and displayed within the browser window by an external application. Plug-ins are associated with MIME types and are launched when a particular type of document is encountered. In this way, they are similar to helper applications. The Netscape <EMBED> tag is used to

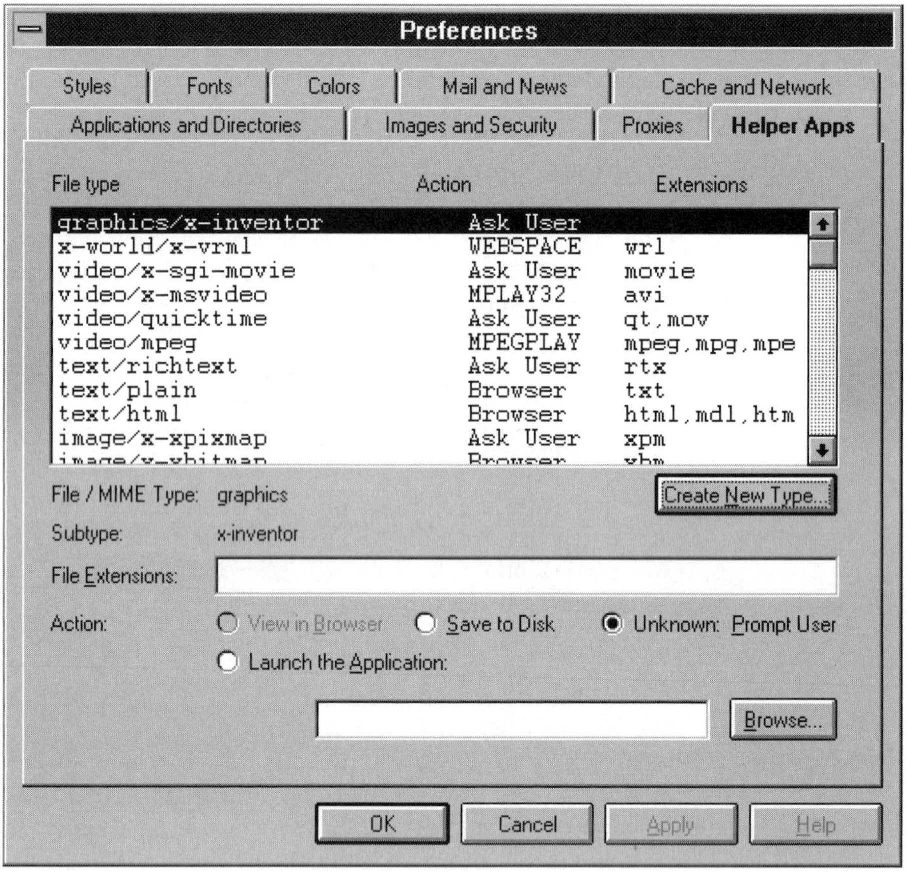

Figure 30-1
Netscape
MIME/Helper
configuration panel

indicate that a data type should be displayed inline but must be processed by an external application before it can be displayed:

```
<EMBED SRC="/images/photo.bmp">
```

In this example, a graphic in the Microsoft Windows bitmap format is embedded in an HTML document. Almost no browsers support this image type inline, but with the <EMBED> tag, the image is rendered externally by a Windows application (Paintbrush) and then displayed inline just as if it were a GIF or JPEG image. Some versions of Mosaic support VRML documents in this manner. Microsoft is working on similar functionality for Internet Explorer.

MIME TYPES

MIME types were developed for use in electronic mail systems. On many UNIX systems, there is a mailcap configuration file that maps MIME types to viewer applications, much like the mechanism found in Web browsers. A typical mailcap entry would be:

image/*; xv %s

which tells the system to launch the graphics viewing program xv when any file
of type image is encountered, whether it is image/gif, image/jpeg, or any other
image format. The %s tells the mail program to place the name of the data file
on the command line with the viewer program, which is how a user would run
the program, for example:

xv logo.gif

MIME types that have not yet been registered begin with the prefix x-. The
MIME type for the Virtual Reality Modeling Language (VRML) is x-world/x-vrml.
Once registered with the Internet Assigned Number Authority (IANA), an official registry of MIME types, the prefix is removed. When VRML is registered
with the IANA, its MIME type and subtype will likely become world/vrml.

Most Web browsers and Web servers are preconfigured to support a number
of MIME types including many of those registered with IANA. In many cases,
you will still have to specify helper applications at the client end since the Web
browser may not be able to locate them automatically.

**TABLE 30-1   MIME TYPES REGISTERED WITH THE INTERNET ASSIGNED
NUMBER AUTHORITY**

Type	Subtype	Type	Subtype
text	plain	application	applefile
	richtext		mac-binhex40
	enriched		news-message-id
	tab-separated-values		news-transmission
			wordperfect5.1
multipart	mixed		pdf
	alternative		zip
	digest		macwriteii
	parallel		msword
	appledouble		remote-printing
	header-set		mathematica
			cybercash
message	rfc822		commonground
	partial		iges
	external-body		riscos
	news		eshop
			x400-bp
application	octet-stream		
	postscript	image	jpeg
	oda		gif
	atomicmail		ief
	andrew-inset		g3fax
	slate		tiff

**TABLE 30-1   MIME TYPES REGISTERED WITH THE INTERNET ASSIGNED
NUMBER AUTHORITY, CONT.**

Type	Subtype	Type	Subtype
application, cont.	wita		
	dec-dx	audio	basic
	dca-rft		
	activemessage	video	mpeg
	rtf		quicktime

MULTIMEDIA FORMATS SUPPORTED ON THE WEB

Virtually any type of data for which two parties establish a MIME type can be exchanged and viewed on the Web. The new type simply has to be added to the server configuration file and the client needs to be configured to recognize the type and launch an external helper application. But when you are publishing documents on the Web, you will probably want to use established data formats for your multimedia content. Let's examine four of the MIME types most commonly published on the Web: application, image, audio, and video.

Application types   Application data types are often platform specific. Some types are more widely supported than others. PostScript (subtype postscript) and Acrobat's PDF (subtype pdf) file formats are more widely supported than subtypes such as rtf, wordperfect5.1, or msword for delivering formatted text and graphics. Acrobat Reader is available for many computer platforms (see Chapter 35). PostScript can be viewed using a freeware program called Ghostscript, which runs under most operating systems. PostScript files can also be sent to a PostScript printer if no viewer is available. So PDF and PostScript are probably the best choices for delivering formatted documents if HTML is not sufficient.

Compressed data is also classified under the type application but there is no single subtype that is globally supported. The zip subtype is supported by more platforms than the Macintosh BinHex format (subtype mac-binhex40). BinHex is actually not a compression format but is used to encode Macintosh binaries including files compressed with StuffIt or other Macintosh-specific compression applications, so zip is a better choice. The application/x-gzip format is probably the best choice for exchanging compressed data since there are versions of gunzip, the program that uncompresses gzipped data, for most platforms.

Image types   Several types of image data are supported inline by Web browsers. The most widely supported inline image subtype is GIF (subtype gif). GIF was the first color-image format adopted by the Web community. JPEG (subtype jpeg) has been gaining in popularity and is very widely supported as well. Many Web browsers support the old x-xbitmap subtype from the days when Mosaic was first developed on UNIX workstations running the X-windows graphical user interface. A new graphics format has recently been designed specifically for the Web, called PNG (Portable Network Graphics), and its acceptance has been rapid. The best strategy for including inline images is to use GIFs for icons and small images with fewer than 256 colors, and JPEG or PNG for high-resolution, high-color images.

Audio types   There are few widely accepted standards for audio on the Web. Until recently, most users had to purchase additional hardware to play back audio data. Most computer systems sold today include an audio card and a pair of speakers, or an output jack to which speakers can be attached. Because audio is a relatively recent addition to most desktop computers, the only registered audio subtype is basic. The basic audio format is an audio format developed by Sun Microsystems for use with Sun workstations. Basic audio files end with an au or snd extension and are supported by a helper application called Naplayer that is bundled with Netscape Navigator. This is the best format for distributing audio files on the Internet. AIFF (subtype x-aiff) and Microsoft's WAV format (x-wav) are also supported by Naplayer.

Video types   Motion video is often published in the Apple QuickTime format (subtype quicktime). QuickTime includes support for synchronized audio and video tracks, as well as various compression schemes. MPEG (subtype mpeg) is probably more widely supported but currently does not include support for synchronized audio. If an audio track is not included with the image, then MPEG should be used. A third option is Microsoft's AVI format (subtype x-msvideo), but this is essentially a proprietary format that users may not be able to find a helper application for on systems not running Microsoft Windows.

BANDWIDTH AND ETIQUETTE ISSUES

When including application subtypes   If you are including links to document subtypes such as Acrobat PDF or PostScript file format, you should include links to helper applications. It is also a good idea to include some basic instructions for installing and configuring the helper application since this might be the first time some users have had to perform this task. The same goes for compressed data, which saves connect time for users with slow connections, but might arrive in an unusable format. Do some research: locate some sites that distribute decompression utilities for multiple platforms (at least Windows and Macintosh), and include a link to these sites in your HTML documents.

When including image subtypes   Image files should be small and compressed, allowing for your own personal quality requirements. Use the GIF format whenever possible and be sure to store all images as interlaced GIFs so they will begin displaying immediately. This allows users to stop transfer if they decide they've seen enough of the image. You may wish to use PNG instead of JPEG for high-color images, since it supports an interlaced file format as well. Use the highest compression you can, but be sure to view the resulting image since higher compression can result in a lower-quality image. Consider making large images external files that are the target of descriptive anchors. And include an ALT attribute with all inline images both for users with slow connections and for visually impaired users.

When including audio subtypes Audio formats are often stored in a compressed mode, so they are probably as small as they can be. You can reduce the sampling rate if a file is too large. Sampling rates as low as 8MHz are suitable for lectures, readings, or other audio that has a low sound to background-noise ratio. Plan to distribute audio in mono rather than stereo as stereo consumes a lot more storage and will take longer to transmit. Make sure you annotate all audio links as such and provide transcriptions if possible, so that hearing-impaired users can access the content.

When including video subtypes MPEG videos are, by definition, compressed since MPEG is a digital video compression scheme. You can reduce the size of MPEG and QuickTime clips by reducing the number of frames, but this results in a jerky motion so be sure to preview the results before you publish them. If you are publishing QuickTime movies, be sure to save them as "flattened" QuickTime movies. Macintosh files actually have two parts (a data fork and a resource fork), and QuickTime movies in the native Macintosh file format are not suitable for distribution on the Web. Flattening the movie places the information stored in the two forks into one file containing the entire movie, which can be opened and viewed on any system with a QuickTime viewer. Consider providing file size information in brackets next to the link targeting the movie. This allows the reader to decide if they have disk space and a fast enough connection to retrieve and view the video:

```
<A HREF="ostrich.mov">Ostrich in motion [3.2Mb]</A>
```

Also identify the target as a video clip and provide a transcription/description of the video and a closed-captioned version if at all possible.

The Web supports and encourages hypermedia data. If you plan carefully, you can select data formats that most users will be able to accept. MIME and helper applications are often taken for granted but they are an essential part of the Web.

31

Introducing Java

CHAPTER AT A GLANCE

- Java versus HotJava
- Features of Java-compatible browsers
- Introducing the Java programming language
- *JavaScript: Inline Browser Scripting*
- Table 31-1: *Object-Oriented Terminology*

Not since the arrival of Mosaic has there been such a buzz as has engulfed Java and catapulted it into the spotlight. But enthusiasm for Java is grounded in expectations of what it might be able to do as much as what it can do. Are those expectations too high? What can client-side scripting offer that CGI scripts cannot deliver? What is Java?

Sun Microsystems initially developed Java, originally known as Oak, to control information and household appliances. They have since groomed Java to be the programming language of the Internet. Java is a full-fledged, object-oriented programming language. Object-oriented languages bundle functions and variables into discrete entities that perform a particular task. Objects are an attempt to model computer tasks after the real world. An object describes a task as a set of data and a set of actions, or *methods*, that can be performed using that data. For example, a refrigerator can be described in object-oriented terms by assigning dimensions, shelf space, and temperature to variables, and by the actions it can perform, which include making ice, adjusting its temperature, and turning the light off and on. Figure 31-1 shows how to "reinvent the wheel" in object-oriented terminology. Another important characteristic of objects is that no object can directly manipulate the data contained in another object. The dishwasher cannot check or adjust the refrigerator's thermostat. If object A wants to know the value of a set of strings that belongs to object B, then there has to be a method in object B for retrieving and returning those values. A method is virtually the same as a function or procedure in non object-oriented languages. The big difference is that when a method is called, the object name precedes the method name, like this:

```
objectA.return_values();
```

This mode of calling a procedure owned by an object is called messaging. Furthermore, objects can have public methods and private methods. The only methods a message originating outside the object can target are public methods. This practice of bundling public and private methods together with the data they manipulate is called encapsulation. It is one of the reasons objects are superior to procedural programs. Once an object is created and debugged, it can be used and reused without any further development.

Another feature of object-oriented programming languages is the ability to extend existing objects. Extending an existing object to enable it to do new things is called subclassing. While methods are similar to functions, there is no comparable procedural language equivalent to subclassing. Java, like most object-oriented languages, builds on a suite of predefined objects. Like a family tree, all objects descend from a common ancestor called the Object class.

Figure 31-1 Wheel object with four methods and five encapsulated instance variables

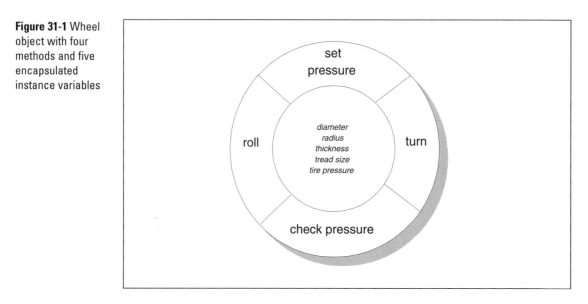

Objects are referred to as classes but they are not precisely the same thing. A class is a definition of an object. It is a set of source code that declares the object, its variables, and methods. When an object is used in a program, even if it is not extended, it is usually *instantiated*. That is, a copy of the object (mainly its variables) is created in memory for the program. Most activities are performed with and by instances of objects. A few objects have components that can be used without creating an instance of the class. Of course, without an instance, the object has no data available to it, but this is not always necessary. One such class in Java is the System class. It has input and output methods (remember Perl's print() command?) that can be referenced without creating an instance of the System class:

```
System.out.println("Hello, World Wide Web");
```

If you need an instance of an object, use the new operator with the name of the class you want to create an instance of:

```
System My.System = new System;
```

This line performs two actions. First it declares a variable called My.System to be of type System. Then it assigns it the value of a System object, that is, a My.System object is created that has all of the variables and methods declared in the System class available in memory.

Objects are a very different way to create computer programs than the traditional step by step approach of procedural languages, but they are very similar to the methods we use in other endeavors. Here's an example: think of class as the prototype of a Mars rover (Figure 31-2). It's been driven around in a stone-

Figure 31-2
Inheritance hier-
archy for Mars
rover

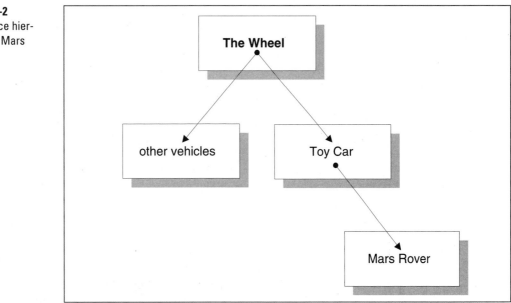

filled sandbox, but it won't be leaving Earth. Once the rover is tested, and changes are made to it so its camera lenses repel dust and it can remain upright on steep terrain, then it has been debugged. This final prototype represents the Mars rover class from which rovers destined for the red planet will be instantiated. The developers would take this final prototype and revise their specifications for a Mars rover. Manufacturers take the specifications (the class), and create duplicates of it (instances) which they pack, set atop a powerful rocket, and launch into space. Unless something goes wrong with the rocket, each rover delivered to the planet will behave exactly as planned.

Inheritance can be explained using the same analogy. The Mars rover might have been inspired by a child's radio-controlled toy car. In fact, the designers might have purchased and modified such a toy to work out some of the problems. After all, both devices have some characteristics in common: four wheels, forward motion, internal motors. The toy car represents a superclass of this Mars rover. The Mars rover inherits the characteristics of the toy car, but is then extended to allow it to function in a cold, dry, rocky environment by adding larger wheels, shielding, and more-advanced radio-control circuitry. New characteristics such as a video camera and stabilizers are represented by both variables describing them and methods that allow them to be controlled. But by inheriting the basic characteristics of a small, motorized vehicle, the developers didn't have to "reinvent the wheel."

Browsers and Applets

Java is one example of the client-side scripting allowed for but not specified in the HTML 3 specifications. It is a programming language that can be used to perform specific tasks but it is robust enough to be used for designing entire applications that can run inside a Web browser window or in their own window. In order for a browser to support Java, or to be Java capable, it must include a Java interpreter. However, Java is not an interpreted language in the same sense as Perl is. Java programs are not delivered as text files, but rather as Java machine code files. The Java interpreter pretends to be a computer called the Java virtual machine. So Java programs must be compiled into what is referred to as a class file, that actually contains Java machine code, before they can be distributed over the Web.

Among the Java-aware browsers currently available are HotJava (Figure 31-3) and Netscape 2.0 (Figure 31-4). HotJava was the first Java Web browser, developed by Sun Microsystems. The browser itself is actually a standalone Java application, which demonstrates just how powerful the language is.

Java browsers work just like regular Web browsers. But they include the Java virtual machine interpreter, which allows them to run Java applications and applets.

Java programs that run inside a Web browser are called applets. Applets can do virtually anything a regular Java application can do, but they use the Web browser window as their environment instead of the user's operating system desktop. Applets are embedded in Web documents with the <APPLET> tag.

Figure 31-3
HotJava with an
embedded applet

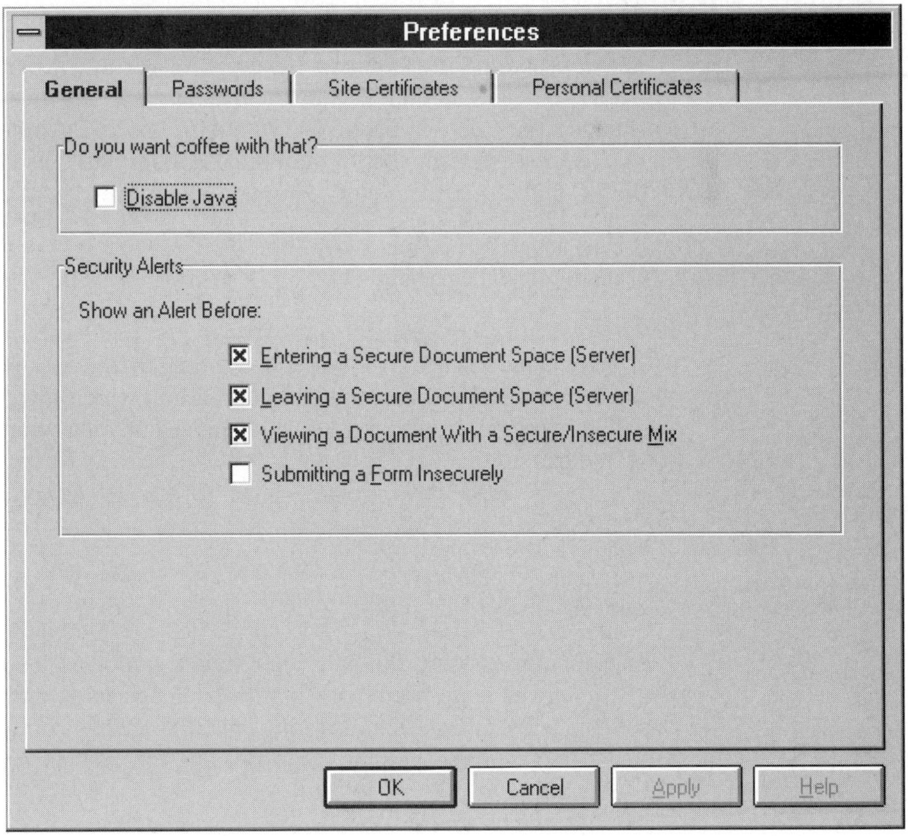

Figure 31-4
Netscape 2.0
Options—Security
Preferences panel
where Java sup-
port can be
enabled or
disabled

<APPLET> has four attributes: WIDTH, HEIGHT, CODE, and CODEBASE. HEIGHT and WIDTH are required and should be assigned a value in pixels. CODE or CODEBASE must then be used to specify either a class files path on the server and a class name, or the name of a class in the same directory as the HTML file. The <PARAM> tag is used within the <APPLET> tag to specify name/value pairs that control the behavior of the Java applet. It is up to the programmer who wrote the applet to retrieve these values and use them appropriately. Text and other HTML markup can also be included between the <APPLET> start and end tags. This data is displayed by browsers that do not support Java, but ignored by Java browsers. So you can embed messages within this tag to users without Java-capable browsers to let them know why they cannot see a portion of the document content:

```
<APPLET CODE="searcher.class" WIDTH=300 HEIGHT=300>
<PARAM NAME="sites" VALUE="5">
<P>
<EM>A Java-based search agent applet would be displayed here if you were
using a Java-capable browser</EM>
</APPLET>
```

The Java Language

The Java programming language is very similar to C. Program statements and expressions resemble their C equivalents. Java statements end with semicolons (;), include parentheses around arguments, use curly braces to group statements, and use the same set of mathematical operators as C.

Both C and C++/Objective C comment styles are supported:

```
/* a comment */
x_coord= 10; // a comment
```

Variables in Java must be declared before use just as in C. Variables can begin with letters, underscore (_), or dollar sign ($). Letters can include any Unicode character other than typographical characters, which means variables can be specified in the programmer's native language and character set if desired. Here are some examples:

```
int $counter;
boolean _test;
Homepage_counter+=1;
épreuve=false;
```

And of course, string and character values can be assigned any Unicode values. Unicode is supported both at the language level and in preconstructed classes for easy internationalization. Java, like C, has some keywords that are part of the language and not appropriate for use as variable names. See

Appendix C for a list of Java keywords.

Java includes many control structures familiar to C programmers including if-else, switch, for, while, and do-while:

```
if (test=true)
    test=false;
else
    test=true;
for ($counter=1; $counter<100; $counter++) {
    // some Java statements
}
```

Java uses different string operators than C. You can concatenate two strings with the + operator. The += operator lets you append the contents of the string after the equal sign to the contents of the variable to the left of it. Arrays are also declared differently in Java. Array declarations must include the new operator:

```
int row[] = new int[12];
```

If you've written programs in C, you are already familiar with most aspects of the Java language. More information about the Java language is included in Appendix C.

JAVASCRIPT: INLINE BROWSER SCRIPTING

Netscape Navigator was the first commercial browser to include support for the Java programming language. Prior to their adoption of Java, Netscape was working on a scripting language called LiveScript that would allow authors and programmers to provide client side scripts inside HTML documents and control the behavior of the Navigator Web browser. Once Java appeared, LiveScript quickly became JavaScript—a "light" version of Java for Web pages. JavaScripts can be embedded in HTML documents between the <SCRIPT> start and end tags or accessed via a <SCRIPT SRC="http://server/script.js"> element in the document header. When an SRC attribute is provided, the script is retrieved from a Web server, where it is stored with the file extension .js identifying it as a JavaScript. JavaScripts are plain text files containing script source, unlike Java applets, which are binary class files that cannot be viewed, only executed. The Netscape browser interprets the contents of a script as it renders the HTML page associated with it. JavaScripts can perform animations, extend the browser or Java applets, check form input, and perform many of the same functions that CGI scripts normally perform. But since the action takes place on the client machine, bottlenecks such as heavy network traffic and busy servers are avoided. Here is a brief example of a JavaScript embedded in an HTML file:

Continued on next page

```
Continued from previous page
   <HTML>
   <HEAD>
   <TITLE>Malay Test 1: JavaScript Version</TITLE>
   </HEAD>
   <BODY>
   <SCRIPT LANGUAGE="JavaScript">
   function score(form) {
      answer=form.q3.value;
      answer=answer.toLowerCase();
      if ((answer == "nasi") || (answer == "beras")) {
         form.result.value = "Correct!";
      }
   }
   </SCRIPT>
   <H1>Malay Test 1</H1>
   <FORM>
   3. What is the Malay word for rice? <INPUT NAME="q3" TYPE=TEXT>
   <HR>
   <INPUT TYPE="reset">
   <INPUT TYPE="button" VALUE="Check my answer"
   onClick="score(form)">
   <P>
   Your response was <INPUT TYPE=TEXT NAME="result">
   </FORM>
   </BODY>
   </HTML>
```

To learn more about JavaScript, access Netscape's *JavaScript Authoring Guide* at http://home.netscape.com/eng/mozilla/Gold/handbook/javascript/index.html

Using Java: An Introduction

As you have seen, Java is a complete programming language that can be used to create software as well as interactive Web content. In this text, we will only concern ourselves with elements of the Applet class and a few others. The goal is to give you some idea of the possibilities that Java presents for embedded Web content. The real key to becoming proficient with Java is becoming familiar with the application programming interface (API). This consists of a set of packages containing groups of objects used to perform certain tasks. Java packages are text files containing source code for several Java class definitions. When an object from a class is used or extended, that class must be imported. The import statement should be placed at the beginning of your Java source file and its argument must start with a package name, followed by a period, followed by a class name or an asterisk to use more than one class in the package without having to specify each class name. Our "Hello WWW!" applet (complete source listing is at the end of this chapter) uses classes from the awt and applet packages; here are its import statements:

```
import java.awt.*;
import java.applet.Applet;
```

The awt (abstract window toolkit) class is used to create and manipulate elements found in a graphical user interface such as windows, text fields, buttons, pull-down menus, etc. This package can be used to construct elements of an applet and also to build standalone applications with Java.

Now let's look at more of the "Hello, WWW!" applet source:

```
public class HelloWorld extends Applet
```

This line declares a class for the new applet called HelloWorld. It is a subclass of the Applet class, which allows it to exist within a Web browser window if the browser has a Java interpreter.

Every Java application is a class. Classes can be new or inherited from existing classes. New classes inherit from the Object class if the extends modifier is not present in a class definition. The interpreter views the declaration like this:

```
class doSomething extends Object {
```

The Object class allows Java code to know how to be an object, that is, how to put itself into memory, interact with other objects, and keep track of its variables and methods.

You can also create classes with incomplete methods . You might want to do this if you are working with a team of programmers and want to define an interface to an object, without going to the trouble of writing the code to implement the object; this is called an abstract class:

```
class someObject {
    abstract int someMethod( argument1, argument2) {
```

By doing this, you know what messages you could send to an object of that class and what arguments they require. Others can then subclass your abstract class to create the objects that will actually be instantiated at runtime. A variation on abstract classes is the interface. An interface is a class that contains only abstract methods:

```
public interface interfaceName {
    abstract int method1 ();
    abstract boolean method2();
```

These constructs demonstrate a feature common to all object-oriented programming languages: the concept of programming with objects is often easier than implementing the concepts in a programming language. It takes a bit of practice to link the terminology with what the code is actually doing.

Following the class declaration is a declaration for a method in the HelloWorld class. init() is actually a method defined in the Applet class. HelloWorld is extending this method so that it can initialize itself in a certain way. In this case, when the class is created and the init() method called, it calls another method of the Applet class called resize(). The resize() method sets up the applet screen area to be an area 400 pixels wide by 70 pixels high. The init() method is one of a class of methods that are called automatically during the life span of an object, if they exist. The init() method is the first method called for an object.

Let's look at the second method declaration in Hello, WWW!:

```
public void paint (Graphics g) {
```

This creates a new paint() method in the HelloWorld class. The method is public, meaning it can be messaged by objects other than HelloWorld. If an object wished to ask HelloWorld to paint itself, it would include a statement like this:

```
HelloWorld.paint(g);
```

Here again, paint() is a method called automatically by the interpreter. Graphics g declares an argument of the class Graphics for the paint() method. Classes can be used to declare types just like variable type names (int, Boolean, etc.).

The paint() method sends messages to the Graphics object g:

```
g.drawRect(10,10, 320, 40);
g.drawString("Hello, World Wide Web!", 100, 34);
```

The first message tells the graphics object to draw a rectangle starting at coordinate 10,10 and to make it 320 pixels wide by 40 pixels high. The second message tells the graphics object to display a string "Hello, World Wide Web!" starting at the specified coordinates 100, 34.

Once the applet completes the assigned task, it exits. The Java runtime environment also runs other objects that manage your Applet objects. For example, a garbage collection object is running alongside your Applet to manage memory and clean up after objects that have completed their task. Otherwise they would continue to use up system memory until you reboot your computer!

The garbage collector illustrates another feature of the Java language: it is multithreaded. A multithreaded programming language allows you to write programs that have components which can execute simultaneously and independently of one another. For example, if you had a word processor that was multithreaded, it might allow you to edit another document while you are spell checking a document. It is almost as though the spell checker were a separate program altogether. Threads are not quite as easy as they seem, since the order in which actions are performed can affect the outcome. If you were spell checking a document and saved the same document while the spell checker was running, then the document would be saved before the spell checker completed, possibly with spelling errors. This problem is handled by declaring certain threads to be thread-safe. Thread-safe threads can perform their task without any concern of the actions of another thread. But of course, not every task can be thread-safe.

Threads are an advanced topic and you should consult the online Java programming guide for implementation information. The Java programming guide also documents the complete Java API. The API lists packages, classes in the package, and the methods and instance variables of each class using an easy-to-navigate tree structure. Once you become familiar with the API, you will find that much of the work has already been done for you. More often than not, rather than create your own classes, you will be extending classes in the API to suit your needs.

The next chapter will continue with further discussion of the Java API. We will develop a simple, interactive applet that demonstrates many aspects of the Java language. We will also take a closer look at the applet and awt classes.

Here is the complete source for the Hello, WWW! Applet:

```java
import java.awt.*;
import java.applet.Applet;

public class HelloWorld extends Applet {
    public void init() {
        resize(400, 70);
    }
    public void paint(Graphics g) {
        g.setColor(Color.black);
        g.drawRect(10,10, 320, 40);
        g.drawString("Hello, World Wide Web!", 100, 34);
    }
}
```

Here is the HTML document that calls it:

```html
<HTML>
<HEAD><TITLE>Hello, WWW!</TITLE></HEAD>
<BODY>
<H1>Hello world applet</H1>
<APPLET code="HelloWorld" WIDTH=400 HEIGHT=70>
</APPLET>
</BODY>
</HTML>
```

TABLE 31-1   **OBJECT-ORIENTED TERMINOLOGY**

Term	Definition
abstract class	a class with some incomplete methods
class	specification for an object
encapsulate	variables are concealed within the object and accessible only through class methods
instance variable	a variable belonging to an instance of an object
interface	a class consisting solely of incomplete method definitions
method	defines a group of statements to perform a task
object	an instance of an object, a class loaded into memory
public	a variable or method visible to other objects

Building
Java Applets

CHAPTER AT A GLANCE

- Introducing the Java Development Kit
- Inside the Java API
- Developing active content for a Web page using the Java language and API
- Table 32-1: *Components of the Java Development Kit*
- Project: *English to Malay Word Translator*
- *Intelligent Agents*

Java is all about dynamic content. Web pages created with HTML are static. Even Web forms offer a static input interface, depending on a remote CGI script to generate content. Web pages are only interactive in that they present hypertext links with which users may navigate. Java allows authors to embed interactive content in the form of applets directly into a Web page. Interactive content can be animations, live data feeds, or real software applications appearing alongside HTML text. This allows a Web browser to become a networked applications desktop, not just a document browser.

Since Java is a virtual computer that sits atop the operating system, Java applications can run on any computer to which this virtual Java machine has been ported. This makes it possible that Web browsers will usurp operating systems and graphical user interfaces as the default user environment. Indeed, Microsoft is already revising the Windows 95 interface to appear more Weblike in its next release. Instead of interacting with icons representing files as in a traditional graphical user interface, users might immediately run a Web browser allowing them to interact with their local computer and network documents and applications using a familiar hypertext interface. Applications such as word processors or spreadsheets might reside on a central server at their site or be rented from a remote vendor by the hour.

Java can be paired with other technologies such as VRML to construct wholly new and unimagined interfaces to applications and files (Figure 32-1). A virtual reality database system might be implemented on the Internet as a virtual hall of records where users meet and interact within the database and database functions are performed with controls that are as real as a steering wheel or brakes are in a car in the physical world. Java-powered search engines might render database records in a mode as familiar as a set of file cabinets or as abstract as a collection of objects floating in space with each record appearing like a mini solar system, fields revolving around a sphere much like electrons circling the nucleus of an atom. New users might be directed to a training amphitheater where the new tools are demonstrated. Java-driven database management tools and environments might make managing a database as immersive and experiential as gardening or driving a car.

Figure 32-1 A 3-D object that can be manipulated with mouse actions, created by a Java applet

All of the components required for us to make such a leap en masse to a new mode of interacting with applications and data now exist. Java is the missing piece of the puzzle—allowing users to interact with one another over a network regardless of their preferred computing environment. Hardware differences become irrelevant as do operating system differences, except for the ways they can facilitate or hinder the operation of the Java Virtual Machine and network connectivity.

Java has many implications for the Web. It also has implications for other Internet data formats. VRML worlds are currently static "places" in which a user may travel, examine objects, and explore. Java is already being explored as a mechanism for the next generation of VRML. Future worlds might allow visitors to virtually exist in a world, appearing as a simple wire-frame entity with a photograph for a head like the visitors to the cathedral-like hall of data in the popular movie *Disclosure*, or any number of rendered entities whose complexity depends on available computing power and network bandwidth. Objects within a Java-powered VRML world could move, fly, and be manipulated by visitors. Java classes might map to VRML objects in a world where object-oriented programming may be synonymous with objects we can see, touch, and manipulate.

The Java Development Kit

Current Java development tools are primitive when compared with graphical object-oriented development systems such as NEXTSTEP's InterfaceBuilder or Delphi for Windows. There are no graphical design tools included with Sun's free Java Development Kit. But there are many programming examples available, and the Application Programming Interface is detailed on the Web as a hierarchy of packages and classes. Today's Java programmers must delve into the online API (application programming interface) in order to create even the most basic applet. Luckily, interest in Java is high, so better development tools will be forthcoming. Currently, the only choice for developing Java applications is Sun's Java Development Kit.

Java Development Kit (JDK) includes most of the tools necessary to create and test both standalone applications and applets for Java-capable Web browsers. The kit for Windows NT or Windows 95 (Figure 32-2) is 2.5MB compressed and uses 6MB of disk space when installed. It is available as a self-extracting archive at ftp://java.sun.com/pub/JDK-beta-win32-x86.exe. Sun also distributes a JDK for Sun workstations running Solaris 2.3 or higher and PowerPC-based Macintosh systems. The Sun kit is 4.5MB compressed and 9MB installed. It is available from ftp://java.sun.com/pub/JDK-beta-solaris2-sparc.tar.Z. You can learn about other sites distributing the JDK and about new versions of the kit by accessing Sun's Java page at http://java.sun.com/.

The first step in developing a Java application is identifying the objects needed to perform various tasks required of the application. Then you implement new classes, subclass classes similar to those you actually need, or utilize existing classes as they are for each object identified. Java classes are contained

Figure 32-2 Add the java\bin directory to your path so JDK components are accessible (Windows NT shown).

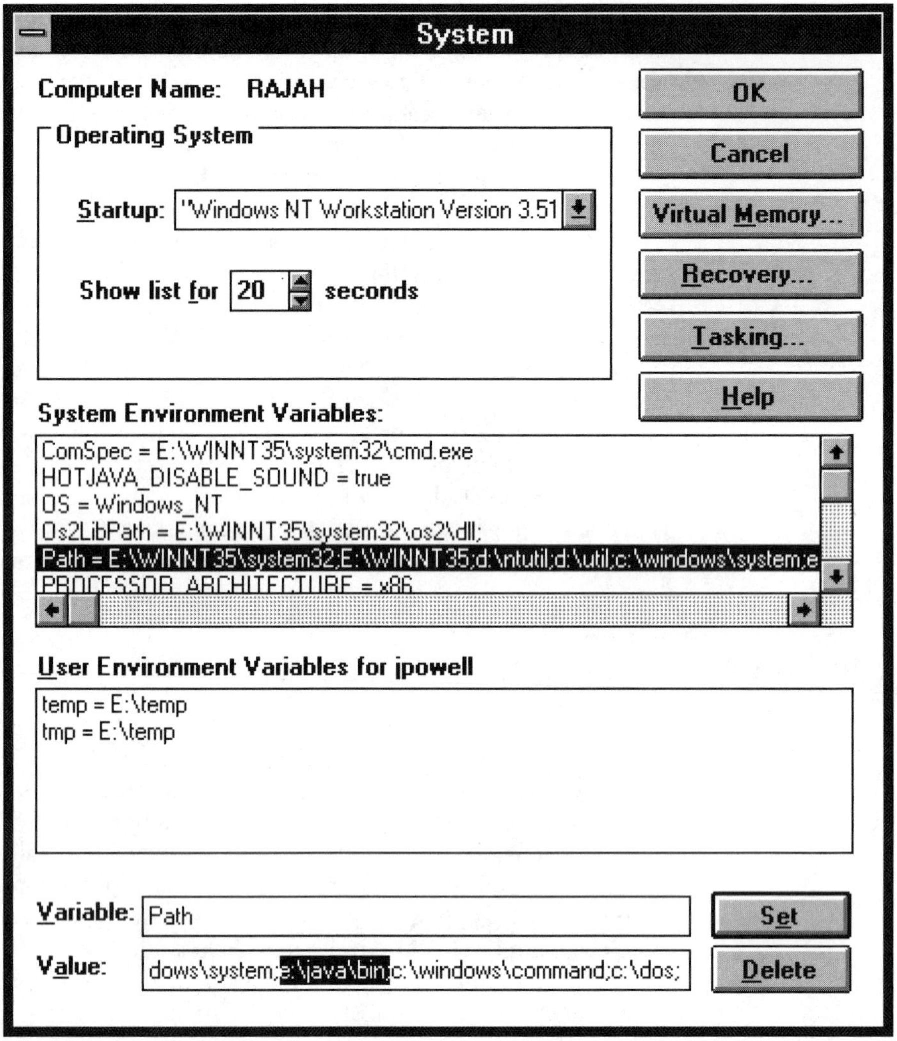

in packages, which are collections of similar objects. These packages constitute the API. The API documentation will help you decide if you can simply use a class as is (static or instance of the class), subclass an existing class (extends), or will need to create a new class.

Next, you will need a text editor to input your Java source code. The text editor is the only item not included with the kit, since it is assumed that you've already installed an editor on your system for other projects. Any program that can output plain ASCII text files will suffice. You can then compile your program into the Java machine language, referred to as bytecode, using the javac compiler. javac compiles Java code stored in programs named something.java and generates something.class files that can be served over the Web or used as standalone programs with the Java interpreter, which emulates the Java virtual machine on your computer. The JDK also includes an applet viewer that implements enough of the java.browser class to simulate a Web browser so you can test applets.

If you run into problems not detected at compile time, there is a Java language debugger (jdb) that you can use to locate and correct problems with your applications or applets.

If you create a new set of classes and save them as a package, you can use the javadoc application to generate documentation for them. javadoc can also be used to generate API documentation from the API included with the development kit.

Other kit components include a dissassembler (javap) and a program to create C header files from Java classes so you can combine Java and C code to create applications.

TABLE 32-1   COMPONENTS OF THE JAVA DEVELOPMENT KIT

Program	Purpose
javac	Java language compiler
java	Java interpreter for running java applications
jdb	Java language debugger
javah	Creates C header files and C stub files from a Java class
javap	Java language dissassembler
javadoc	API documentation generator
appletviewer	Java applet viewer

Each of these programs is run from the NT or Sun command line along with the appropriate arguments; for example, to compile a Java program, type:

    javac Translator.java

and to view it, type:

    appletviewer LangTrans.html

after creating an HTML file with the appropriate <APPLET> tag pointing to the newly created Java class.

PROJECT: ENGLISH TO MALAY WORD TRANSLATOR

An applet can serve live data, interactive documents, or applications within a browser window. Java also lets you develop standalone applications that can be delivered across the Internet. But our project will focus on building a browser applet: a simple language translator that can be retrieved and used on any computer platform that has a Java-capable browser. The applet could easily be extended to support additional vocabulary or even multiple languages. This demo version supports ten words.

Identify the objects This translator will accept words in English and attempt to locate an equivalent word in the Malay language. The first text field on the screen accepts keyboard input once the user has selected the field. The user can then select the "Translate" button, which sends a message to the translate object, which attempts to locate an equivalent word in the other language. The second text field is not for user input but displays the translation of the word the user has entered in the output language. If no match is found in the dictionary, then the translate object tells the second text field to display an error message.

Design the interface The translator interface (Figure 32-3) is very simple. As mentioned above, it utilizes two text fields and a single button. One text field is editable, that is, the user can enter or replace text in the field. The second field only displays output from the translator. Each field is 15 characters wide.

When designing an interface for a Java applet, remember that you can use HTML to create much of the interface. The HTML document containing the embedded applet might include documentation for the applet, access to its source code, or hypertext links to other applets that might provide similar services or even allow you to modify the behavior of this applet. For example, you might want to extend the translator applet by creating a second applet that allows you to teach it new words.

Create classes There are Java classes in the Abstract Window Toolkit (awt) package that we can subclass and use to create our user interface. Our job will be to create appropriate subclasses and instantiate those classes to construct an interface and translation engine at runtime. The hard part will be to build the translation class, which will be a new class (inheriting only from the object class). We will have to design it from the ground up, deciding what data (the characteristics of the object) it will know about, and what methods (the behavior of the object) it needs to implement in order to get the work done and communicate with other objects. And of course we will have to instantiate this object at runtime to actually perform requested translations.

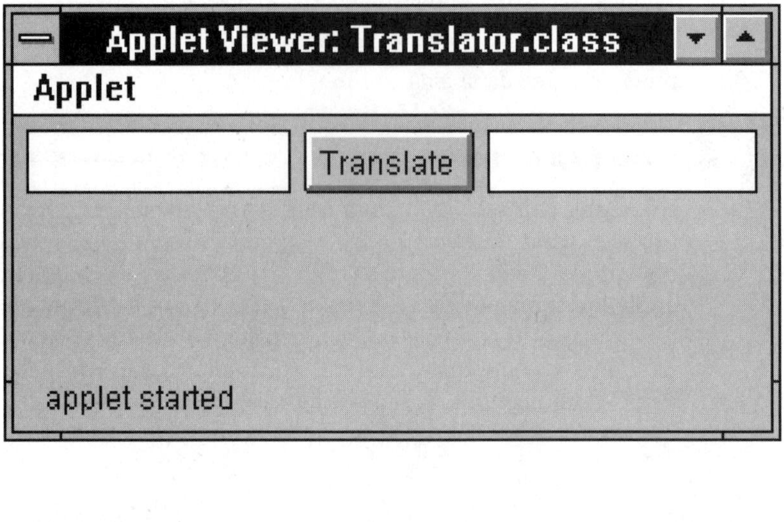

Figure 32-3 The Translator applet interface displayed with the JDK applet viewer

Put together the interface First, we must import the packages and/or classes we will be using in this applet. By doing this, we can use or extend existing classes rather than write new code to create buttons and text fields. Here are the import statements for the Translator.java program:

```
import java.awt.*;
import java.util.Hashtable;
import java.applet.Applet;
```

We import the entire awt package since we will be using several classes from it including Button, TextField, and the layout manager classes to place our components into the browser window. Hashtable is a data structure class that relates items to key values. We can use this to pair English words with their Malay equivalents. Finally, we import the Applet class, which allows us to make our application an embedded applet rather than a standalone application.

Next, let's create a place for the applet to be drawn within the browser window:

```
public class Translator extends Applet
{
    Button translateButton;
    TextField tfWord;
    TextField translation;

    public void init()
    {
        translateButton = new Button("Translate");
        tfWord = new TextField(12);
        translation = new TextField(12);
        add("Left", tfWord);
        add("Center", translateButton);
        add("Right", translation);

        resize(500, 250);
    }
}
```

First, we extend the Applet class, from the java.applet.Applet package. We then declare five object-instance variables including translateButton of the Button class, and word and translation of the TextField class. Both of these classes are part of the awt package. Next we instantiate these objects in the init() method. We use the add method to place and position our button and text fields in the Web browser window.

Now we have our interface done. You can even enter text in the text fields and press the Translate button. These objects know how to do this without us writing any code. We just create instances of the classes we need to add controls to our interface. But our controls don't work together yet and although the button can be pressed, no action is taken when this occurs. So next, let's have our class copy the contents of the word text field to the translation text field when the Translate button is pressed. Insert this method before the main method in the source:

```
public synchronized boolean handleEvent (Event evt)
{
    if ("Translate".equals(evt.arg))
    {
        translation.setText(tfWord.getText());
        show();
        return true;
    }
    return false;
}
```

All interface objects such as Applet, Button, and TextField have an event handler method that checks for and responds to actions such as text entry in a text field, mouse pointer location, and button press events. You can override this method to make your class respond to user input. In our case, we want our Translator class to check for and respond to its Translation button being pressed. So we override the handleEvent method to do what we need. To override a method, you just declare it, putting your own code in the body of the method. In our version of handleEvent, we check the label of the component that was the target of an event. The object evt contains this information, so we send it a message to get it: evt.arg. If the label is "Translate" then we execute the code following the if statement. The first line sends a message to the word text field tfWord.getText(). This returns the contents of the field. We then send a message to the translation text field to set its contents to the value contained in the word text field translation.setText. getText and setText let you interact with the contents of a text field. The contents are encapsulated within the text field component class, so you must call these methods to get and replace this data.

Create the translation engine Now all that is left to do is to build a translation engine. First, we need a place to store our dictionary. Java has a class called Hashtable that lets you associate value pairs, similar to Perl's associative array. The Hashtable class associates objects. Value pairs can be numbers, words, phrases, images, audio clips, anything that can be contained by an object. Our instance of the Hashtable class will be used to associate an English word with a Malay word. Insert the following declaration after the declarations for the button and text fields:

```
Hashtable malayDictionary;
```

Now we need to fill our dictionary with some translation pairs. To do this, we will add code to the init() method for the Translator class and initialize the dictionary with it. The init() method is automatically called once per execution for any class.

```
malayDictionary = new Hashtable();
malayDictionary.put("book", "surat");
malayDictionary.put("bread", "roti");
malayDictionary.put("cat", "kucing");
malayDictionary.put("english", "ingerris");
malayDictionary.put("good", "baik");
malayDictionary.put("heavy", "berat");
malayDictionary.put("how much", "berapa");
malayDictionary.put("mountain", "gunung");
malayDictionary.put("prince", "raja");
malayDictionary.put("thanks", "terima kasih");
```

Each malayDictionary.put message inserts a pair of strings into the Hashtable. The first string is the key, which can be used to locate the second string, the value. In our case, the English word serves as a key and the equivalent Malay word is the value associated with it. Notice that one entry inserts the phrase "how much" into the Hashtable. We have inserted pairs of string objects into the Hashtable, so we don't need to be concerned with the length of the string or number of words. The string object takes care of this.

One more step is required to activate our translation engine. We need to update our event handler method to use the Hashtable to retrieve translations. Replace the handleEvent method we used previously with this one:

```
public synchronized boolean handleEvent (Event evt)
{
    if ("Translate".equals(evt.arg))
    {
     String userWord = (String)malayDictionary.get
        (tfWord.getText());
     if (userWord != null) {
        translation.setText(userWord);
     } else
     {
        translation.setText("Word not known");
     }
     show();
     return true;
     }
   return false;
}
```

This method first checks to see if the user pressed the "Translate" button. If so, the text the user placed in the word field is used as a key to retrieve a string from the dictionary. This string object is placed in userWord. We have to be sure to cast the value returned by our instance of the Hashtable object so that it can be used later to set the output text field. That's why (String) precedes the get message we send to the Hashtable:

```
(String)malayDictionary.get(tfWord.getText());
```

A second if statement checks the translation value returned by the Hashtable. If there was no entry for the word the user entered, the Hashtable object returns. So we check for null, and return the string "Word not known" if it is found. Otherwise, we send a message to the translation field to set its contents to the value in userWord.

Use the applet   Finally, let's build a Web page in which we will embed the content:

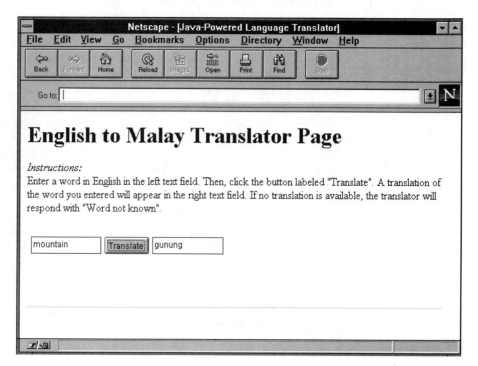

```
<HTML>
<HEAD><TITLE>Java-Powered Language Translator</TITLE></HEAD>
<BODY>
<H1>English to Malay Translator Page</H1>
<EM>Instructions:</EM><BR>
Enter a word in English in the left text field.
Then, click the button labeled "Translate". A translation of the word you entered
will appear in the right text field. If no translation is available, the translator will
respond with "Word not known".
<P>
<APPLET CODE="Translator.class" WIDTH=300 HEIGHT=100>
Java-powered English to Malay translator
```

```
</APPLET>
<HR>
</BODY>
</HTML>
```

Although we created a page specifically for this applet, it could just as easily have been inserted into an existing Web page. Non-Java-capable browsers would simply display the contents of the <APPLET> tag.

INTELLIGENT AGENTS

Today, most users actively pursue information on the Web. Whether they access a search service or follow the hypertext links in a document to other documents, the user must retrieve and filter the information in order to determine whether it is useful. This is an inefficient, time-consuming process. One of the next leaps forward in information technology will be intelligent agents.

An intelligent agent is a software application that maintains detailed information about topics a user is interested in. The agent may determine topics automatically by monitoring the Web pages and resources a user consults most often, or specified by the user using some type of configuration file. The agent then pursues documents on the Web on a regular basis by following hypertext links, consulting search engines, and other methods. An intelligent agent could be as simple as a smart Web browser, or as complex as a distributed application with permission to run on dozens of remote servers in order to examine the contents of archives. Java is an ideal candidate for building intelligent agents, since it includes network classes that allow it to retrieve information from the Web, and is a secure language that other computers need not be too concerned with executing. Pretty soon, Java applets and programs will crop up that can do this, and the futuristic TV commercials predicting that we'll all have our own digital assistant that greets us each morning with selections of newspaper articles, video clips, and other information will become a reality.

Java lets you embed applications as active content within an HTML page. This applet could be extended to learn new words. Or it could be modified so that multiple Hashtable instances exist for multiple languages. We could then add a menu component to the interface and let the user select the language. By using other packages such as the java.net package, we could even have the applet load dictionary instances only as needed from the server. With additional effort, the applet could even be extended to function as a crude Web page translator. Perhaps it could attempt to determine the language of a targeted Web page and translate it into the reader's native language. It is not a big leap from active content to intelligent browsers. In this and many other ways, Java points the way to the Web of the future.

Complete source listing for Translator class:

```java
import java.awt.*;
import java.util.Hashtable;
import java.applet.Applet;
public class Translator extends Applet
{
    Button translateButton;
    TextField tfWord;
    TextField translation;
    Hashtable malayDictionary;

    public void init() {
        translateButton = new Button("Translate");
        tfWord = new TextField(12);
        translation = new TextField(12);
        add("Left", tfWord);
        add("Center", translateButton);
        add("Right", translation);

        malayDictionary = new Hashtable();
        malayDictionary.put("book", "surat");
        malayDictionary.put("bread", "roti");
        malayDictionary.put("cat", "kucing");
        malayDictionary.put("english", "ingerris");
        malayDictionary.put("good", "baik");
        malayDictionary.put("heavy", "berat");
        malayDictionary.put("how much", "berapa");
        malayDictionary.put("mountain", "gunung");
        malayDictionary.put("prince", "raja");
        malayDictionary.put("thanks", "terima kasih");
    }
    public synchronized boolean handleEvent (Event evt)
    {
        if ("Translate".equals(evt.arg))
        {
        String userWord = (String)malayDictionary.get(tfWord.getText());
        if (userWord != null) {
            translation.setText(userWord);
          else
          {
              translation.setText("Word not known");
          }
          show();
          return true;
        }
        return false;
    }
}
```

Non-HTML Content on the Web

33

Introduction
to VRML

CHAPTER AT A GLANCE

- The purpose of VRML and its relationship to the Web
- Introducing various VRML language constructs
- VRML Primer
- Table 33-1: *Field Value Types*
- VRML Node Summary

The Virtual Reality Modeling Language is a computer language for describing three-dimensional objects and spaces. VRML includes language elements for creating simple shapes, various lighting effects, applying textures to shapes, and various points of view (also referred to as cameras). Rooms, houses, and even entire cities can be duplicated in VRML. When a user enters a VRML world, they can walk or fly through the space and examine objects. Objects such as virtual furniture, doorways, or 3-D controls within a VRML world can be configured as hypertext links, leading a visitor to other virtual worlds. VRML documents can be delivered on floppy, CD-ROM, and most importantly, via the Web. Indeed, VRML relies heavily on three key elements of the Web: the Web server as a means to publish documents, the URL to locate pieces of a virtual world and link to VRML and non-VRML data on the Internet, and the Web browser for retrieving the VRML document from a Web server. Some VRML browsers can directly address Web servers. Others are being developed as plug-ins to HTML Web browsers so that a browser such as Mosaic or Netscape can display and allow a user to navigate both the Web and VRML space with the same browser.

VRML documents can be constructed with any text editor just like HTML documents. As you will see in this and the next chapter, VRML documents can become quite large. Most complex virtual worlds are developed with graphical world editors. But if you learn the language behind the objects produced by this type of software, you will not only be able to utilize it to its fullest potential but will also be able to create objects and scenes that some editors may not support. This chapter covers VRML version 1.0. Version 2.0 is already in the works. It will include the ability to interact with objects in virtual worlds and support for moving, interactive objects using Java. Like HTML, there are also a few browser-specific extensions to VRML in use, but these are not covered in this book.

VRML documents start with the line

```
#VRML V1.0 ascii.
```

VRML files usually have the file extension .wrl (which is short for world). Web clients should have a MIME type entry that relates x-world/x-vrml to the file extension .wrl and to a VRML browser. If you are publishing VRML files, you may also need to ask your Web server administrator to add an entry to the Web server's mime.types configuration file. This entry ensures that the Web server prepends the appropriate header to the .wrl file when delivering it to a Web client:

```
x-world/x-vrml        .wrl
```

VRML describes objects in a world. Each object, referred to as a node, has a number of modifying properties that precede it. Here is an example of a Sphere node with a color parameter:

```
Material {
    emissiveColor 1.0 1.0 1.0
}
Sphere {
    radius 2
}
```

This node describes a glowing white sphere, 2 meters in radius. All size and distance values are considered to be in meters. Nodes are listed in a hierarchy called scene graphs. This hierarchy determines the order of the nodes. Nodes above other nodes can affect where later nodes are placed in a world and how they look. For example, one node might describe a glowing sphere that reflects off of a second. Here are a pair of Sphere nodes, one describing a smaller sphere in orbit around another:

```
Separator {
   Material {
      emissiveColor 1.0 1.0 1.0
   }
   Sphere {
      radius 3
   }
   Transform {
      translation 5 0 0
   }
   Sphere {
      radius 1
   }
}
```

Notice the two Sphere nodes are contained by a Separator node and curly braces ({}). When two nodes are grouped with the Separator node, they can also be treated as one node by other objects. This also serves to limit the effect of properties. In this example, the Material node modifies only the Spheres defined within this Separator node.

Nodes have the following characteristics:

- *Type of object:* Sphere, Transform, Material, and Separator are all object, or node types. All node type names start with an uppercase letter.

- *Fields:* Translation, emissiveColor, and radius are all node fields. They control the appearance of an object.

- *Name:* The DEF keyword is used to assign a name to an object, for example, DEF orbit Separator defines a separator node called orbit. This object can be reused later (or instantiated) when referred to with the USE keyword. If an object or group of objects called orbit has been defined, you can place a second object of this type in your VRML world by simply inserting the line USE orbit.

- *Child nodes:* Unless contained by a Separator node, each subsequent node in a file is a child of the previous node. Separators let you clarify and alter these relationships.

Let's revise the basic sphere example we considered earlier and make it a valid VRML file. Notice also the Separator node is now called orbit, and is preceded by a comment, which begins with a pound sign (#):

```
#VRML V1.0 ascii
# A pair of sphere nodes, one orbitting the other
DEF orbit Separator {
   Material {
      emissiveColor 1.0 1.0 1.0
   }
   Sphere {
```

```
        radius 3
    }
    Transform {
        translation 5 0 0
    }
    Sphere {
        radius 1
    }
}
```

Here's the rendering of this code as displayed by the WorldView VRML browser (Figure 33-1):

Figure 33-1 A pair of spheres

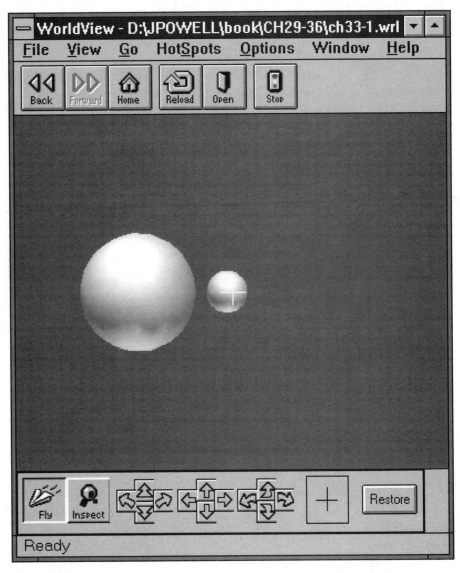

VRML places great demands on the client computer. Complex worlds are slower to navigate because they take longer to draw and redraw as the user moves through them. VRML worlds can quickly become so complex that they take more time to download. There are a few things you can do to make your world easier to navigate. Be aware that every object in a world is constructed of polygons (even spheres!). Every object adds new overhead to the world. The smaller an object is, the quicker it can be drawn, so scaling down the world is one way of speeding up redraw and navigation for the user. Bitmapped graphics such as GIFs or JPEGs can be used as textures in VRML, but use them sparingly. For example, you might find an image of carpet and apply it to the floor within a virtual home. Always use the smallest image possible for texturing. Finally, distribute your world as a compressed document whenever possible. Most VRML browsers support the gzip compression standard. This will speed up downloading so users don't have to wait as long to enter your VRML world.

The remainder of this chapter is a VRML primer. Chapter 34 includes a project implementing some of these language elements. Keep in mind that there are graphical tools that allow you to draw worlds and save them as VRML files, so learning the VRML language is not the only way to create worlds. Indeed, it would be extremely difficult to create and maintain complex worlds by creating VRML documents in a text editor, but occasionally you will find that you need to get inside a VRML file to refine an object or space, so it is helpful to be familiar with the language.

Virtual Reality Modeling Language Primer

FIELDS

Fields control the appearance of an object. There are two types of fields: fields having only one value, and fields having multiple values. We have seen both types in the sphere example above. The radius field requires only one numeric value, while coordinate fields such as translation require three numeric values. As we look at the various object types, we will also consider the types of fields appropriate for them. Table 33-1 relates the defined field value types with their VRML specification names, descriptions, and expected values:

TABLE 33-1   FIELD VALUE TYPES

Field Type Name	Description	Example Values
SFBitMask	a bit mask	mnemonic names for one or more bit flags
SFBool	a Boolean value	1, 0, TRUE, FALSE
SFColor	an RGB color value	triplet of color values from 0.0 to 1.0: gray is .9 .9 .9
SFEnum	an enumerated type name	mnemonic value
SFFloat	a single precision, floating point number	3.1415926

TABLE 33-1   FIELD VALUE TYPES, CONT.

Field Type Name	Description	Example Values
SFImage	color or gray scale pixel map definition: width, height, depth, color value for each pixel	2 2 1 255 0 255 0 is a 2 pixel wide by 2 pixel high by 1 pixel deep (gray scale) checkerboard
SFLong	32-bit (long) integer	1200263
SFMatrix	transformation matrix	—
SFRotation	arbitrary rotation: axis of rotation x y z, right-handed rotation,	0 0 1 -0.4 rotates -.4 radians on the z axis
SFString	ASCII character sequence	"Exit here"
SFVec2f	2-dimensional vector	—
SFVec3f	3-dimensional vector	—
MFColor	any number of RGB color values	1 0 0 0 1 1 0 1 0 is red, yellow, and green
MFLong	any number of 32-bit integers	3.1415926 3.1415926
MFString sequences	any number of ASCII-character	"Red - stop" "Yellow - caution" "Green - go"
MFVec2f	any number of 2-dimensional vectors	—
MFVec3f	any number of 3-dimensional vectors	—

VRML NODES

There are 36 types of nodes that fall into six basic categories. Shape nodes draw objects in a virtual world. Geometry, material, transformation, camera, and lighting nodes control how shape objects are drawn. They are also referred to collectively as property nodes. Grouping nodes gather shape and property nodes into collections of objects that can behave and be addressed as one single object.

Shape nodes There are eight types of shape nodes in VRML 1.0. Each defines a type of object that is to be drawn, or rendered by a VRML browser. More complex objects are constructed of these simple shapes, which are themselves made up of flat polygons. The AsciiText node draws a string of ASCII text in the world at the current x, y, z location. It has four possible fields. The text that is to be drawn is of type MFString. Three fields control the placement and size of the text: spacing (SFFloat), justification (SFEnum), and width (MFFloat). Possible values for justification are LEFT, CENTER, and RIGHT. Cone nodes draw conical-shaped objects. Cone nodes have three fields: parts (SFBitMask), bottomRadius (SFFloat), and height (SFFloat). The parts field controls where materials node properties will be applied, while bottomRadius and height control the size of the cone. The Cube node draws a cube-shaped object. You can specify the cube dimensions with the width (SFFloat), height (SFFloat), and depth (SFFloat) fields. The Cylinder node draws a cylinder. It has three fields: parts (SFBitMask), radius (SFFLoat), and height (SFFloat). The IndexedFaceSet and IndexedLineSet nodes are used to create polygons constructed of multiple two-dimensional polygons or multiple lines. Each has four fields: coordIndex (MFLong), materialIndex (MFLong), normalIndex (MFLong), and textureCoordIndex (MFLong). The PointSet node is used to draw a set of points. These points are drawn using coordinate sets. The first point to be drawn is specified using the startIndex field (SFLong), and the number of points to be drawn is specified by numPoints (SFLong). If numPoints is set to -1, then all remaining points defined in the coordinate node will be drawn. The Sphere node is used to draw a sphere. Sphere has a single field, radius (SFFloat), which determines the size of the sphere.

Geometry nodes   There are five types of geometry nodes for defining coordinates sets or other geometric attributes that can be utilized by or applied to a shape node. The Coordinate3 node defines a set of three-dimensional coordinates. This coordinate set is used by shape nodes such as IndexedFaceSet or PointSet to create objects. It has one field, point (MFVec3f). FontStyle nodes define various font characteristics that are then applied to any AsciiText shape nodes that follow. They have three fields: size (SFFloat), family (SFEnum), and style (SFBitMask). Defined family field values are SERIF, SANS, or TYPEWRITER. Style field values are NONE, BOLD, and ITALIC. The Normal node defines a set of three-dimensional surface vectors that can be used by shape nodes such as IndexedFaceSet or PointSet to create objects. It has one field, vector (MFVec3f). NormalBinding specifies how normals are bound to shapes made from faces and vertices, such as IndexedFaceSet. It has only one field (SFEnum) which has a number of possible binding values: DEFAULT, OVERALL, PER_PART, PER_PART_INDEXED, PER_FACE, PER_FACE_INDEXED, PER_VERTEX, and PER_VERTEX_INDEXED. The ShapeHints node applies to IndexedFaceSets and specifies the type of faces found in the object, such as solid or convex. The browser can use this information to skip the process of rendering certain information that is either obscured by other faces, or not yet visible at this distance. This improves browser performance while redrawing complex objects. There are four ShapeHints fields: vertexOrdering (SFEnum), shapeType (SFEnum), faceType (SFEnum), and creaseAngle (SFFloat). Each of these fields has several predefined values: vertexOrdering can be set to UNKNOWN_ORDERING, CLOCKWISE, or COUNTERCLOCKWISE, shapeType can be set to UNKNOWN_SHAPE_TYPE or SOLID; faceType can be set to UNKNOWN_FACE_TYPE or CONVEX.

Material nodes   Material nodes, of which there are six types, store information about a particular object such as what color it should be rendered in or what texture should be applied to its surface. Info nodes are used to store nondisplaying information used by a specific type of browser. They are sometimes used to include copyright or authorship information. Info nodes have one field, string (SFString). Level of detail (LOD) specify different shape, materials, and transformation nodes depending on the distance between the person and the object. Material nodes define various properties of the surface of any shape nodes that follow it. Each field corresponds to a surface characteristic: ambientColor (MFColor), diffuseColor (MFColor), specularColor (MFColor), emissiveColor (MFColor), shininess (MFFloat), and transparency (MFFloat). MaterialBinding nodes specify selective application of material node information to shapes, using its value (SFEnum) field. This field can be assigned one of the following values: DEFAULT, OVERALL, PER_PART, PER_PART_INDEXED, PER_FACE, PER_FACE_INDEXED, PER_VERTEX, and PER_VERTEX_INDEXED.

Other material nodes let you apply textures to objects. Textures are image files that are placed onto objects by the VRML browser. A Texture2 node specifies a texture image that should be applied to nodes that follow it. Textures can be specified pixel by pixel using the image (SFImage) field, or an image file can be used when specified with the filename (SFString) field, which can specify a URL for a GIF, RGB, or other image file supported by the browser. Other fields include the horizontal coordinate for the texture, wrapS (SFEnum) and the vertical coordinate, wrapT (SFEnum), which control wrapping of the texture image on an object. Wrapping can REPEAT, or CLAMP to a spot on the face. Texture2Transform nodes can be used to specify the size and position of a texture on a shape node. Its fields include translation (SFVec2f), rotation (SFFloat), scaleFactor (SFVec2f), and center (SFVec2f). TextureCoordinate2 specifies coordinates for textures being applied to objects created from PointSet, IndexedLineSet, or IndexedFaceSet nodes. The coordinates are specified with a point (MFVec2f) field.

Transformation nodes   Transformation nodes (there are five types) let you specify the location of objects in relation to each other. A MatrixTransform node specifies a three-dimensional transformation with a matrix (SFMatrix) field. Rotation nodes cause the nodes that follow to be rotated in three dimensions around an arbitrary axis through the origin of the object, using the rotation (SFRotation) field. A Scale node specifies three-dimensional scaling information for an object with its scaleFactor (SFVec3f) field. Transform combines several types of transformation nodes into one, specifying various transformations with its fields: translation (SFVec3f), rotation (SFRotation), scaleFactor (SFVec3f), scaleOrientation (SFRotation), and center (SFVec3f). A Translation node controls spatial positioning of the current object relative to the previous object drawn. It has one field, translation (SFVec3f).

Camera nodes   Cameras are default viewpoints for a world, that define where a user enters a world and how the space is presented. When a user enters a world, they typically start at a camera viewpoint selected by the browser, but you can specify alternate entry points. There are two types of camera nodes. An OrthographicCamera node specifies a flat view into a world. Objects in the space do not diminish as the viewer moves away from them. A PerspectiveCamera node specifies that objects are viewed in perspective, that is diminishing at a distance. This type of node lends a more realistic appearance to a virtual world. Each camera node type has four fields: position (SFVec3f) and orientation (SFRotation) control the xyz coordinates of the camera and the direction it is aimed, focalDistance (SFFloat) controls the distance at which objects can be seen, and heightAngle (SFFloat) controls the height of the viewing area.

Lighting nodes The three lighting source nodes are used to illuminate objects and scenes. DirectionalLight nodes control a source of light that emits many parallel rays in a specific direction. Its fields include on (SFBool), intensity (SFFloat), color (SFColor), and direction (SFVec3f). PointLight nodes specify a single light-emitting point that illuminates uniformly in all directions. PointLight fields include on (SFBool), intensity (SFFloat), color (SFColor), and location (SFVec3f). A SpotLight node specifies a spotlight that illuminates in a certain direction with a beam shaped like a cone, gradually dropping off with increased distance. SpotLight fields include on (SFBool), intensity (SFFloat), color (SFVec3f), location (SFVec3f), direction (SFVec3f), dropOffRate (SFFloat), and cutOffAngle (SFFloat).

Group nodes Group nodes (there are four types) contain other types of nodes. When you group nodes together, they are drawn and move about as one object. You can reuse groups if you use the DEF keyword to give the group a name. You can then use the group elsewhere by using the USE keyword when a named group of objects should be drawn in a new location. Reusing a set of objects in a VRML world is called *instancing*, and it speeds up navigation for the end user. Group nodes tie a set of nodes together. Group is simply an invisible binding box that can be used in conjunction with DEF to make a region of space containing objects reusable. Separator nodes group items and allow you to specify transformation and materials nodes within the group that will not affect the rendering of subsequent nodes outside the group. Separator has only one field: renderCulling (SFEnum), which can be assigned ON, OFF, or AUTO, which determines whether objects and object faces that are not visible should be drawn. A Switch node groups a set of nodes and specifies which of those nodes should be rendered in the space, with its whichChild (SFLong) field. The first node in the group would be rendered if whichChild were set to 0, the second if it were assigned 1, etc. TransformSeparator nodes are nearly identical to Separator nodes, except they only save transformation node values, not any others that occur before the grouping.

Finally, VRML has two node types that point to or retrieve data from the Web: WWWAnchor and WWWInline. A WWWAnchor node indicates that the node(s) which follow it should act as a hypertext link. Its name (SFString) field points to the URL of a target document, description (SFString) is a text description of that target document displayed by some browsers in a status field, and map (SFEnum) can be set to NONE or POINT to make the object anchor an image mapping field that passes the xyz coordinates of the user's click to the target. The targeted file can be another VRML file or any other type of file. WWWInline points to a VRML document that should be loaded at this point in the current world. It is similar to the HTML <IMG> tag. WWWInline fields include name (SFString), which is the URL of the .wrl document to be loaded, bboxSize (SFVec3f), and bboxCenter (SFVec3f), which specify a bounding box that tells the browser how much space the inline document will consume so it can continue rendering other objects while it is retrieving this one from the Web.

VRML NODE SUMMARY

Node	Type	Fields
AsciiText	shape	string, spacing, justification, width
Cone	shape	parts, bottomRadius, height
Coordinate3	geometry	point
Cube	shape	width, height, depth
Cylinder	shape	parts, radius, height
DirectionalLight	lighting	
FontStyle	geometry	size, family, style
Group	group	
IndexedFaceSet	shape	coordIndex, materialIndex, normalIndex, textureCoordIndex
IndexedLineSet	shape	coordIndex, materialIndex, normalIndex, textureCoordIndex
Info	material	string
LOD	material	range, center
Material	material	ambientColor, diffuseColor, specularColor, emissveColor, shininess, transparency
MaterialBinding	material	value
MatrixTransform	transformation	matrix
Normal	geometry	
NormalBinding	geometry	
OrthographicCamera	camera	position, orientation, focalDistance, height
PerspectiveCamera	camera	position, orientation, focalDistance, heightAngle
PointLight	lighting	on, intensity, color, location
PointSet	shape	startIndex, numPoints
Rotation	transformation	rotation
Scale	transformation	scaleFactor
Separator	group	renderCulling
ShapeHints	geometry	vertexOrdering, shapeType, faceType, creaseAngle
Sphere	shape	radius
SpotLight	lighting	on, intensity, color, location, direction, dropOffRate, cutOffAngle
Switch	group	whichChild
Texture2	material	filename, image, wrapS, wrapT
Texture2Transform	material	translation, rotation, scaleFactor, center
TextureCoordinate2	material	point
Transform	transformation	translation, rotation, scaleFactor, scaleOrientation, center
TransformSeparator	group	
Translation	transformation	
WWWAnchor	group	name, description, map
WWWInline	group/other	name, bboxSize, bboxCenter

34

Touring and Building Virtual Worlds

CHAPTER AT A GLANCE

- Navigation issues in virtual space
- Rendering controls and their impact on navigation
- VRML browsers and how they deal with 3-D navigation
- VRML editors
- Project: *Building a Virtual World*

VRML Browsers

VRML browsers let you retrieve and enter the home spaces (the VRML equivalent of home pages) and virtual worlds being created and published on the Web. VRML worlds are often single, self-contained files with links to other worlds. When you retrieve a world, the browser downloads a text file containing VRML code, which it then uses to render a copy of that world on your local computer. You navigate through this locally stored copy until you encounter a link to another world. This is similar to the way you navigate through HTML documents.

As with Web browsers, there are a number of VRML browsers available for most popular computing platforms. Unlike Web browsers, navigational controls are more varied from VRML browser to browser. These variations are due to the fact that navigating a three-dimensional space with the typical input devices (keyboard and mouse) on a two-dimensional screen is not a task with one straightforward solution. We will look at the solutions developed for three VRML browsers: WebSpace and WorldView for Microsoft Windows, and Whurlwind for the Macintosh, each of which tackles navigation somewhat differently.

VRML browsers provide three types of navigation controls. The first two types control movement of the viewer and objects within the space. The viewer can move along three dimensions as they tour a site. Some browsers refer to this as *walk-through* or *fly* mode. Objects can be manipulated with examiner tools. They can be made to spin on their x, y, or z axis so the viewer can look at all sides of the object. The third type of controls allows users to follow hypertext links to other worlds as well as HTML and other non-VRML document formats.

VRML browsers also include a set of standard Web browser–like controls. These include bookmark-like tools and rendering styles. Most VRML browsers support the virtual equivalent of bookmarks in the form of *hotspot* or *viewpoint* lists. These viewpoints usually correspond to the entry point in the virtual world, rather than a specific location as the name implies. Most browsers also support various rendering and shading levels that increase the detail of the objects while decreasing the speed with which a viewer can move through a world. The simplest rendering model is wireframe. Wireframe rendering simply displays outlines of the polygons used to construct an object. Solid rendering places surfaces on objects, including colors and textures if specified with a Material or Texture2 node. Flat shading is the default shading type applied to solid objects. With flat shading, each polygon is colored, rather than transparent. VRML browsers usually support two other types of shading: Gouraud and Phong. Gouraud shading averages the shading from one polygon face to the next, based on lighting and texture node information. This produces a more realistic image, but one that still tends to exhibit a faceted appearance. Gouraud will noticeably slow a VRML browser but not as much as Phong shading. Phong calculates averages for each corner of a polygon and its neighbors in order to improve shading. This results in very realistic objects, but slows navigation substantially. However, it is easy to switch between shading modes during navigation.

WORLDVIEW FOR WINDOWS

The WorldView browser for Windows (Figure 34-1) uses a matrix of directional buttons for both fly and inspect mode. In fly mode, buttons work as a steering mechanism. In this mode, the user can move through a scene traveling forward, backward, left, right, up, and down. In inspect mode, the directional controls determine along which axis an object will be rotated. Objects can be rotated left, right, flipped over, or looped in front of the user. The large plus sign to the

Figure 34-1
WorldView VRML
browser displaying
VRML logo

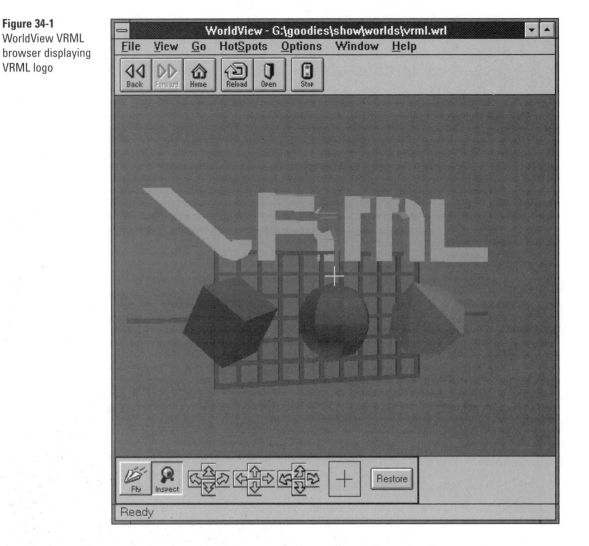

right of the other controls is a mouse-controllable pointer which can be used instead of the button controls. WorldView is capable of communicating directly with Web servers, so it has a familiar set of Weblike navigational aids across the top of the viewing window as well. Hypertext links are not visible or highlighted in any way in the view unless the creator of the space has constructed them with some texture or text that identifies them as links. Instead, the text description or URL of the link is displayed in a status field at the bottom of the window when the crosshairs pass over an object that has a WWWAnchor node.

WEBSPACE FOR WINDOWS

WebSpace (Figure 34-2) is a VRML client that depends on Web browsers such as Netscape to retrieve data for it. Like WorldView, WebSpace has two naviga-

Figure 34-2
WebSpace VRML
browser display-
ing VRML logo

tional modes: walk (fly) and examine (inspect). The browser can be toggled between these two modes from the *View* menu. Navigation controls for each mode are displayed across the bottom of the viewing window. WebSpace presents the user with a pointer, a steering handle, and a directional arrow for navigation. The controls function as though you were in a spacecraft flying through the world. WebSpace has a set of Web browser–like controls for initiating or ending load requests. Requests are passed to a Web browser that must have been launched prior to running WebSpace, such as Netscape Navigator. Objects serving as hypertext links are displayed in bright orange when the user points at them.

Figure 34-3
Whurlwind VRML
browser for
Macintosh display-
ing VRML logo

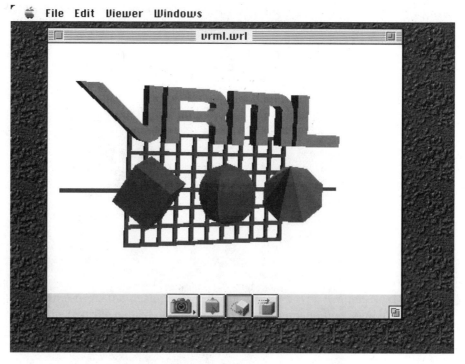

WHURLWIND FOR MACINTOSH

Whurlwind (Figure 34-3) was the first VRML browser developed for the Macintosh environment. It requires the QuickDraw 3-D extensions (freely available from Apple). Like WebSpace, Whurlwind functions as a Web browser helper application, depending on a Web browser to retrieve documents for it. Whurlwind allows you to travel through a world and manipulate objects using a minimalistic set of controls combined with mouse clicks and drags. It has four simple controls: camera to return you to the world's starting point, distance to switch to a walker or flyinglike mode, rotation to switch to an examinerlike mode, and panning to change the position of an object on the screen.

VRML Editors

It is possible to construct an entire VRML world with nothing more than a text editor, and we will do so momentarily. However, complex worlds are difficult to code and maintain by hand. There are a number of 3-D graphics editors under development or already on the market that allow you to draw your world, rather than write hundreds or thousands of lines of VRML code to create it. One such program is HomeSpace 3-D (Figure 34-4). This Windows-based graphics editor provides both a VRML browser–like view and a top-down view of the world as

Figure 34-4
HomeSpace 3-D editor can save documents in VRML format.

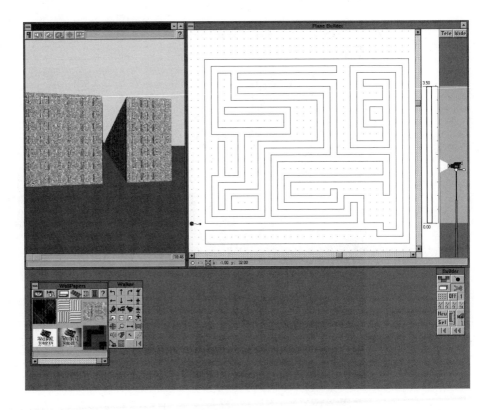

you construct it. Several tool palettes float beneath these windows providing quick access to texture maps, image placement, and wall building tools. HomeSpace can save 3-D worlds in several formats, including VRML.

The Virtus VRML Editor (Figure 34-5) for Windows and Macintosh systems provides multiple views of a scene as well as an object template and object inspector. The design view window lets you place objects in a space. You can position and rotate objects, as well as apply colors or textures to objects or surfaces in design view. The walk view presents the world just as it would appear in a VRML browser. You can navigate the space and examine objects. The Virtus VRML Editor includes a gallery of shapes and objects including geometric shapes for designing structures, and special-purpose objects such as household furniture. The gallery includes a preview area where you can inspect objects more closely. By default, this editor saves its 3-D worlds in its own native format, but it can just as easily export worlds to VRML format.

Graphical VRML editors manage to do most of the work for you, but many lack complete support for all VRML node types such as WWWInline or WWWAnchor nodes. That's when knowing how to construct a VRML world without a graphical editor comes in handy.

Figure 34-5 Virtus
VRML Editor

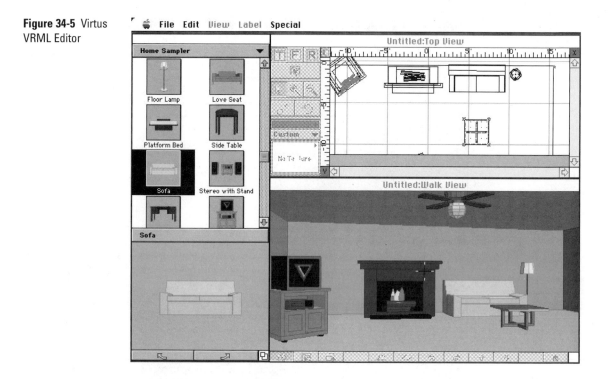

PROJECT: BUILDING A VIRTUAL WORLD: OUR SOLAR SYSTEM

If you create worlds in VRML, it is likely that you will use a graphical tool to construct three-dimensional spaces and objects, and save them in the VRML world format. But these tools are still in the earliest stages of development. Some lack the ability to create anchor nodes, others have numerous palettes and design panels for constructing buildings and spaces, but little support for designing objects to reside in these spaces. Once you have become familiar with VRML, you can easily edit your files to add these features. This is much easier if you are familiar with most of the node types and have created a few small worlds or modified existing VRML files. So to give you a chance to build a VRML world, we will construct a model of the solar system.

Building a virtual solar system is destined to become the virtual reality equivalent of the "Hello, World" program taught in programming language courses. It is simple enough that it can be constructed with less than 200 lines of VRML code, but there are many possibilities for expanding such a project, so it lends itself to further experimentation. This project's goal is to construct a not-to-scale version of the solar system. It includes examples of all node types: shape, geometry, material, transformation, camera, lighting, and group. You can create this file with any text editor or word processor that has a text-only save option. Figure 34-6 shows a view of the completed solar system VRML world embedded in an HTML document.

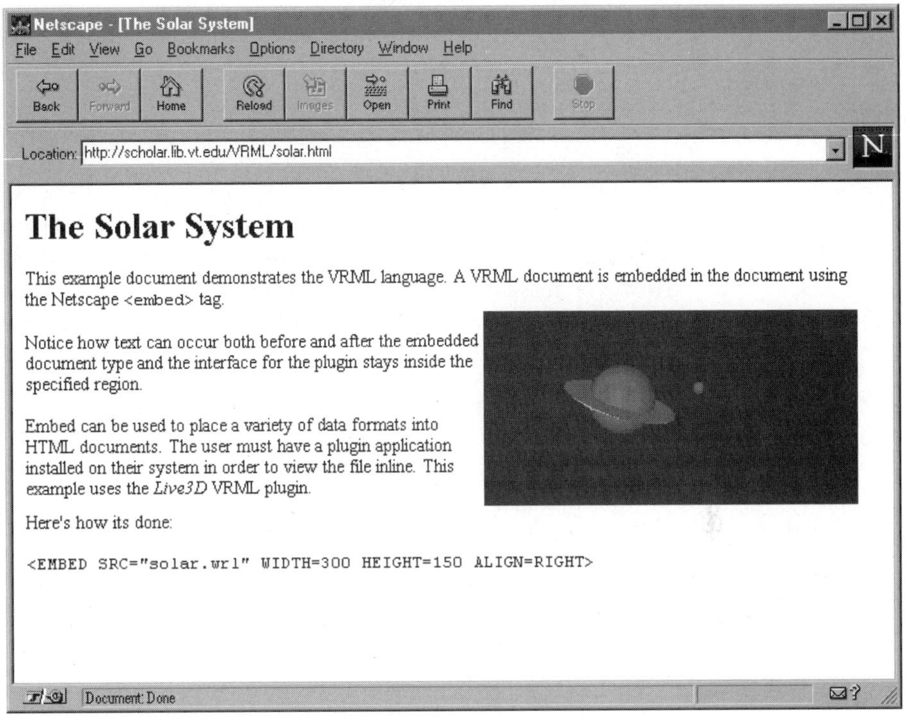

Figure 34-6 Live3D
Netscape plug-in
displaying a view
of the solar sys-
tem alongside
HTML using the
Netscape
<EMBED> tag

Start your document with:

#VRML V1.0 ascii

to indicate that it is a VRML document. Next we'll add a series of spheres representing the Sun and its children, the planets. Some of the highlights are covered here, and the complete source follows at the end of the chapter. The Sun is the first shape node defined, preceded by a material node that paints the sphere with a glowing, shiny yellow color. A lighting node also modifies the sphere to increase its brightness. The Sun has a radius of 114 meters in this simulated solar system:

```
# The sun
DEF sun Separator {
    Material {
        emissiveColor 1 1 0
        shininess 1
    }
    PointLight {
        on TRUE
        intensity 1
```

Continued on next page

Continued from previous page

```
        color 1 1 0
    }
    Sphere {
        radius 114
    }
```

The planet nodes follow the Sun node. Each planet node is preceded by a geometry transformation node that moves the rendering position away from the Sun. However, most spheres will be displayed in relation to the Sun and will orbit it if the space is rotated. Separator group nodes encapsulate each planet as a separate object. Here is Mercury:

```
# Mercury comes next
  DEF mercury Separator {
      Transform { translation 269 0 0 }
      Material {
          diffuseColor .3 .3 0
      }
      Sphere { radius 3 }
  }
```

Some planets, such as Earth, have their own moons. Here is Earth with its child Moon node:

```
# Then Earth and around it circles the moon
  DEF earth Separator {
      Transform { translation 401 0 -15 }
      Material {
          diffuseColor 0 .3 .7
          shininess 1
  }
  sphere { radius 5 }
      DEF Moon Separator {
      Transform {translation 7 0 0 }
      Material {
          diffuseColor .9 .9 .9
          shininess 1
      }
      Sphere { radius 1 }}
  }
```

Notice the transformation node preceding the Moon. This transformation is relative to Earth's coordinates, and has no effect on the next transformation node, for Mars, since it is contained by Earth's separator node. In other words, the Moon orbits Earth, not the Sun. Next we skip outward to Saturn. In order to simulate Saturn's rings, we create a nearly flat cylinder that is centered on the same spot as Saturn's sphere:

```
# Saturn with its rings and Titan
   DEF saturn Separator {
       Transform { translation 1030 0 10 }
       PerspectiveCamera {
           position 330 50 190
           orientation 0 4.5 0 1.9
           focalDistance 400
   }
   Material {
           emissiveColor .8 .7 0
           shininess .7
       }
       Sphere { radius 13 }
       DEF rings Separator {
           Material {
               emissiveColor .9 .9 .9
           }
           Transform { rotation 0 0 1 -.4 }
           Cylinder { radius 22 height .1}
       }
       DEF titan Separator {
           Transform { translation 32 3 -3 }
           Material {
               emissiveColor .9 .7 0
           }
           Sphere { radius 2 }
       }
   }
```

Notice that this node also has a Camera node. A PerspectiveCamera node is defined near Saturn so visitors can have a closeup view as soon as they enter the world. The camera is positioned away from Saturn but pointing back toward it.

Finally, we leap out to the edge of the solar system where we use another shape node, Cone, to create a few comets near Pluto. We only need one comet node because we can use the USE keyword to make more comets:

```
Transform { translation 1550 20 -5 }
   # Throw in the Oort cloud past Pluto
   DEF comet Separator {
       Transform {
           rotation 1 0 1 1.5
       }
```

Continued on next page

Continued from previous page

```
            Material {
                    emissiveColor 1 1 1
            }
            Cone { bottomRadius 1
                            height 27 }
        }
        Transform { translation 40 21 1 }
        USE comet
        Transform { translation 40 27 1 }
        USE comet
    }
```

The best way to understand VRML is to modify a file like this, where objects on the screen are easily mapped to nodes in the VRML file. After you enter the complete source, try changing the color and location of planets, add moons, or place textures on the spheres. Once you have experimented with this project, you will be able to open and add features to more complex worlds as you start developing spaces with graphical editors.

Here is the complete VRML source for this project:

```
#VRML V1.0 ascii

# Chapter 34: solar.wrl
# Simple VRML of the solar system
# The sun
DEF sun Separator {
    Material {
        emissiveColor 1 1 0
        shininess 1
}
    Sphere {
        radius 114
}
    # Mercury comes next
    DEF mercury Separator {
        Transform { translation 269 0 0 }
        Material {
            diffuseColor .3 .3 0
        }
        Sphere { radius 3 }
    }
    # Then Venus
    DEF venus Separator {
        Transform { translation 358 -1 0 }
        Material {
            diffuseColor .4 .7 0
        }
```

```
        Sphere { radius 5 }
}
# Then Earth and around it circles the moon
DEF earth Separator {
        Transform { translation 401 0 -15 }
        Material {
            diffuseColor 0 .3 .7
        shininess 1
        }
        Sphere { radius 5 }
        DEF Moon Separator {
        Transform {translation 7 0 0 }
        Material {
                diffuseColor .9 .9 .9
                shininess 1
        }
        Sphere { radius 1 }}
}
# Mars is next
DEF mars Separator {
        Transform { translation 502 0 -31 }
        Material {
            diffuseColor 1 0 0
            shininess .7
        }
        Sphere { radius 4 }
}
# Here's Jupiter and one moon: Io
DEF jupiter Separator {
        Transform { translation 709 0 -22 }
        Material {
            emissiveColor 1 0 0
            shininess .9
    }
        Sphere { radius 26 }
        DEF io Separator {
            Transform { translation 22 0 0 }
            Material {
                emissiveColor .7 .7 0
                shininess .3
            }
            Sphere { radius 2 }
        }
}
# Saturn with its rings and Titan
DEF saturn Separator {
```

Continued on next page

Continued from previous page

```
        Transform { translation 1030 0 10 }
        PerspectiveCamera {
            position 330 50 190
            orientation 0 4.5 0 1.9
            focalDistance 400
        }
    Material {
        emissiveColor .8 .7 0
    shininess .7
        }
        Sphere { radius 13 }
        DEF rings Separator {
            Material {
                emissiveColor .9 .9 .9
            }
            Transform { rotation 0 0 1 -.4 }
            Cylinder { radius 22 height .1}
        }
        DEF titan Separator {
            Transform { translation 32 3 -3 }
            Material {
                emissiveColor .9 .7 0
            }
            Sphere { radius 2 }
        }
    }
    # Uranus with its tilted rings
    DEF uranus Separator {
        Transform { translation 1220 0 10 }
        Material {
            emissiveColor 0 0 1
            shininess .9
        }
        Sphere {radius 8 }
        DEF u_rings Separator {
            Material {
                emissiveColor .8 .8 .8
            }
            Transform { rotation 0 0 1 1.3 }
            Cylinder { radius 11 height .1 }
        }
    }
    # Neptune near the edge
    DEF neptune Separator {
        Transform { translation 1395 0 -10 }
```

```
        Material {
            emissiveColor 0 1 0
            shininess .9
        }
        Sphere { radius 8 }
    }
    # Last of all, Pluto
    DEF pluto Separator {
        Transform { translation 1430 30 -25 }
        Material {
            diffuseColor 0 0 0
        }
        Sphere { radius 2 }
    }
    Transform { translation 1550 20 -5 }
    # Throw in the Oort cloud past Pluto
    DEF comet Separator {
        Transform {
            rotation 1 0 1 1.5
        }
        Material {
            emissiveColor 1 1 1
        }
    Cone { bottomRadius 1
            height 27 }
    }
    Transform { translation 40 21 1 }
    USE comet
    Transform { translation 40 27 1 }
    USE comet
}
```

35

Adobe Acrobat

CHAPTER AT A GLANCE

- How to create Acrobat-compatible documents
- Table 35-1: *Acrobat Reader Versions*
- Description of PDF, the Acrobat portable document format
- How Acrobat interacts with the Web

HTML was developed to allow users to share documents regardless of the type of computer they are using. But it provides only the most basic page layout and formatting control, leaving most of it up to built-in style sheets applied by the Web browser when the user opens a document. Netscape has developed numerous markup extensions to HTML which, while touted as cross-platform, are only supported by Netscape browsers and on computers on which the Netscape browser can run. Microsoft has recently entered the fray as well, developing its own nonstandard extensions to HTML for its own browser, Internet Explorer. HTML 3 includes cascading style sheets, providing formatting control superior to both Netscape and Internet Explorer, while allowing users with special needs or preferences to maintain a local style sheet to override certain settings for better readability. All of these efforts, both open and proprietary, are driven by demand from authors and readers for better electronic documents.

Adobe Systems launched a new electronic document-publishing system just as the Web was gaining momentum. Acrobat describes both a document format and a suite of applications that allow users to create and view documents that retain the formatting and presentation elements comparable to a printed page. At the heart of Acrobat is the portable document format (PDF). This page-description format captures the text of a document, each image, and all of the information about its layout, including font styles and sizes, and encodes it in a single compressed file. The result is a visually rich document that can contain full-color images, looks very much like the original document even if a user does not have the fonts used by the author, and can be searched like a text file. PDF files can also include internal and external hypertext links from portions of text or graphics, thumbnail page images for navigation, and comments from other readers inserted as "sticky" notes alongside document text.

The Acrobat software suite includes an application called *Distiller* (Figure 35-1) for converting PostScript documents to the PDF format. PostScript is a page-description language used by printers and by a few operating systems for displaying text and graphics on the screen. It is a true programming language requiring an interpreter to execute the program and generate output on paper or to the screen. Distiller includes a PostScript interpreter that creates the pages and then converts each page to the PDF format.

Distiller has controls for managing the quality of PDF output. You can automatically compress text, generate thumbnails, or generate an ASCII-encoded PDF file suitable for attaching to electronic mail. You can also control the resolution and compression level of images within the original PostScript file (Figure 35-2).

Figure 35-1
Acrobat Distiller

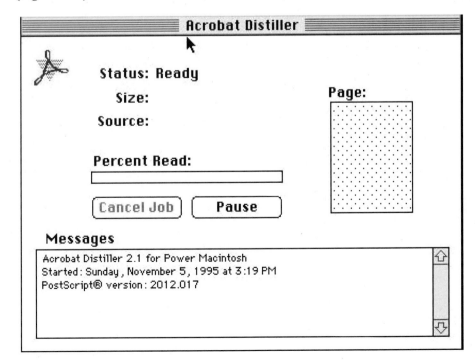

Figure 35-2
Distiller options for
text and image
compression

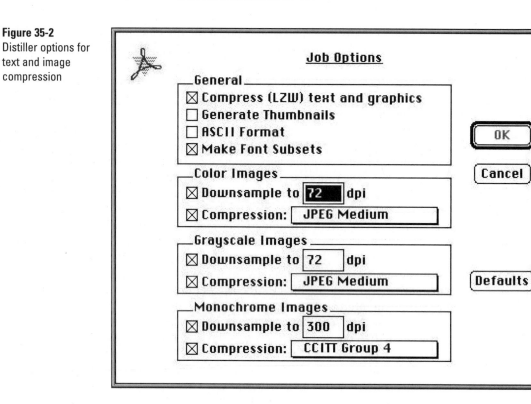

Another product, Acrobat Exchange (Figure 35-3), allows users to open, view, and edit PDF files.

A toolbar across the top of the screen allows you to access different navigational aids, pan around the page, enlarge or shrink text and graphics, search for or extract text, add or edit links, and move through the document. Exchange allows users to interactively annotate documents, create thumbnails and hypertext links, and add or delete pages. Exchange also includes a virtual PDF printer driver that allows a user to convert the output of any program, such as a spreadsheet, word processor, or presentation application to a PDF file. The PDF writer shows up as a printer, which the user can select to use for printing.

Acrobat Reader (Figure 35-4) is the enabling component of the Acrobat software suite. It is a free reader application that allows a user to open and view Acrobat files on a number of different computer platforms. Reader allows printing, navigating hypertext links, searching, and enlarging text and graphics for easier readability.

Table 35-1 lists the platforms for which Acrobat Reader is available.

Figure 35-3
Acrobat Exchange

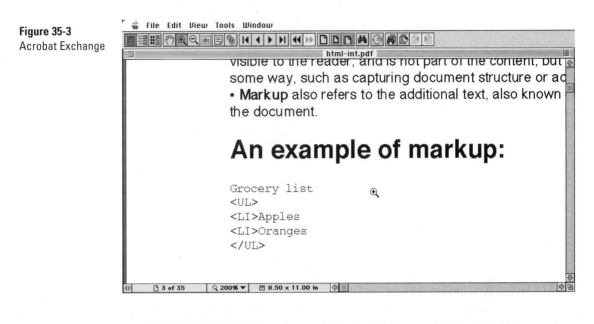

Figure 35-4
Acrobat Reader

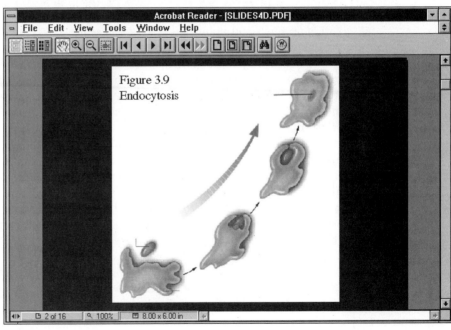

TABLE 35-1   ACROBAT READER VERSIONS (AVAILABLE AT FTP.ADOBE.COM)

Platform	Reader filename	Version
DOS	acrodos.exe	2.1
Windows 3.1, OS/2	ACROREAD.EXE	2.1
Windows NT, Windows 95	ACROREAD.EXE	2.1
Macintosh and PowerMac	ACROREAD.MAC.hqx	2.1
Sun SunOS and Solaris	SunOSReader.TAR.Z	
	SolarisReader.TAR.Z	2.1
Hewlett Packard HP-UX	HPUXReader.TAR.Z	2.1
Silicon Graphics SGI	sgireader1.0.1.tar.Z	1.0.1

Acrobat appears to have all of the features of an HTML killer: cross-platform support, free browser software, hypertext capability, and full presentation control. So why hasn't it replaced HTML? Well, Acrobat Reader arrived on the scene just as Mosaic was heating up the Web, bearing a price tag. Even today, there are no free Acrobat creation tools and understandably so, since Acrobat is a commercial product. Many aspects of Acrobat, such as the document format and the API, are published and could be considered open standards. HTML was and is an open and published standard and has never been the property of a company or required a licensing fee.

Acrobat and PDF are good at what they do. They represent major advances in electronic publishing. But they are not necessarily suitable for every electronic publishing project and have only recently become full-fledged Web documents with the addition of the Weblink plug-in for Reader and PDF creation software. Weblink allows authors to embed URLs in PDF documents so they can contain not only local hypertext links but also links to other PDF, HTML, and multimedia documents on the Web. Thanks to the Weblink technology and free readers for many popular computing platforms, Acrobat is now becoming a viable publishing medium for the World Wide Web.

Another recent development that will place Acrobat squarely into the mainstream of Web publishing is the release of Adobe's Amber Netscape plug-in (Figure 35-5). Amber embeds an Acrobat reader into the Web browser window. The embedded reader has the same functionality of a regular Acrobat Reader, but is essentially part of the Web browser. Users can freely navigate between PDF and HTML files without the extra overhead of running and interacting with two separate applications on the desktop.

When to Use PDF

There are several instances when PDF is an acceptable alternative to HTML. One is when presentation and appearance are as important as the document content. Commercial sites often use Acrobat to distribute catalogs and bro-

Figure 35-5
HTML in left
frame, Acrobat
Amber in right

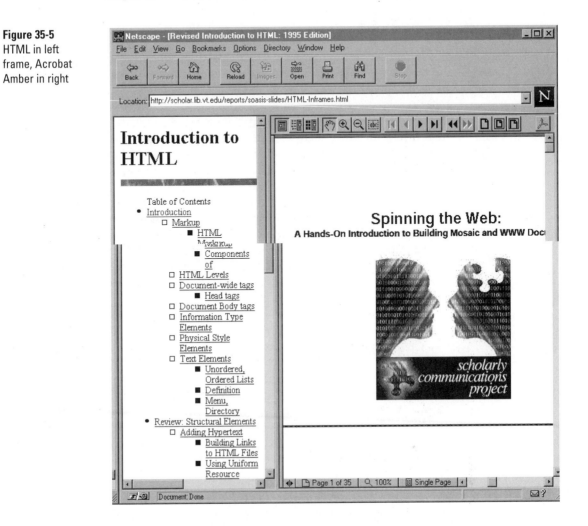

chures. They are able to maintain the look and feel of these materials into which they have already invested a significant amount of time and effort. PDF is also suitable for publishing materials already prepared as word processor documents or spreadsheets. The PDF writer bundled with Exchange can be used to output complex documents to PDF in seconds, whereas a good deal of time and effort would be required to convert the material to HTML. Acrobat is also useful for electronically editing documents. Multiple editors could each embed "sticky" notes in a document containing a list of changes or comments, all without printing a single page. PDF documents can be restricted with license keys so you can limit access to the content. Publishers of electronic books and magazines can charge for the license key, which allows them to provide documents over the Web but charge a subscription fee.

WHEN NOT TO USE PDF

When is PDF a poor choice for Web publishing? When cross-platform access is a major issue. There are many operating environments for which no Acrobat Reader application exists or is planned. Users of those environments would have to save the document and take it to another computer running an operating system for which a reader exists. Acrobat documents are less accessible than HTML for the visually impaired. Text reader software is only now being developed to allow Acrobat documents to be converted to speech. Multicolumn PDF files will often be read left to right with column 1 line 1 followed by column 2 line 1, if they can be read by software at all. Adobe is working on several solutions to this problem. One solution is to encode document structure information in the PDF file, something HTML already allows. Another reason PDF may be a poor format for Web publishing is that it is not capable of representing interactive documents. You cannot build forms or database frontends to resources as PDF files. Acrobat Reader relies on a Web browser to retrieve data pointed to by URLs embedded in PDF files. So PDF is not a good format for publishing large multifile hypertext collections.

Browsing and Publishing on the Web with Acrobat

Acrobat documents can be published on the Web using Web servers in the same way that VRML and other document formats are served. To ensure proper transfer and that Web browsers will recognize PDF files correctly, the MIME types file for the Web server must contain a PDF entry like this:

```
application/pdf       pdf PDF
```

This associates a MIME type with the .pdf file extension for Acrobat documents stored in the Web server's archives. The Web server will deliver documents with filenames ending in pdf with a Content-type header like this:

```
Content-type: application/pdf
```

The user will need to configure a PDF viewer such as Acrobat Reader for their Web browser in order to view the document. Here's an example configuration for Netscape:

Configuring a helper for PDF ensures that the Acrobat Reader or Amber plug-in is launched when you select a link that targets a PDF file. If the user wishes to follow Web hypertext links then they will need to make sure they have the Weblink plug-in. Weblink is distributed with Acrobat Reader 2.1, so all that is necessary to activate it is to configure a default Web viewer for it. It is built into the Amber plug-in for Netscape. The Weblink configuration panel is accessible from the *Edit/Preferences* menu of Reader:

Once configured, when a user selects a hypertext link that uses a URL to target a document on the Web, Acrobat Reader forwards the request to the Web browser. Reader relies on the Web browser to retrieve the document and select an appropriate viewer based on the returned document's Content-type. If the document is another PDF file, then the Web browser will deliver the contents back to Acrobat Reader. With the Weblink plug-in, PDF files can function as networked hypertext documents just like HTML.

Acrobat Exchange is required for creating hypertext links within PDF files. The Weblink plug-in enables Exchange to embed URL information with hypertext links.

```
┌──────────────────────────────────────────────────┐
│ ▪▫            Create Link                          │
│ ┌─ Appearance ──────────────────────────────────┐ │
│ │                     Color:  ┌ Black      ▼ ┐   │ │
│ │   ⦿ Visible                                    │ │
│ │                     Width:  ┌ Thin       ▼ ┐   │ │
│ │   ○ Invisible                                  │ │
│ │                     Style:  ┌ Solid      ▼ ┐   │ │
│ └────────────────────────────────────────────────┘ │
│ ┌─ Action ──────────────────────────────────────┐ │
│ │   Type:  ┌ WorldWideWeb Link  ▼ ┐             │ │
│ │   Link to a document using a World Wide Web    │ │
│ │   "Uniform Resource Locator".          ▶       │ │
│ │   ─────────────────────────────────────────    │ │
│ │           ┌     Edit URL...     ┐              │ │
│ │   Use the button above to define the target URI for │ │
│ │   the link.                                    │ │
│ └────────────────────────────────────────────────┘ │
│                        ┌ Cancel ┐  ┌ Set Link ┐   │
└──────────────────────────────────────────────────┘
```

Unlike HTML hypertext links, Acrobat gives the author control over how a link is made visible. Authors can even choose to make links invisible, so that the user is aware of a link only when the cursor becomes a hand as it passes over link text. Acrobat links are rectangular areas that, when visible, are surrounded by a solid or dashed line in the color specified by the author. Link types include *Local* (inside the same document) and *WorldWideWeb Link*. If a Web link is specified, then the author must select *Edit URL* to provide the URL for the target document:

```
┌──────────────────────────────────────────────────┐
│ Enter a Universal Resource Locator for this link: │
│ ┌────────────────────────────────────────────────┐│
│ │ http://scholar.lib.vt.edu/                     ││
│ └────────────────────────────────────────────────┘│
│ □ Mapped Coordinates Link      ┌ Cancel ┐ ┌ OK ┐ │
└──────────────────────────────────────────────────┘
```

Acrobat and the portable document format are an excellent way for businesses and institutions to reduce the amount of paper they use and archive, while increasing the accessibility of the information they contain. New Acrobat products such as Acrobat Capture, a combination scanning/OCR package for converting existing paper documents to PDF, and Acrobat Search for indexing collections of PDF files are further proof that Adobe is a leader in the electronic document field. However, HTML is an open standard describing a markup language that anyone can create on any computer they choose. Many inexpensive and free tools are available for creating such documents, which are small and well-suited for today's Internet. Acrobat is a business solution that is being migrated to the Web because it makes good business sense. Both PDF and HTML are evolving toward a future standard that incorporates structure and presentation control. PDF excels at formatting while HTML provides structures that, while primitive by some SGML application standards, do allow authors to tag some of the logical structures within a document. With the adoption of HTML 3, the hypertext markup language will continue to be the standard document interchange language for the Web.

HTML and SGML

CHAPTER AT A GLANCE

- The relationship of SGML to HTML
- Table 36-1: *Components of an SGML Application*
- Configuration and functionality of Panorama SGML browser
- Other SGML markup languages
- Table 36-2: *Some Example TEI Lite Tags and Their HTML Equivalents*

HTML is SGML.

Some people don't know this. Others deny it because they know too little about SGML (Standard Generalized Markup Language) or think HTML has strayed too far from SGML. HTML is an SGML-based markup language that was originally designed to allow users to encode the structure of documents in a platform-independent manner, without formatting information. SGML allowed HTML, and therefore the Web as we know it, to be born. And SGML promises more surprises for the Web. There are many other markup languages born of SGML making their way onto the Web. In this chapter we will look at one of them, the Text Encoding for Interchange markup language. You may find it or some other SGML application more suitable for some projects, or you may even choose to extend a language or even create your own. That's what SGML is all about.

SGML is a language used to define markup languages. It is often referred to as a metalanguage. SGML-defined markup languages are often referred to as applications of SGML. Far fewer people use SGML than use applications of it like HTML. But all documents tagged in any SGML markup language are loosely referred to as SGML documents.

TABLE 36-1   COMPONENTS OF AN SGML APPLICATION

Term	Meaning
DOCTYPE	Declaration of the DTD used by a document
DTD	SGML document defining a markup language
Entity Definition	Character and string (document parts) mapping file
Style Sheets	Formatting information
Navigator	Alternate view of a file
SGML document	Document tagged with markup defined in an SGML DTD

Most of this book has been about SGML, specifically one markup language defined with SGML, called the HyperText Markup Language. As is the case with other SGML applications, most people who work with SGML markup languages are concerned with tagging documents, rather than with designing markup languages. But SGML does allow you to design and define markup languages according to the structures found in a set of documents. The designer takes into account the type of information the document communicates, its structure, relationships with other documents, and even the workflow of the organization creating documents. The designer develops a markup language using SGML and records this language in a Document Type Declaration (DTD).

The DTD describes the markup elements of the language, the attributes, their values, and the structures found in the document. HTML 2 and HTML 3 both have DTDs just like ICADD (Chapter 22) and TEI (Text Encoding for Interchange). It is from these DTDs that HTML markup specifications, browsers, editors, and even books like this are derived. But DTDs do not concern themselves with the formatting of a document or the way in which a specific tag might be displayed by a browser, they only define elements and relate them to document structures. Here is an excerpt from the TEI Lite Document Type Definition defining two markup elements, <TEI.2> and <GI>, and their attributes:

```
<!— The public identifier I currently use for this is
    -//TEI/DTD TEI Lite 1.0//EN
    but it may change ... (LB, 18 May 95) —>
<!ELEMENT TEI.2 - O (teiHeader, text)>
<!ATTLIST TEI.2
        ana IDREFS #IMPLIED
```

```
        corresp IDREFS #IMPLIED
        next IDREF #IMPLIED
        prev IDREF #IMPLIED
        id ID #IMPLIED
        n CDATA #IMPLIED
        lang IDREF #IMPLIED
        rend CDATA #IMPLIED
        TEIform CDATA "TEI.2" >
<!ELEMENT gi - O (#PCDATA)>
<!ATTLIST gi
        ana IDREFS #IMPLIED
        corresp IDREFS #IMPLIED
        next IDREF #IMPLIED
        prev IDREF #IMPLIED
        id ID #IMPLIED
```

There are many advantages to publishing with SGML. An author can utilize any defined DTD to tag and publish a document or set of documents to the Web. If no DTD exists for the type of data she wishes to publish, then she can design her own markup language using SGML to create a DTD. She can develop as rich a set of tags as is needed to tag her documents. And regardless of the DTD, the documents are guaranteed to be platform independent. Then the author can publish the DTD, the documents themselves, and one or more style sheets for the materials on a server. Web servers can be, and in fact are, used today to publish DTDs, style sheets, and SGML document applications other than HTML. SGML also provides many more advanced hypertext link mechanisms such as cross-reference links and tree links where the user is given a menu of possible targets to choose from (Figure 36-1).

Figure 36-1
Panorama displays link targets in a pop-up window.

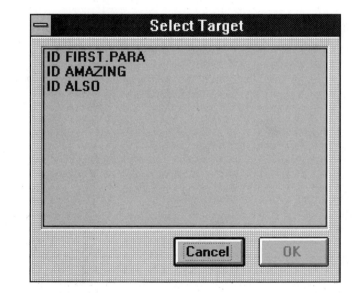

Like HTML, other SGML applications require specialized browsing software for viewing and navigating documents. Web browsers are specialized SGML browsers. They are capable of displaying only one type of SGML document: HTML files. Most SGML browsers need access to a copy of a document's DTD so they know how to process the markup. They also refer to a style sheet—a default or a user- or author-specified document not unlike HTML 3's Cascading Style Sheets (CSS)—to tell them how to format the contents of a specific tag. Web browsers such as Netscape Navigator have the DTD for HTML and a style sheet for presenting it "hard coded" into the browser. They are unable to adapt to other SGML applications by accessing a DTD and style sheet. SGML browsers can tackle HTML if they have the HTML DTD, since it will tell them everything they need to know about HTML documents.

Panorama

Panorama is an example of an SGML browser. It is capable of displaying any SGML document for which a DTD is provided (including HTML). Panorama is the first SGML browser to be developed for accessing Web-based SGML documents in cooperation with a Web browser. Like many VRML browsers, Panorama depends on the Web client to perform network file transactions such as retrieving DTDs or SGML documents. Future versions of Netscape will support Panorama as a plug-in, which means SGML documents will be processed by a Panorama engine, but displayed in a Netscape window.

Panorama can support math, tables, and a feature similar to the frames capability found in Netscape 2.0, called *navigators* (Figure 36-2). Panorama navigators are separate files derived from the DTD that provide alternate views of the

Figure 36-2 The same SGML document with two different navigators

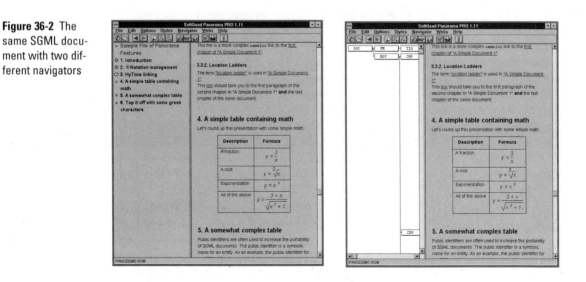

current document. The view can be an overview, outline, table of contents, or other view defined by the author. The navigator document is displayed in the left side of the browser window. Multiple navigators are often available for a document and they are accessible from the Panorama Navigator menu. In Figure 36-2 the same document is displayed with a contents navigator and an SGML tree navigator illustrating the structure of the document by using its elements.

Other navigators can be created by the user and accessed in the same way. Panorama also lets you select alternate style sheets that are applied both to the document and the navigator text. Like HTML 3 style sheets, these can be used to change the font style, size, color, and many other document formatting characteristics.

Panorama can also display the tagged source document (Figure 36-3). It displays each element and its contents. Tag attribute lists are represented by a small selectable square within the tag icon. When selected, the list is displayed in a panel similar to the one displayed when a user selects a hypertext link with multiple targets.

Figure 36-3 SGML document with Show Tags option activated, and an attribute panel for a <CLINK> hypertext anchor element

Panorama is freeware, available on the Internet for Microsoft Windows–based computers. It can be configured to work with many Web browsers, including Mosaic and Netscape Navigator. The company that developed Panorama sells many other SGML authoring products including Panorama Pro, which can be used to publish SGML documents on the Web. It can also be used to create style sheets and navigators for those documents.

Publishing documents on the Web involves several steps. Every SGML document published on the Web should include a DOCTYPE declaration defining the DTD used. The Web server's mime.types file should include a line like this:

```
text/x-sgml sgm sgml
```

Next install your document instance, that is the document you've tagged using a specific DTD, its DTD, navigator, and style sheets (if applicable) on the server with the documents. Make sure all tags in the SGML documents include start and end tags, and be sure to validate your document (validation confirms proper use of tags and attributes, etc.). Like VRML documents, SGML documents can be served by Web servers with minimal effort.

TEI Lite

Panorama is bundled with many DTDs so it can quickly process and display many common SGML application types. One of these types is TEI Lite. TEI Lite is a subset of the TEI SGML application developed by the Association for Computers and the Humanities, the Association for Computational Linguistics, and the Association for Literary and Linguistic Computing. TEI Lite consists of only a core set of markup elements from TEI; even then it is a huge set of tags compared to HTML. TEI was designed to be applied to a wide variety of documents, but especially literary documents such as poems, works of fiction, plays, and other texts. Even TEI Lite would take a book to describe in sufficient detail to enable you to use it effectively. However, we can consider the structure of a TEI document and some core TEI elements to give you an idea of what TEI markup is like. Figure 36-4 outlines the basic structure of a TEI document.

TEI DOCUMENT STRUCTURE

TEI allows markup of three types of texts. The simplest text is referred to as a unitary text. A unitary text contains only one document. Examples of unitary texts include novels and plays. The document is surrounded by the <TEI.2> element. It is equivalent to the <HTML> tag for HTML 2 and HTML 3 documents. This is followed by a header which is tagged with the <teiHeader> element. TEI elements work like HTML elements in that they are containers, with start and end tags and attributes. Many of the elements discussed are displayed in lowercase because that is how they are noted in TEI documentation, but in fact the elements are case-insensitive just like HTML, so <teiHeader> and <TEIHEADER> are equivalent just as <head> and <HEAD> are identical in HTML. The TEI header has many more elements than an HTML document header; its contents are

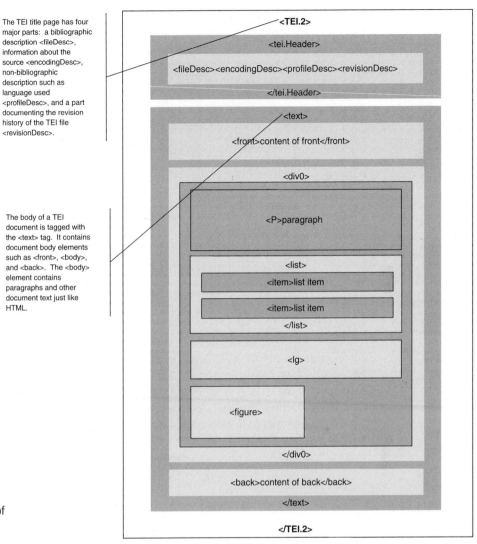

The TEI title page has four major parts: a bibliographic description <fileDesc>, information about the source <encodingDesc>, non-bibliographic description such as language used <profileDesc>, and a part documenting the revision history of the TEI file <revisionDesc>.

The body of a TEI document is tagged with the <text> tag. It contains document body elements such as <front>, <body>, and <back>. The <body> element contains paragraphs and other document text just like HTML.

Figure 36-4
Basic structure of
a TEI document

roughly equivalent to a printed book's title page. We will consider the TEI header in more detail in a moment. The remainder of the TEI document is enclosed by the <text> element. This part of the text is further subdivided into front matter with the <front> element, the body of the text <body>, and the back matter, which is tagged with the <back> element:

```
<TEI.2>
    <teiHeader>title page information</teiHeader>
    <text>
        <front></front>
        <body>body of the text</body>
        </back></back>
    </text>
</TEI.2>
```

Composite texts, such as collections of short stories or anthologies, are tagged somewhat differently than unitary texts. The collection is assumed to share the same title page, so only one header is included. The entire collection is enclosed by the <group> element. Each story or poem is tagged with a <text> element that includes <front>, <body>, and <back> elements:

```
<TEI.2>
    <teiHeader>title page information</teiHeader>
    <group>
        <text>
            <front></front>
            <body>body of the text</body>
            </back></back>
        </text>
        <text>
            <front></front>
            <body>body of the text</body>
            </back></back>
        </text>
    </group>
</TEI.2>
```

The third type of text TEI supports is called a corpus. A corpus is a number of texts that can be grouped together, but each text constitutes a distinct work. Each text in the collection should be a unitary text. The collection is referred to as a TEI corpus. Notice that the <TEI.2> element is contained within the <teiCorpus> element. The corpus can have a header that describes the entire collection, and each text has its own header as well:

```
<teiCorpus>
    <teiHeader>title page information</teiHeader>
    <TEI.2>
        <teiHeader>title page information</teiHeader>
        <text>
            <front></front>
            <body>body of the text</body>
            </back></back>
        </text>
    </TEI.2>
    <TEI.2>
        <teiHeader>title page information</teiHeader>
        <text>
            <front></front>
            <body>body of the text</body>
            </back></back>
        </text>
    </group>
```

```
    </TEI.2>
  </teiCorpus>
```

HEADER ELEMENTS

The TEI header is of interest to authors and library catalogers in particular because of the amount of detail about the document that can be included with it. In contrast, HTML 2 offers only the body element <ADDRESS> and the header element <LINK MADE> as multipurpose containers in which authors might record their name, and the header's <TITLE> tag for the document title. It is often quite difficult to identify the authorship and origin of a particular document on the Web unless the author has taken great pains to highlight this information. It is virtually impossible to automatically determine the authorship of a randomly selected HTML 2 document, or even uniquely identify the document with so little information!

TEI has a structured, four-part header. The part that generates the most interest is the <fileDesc> element, which contains full bibliographic information about the contents of the electronic file. This includes the title, author, subject information, date, and place of publication. The second part, <encodingDesc>, documents the relationship between the electronic text and the original source. The <profileDesc> includes information about the language of the document, who tagged it, and what software was used to tag and validate it. Finally, the <revisionDesc> element contains information about the revision history for the electronic file.

Here is a simple TEI header for this book:

```
<tei.Header>
<fileDesc>
   <titleStmt>
      <title>HTML Plus!</title>
      <author>Powell, James 1965-</author>
   </titleStmt>
   <editionStmt>
<edition>Second draft</edition>
<date>1996</date>
</editionStmt>
<publicationStmt>
   <publisher>Integrated Media Group</publisher>
   <pubPlace>Belmont, California, USA</pubPlace>
</publicationStmt>
</fileDesc>
<encodingDesc>
   <projectDesc>Constructed as an example header for this text which
does not actually exist as a TEI document</projectDesc>
</encodingDesc>
<profileDesc>
```

Continued on next page

Continued from previous page

```
<creation>
    <date value='1996-02'>February 1996</date>
    <name type=place>Christiansburg, Virginia</name>
</creation>
<revisionDesc>
    <change><date>02/29/96</date>
    <respStmt><name>JEP</name><resp>author</resp>
<item>added profile information to header</item></respStmt>
</revisionDesc>
</teiHeader>
```

BODY ELEMENTS

The TEI document body can contain paragraphs and divisions. Paragraphs are tagged with the <P> tag, just like HTML. Unnumbered divisions are tagged with the <DIV> tag, which is also found in HTML 3. Numbered divisions can range from <DIV0> to <DIV7> and should be nested, since the lowest-numbered division contains the largest subdivision of the text. Divisions may have a header and a trailer, <head> <trailer>, and contain elements such as paragraphs, quotes, lists, as well as structural elements for the components of plays, poems, scripts, etc. Literally dozens of elements are available for tagging content. Table 36-2 gives a few more examples that should give you some idea of the variety of texts that can be tagged with TEI.

TABLE 36-2   SOME EXAMPLE TEI LITE TAGS AND THEIR HTML EQUIVALENTS

TEI Tag	HTML 2/HTML 3 Equivalent	Content
<l>	none	line of verse
<lg>	none	group of verse lines
<sp>	none	a speech
<emph>	<em>	emphasized word or phrase
<foreign>	none	word or phrase in different language than surrounding text
<q>	<blockquote> <q>	a quotation
<note>	<note>	various notes or annotations
<corr>	<strike> (partially duplicates)	marks a correction
<name>	<author> or <person> (partially)	a proper noun
<date>	none	a date
<abbr>	<abbr>	contains an abbreviation
<list>	<ul>	marks a list
<item>	<li>	tags an item within a list
<address>	<address>	contains an address of some type
<table>	<table>	a table
<code>	<code>	a segment of programming language code
<formula>	<math>	contains a mathematical formula

IMAGES AND ANCHORS (FIGURES AND POINTERS!)

TEI utilizes the same structures and types of elements as HTML. TEI simply defines many more elements for a finer granularity of structural markup. So it should come as no surprise that TEI has support for images and anchors. Images can be included inline with the <figure> tag. If the figure is not to be displayed, then you can use the <figDesc> to indicate that an image would have occurred at this location and describe it with its contents. TEI Lite supports three image types by default: CGM, TIFF, and JPEG. Each embedded image must have an entity declaration in the entity file accompanying the TEI document like this:

```
<!ENTITY usmap SYSTEM "usmap.tiff" NDATA tiff>
```

Then the entity is referenced in the HTML document with the <figure> tag to embed the graphic:

```
<figure entity=usmap>
    <p>Map of the United States</p>
</figure>
```

TEI has three types of links. Simple cross-references link text from one point to another within the same document. These types of links are specified with the <ref> or <ptr> element. These elements have several attributes, the most important one being the TEI equivalent of the HTML HREF attribute: target. target is assigned an SGML identifier value that corresponds to the tag marking the text that should be linked to, or targeted. This id is set with the global id attribute (also found in HTML 3). The main difference between <ref> and <ptr> is that only <ref> allows you to specify anchor text:

HTML:
See also <A HREF="#SGML">glossary entry for <ABBR>SGML</ABBR></A>

TEI:
See also <ref target="SGML">glossary entry for <ABBR>SGML</ABBR></ref>

Another type of link in TEI is the extended pointer. HTML relies on the value assigned to the HREF, a URL, to provide a link to other documents. TEI extended pointers are tagged with <xptr> or <xref>, which are essentially extended pointer versions of the simple cross references elements we've just seen. The critical attribute for these elements is the doc attribute. It is assigned the name of a document to which the link points:

```
Refer to <xref doc="chapter3">Chapter 3</xref>.
```

Extended pointers can also point to sections with a document using the from and to attributes.

Finally, there are also special links used to link texts with translations or alternate versions. These links are indicated with linking attributes including:

ana	link element to its interpretation
corresp	link element to a corresponding element
next	link to the next occurrence of this element

Neither HTML 2 nor HTML 3 has a link type like this, although it can be roughly duplicated with anchors.

This is just a small portion of the TEI Lite markup language. As you can see there are differences both in the number of tags and in the way in which content is tagged. Still, both TEI and HTML are SGML applications and as such they share many features. Both are platform-independent text markup languages utilizing ASCII strings as markup elements and attributes, whose elements have start and end tags for tagging document structures. Both TEI and HTML can be validated, and they are processed by a browser application when viewed, leaving formatting up to the browser software and style sheets. These are all features imparted by SGML.

In learning HTML you have been exposed to elements and attributes, editors that include automatic validation (SoftQuad HoTMetaL Pro, InContext Spider), and browsers such as Netscape Navigator. As you start to learn other SGML applications, you will find that many include extensive comments or additional documentation. The DTDs of many SGML applications are, to say the least, difficult to read, and are not sufficient to impart the finer points of analyzing and tagging documents to ordinary humans. How many people do you know who learned HTML from its DTD? Rest assured that you will find equally helpful tools and learning aids for TEI and other SGML applications. So if you are comfortable with HTML markup, validators, browsers, and editors, you have a giant head start into the world of SGML!

Character and Numeric Entity Table

Hex	Decimal	Char	Entity	Hex	Decimal	Char	Entity
00	000	NUL		01	001	SOH	
02	002	STX		03	003	ETX	
04	004	EOT		05	005	ENQ	
06	006	ACK		07	007	BEL	
08	008	BS		09	009	HT	
0A	010	NL		0B	011	VT	
0C	012	NP		0D	013	CR	
0E	014	SO		0F	015	SI	
10	016	DLE		11	017	DC1	
12	018	DC2		13	019	DC3	
14	020	DC4		15	021	NAK	
16	022	SYN		17	023	ETB	
18	024	CAN		19	025	EM	
1A	026	SUB		1B	027	ESC	
1C	028	FS		1D	029	GS	
1E	030	RS		1F	031	US	
20	032	SP		21	033	!	
22	034	"	"	23	035	#	
24	036	$		25	037	%	
26	038	&	&	27	039	'	
28	040	(		29	041	)	
2A	042	*		2B	043	+	
2C	044	,		2D	045	-	
2E	046	.		2F	047	/	
30	048	0		31	049	1	

Hex	Decimal	Char	Entity	Hex	Decimal	Char	Entity
32	050	2		33	051	3	
34	052	4		35	053	5	
36	054	6		37	055	7	
38	056	8		39	057	9	
3A	058	:		3B	059	;	
3C	060	<	<	3D	061	=	
3E	062	>	>	3F	063	?	
40	064	@		41	065	A	
42	066	B		43	067	C	
44	068	D		45	069	E	
46	070	F		47	071	G	
48	072	H		49	073	I	
4A	074	J		4B	075	K	
4C	076	L		4D	077	M	
4E	078	N		4F	079	O	
50	080	P		51	081	Q	
52	082	R		53	083	S	
54	084	T		55	085	U	
56	086	V		57	087	W	
58	088	X		59	089	Y	
5A	090	Z		5B	091	[	
5C	092	\		5D	093	]	
5E	094	^		5F	095	_	
60	096	`		61	097	a	
62	098	b		63	099	c	
64	100	d		65	101	e	
66	102	f		67	103	g	
68	104	h		69	105	i	
6A	106	j		6B	107	k	
6C	108	l		6D	109	m	
6E	110	n		6F	111	o	
70	112	p		71	113	q	
72	114	r		73	115	s	
74	116	t		75	117	u	
76	118	v		77	119	w	
78	120	x		79	121	y	
7A	122	z		7B	123	{	
7C	124	|		7D	125	}	
7E	126	~		7F	127	DEL	
A0	160			A1	161	¡	¡
A2	162	¢	¢	A3	163	£	£
A4	164	¤	¤	A5	165	¥	¥
A6	166	¦	¦	A7	167	§	§
A8	168	¨	¨	A9	169	©	©
AA	170	ª	ª	AB	171	«	«
AC	172	¬	¬	AD	173	-	­
AE	174	®	®	AF	175	¯	¯
B0	176	°	°	B1	177	±	±

Hex	Decimal	Char	Entity	Hex	Decimal	Char	Entity
B2	178	²	²	B3	179	³	³
B4	180	´	´	B5	181	µ	µ
B6	182	¶	¶	B7	183	·	·
B8	184	¸	¸	B9	185	¹	¹
BA	186	º	º	BB	187	»	»
BC	188	¼	¼	BD	189	½	½
BE	190	¾	¾	BF	191	¿	¿
C0	192	À	À	C1	193	Á	Á
C2	194	Â	Â	C3	195	Ã	Ã
C4	196	Ä	Ä	C5	197	Å	Å
C6	198	Æ	Æ	C7	199	Ç	Ç
C8	200	È	È	C9	201	É	É
CA	202	Ê	Ê	CB	203	Ë	Ë
CC	204	Ì	Ì	CD	205	Í	Í
CE	206	Î	Î	CF	207	Ï	Ï
D0	208	Ð	Ð	D1	209	Ñ	Ñ
D2	210	Ò	Ò	D3	211	Ó	Ó
D4	212	Ô	Ô	D5	213	Õ	Õ
D6	214	Ö	Ö	D7	215	x	×
D8	216	Ø	Ø	D9	217	Ù	Ù
DA	218	Ú	Ú	DB	219	Û	Û
DC	220	Ü	Ü	DD	221	Ý	Ý
DE	222	Þ	Þ	DF	223	ß	ß
E0	224	à	à	E1	225	á	á
E2	226	â	â	E3	227	ã	ã
E4	228	ä	ä	E5	229	å	å
E6	230	æ	æ	E7	231	ç	ç
E8	232	è	è	E9	233	é	é
EA	234	ê	ê	EB	235	ë	ë
EC	236	ì	ì	ED	237	í	í
EE	238	î	î	EF	239	ï	ï
F0	240	ð	ð	F1	241	ñ	ñ
F2	242	ò	ò	F3	243	ó	ó
F4	244	ô	ô	F5	245	õ	õ
F6	246	ö	ö	F7	247	÷	÷
F8	248	ø	ø	F9	249	ù	ù
FA	250	ú	ú	FB	251	û	û
FC	252	ü	ü	FD	253	ý	ý
FE	254	þ	þ	FF	255	ÿ	ÿ

Color Codes for Netscape and VRML

Colors of a set of 32 crayons, with their approximate Netscape RGB and VRML RGB triplet color values.

Color Name	Netscape RGB Value (Hexadecimal)	VRML RGB Triplet (Decimal)
black	000000	0.0,0.0,0.0
white	ffffff	1.0,1.0,1.0
gray	c0c0c0	.750,.750,.750
red	ff0000	1.0,0.0,0.0
maroon	8e236b	.556,.137,.420
violet red	db7093	.859,.439,.576
fuschia	ff6ec7	1.0,.431,.780
carnation pink	bc8f8f	.737,.561,.561
magenta	ff00ff	1.0,0.0,1.0
red violet	cc3299	.800,.196,.600
violet (purple)	871f78	.529,.122,.471
blue violet	9f5f9f	.624,.373,.624
blue	0000ff	0.0,0.0,1.0
cerulean	38b0de	.220,.690,.871
midnight blue	00009c	0.0,0.0,.612
turquoise blue	5f9f9f	.373,.624,.624
jungle green	70db93	.439,.859,.576
pine green	238e23	.137,.556,.137
blue green	426f42	.259,.435,.259

Color Name	Netscape RGB Value (Hexadecimal)	VRML RGB Triplet (Decimal)
green	00ff00	0.0,1.0,0.0
olive green	9f9f5f	.624,.624,.373
yellow green	7fff00	.498,1.0,0.0
green yellow	99cc32	.600,.800,.196
yellow	ffff00	1.0,1.0,0.0
dandelion	eaeaae	.918,.918,.682
yellow orange	e9c2a6	.914,.761,.651
orange	ff7f00	1.0,.498,0.0
vivid tangerine	ff9000	1.0,.565,0.0
red orange	ff2400	1.0,.141,0.0
peach	ebc79e	.922,.780,.620
brown	a62a2a	.651,.165,.165
burnt sienna	8e6b23	.557,.420,.137

Java Keyword Summary and API Overview

Java Keywords

abstract	interface
boolean	long
break	native
byte	new
case	null
catch	package
char	private
class	protected
continue	public
default	return
do	short
double	static
else	super
extends	switch
false	synchronized
final	this
finally	threadsafe
float	throw
for	transient
if	true
implements	try
import	void
instanceof	while
int	

JAVA API OVERVIEW

Refer to the Java 1.0 API Documentation at http://java.sun.com/JDK-1.0/api/packages.html for complete API documentation.

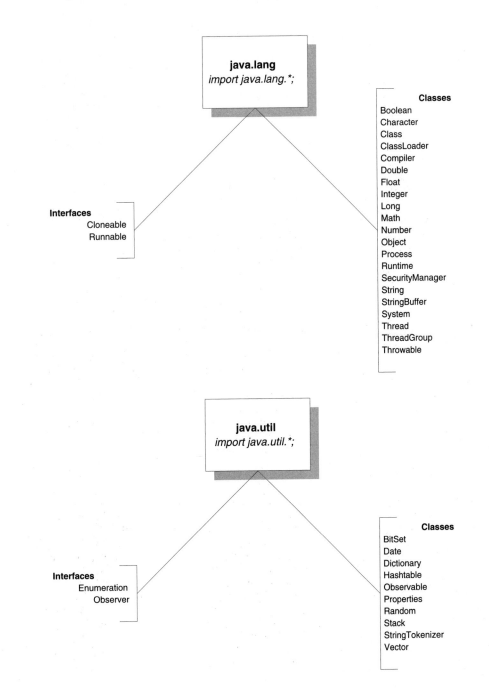

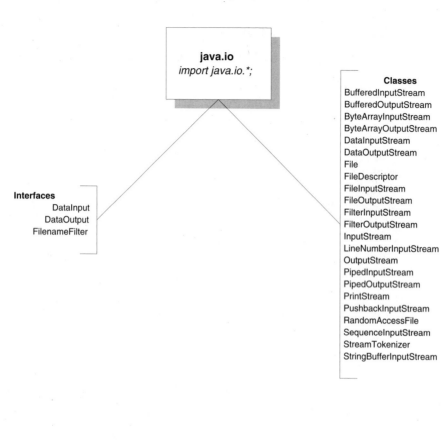

java.io
import java.io.;*

Interfaces
DataInput
DataOutput
FilenameFilter

Classes
BufferedInputStream
BufferedOutputStream
ByteArrayInputStream
ByteArrayOutputStream
DataInputStream
DataOutputStream
File
FileDescriptor
FileInputStream
FileOutputStream
FilterInputStream
FilterOutputStream
InputStream
LineNumberInputStream
OutputStream
PipedInputStream
PipedOutputStream
PrintStream
PushbackInputStream
RandomAccessFile
SequenceInputStream
StreamTokenizer
StringBufferInputStream

java.net
import java.net.;*

Interfaces
ContentHandlerFactory
SocketImplFactory
URLStreamHandlerFactory

Classes
ContentHandler
DatagramPacket
DatagramSocket
InetAddress
ServerSocket
Socket
SocketImpl
URL
URLConnection
URLEncoder
URLStreamHandler

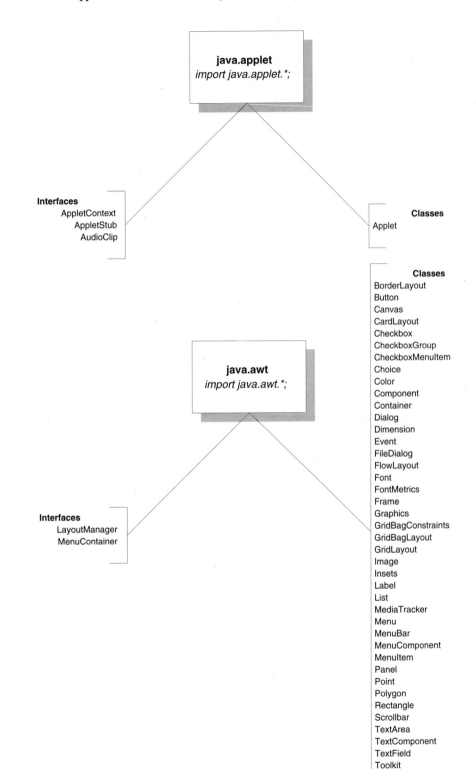

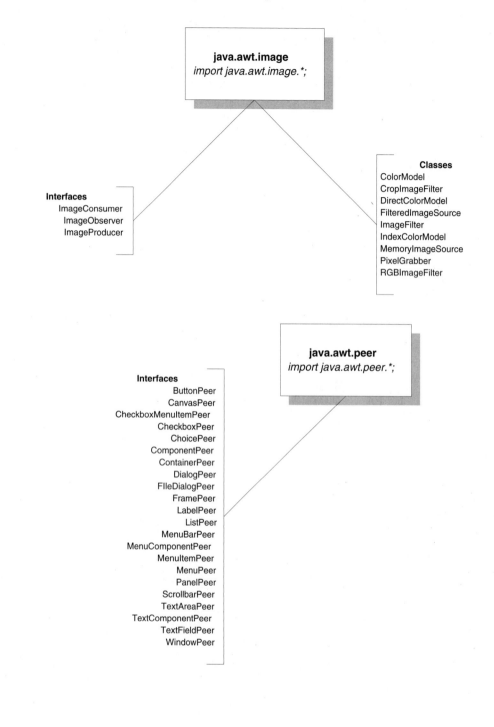

java.awt.image
import java.awt.image.;*

Interfaces
ImageConsumer
ImageObserver
ImageProducer

Classes
ColorModel
CropImageFilter
DirectColorModel
FilteredImageSource
ImageFilter
IndexColorModel
MemoryImageSource
PixelGrabber
RGBImageFilter

java.awt.peer
import java.awt.peer.;*

Interfaces
ButtonPeer
CanvasPeer
CheckboxMenuItemPeer
CheckboxPeer
ChoicePeer
ComponentPeer
ContainerPeer
DialogPeer
FIleDialogPeer
FramePeer
LabelPeer
ListPeer
MenuBarPeer
MenuComponentPeer
MenuItemPeer
MenuPeer
PanelPeer
ScrollbarPeer
TextAreaPeer
TextComponentPeer
TextFieldPeer
WindowPeer

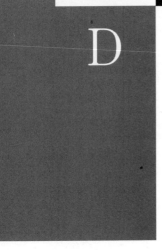

D

Internet
Resources

Where to go for more information

Chapter 1   Windows on the Web: Web Browsers
NCSA Mosaic Home Page
http://www.ncsa.uiuc.edu/SDG/Software/Mosaic/NCSAMosaicHome.html

Welcome to Netscape
http://www.netscape.com/

Chapters 2–5   [Introduction to HTML 2]
A Beginner's Guide to HTML
http://www.ncsa.uiuc.edu/General/Internet/WWW/HTMLPrimer.html

HTML Quick Reference
http://www.ncsa.uiuc.edu/General/Internet/WWW/HTMLQuickRef.html

HyperText Markup Language (HTML): Working and Background Materials
http://www.w3.org/hypertext/WWW/MarkUp/MarkUp.html

The HTML Language
http://union.ncsa.uiuc.edu/HyperNews/get/www/html/lang.html

The Art of HTML
http://www.thecoo.edu/~menon/html.html

Chapter 6   Making Connections
Introduction to HTML and URLs
http://www.utirc.utoronto.ca/HTMLdocs/NewHTML/intro.html

A Beginner's Guide to URLs
http://www.ncsa.uiuc.edu/demoweb/url-primer.html

A Guide to URLs
http://www.netspace.org/users/dwb/url-guide.html

Chapter 7   Adding Images
Transparent/Interlaced GIF Resources
http://dragon.jpl.nasa.gov/~adam/transparent.html

Randy's Icon and Image Bazaar
http://www.infi.net/~rdralph/icons/

Free Art, Photoshop, and Corel Tips, and More
http://www.mccannas.com/newtips.htm

PNG (Portable Network Graphics) Home Page
http://quest.jpl.nasa.gov/PNG/

Chapter 8   Introduction to HTML Forms
Mosaic for X version 2.0 Fill-Out Form Support
http://www.ncsa.uiuc.edu/SDG/Software/Mosaic/Docs/fill-out-forms/overview.html

Forms Tutorial
http://www.webcom.com/~webcom/html/tutor/forms/start.html

Chapter 9   Image Maps
NCSA Tutorial: Imagemap
http://hoohoo.ncsa.uiuc.edu/docs/tutorials/imagemapping.html

Imagemap Help Page—Instruction
http://www2.ncsu.edu/bae/people/faculty/walker/hotlist/imagemap.html

How to Do Imagemaps
http://www.hway.net/ihip/

Chapter 10   Netscape and Other Browser-Specific Extensions
Netscape Extensions to HTML
http://www.netscape.com/assist/net_sites/html_extensions.html

How To... (Netscape extensions)
http://home.teclink.net/~rets/indy.html

Microsoft Internet Explorer HTML Support
http://www.microsoft.com/windows/ie/html_toc.htm

WebExplorer Home Page
http://www.raleigh.ibm.com/WebExplorer/webhome.htm

Chapters 11–13   [HTML 3]
HyperText Markup Language Specification Version 3
http://www.w3.org/pub/WWW/MarkUp/html3/CoverPage.html

A Quick Review of HTML 3
http://www.w3.org/hypertext/WWW/Arena/tour/start.html

All Elements in HTML 3 DTD
http://www.halsoft.com/sgml/html-3.0/ALL-ELEM.html

HTML 3 for NETSCAPE
http://www.sirius.com/~paulus/html30.html

WRL: HTML 3 and Netscape 2.0
http://webreference.com/html3andns/

Chapter 14   HTML 3 Style Sheets
Cascading Style Sheets, Level 1
http://www.w3.org/pub/WWW/TR/WD-css1.html

Cascading HTML Style Sheets—A Proposal
http://www.w3.org/hypertext/WWW/People/howcome/p/cascade.html

Web Style Sheets
http://www.w3.org/hypertext/WWW/Style/

Chapter 15 HTML 3 Table Primer
The HTML 3 Table Model
http://www.w3.org/pub/WWW/TR/WD-tables.html

Tables
http://amelia.db.erau.edu/~andrew/http/HTML_3.0/tables.html

Tables in Netscape 1.1
http://www.netscape.com/assist/net_sites/tables.html

Chapter 16 Overview of HTML Math
MATH
http://www.halsoft.com/sgml/html-3.0/math.html

HTML Math Entities
http://www.hpl.hp.co.uk/people/dsr/html3/mathsym.html

HTML Math
http://amelia.db.erau.edu/~andrew/http/HTML_3.0/maths.html

NCDesign HTML Design Guide—Math
http://ncdesign.kyushu-id.ac.jp/howto/text/Table/math.html

Chapter 17 Document Frames Tutorial
Frames—An Introduction
http://www.netscape.com/assist/net_sites/frames.html

Netscape Frames
http://pel.cs.byu.edu/~sharky/frames/menu.htm

NCDesign HTML Design Guide—Frames
http://ncdesign.kyushu-id.ac.jp/howto/text/Frame/frame/index.html

Chapter 18 Special Characters and Multilingual Documents
Special Characters in HTML
http://www.utirc.utoronto.ca/HTMLdocs/NewHTML/entities.html

The Unicode Standard
http://www.stonehand.com/unicode/standard.html

The Multilingual WWW
http://www.yars.free.net/multilang.html

Chapter 19 The Home Page
How to Create Your Own Home Page: Part 1
http://www.intergalact.com/hp/part1.html

Style Guide for Online Hypertext
http://www.w3.org/hypertext/WWW/Provider/Style/Overview.html

Composing Good HTML (Version 2.0)
http://www.cs.cmu.edu/~tilt/cgh/

Chapters 20–21 [Hypertext]
What Is Hypertext?
http://www.w3.org/hypertext/WWW/WhatIs.html

Hypertext Sources
http://www.uoregon.edu/~heroux/ici/Hypertext.html

Yale C/AIM WWW Style Manual
http://info.med.yale.edu/caim/StyleManual_Top.HTML

Introduction to HTML: Table of Contents
http://www.cwru.edu/help/introHTML/toc.html

Chapter 22 Considerations for Users with Special Needs
Design of HTML (Mosaic) Pages to Increase Their Accessibility to Users With Disabilities
http://trace.wisc.edu/HTMLgide/

WEB Server for the Visually Handicapped
http://biomed.nus.sg/vh/vh.html

Chapter 23 Making Your Documents Public
EFF "Intellectual Property Online: Patent, Trademark, Copyright" Archive
http://www.eff.org/pub/Intellectual_property/

WWW Multimedia Law
http://www.batnet.com/oikoumene/

NCSA HTTPd: Security Concerns on the Web
http://hoohoo.ncsa.uiuc.edu/security/

How to Set up Protected W3C httpd
http://www.w3.org/hypertext/WWW/Daemon/User/Config/AccessAuth.html

Submit It!
http://www.submit-it.com/

Chapter 24 Publishing HTML on CD-ROM
Multimedia File Formats on the Internet
http://ac.dal.ca/~dong/intro.htm#intro.1

CD Archive, Inc. (Frequently asked questions about CD-ROMs)
http://www.cdarchive.com/info/cd_rom_faq/cd_faq.htm

Apple Extensions to ISO-9660 (TechNote FL 36)
http://dev.info.apple.com/technotes/Archive/Files/fl_36.html

Chapter 25 HTML Editors
Yahoo—Computers and Internet:Internet:World Wide Web:HTML Converters
http://www.yahoo.com/Computers_and_Internet/Internet/World_Wide_Web/HTML_Converters/

Yahoo—Computers and Internet:Internet:World Wide Web:HTML Editors
http://www.yahoo.com/Computers_and_Internet/Internet/World_Wide_Web/HTML_Editors/

Chapter 26 Processing Forms Data
The Common Gateway Interface
http://hoohoo.ncsa.uiuc.edu/cgi/

CGI Overview
http://www.bio.cam.ac.uk/web/form.html

CGI Form Handling in Perl
http://www.intergalact.com/hp/part3/overview.html

Learn to Write CGI-Forms
http://www.catt.ncsu.edu/~bex/tutor/index.html

Chapter 27 Very Gentle Introduction to Perl
PERL — Practical Extraction and Report Language
http://www.cs.cmu.edu/htbin/perl-man

perl5 Manual Page
http://www.metronet.com/0/perlinfo/perl5/manual/perl.html

Learning Perl: References

http://www.teleport.com/~rootbeer/perl.html

CPAN: Comprehensive Perl Archive Network
ftp://uiarchive.cso.uiuc.edu/pub/lang/perl/CPAN/README.html

Chapter 28 Search Systems and HTML
Index of /pub/NIDR.tools/freewais/
ftp://ftp.cnidr.org/pub/NIDR.tools/freewais/

Son of WAIS.pl
http://dewey.lib.ncsu.edu/staff/morgan/son-of-wais.html

The Harvest Information Discovery and Access System
http://harvest.cs.colorado.edu/

Chapter 29 HTML on the Fly
An Exploration of Dynamic Documents
http://www.netscape.com/assist/net_sites/pushpull.html

Malcom's Guide to Server PushPull & CGI Animation
http://www.emf.net/~mal/animate.html

Yahoo—Computers and Internet:Internet:World Wide Web:Gateways
http://www.yahoo.com/Computers_and_Internet/Internet/World_Wide_Web/Gateways/

Chapter 30 Hypermedia with HTML
MIME Documentation
http://www.netscape.com/assist/helper_apps/mime.html

comp.mail.mime FAQ, part 1 of 3 (frequently asked questions list)
http://www.cis.ohio-state.edu/text/faq/usenet/mail/mime-faq/part1/faq.html

WebMuseum: Technical: Setting Properly Your Web Reader
http://sunsite.unc.edu/louvre/about/tech.html

WWW Viewer Test Page
http://www-dsed.llnl.gov/documents/WWWtest.html

Chapter 31 Introducing Java
Java: Programming for the Internet
http://java.sun.com/

Shlurrrpp......Java Learning Java : The Java Tutorial for Java Programming
http://www.neca.com/~vmis/java.html

JavaScript
http://home.netscape.com/comprod/products/navigator/version_2.0/script/index.html

Chapter 32 Building Java Applets
Perpetually Unfinished Guides to Java
http://ugweb.cs.ualberta.ca/~nelson/java/JavaGuides.html

Gamelan: Earthweb's Java Directory
http://www.gamelan.com/

Java Class Warehouse
http://www.entmp.org/jcw/

Chapter 33 Introduction to VRML
VRML 1.0 Specification
http://www.virtpark.com/theme/vrml/

VRML FAQ
http://www.oki.com/vrml/VRML_FAQ.html

VRML Test Suite
http://www.chaco.com/vrml/test/

Chapter 34 Touring and Building Virtual Worlds

Grafman's VRML Tools Review
http://www.graphcomp.com/vrml/review.html

VRML Repository
http://www.sdsc.edu/vrml/

Yahoo—Computers and Internet:Internet:World Wide Web:Virtual Reality Modeling
Language (VRML):Authoring
http://www.yahoo.com/Computers_and_Internet/Internet/World_Wide_Web/Virtual_Reality_
Modeling_Language__VRML_/Authoring/

Chapter 35 Adobe Acrobat

Adobe Acrobat
http://w1000.mv.us.adobe.com/Acrobat/Acrobat0.html

xpdf: A PDF Viewer for X
http://www.contrib.andrew.cmu.edu/usr/dn0o/xpdf/xpdf.html

Acrobat Reader Tutorial
http://w3.ag.uiuc.edu/AIM/SLOAN/tutorials/Acrobat/index.html

Chapter 36 HTML and SGML

SGML on the Web
http://www.ncsa.uiuc.edu/SDG/Software/Mosaic/WebSGML.html

SoftQuad: SGML: Your Multiplatform Publishing and Information Management Solution
http://www.sq.com/htmlsgml/htmlsgml.htm

SoftQuad: Panorama Free
http://www.sq.com/products/panorama/pan-free.htm

Text Encoding Initiative Home Page
http://www.uic.edu:80/orgs/tei/

SGML: Academic Projects
http://www.sil.org/sgml/acadapps.html#tei

INDEX